CONSULTATION AND CO-OPERATION
IN THE COMMONWEALTH

CONSULTATION
AND
CO-OPERATION
IN THE
COMMONWEALTH

*A Handbook on
Methods and Practice*

BY

HEATHER J. HARVEY

*Issued under the auspices of the
Royal Institute of International Affairs*

OXFORD UNIVERSITY PRESS

LONDON NEW YORK TORONTO

1952

Oxford University Press, Amen House, London E.C.4

GLASGOW   NEW YORK   TORONTO   MELBOURNE   WELLINGTON
BOMBAY   CALCUTTA   MADRAS   CAPE TOWN

Geoffrey Cumberlege, Publisher to the University

First published 1952.
*An earlier handbook on this subject
compiled by Gerald E. H. Palmer
was published in* 1934 *under the title
'Consultation and Co-operation in
the British Commonwealth'*

*Printed in Great Britain by
Latimer Trend & Co. Ltd., Plymouth*

PREFACE

A HANDBOOK under the title of *Consultation and Co-operation in the British Commonwealth*[1] was issued under the auspices of the Royal Institute of International Affairs in 1934. It was compiled by Mr Gerald E. H. Palmer, assisted by members of the staff of the Institute, with generous help also from the sister Institutes in the Commonwealth. The compiler of the present handbook gratefully records her indebtedness to that pioneer team.

This book, like its predecessor, was first prepared as background material for one of the series of unofficial British Commonwealth Relations Conferences organized by the Institutes of International Affairs in the Commonwealth. It was issued in mimeographed form to participants in the fourth Conference, held at Bigwin Inn, Ontario, from 8–18 September 1949. As a result, valuable comments on the text, and, in some cases, material and documents not readily available in the United Kingdom, were received by the Royal Institute from participants in the Conference, and from other members of the sister Institutes.

In view of this helpful attitude and of the fact that the Bigwin Inn Conference gave considerable attention to problems of Commonwealth consultative and co-operative machinery, and deplored the prevailing ignorance of its nature and scope,[2] the Council of the Royal Institute felt justified in putting in hand the revision and amplification of the mimeographed material for publication.

The object to be attained by the compiler was, at first sight, simple and straightforward: to collect, in one volume, the facts about the machinery of consultation and co-operation in the Commonwealth which would otherwise have to be sought in a multitude of other publications; and to present them without comment, save in the form of quotations from official and ministerial statements.

But the task was far less simple than it appeared. 'Terminology', Mr Attlee has said, 'if it is to be useful, keeps step with developments without becoming rigid or doctrinaire';[3] but this flexibility can be an embarrassment when it comes to defining the scope of a book. The first question was the content to be given to the word 'Commonwealth' for this purpose. There was always implicit in the word the modern, more catholic and richer inter-

[1] London, Oxford University Press, 1934.
[2] *The Changing Commonwealth: proceedings of the fourth unofficial British Commonwealth Relations Conference*, ed. by F. H. Soward (London, Oxford University Press for Canadian Institute of International Affairs, 1950) pp. 154 and 183 ff. [3] See p. 2, below.

pretation; but to include in the book an account of the working of consultation and co-operation in respect of all dependent territories would have made it unwieldy to the point of uselessness. 'Commonwealth' in this book, therefore, covers only the present fully self-governing membership. Even so, the traditional British latitude to be illogical has been invoked, for certain material on pre-republican Eire is included.

It was soon evident, however, that, if the task of compilation were not to become a Penelope's web, some further practical limitation would have to be devised. The compiler therefore deliberately adopted an arbitrary general convention: the exclusion of co-operative and consultative arrangements under treaties or agreements to which only one self-governing Member of the Commonwealth was a party, even though others might be involved informally or with observer status.

One problem defied solution: that of relating the space allotted in the book to the importance of the organ of co-operation described. In some cases the factual background may be short and simple, in others confused and complicated. The account of the origins of the latter must inevitably occupy greater space. In the interest of reducing space, the briefer expression 'Dominions' has occasionally been employed where the phrase 'fully self-governing Members of the Commonwealth' would have been correct.

Responsibility for the text, for selecting what should be included and what omitted, and for any indication of opinion which the act of selection involves, lies squarely on the compiler. Responsibility for deciding that the handbook would be a useful publication lies with the Council of the Royal Institute, which is aware that the printing delays inevitable in the United Kingdom to-day mean that no book dealing with current affairs can be completely up to date. Having made clear where responsibility rests, the Council, warmly seconded by the compiler, desires to make equally clear its appreciation of the generosity of those authorities who read and commented upon the material in draft, and supplied additional information from their knowledge and experience. Many of these authorities have held official positions in the countries of the Commonwealth, and for this reason and on account of the large number of those who collaborated in this way, the Council must limit itself to this general expression of gratitude.

Special thanks are due to Mrs E. Margaret Meade who prepared the bulk of the material contained in Chapters VII and XI, and parts of Chapter VIII.

HEATHER J. HARVEY

April 1951

CONTENTS

Part III

MACHINERY OF COMMONWEALTH PARTICIPATION IN INTERNATIONAL ACTION

CHAPTER I

INTRODUCTION

Membership of the Commonwealth

THE logical introduction to a handbook on the machinery of consultation and co-operation between the members of an association would be a description of the constitution and rules of the association, and the conditions and consequences of membership. But in the case of the British Commonwealth of Nations it is not possible to reduce its nature to a definition, nor its working arrangements to a list of legal or conventional rules. All, therefore, that this opening chapter attempts is to draw attention to some among the recent events bearing on its nature and membership.

The Members of the Commonwealth

The Members of the British Commonwealth of Nations are nowhere legally enumerated as such. Paragraph 1 of the Preamble to the Statute of Westminster[1] enumerates His Majesty's Governments in the sovereign States Members, and Section 1 of the Statute enumerates the overseas Dominions but omits the United Kingdom. The Balfour Declaration of 1926 defined the 'position and mutual relation' of the Members without enumerating them. The fully self-governing Members of the Commonwealth enumerated in December 1931 were: the United Kingdom of Great Britain and Northern Ireland; the Dominion of Canada; the Commonwealth of Australia; the Dominion of New Zealand; the Union of South Africa; the Irish Free State; and Newfoundland.

Since that date: the Irish Free State in 1949 became the Republic of Ireland and withdrew from membership; Newfoundland entered into union with Canada as a tenth province in 1949; British India was divided into two States, the Union of India and Pakistan, which became Dominions on 15 August 1947; the Union of India became a Republic in 1950; and the island colony of Ceylon became a Dominion on 4 February 1948.

The Meaning of 'Commonwealth'

The usage and content of the word 'Commonwealth' is not defined in law. Possibly the nearest to a legal definition is 'free association', used in paragraph 2 of the Preamble to the Statute of Westminster; but the Preamble is, in fact, not law but con-

[1] For the text of the Statute, see Appendix.

stitutional convention. There has been no formal official definition or demarcation of the content of the expressions 'Commonwealth' or 'British Commonwealth of Nations': on the contrary, there has been official recognition, instances of which will be found below, of evolution and fluidity in the use of these expressions, of the term 'Dominion', and of the words 'the British Empire'.

A step in the evolution of the meaning of the word 'Commonwealth' was taken, in a curiously remote connexion, on 18 November 1947. In the provisions for registration of medical practitioners in the Medical Act of 1886, it was laid down that the medical register should have separate lists for 'colonial' and 'foreign' practitioners. In the Medical Practitioners and Pharmacists Bill of 1947 the same phraseology slipped into Clause I, section 3. Attention was drawn by Lord Altrincham to this anomalous use of the word 'colonial', and Lord Henderson, accepting the correction on behalf of His Majesty's Government, moved an amendment (which was agreed to) to substitute 'Commonwealth' (with a capital 'C') for 'colonial'. In doing so he said:

It has not been easy to find an expression which exactly fulfils the intention, but consultations with the Department of Commonwealth Relations and the Colonial Office have taken place and have led to the joint conclusion that 'Commonwealth' as a general term, is the best. It is true that the term 'British Commonwealth of Nations' is recognized and accepted as connoting the present association of the Dominions and the United Kingdom as independent nations, but I am advised that the word 'Commonwealth' alone can properly be given the wider meaning of all territories within the Empire, including the Dominions.[1]

On 2 May 1949, after the Declaration of 27 April 1949 (see p. 25 below), which employed the expression 'Commonwealth' both alone and with the prefixed adjective 'British', the Prime Minister, Mr Attlee, was asked whether it was intended officially to abandon the use of the expression 'British Empire', and whether the other Commonwealth Governments had agreed to its progressive substitution in official usage by the term 'Commonwealth'. Mr Attlee replied:

Terminology, if it is to be useful, keeps step with developments without becoming rigid or doctrinaire. All constitutional developments in the Commonwealth, the British Commonwealth, or the British Empire—I use the three terms deliberately—have been the subject of consultations between His Majesty's Governments, and there has been no agreement to adopt or to exclude the use of any one

[1] *Hansard* (Lords), vol. 152, col. 751.

of these terms, nor any decision on the part of His Majesty's Government in the United Kingdom to do so.[1]

The use of the word 'Dominion' has also been affected by changes of fact and opinion. On 2 July 1947, the Prime Minister, Mr Attlee, stated in the House of Commons:

It has for some time past been clear that in certain quarters, both here and overseas, the view has been taken that the titles of the Secretary of State for Dominion Affairs and the Dominions Office are no longer entirely appropriate and are liable to convey a misleading impression of the relations between the United Kingdom and the other Members of the Commonwealth.

The titles, he continued, would be altered to 'Secretary of State for Commonwealth Affairs and Commonwealth Relations Office'.[2]

The question was raised in Canada in 1947, and again in 1950, whether the use of the phrase 'the British Dominions beyond the seas' in the Royal Style and Titles was still fully appropriate. On 2 May 1950, in the House of Commons, the Canadian Prime Minister, Mr St Laurent, indicated that Canada was unlikely to take the initiative in proposing any change, although 'we are not under the dominion of any but ourselves and his gracious Majesty the King of Canada . . .'[3] 'There was no question of dissatisfaction, but merely a desire for accuracy.'[4] Although 'Canada' is no longer prefixed by 'Dominion of', the Canadian House of Commons on 2 June 1950 voted by 73 to 39 to retain the name 'Dominion Day' for Canada's national day.

Variations and inconsistencies in the use of 'Dominion' continue, for the word is a convenient and brief, if not wholly accurate, alternative to the more cumbrous 'fully self-governing Member of the British Commonwealth'. In the absence of formal decisions, it is not particularly rewarding to pursue these variations further.

The Statute of Westminster

There is no comprehensive legal instrument which is the constitutional foundation of the British Commonwealth. Apart from the general influence towards conformity in public law exerted by English Common Law, 'the Commonwealth . . . is a singularly lawless association. . . . The Statute of Westminster is all there is of the Commonwealth in law, and it is not very much. . . . The

---

[1] *Hansard* (Commons), vol. 464, col. 644.
[2] ibid. vol. 439, col. 1320.
[3] *The Times*, 3 May 1950.
[4] *Manchester Guardian*, 4 May 1950.

Statute, however creative in the political sphere, brought a purely negative contribution in law.'[1]

The text of the Statute will be found in the Appendix. It has been described as having the character of an instrument designed to bring the law into conformity with facts and practice whose progress had outstripped the law. The developments which the Statute recognized and complied with belonged generally to the field of constitutional convention.

Some Statements of Commonwealth Convention

Some account of the international recognition, up to 1919, of the Members of the British Commonwealth as sovereign independent States will be found in Chapter XII. It was felt desirable that the facts should also be explicitly asserted, by common consent, within the Commonwealth association itself. This view, which was several times affirmed during the Imperial War Conferences of 1917 and 1918,[2] led in due course to the study of the matter undertaken at the Imperial Conference of 1926 by its Inter-Imperial Relations Committee under the chairmanship of the first Earl Balfour.

The report of this Committee stated that: 'Equality of status, so far as Great Britain and the Dominions are concerned, is . . . the root-principle governing our inter-imperial relations.' The most famous passage in the Committee's report, known generally as the Balfour Declaration, stated the convention governing the position and mutual relation of the Members of the Commonwealth:

They are autonomous communities within the British Empire, equal in status, in no way subordinate one to another in any aspect of their domestic or external affairs, though united by a common allegiance to the Crown, and freely associated as members of the British Commonwealth of Nations.[3]

Law had to be brought into line with this constitutional convention, for 'existing administrative, legislative, and judicial forms are admittedly not wholly in accord with the position as described'.[4] The major part of the task of examining and recommending changes in forms was entrusted to the Conference on the Operation of Dominion Legislation and Merchant Shipping

---

[1] R. T. E. Latham, *The Law and the Commonwealth* (London, Oxford University Press for the Royal Institute of International Affairs, 1949) p. 513. (This work was first published in the first volume of W. K. Hancock, *Survey of British Commonwealth Affairs*, 1937.)
[2] See Chapter IV, below.
[3] Cmd. 2768 (1926) p. 14
[4] ibid. p. 15.

Legislation, which met in the autumn of 1929. Its report, presented in January 1930,[1] was considered by the Commonwealth countries in preparation for the Imperial Conference of 1930; and the Conference substantially adopted the report, making certain small amendments in the draft clauses proposed for statutory enactment. The resultant statute was considered in draft by the Dominion Parliaments, and debated and finally adopted in its agreed form by the Parliament at Westminster in December 1931, as the Statute of Westminster.

Consequential Changes in Law and Convention relating to Equality of Status

The Statute of Westminster formally disposed of the following inequalities of status:

By Section 2 (1):
The Colonial Laws Validity Act of 1865 ceased to apply to any future Dominion legislation.

By Section 2 (2):
No future Dominion legislation could be invalid on the ground of repugnance to the law of England or to any past or future United Kingdom legislation; and any Dominion might repeal any such United Kingdom legislation which is part of the law of the Dominion.

By Section 3:
The Dominions were given full power to legislate with extraterritorial operation.

By Section 4:
The United Kingdom Parliament might not legislate for a Dominion except at its express request and consent.

By Sections 5 and 6:
The amplitude of the Dominions' powers under Sections 2 and 3 were expressly clarified in relation to legislation affecting shipping and Courts of Admiralty.

By Section 11:
It was made clear that in future the expression 'Colony' in any United Kingdom legislation shall not apply to a Dominion or any Province or State forming part thereof.

At the desire of the Dominions of Canada, Australia, and New Zealand, the bases of their constitutions were at this time excepted from the operation of the Statute by Sections 7, 8, and 9, despite the fact that this involved the maintenance of certain technical legal inequalities.

The Statute of Westminster by itself did not dispose of all formal survivals of inequality of status. The Imperial Conferences

[1] Cmd. 3479.

of 1926 and 1930 had already made explicit, in terms agreed by the Conference participants, certain conventions of equality, mostly habitually established but not necessarily or previously set out. One or two of these declarations required imperial legislation in order to bring law and convention into harmony. The Irish Free State objected to the form of the title of His Majesty the King, as established under the Royal Titles Act of 1901, and in which the expression 'the United Kingdom of Great Britain and Ireland' was used. Since this style was incompatible with the position of the Irish Free State as a separate Dominion, it was altered by the Royal and Parliamentary Titles Act, 1927. His Majesty's title then read: 'George V, by the Grace of God, of Great Britain, Ireland and the British Dominions beyond the Seas, King, Defender of the Faith, Emperor of India.'

By the same Act, the title of the Parliament at Westminster was altered to 'Parliament of the United Kingdom of Great Britain and Northern Ireland'.

The Conferences of 1926 and 1930 dealt with the functions of the Governor-General. The first point in those functions was dealt with by reference: the 1926 Conferences declared that the Governor-General must follow, in relation to the Cabinet in the Dominion, the same rules as are followed by the King in his relations with his Ministers in the United Kingdom. The same Conference declared that the Governor-General was the representative of the King alone: not in any way of His Majesty's Government in the United Kingdom. The 1930 Conference declared that the Governor-General should be appointed, after informal consultation with the King, on the formal advice of His Majesty's Government in the Dominion.

The formal inequalities resulting from the powers of disallowance and reservation of Dominion legislation were dealt with by the 1930 Conference, and subsequently, by a mixture of conventional pronouncement and legal enactment. The Conference declared that a Dominion could remove disallowance from its constitution, either in accordance with the procedure for amendment prescribed by its constitution, or—if the required powers and forms were not prescribed—by inviting the United Kingdom Parliament to pass the necessary legislation. One point of strict law, however, had to be dealt with. The Dominions had in the past enjoyed considerable advantages by being able, on compliance with certain conditions, to obtain trustee status for their stocks. One of these conditions was the formal acceptance[1] of disallowance of any Dominion legislation which would break the contractual terms of the trustee issue, or otherwise injure the

---

[1] Under Section 9 of the Colonial Stock Act, 1900.

stockholders in the view of the United Kingdom Government. This right of disallowance generally remains, the Governments of Canada, Australia and New Zealand having accepted it as a kind of business obligation not derogatory to equality of status. The Union of South Africa is an exception. It removed disallowance from its constitution by Section 11 (2) of the Status of the Union Act, 1934, and, at the request of the Union, His Majesty's Government in the United Kingdom previously obtained, by the Colonial Stock Act, 1934,[1] statutory power to accept, in lieu of the right of disallowance, an undertaking confirmed by Dominion statute that legislation which appeared to the United Kingdom Government to involve departure from the original contract or otherwise to affect the interests of stockholders should not be submitted for the Royal Assent until after agreement had been reached with the United Kingdom Government; and that any Dominion legislation which inadvertently had such effect should be amended to the satisfaction of the United Kingdom Government. The Union Government passed the necessary confirmatory statute before the passage of the Status of the Union Act.

The powers of reservation of Dominion legislation were of three kinds: discretionary, obligatory on instructions from the United Kingdom Government, and obligatory by statute. In the matter of discretionary reservation, the usage which had grown up steadily over many years—that the Governor-General should act on the advice of the Dominion Cabinet—was explicitly recognized by the 1930 Conference. With regard to reservation on instructions, it was declared by the same Conference that 'His Majesty's Government in the United Kingdom will not advise His Majesty the King to give the Governor-General any instructions to reserve Bills presented to him for assent'. Statutory obligatory reservation, which arose in the bulk of cases from provisions in Dominion constitutions, required legislation to abolish it. Where a prescribed course for constitutional amendment was embodied in the constitution of a Dominion, it was agreed in 1930 that the Dominion was free to abolish reservation by following this course. Where no course other than an Act of the United Kingdom Parliament was prescribed, the Dominion could request the passage of the required Act.

As mentioned above (p. 5), Section 3 of the Statute of Westminster gave the Dominions full power to legislate with extra-territorial effect; while Section 2, (1) and (2), set out their power to repeal imperial legislation applying to them, and the end of repugnancy under the Colonial Laws Validity Act of 1865. Nevertheless, it seemed desirable to make the position unequivocal,

[2] 24 & 25 Geo. V, c. 47, s. 1 (1).

specially to cite, in Sections 5 and 6 of the Statute, those sections of the Merchant Shipping Act, 1894, and the Colonial Courts of Admiralty Act, 1890, to which controversy might attach.

With regard to legislation by one Member which might affect the interests of the other self-governing Members, it was agreed at the 1926 Imperial Conference that 'the appropriate procedure with regard to projected legislation in one of the self-governing parts of the Empire which may affect the interests of other self-governing parts is previous consultation between His Majesty's Ministers in the several parts concerned'.

Merchant shipping legislation was one of the cases to which this convention applied, and the Conference on the Operation of Dominion Legislation, 1929, recommended the framing of an agreement covering points of common interest. The Imperial Conference of 1930 pursued this recommendation in the general field as well as in the particular field of merchant shipping. In general it declared that there were 'a number of subjects in which uniformity has hitherto been secured through the medium of Acts of the United Kingdom Parliament of general application. Where uniformity is desirable on the ground of common concern or practical convenience we think that this end should in the future be sought by means of concurrent or reciprocal action based upon agreement.'

In the particular field of merchant shipping legislation, the Conference accepted, after certain alterations, an agreement drafted in the United Kingdom and circulated in draft to all Members prior to the Conference. On 10 December 1931 this Agreement, in the form approved at the Conference,[1] was signed on behalf of the United Kingdom and all the Dominions.

The Imperial Conference of 1930 also gave its attention to another particular field of similar common concern, namely nationality. It agreed that: 'No member of the Commonwealth either could or would contemplate seeking to confer on any person a status to be operative throughout the Commonwealth save in pursuance of legislation based upon common agreement.'[2]

The 1929 Conference on the Operation of Dominion Legislation and Merchant Shipping Legislation considered that, since the freely associated Members of the British Commonwealth of Nations 'are united by a common allegiance to the Crown, it is clear that the laws relating to the succession to the Throne and the Royal Style and Titles are matters of equal concern to all'. The Conference recommended that this position should be formally recognized by a constitutional convention (which it drafted) to be recited in the Preamble to the proposed Statute of West-

[1] Cmd. 3717, pp. 32-7.   [2] See Chapter III, below.

minster,[1] and the 1930 Imperial Conference accepted this recommendation and this draft, which will be found below.

Conventions Relating to Equality of Status and the Crown

The comparative paucity of statute law basic to the Commonweath association is compensated by a wealth of constitutional convention. Some of this convention relates to status and some to consultation and co-operation; but, as all Commonwealth convention is closely interrelated, the drawing of distinctions between conventions of status and conventions of co-operation is not particularly fruitful.

The Preamble to the Statute of Westminster embodies the convention relating to the Succession and the Royal Style and Titles adopted in 1930:

Inasmuch as the Crown is the symbol of the free association of the members of the British Commonwealth of Nations, and as they are united by a common allegiance to the Crown, it would be in accord with the established constitutional position of all the members of the Commonwealth in relation to one another that any alteration in the law touching the Succession to the Throne or the Royal Style and Titles shall hereafter require the assent as well of the Parliaments of all the Dominions as of the Parliament of the United Kingdom.

Occasion for using the convention contained in this passage has arisen twice since 1931. In 1936, on the abdication of King Edward VIII and the accession of King George VI, its actual operation was not entirely smooth. The change of monarch was legally effected by each Member, although the Union of South Africa took a different view, in law, on the question whether the monarch's abdication is effective by his own act. Convention was breached[2] to the extent that the Irish Free State did not indicate its views, whether assent or dissent, to the other Members, but signified its acceptance of the change by an Act of the Oireachtas passed on 12 December 1936. Two of the legal enactments of the accession of King George VI—in South Africa and the Irish Free State—made the accession effective on different days in those Dominions and in the rest of the Commonwealth.

The second occasion for operating this convention was when the Union of India and Pakistan became Dominions, necessitating a change in the Royal Style and Titles. The Prime Minister

---

[1] Cmd. 3479, p. 21.

[2] The late R. T. E. Latham argued that the condoning of the breach of 'the ancillary conventions governing the tendering of advice' makes it clear that they are not fundamental. (*The Law and the Commonwealth*, p. 583.) In the Dáil on 11 December 1936, Mr de Valera declared that his Government was under no obligation to consult other Commonwealth Governments before initiating legislation touching the Succession.

of the United Kingdom, Mr Attlee, speaking on the second reading of the Indian Independence Bill on 10 July 1947, said:

Clause 7 (2) deals with the omission from the Royal Style and Titles of the words 'Indiae Imperator' and the words 'Emperor of India'. . . . A change in the Royal Style and Titles is not a matter for the United Kingdom alone. As the Preamble to the Statute of Westminster makes clear it concerns the other members of the British Commonwealth as well. But for practical reasons it has not been possible for such parliamentary action as may be necessary to be taken in those other countries simultaneously with legislation here. The House will, however, be glad to learn that, as a result of consultation with the Prime Ministers concerned, I am authorized to state that the other Commonwealth Governments agree to the proposed change in the Royal Style and Titles, and are prepared to take such steps as they consider necessary to obtain the consent of their Parliaments. It may be, therefore, that some time will elapse before this subsection becomes operative.[1]

Changes in the Fully Self-Governing Membership: (1) Eire

The terms of Eire's association with the British Commonwealth since 1936, and the circumstances in which the association terminated in 1949 were as follows.

On the occasion of the abdication of King Edward VIII, the Parliament of the Irish Free State passed two Acts. One was the Constitution (Amendment No. 27) Act, 1936, which removed from the Constitution of the Irish Free State all reference to the Crown or its representative, the Governor-General (whose office was abolished); and deprived the Crown of any function whatever, executive or legislative, in the internal affairs of the State. The Oath of Allegiance required of Members of the Dáil by Article 17 of the 1921 Constitution had already been abolished by the Constitution (Removal of Oath) Act of May 1933; and the Irish Nationality and Citizenship Act, 1935, which defined citizens of the Irish Free State, had repealed the British Nationality and Status of Aliens Acts, 1914 and 1918, 'if and in so far as they respectively are or ever were in force in Saorstát Eireann', and stated that 'the common law relating to British nationality . . . shall cease to have effect'. (This action was, of course, without effect in the municipal law of other Commonwealth countries.)

The second Act passed on 12 December 1936 was the Executive Authority (External Relations) Act, which declared that:

So long as Saorstát Eireann is associated with the following nations, that is to say, Australia, Canada, Great Britain, New Zealand, and South Africa, and so long as the King recognized by those nations as

[1] *Hansard* (Commons), vol. 439, col. 2453.

the symbol of their co-operation continues to act on behalf of each of those nations on the advice of the several Governments thereof for the purposes of the appointment of diplomatic and consular representatives, and the conclusion of international agreements, the King so recognized may and is hereby authorized to act on behalf of Saorstát Eireann for the like purposes as and when advised by the Executive Council to do so.

In the following year the Irish Free State adopted and promulgated a new Constitution, which came into force on 29 December 1937. In line with the enactments of December 1936, the new Constitution excluded the Crown entirely from the internal affairs of the State. In fact, it made no explicit mention of the Crown, being republican, in the sense of non-monarchical, in form although it did not declare a republic; nor did it mention any connexion with the British Commonwealth. Its Article 27 authorized the Government, 'for the purpose of the exercise of any executive function . . . in or in connexion with . . . external relations', to make use of 'any organ, instrument or method of procedure used or adopted for the like purpose by the members of any group or league of nations, with which the State is or becomes associated for the purpose of international co-operation in matters of common concern'.

His Majesty's Government in the United Kingdom, having consulted the Governments of the other Members of the Commonwealth, issued a statement on 29 December 1937 that they were 'prepared to treat the new constitution as not effecting a fundamental alteration in the position of the Irish Free State . . . as a Member of the British Commonwealth of Nations'. Mr De Valera declined at the time to make any comment on this statement.[1]

No further official statements were made until the end of the war of 1939-45, during which Eire remained neutral. On 11 July 1945 Deputy James Dillon asked in the Dáil: 'Are we a republic or are we not, for nobody seems to know?' and Mr De Valera replied: 'We are, if that is all the Deputy wants to know.'[2] A week later he amplified his reply, stating that the political classification of a State depended on its institutions and its fundamental laws, and referring Deputies to the definitions of a republic to be found in various standard dictionaries. His Majesty's Governments in the rest of the Commonwealth made no comment. In September 1947 Mr De Valera stated that Eire was 'associated with the States of the British Commonwealth of Nations' but

[1] Nicholas Mansergh, *The Commonwealth and the Nations* (London, Oxford University Press, for the Royal Institute of International Affairs, 1948) p. 203.
[2] Dáil *Debates*, vol. 97, no. 8, col. 2115.

was not a Member of the Commonwealth. On 28 July 1948 Mr Costello, Prime Minister of the coalition government which had succeeded that of Mr De Valera in office, reasserted the same view.[1]

In September 1948, in the course of a visit to Ottawa, Mr Costello stated that his Government intended to repeal the External Relations Act of 12 December 1936. Commenting later on this statement, the Prime Minister of the United Kingdom, Mr Attlee, said: 'It came without any particular notice to us, but I thought that this was a matter which concerned other Commonwealth countries and I took the opportunity of the presence of representatives of Canada, Australia, and New Zealand to discuss the position with them and with representatives of the Eire Government.'[2]

The opportunity referred to was the occasion of the Commonwealth Prime Ministers' Meeting in October 1948. On 17 October, conversations were held informally at Chequers, and were subsequently renewed in Paris at the time of the session of the United Nations General Assembly during November. Mr Séan MacBride and Mr McGilligan, respectively Minister for External Affairs and Minister for Finance in Mr Costello's Government, participated for Eire. The former said afterwards that 'the discussions were cordial and revealed a general desire on the part of the British Commonwealth representatives to examine constructively any problems which may arise following the repeal of the External Relations Act'.[3] The Canadian, Australian, and New Zealand representatives had a special interest in the matter because there are in their countries large numbers of persons of Irish ancestry.[4] Mr Attlee also 'discussed the matter personally with the Prime Minister of Northern Ireland'.[5]

Mr Costello's first statement regarding his Government's intention to repeal the External Relations Act was made in an address to the Canadian Bar Association at the beginning of September 1948, when he said that, for historical reasons, the Crown was anathema in Eire, and the steps taken to remove it from the government and constitution of Eire were steps in a progressive process of bringing the country's political institutions into harmony with national sentiment. The provisions of the External Relations Act were full of 'inaccuracies and infirmities'. At a press conference on 7 September at Ottawa he said that legal

[1] In reply to a question in the Dáil.
[2] *Hansard* (Commons), vol. 464, col. 1854.
[3] *Round Table*, vol. 39, no. 153 (December 1948), p. 47.
[4] *Hansard* (Commons), vol. 464, col. 1854.
[5] ibid. vol. 458, col. 1414.

arrangements would be made to continue Eire's close relations with the Commonwealth countries, but without any formal association.[1]

The Bill to repeal the External Relations Act was introduced into the Dáil on 17 November, and Mr Costello moved the second reading on 24 November in a speech in which he commented extensively on the internal political history of Eire since 1921 and stressed again his view that strife had been fostered by the continuance, even in an emasculated form, of Eire's links with the Commonwealth. The final severance would promote domestic harmony on the one hand, and good relations with the Commonwealth, towards whose Members he emphasized Irish good will, on the other. Regarding the Crown, he said: 'The Bill will end, and end for ever, in a simple, clear and unequivocal way, this country's long and tragic association with the institution of the British Crown, and will make it manifest, beyond equivocation and subtlety, that the national and international status of this country is that of an independent republic.' The Bill was not

conceived in any spirit of hostility to the British people or to the institution of the British Crown. Least of all is there any notion of hostility to the person who now occupies the throne of England, and who has carried out his duties with efficiency and dignity. . . . The harp beneath the Crown was a badge of servitude, and that could not be eliminated from the consciousness of the people. . . . To those who now asked them why they were leaving the Commonwealth [he would reply] We are not leaving it because . . . in my opinion we left it in 1936. To those who say we are cutting the last link with the Crown, I would ask what sort of a link it was—a link made by a rubber stamp? . . . I want to get . . . a symbol round which our people can rally—the idea of a republic.[2]

The Bill received a unanimous second reading on 26 November, was signed by the President of Eire on 21 December, and came into force on 18 April 1949. As from midnight on that day Eire ceased formally to have any place within the Commonwealth association. The position was recognized in United Kingdom legislation by the Ireland Act, introduced into the House of Commons on 3 May 1949, but retrospective to 18 April. It received the Royal Assent on 2 June 1949.

In form this was in the main a declaratory Act, the point being made in the second reading debate by the Lord President of the Council, Mr Herbert Morrison, that it recognized a *de facto*

[1] *Irish Times*, 8 September 1948.
[2] *Irish Press* and *Irish Times*, 25 November 1948.

situation created by the initiative of another country.[1] It is described as

> An Act to recognize and declare the constitutional position as to the part of Ireland heretofore known as Eire, and to make provision as to the name by which it may be known and the manner in which the law is to apply it; to declare and affirm the constitutional position and the territorial integrity of Northern Ireland and to amend, as respects the Parliament of the United Kingdom, the law relating to the qualifications of electors in constituencies in Northern Ireland; and for purposes connected with the matters aforesaid.[2]

By Section 1:

> (1) It is hereby recognized and declared that the part of Ireland heretofore known as Eire ceased, as from the eighteenth day of April, nineteen hundred and forty-nine, to be part of His Majesty's dominions.
>
> (2) It is hereby declared that Northern Ireland remains part of His Majesty's dominions and of the United Kingdom and it is hereby affirmed that in no event will Northern Ireland or any part thereof cease to be part of His Majesty's dominions and of the United Kingdom without the consent of the Parliament of Northern Ireland.

The Act recognized that Eire should henceforth be known 'by the name attributed thereto by the law thereof . . . the Republic of Ireland'.

Section 2 (1) of the Act provided that the Republic of Ireland, although no longer part of His Majesty's dominions, 'is not a foreign country' for the purposes of United Kingdom law and statutory orders. Section 2 (2) provided that the Republic's representative in the United Kingdom shall have the same privileges and exemptions as Dominion High Commissioners. The 'non-alien' status of Irish citizens provided for by the British Nationality Act of 1948[3] was preserved by Section 3 (1) (a) (i), and any Acts confirming past agreements between the United Kingdom, Northern Ireland, and Eire were preserved by the rest of Section 3 (1). Section 3 (2) provided that references to Eire in legislation passed before 31 December 1949 shall be interpreted as referring to the Republic of Ireland; except the Regency Act, 1937, and any law touching the succession to the Throne or the Royal Style and Titles (Section 3 (3)).

Only the United Kingdom passed an Act declaring that Eire had ceased to form part of His Majesty's dominions. This declaration, and that part of the Ireland Act which excluded the new

---

[1] *Hansard* (Commons), vol. 464, col.1951.
[2] 12 & 13 Geo. 6, c. 41.
[3] See Chapter III, below.

Republic from the operation of the Regency Act and of the law touching the succession and the Royal Style and Titles, were of concern to the whole Commonwealth; the other parts of the Act were directly concerned with United Kingdom law. It was clear from Government statements in the House of Commons that the other Commonwealth members were consulted regarding the matters raised by the action of the Government of Eire, Dr Evatt, Mr St Laurent, and Mr Peter Fraser having taken a prominent and constructive part in the discussions.[1] The following statements are also relevant:

MR HERBERT MORRISON: It is the case that the Dominions were consulted broadly about the development which had taken place as a result of the passing of the Republic of Ireland Act by the Dáil of Dublin. There were consultations . . . with representatives of the appropriate Dominions. That was right, because obviously a Commonwealth issue was raised when the new Republic was insisting on going out of the Commonwealth. . . . It raised all sorts of repercussions in the Commonwealth. . . . But with respect to Northern Ireland, . . . that is essentially a United Kingdom matter. Northern Ireland is part of the United Kingdom. Therefore, that is the domestic business of the United Kingdom Government and the Government of Northern Ireland. . . . The Dominions were not consulted about that particular point; but I am sure that they would not expect to be consulted.[2]

MR P. J. NOEL-BAKER (*Secretary of State for Commonwealth Relations*): This Bill results from . . . the decision of the Government of Eire to leave the Commonwealth. . . . That decision being made, we had to settle the future relations between the people and Government of the new Republic and the people and Government of this country.[3]

MR CHUTER EDE (*Home Secretary*): He asked me if before Mr Costello spoke there had been any documents passing between the two countries of Eire and the United Kingdom indicating that any pronouncement was going to be made. I am authorized by my Rt Hon. Friend the Secretary of State for Commonwealth Relations to say this: There were no documents; there were no conversations. My Rt Hon. Friend was in Dublin on the day the report of Mr Costello's speech came through, and it came as a complete surprise to him. . . . We have said: 'Well, we are sorry that you have gone. . . . You have desired to cut the last thread, but we do not bolt any door.' . . . If at any time the Republic of Ireland desires to re-enter the Commonwealth she will find that the door is open, that there will be a warm welcome, and that no questions about the past and recent events will be asked.[4]

[1] As mentioned by Mr Costello in the debate in the Dáil on 24 November 1948, and by Mr Attlee, *Hansard* (Commons), vol. 464, col. 1854.
[2] *Hansard*, (Commons), vol. 464, cols. 1956-7.
[3] ibid. vol. 465, col. 348.
[4] ibid. cols. 391-2.

The bulk of the time in the House of Lords debate was given to a highly technical point of nationality law, affecting the preservation of their status as British subjects of persons born in Ireland before the establishment of the Irish Free State who would be citizens of Eire under the Irish interpretation of that country's laws. The point was finally cleared up by an amendment to the Ireland Bill, which was accepted by the Cabinet. On the more general questions of Commonwealth convention the following may be noted:

SIR WILLIAM JOWITT (*Lord Chancellor*): I have it in command to acquaint this House that His Majesty, having been informed of the contents of this Bill, is prepared to place his Prerogatives and Interests, so far as they concern the matters dealt with by this Bill, at the disposal of Parliament. . . .[1]

We rejoice in the fact that the Member States of the Commonwealth have complete freedom. If any one of those Member States decides that she desires to go out of the Commonwealth, then beyond all argument she has a perfect right to do so. Ireland did so decide. . . .[2]

We may have been right or we may have been wrong . . . but the line we took was the line that every one of the Dominions wanted us to take and pressed us to take. If we had taken any other line than that which we took, about not making [the Irish] foreigners, and the rest of it, we should have been acting in the teeth of advice from Canada, Australia, and New Zealand, three Dominions which have vast masses of Irish people, and we should have found ourselves taking a line different from the line which I have no doubt they in their case will take. . . .[3]

The opinion of every constituent member of the British Commonwealth is that we should accept this title of 'Republic of Ireland'.[4]

Changes in Fully Self-Governing Membership:
(2) India and Pakistan

An account of the welcoming of India to the circle of the Imperial Conferences was given in the first issue of this handbook.[5] In the event, the accession of India to fully self-governing membership of the Commonwealth took a form which had not then been officially contemplated: for the territory of 'British India' was divided into two sovereign States, and the Princely States and the two new Dominions were left free to negotiate together the terms of their future relationship.

[1] *Hansard* (Lords), vol. 162, col. 907. A similar statement had been made in the House of Commons by the Prime Minister; and was made at the second reading of the British North America Bill, 1949 (see pp. 33–4, below).
[2] ibid. col. 910.
[3] ibid. col. 964.
[4] ibid. col. 1265.
[5] G. E. H. Palmer, *Consultation and Co-operation in the British Commonwealth* (London, Oxford University Press, for R.I.I.A., 1934), pp. 13–14.

The creation of the Dominions was by Act of the United Kingdom Parliament, which received the Royal Assent on 18 July 1947, and of which Section 1 (1) ran: 'As from the fifteenth day of August, nineteen hundred and forty-seven, two independent Dominions shall be set up in India, to be known respectively as India and Pakistan.' Section 6 of the Act sets out the powers of the Legislatures of the new Dominions and—in the words of Mr Attlee—'has, in substance . . . precisely the same effect' as Sections 2-6 of the Statute of Westminster.[1]

Prior to the passage of the Indian Independence Act there had been no formal statement that the other Members of the Commonwealth concurred in the action of the United Kingdom Government. As has been seen above, during the second reading debate, Mr Attlee stated that the other Commonwealth Prime Ministers had agreed to the omission from the Royal Style and Titles of the words 'Indiae Imperator' and 'Emperor of India', which may be assumed to indicate that concurrence was obtained through the normal channels of consultation.

The question whether the newly created Dominions would be free, if they so desired, to withdraw later from the Commonwealth association was dealt with in the House of Commons on 3 June 1947. The Prime Minister, Mr Attlee, after outlining the plan and the practical steps to be taken to transfer power in accordance with the wishes of the Indians themselves, stated:

The major political parties [in India] have repeatedly emphasized their desire that there should be the earliest possible transfer of power in India. With this desire His Majesty's Government are in full sympathy, and . . . as the most expeditious, and indeed the only practicable way of meeting this desire, His Majesty's Government propose to introduce legislation during the current session for the transfer of power this year on a Dominion status basis to one or two successor authorities according to the decisions taken as a result of this announcement. This will be without prejudice to the right of Indian Constituent Assemblies to decide in due course whether or not the part of India in respect of which they have authority will remain within the British Commonwealth.[2]

Mr Churchill followed Mr Attlee, stating that, provided the two conditions implicit in His Majesty's Government's offer—agreement among the Indian parties themselves and acceptance of a period of Dominion status—were fulfilled, 'then I say that all parties in this House are equally pledged by the offer and declaration'.

---

[1] *Indian Independence Act* 1947 (10 & 11 Geo. 6, c. 30); *Hansard* (Commons), vol. 439, cols. 2450-1.
[2] ibid. 3 June 1947, vol. 438, col. 40.

His Majesty's Government's statement related only to British India, and the position with regard to the Princely States was that paramountcy lapsed and did not pass to the successor Dominions, and the States, having therefore regained their independence, were free to decide whether they would adhere as 'willing partners'[1] to either successor Dominion, on terms to be negotiated between the two parties. The question of the position of the States in the event of the Dominion to which they had adhered leaving the Commonwealth was raised in the committee stage debate on the Indian Independence Bill by the junior Member for Cambridge University, Mr Wilson Harris. The Attorney-General, Sir Hartley Shawcross, replying, said:

> The position of States which have acceded to a Dominion which subsequently decides to secede from the British Commonwealth is a matter on which it would be impossible to make a definite statement now, since it depends entirely on the terms on which the State has acceded to the Dominion. That will be a matter dependent in part on the Constitution of the Dominion concerned, and in part on any agreement that may be negotiated between it and a particular State. I do not doubt that a State, in negotiating terms on which it could accede to the Dominion, may make it a condition that the accession should be conditional on the Dominion concerned remaining within the Commonwealth.[2]

The Viceroy, Lord Mountbatten, broadcast on All-India Radio on the same day as Mr Attlee's statement. He said: 'I wish to emphasize that this legislation [granting Dominion status] will not impose any restriction on the power of India as a whole or of the two new States if there is partition, to decide in the future their relationship to each other and to other Member States of the British Commonwealth.'

The question of the acceptance by the new Dominions of the matters agreed at past Imperial Conferences was raised in the committee stage of the Bill. A Member asked: 'To what extent do these decisions apply to the new Dominions? Will they accede to them, or do they automatically apply?' Mr Attlee replied: 'It is difficult to answer that question straight off. We are dealing here [Clause 1 of the Bill] with a particular status, not with agreements made by those enjoying that status. Whether the new Dominions accede to those agreements would be a matter for their consideration.'[3]

---

[1] Indian Independence Bill, second reading, *Hansard* (Commons), vol. 439, cols. 2451–2.
[2] ibid. vol. 440, cols. 116–17.
[3] 14 July 1947, *Hansard* (Commons), vol. 440, cols. 45–6.

Changes in Fully Self-Governing Membership: (3) *Ceylon*

By the year 1946 Ceylon's constitutional evolution had reached a condition of full self-government 'in all matters of internal civil administration'. Under the island's latest Constitution, granted in 1946—generally called the 'Soulbury Constitution'—elections were due to take place in August–September 1947; and on 18 June the Secretary of State for the Colonies, Mr Creech Jones announced in the House of Commons that His Majesty's Government in the United Kingdom was preparing to negotiate with the Government of Ceylon, as soon after the elections as possible, for the amendment of the Soulbury Constitution in respect of the subjects which had been reserved under it. Thus Ceylon would attain unlimited self-government and would proceed to full member status inside the Commonwealth. In making the announcement Mr Creech Jones expressly stated that the action was to be taken in consultation with the other Dominions, and that agreements about the reserved subjects 'will have to be ... satisfactory to the Ceylon Government, to ourselves, and the Commonwealth'.[1]

The necessary agreements were signed on 11 November 1947. The Ceylon Independence Bill was presented to Parliament on 13 November, passed through all its stages, and came into force on 4 February 1948. The first of the three agreements of 11 November 1947 between the United Kingdom and Ceylon Governments set out their mutual interest in the protection and security of each other's territory, and provided for mutual military aid for safeguarding this interest against external aggression.[2] By the second agreement, on external affairs, the Government of Ceylon undertook to adopt and follow the resolutions of past Imperial Conferences, and to observe the principles and practice common to Members of the Commonwealth in regard to external affairs generally and to consultation and the communication of information in particular. The United Kingdom undertook to support any application by Ceylon for membership of the United Nations or of its Specialized Agencies. An exchange of High Commissioners was agreed, and the procedure for the exchange of diplomatic representatives between Ceylon and foreign States was set out. All obligations, responsibilities, rights and benefits under valid international instruments hitherto devolving upon or enjoyed by the United Kingdom shall, in so far as the instruments may be held to apply to Ceylon, devolve upon and

---

[1] ibid. vol. 438, col. 2016.
[2] The texts of the three agreements are contained in Cmd. 7257 (1948). The defence agreement is quoted on p. 275, below, and the external affairs agreement on p. 203.

be enjoyed by the Government of Ceylon. The third of the agreements safeguarded the interests of public servants in Ceylon who had hitherto held their appointments from the Secretary of State, or the Crown Agents for the Colonies.

The Lord Privy Seal, Lord Addison, opening the second-reading debate on the Ceylon Independence Bill in the House of Lords on 4 December 1947, said: 'This is the first occasion in our history in which a colony, developing this system of self-government of its own accord, has deliberately sought to become a Dominion State in our Commonwealth . . . but we hope and expect that it will not be the last.'[1]

Commonwealth Convention in Relation to Change in the Political Character of a Member

In the last two years there have been two cases of territories changing their political classification: Newfoundland, which entered into union with Canada as a tenth province of the Canadian federation; and India, which formally became a republic.

Newfoundland was one of the six Dominions enumerated in Section 1 of the Statute of Westminster. It was at that time a unitary State with a Parliament of two Houses, and was constitutionally equal in all respects to the other Dominions. Like Australia and New Zealand, under Section 10 of the Statute it had formally to adopt Sections 2–6. It had not done so by 1933, when a Royal Commission, sent to Newfoundland to examine its financial position, recommended that the Newfoundland Constitution, which was contained in Letters Patent of 1876 and 1905, should be suspended. In accordance with current constitutional convention, the legislation for suspension could only be introduced into the United Kingdom Parliament at the request of Newfoundland.[2] The Newfoundland Parliament therefore passed an Address to the King, asking for the necessary Imperial legislation, and the Newfoundland Act of 1933 (24 and 25 Geo. V, c. 2) was passed by the United Kingdom Parliament. The Newfoundland Parliament's Address to His Majesty is attached as the first schedule to the Act.

Under the authority of this Act, Letters Patent were issued abolishing the Newfoundland Parliament and transferring the power of legislation for the peace, welfare, and good government of Newfoundland to the Governor,[3] acting with the advice and

---

[1] *Hansard* (Lords), vol. 152, col. 1205.

[2] In the committee stage of the British North America Act, 1949, the Attorney-General for the United Kingdom, Sir Hartley Shawcross, said that the provisions of Section 4 of the Statute of Westminster were not applicable (*Hansard*, Commons, vol. 462, cols. 1265–71).

[3] The Governor of Newfoundland, before 1933, had the same status and functions as the Governors-General of other Dominions.

consent of a Commission of Government. This Commission of Government consisted of six members, three from Newfoundland and three from the United Kingdom. 'The Governor is its chairman, and the Governor in Commission—that is, the Governor acting on the advice of the Commission—is responsible to the Secretary of State and, through him, to Parliament.'[1] Newfoundland ceased to have a High Commissioner in London, and was therefore unrepresented at the Dominion High Commissioners' regular meetings with the Secretary of State for Dominion Affairs (see p. 168, below); and was necessarily unrepresented at the various Dominion Prime Ministers' meetings during and since the war. There was a Newfoundland Trade Commissioner in London; the Newfoundland Offices in Ottawa and Washington were closed.

Since Newfoundland had not adopted Sections 2–6 of the Statute of Westminster, the abdication of King Edward VIII and the succession of King George VI became effective in Newfoundland by the Act of the United Kingdom Parliament which effected the change in the United Kingdom.

The war produced, at least temporarily, a condition of great prosperity in Newfoundland, and the island emerged from its financial difficulties. The annex to the first schedule to the Act of 1933 set out two conditions for the restoration of self-government to Newfoundland: financial solvency, and a request from the people of Newfoundland. Neither the schedule nor the Letters Patent establishing Commission Government set out a procedure for the making of the request.

'The arrangements made in 1933 included a pledge by His Majesty's Government that as soon as the island's difficulties had been overcome and the country was again self-supporting, responsible government, on request from the people of Newfoundland would be restored.'[2] Ten years later, however, it was apparent that the Newfoundlanders might wish to consider other choices besides a return to the pre-1934 status, and cognizance was taken of this in a statement made on 2 December 1943. The Under-Secretary of State for the Dominions, Mr Emrys-Evans, told the House of Commons:

As soon as practicable after the end of the war in Europe, machinery must be provided for enabling the Newfoundland people to examine the future of the island and to express their considered views as to the form of Government they desire, having regard to the financial and economic conditions prevailing at the time. . . . If the general wish of

[1] The Under-Secretary of State for the Dominions, Mr Emrys-Evans, 16 December 1943, *Hansard* (Commons), vol. 395, col. 1799.
[2] *Hansard* (Commons), vol. 395, cols. 599–600.

the people should be for a return to full responsible government we for our part shall be very ready, if the island is then self-supporting, to facilitate such a change. If, however, the general wish should be either for the continuance of the present form of Government or for some change of system which would fall short of full responsible government, we shall be prepared to examine such proposals sympathetically and consider within what limits the continued acceptance of responsibility by the United Kingdom could be recommended to Parliament. . . . In accordance with this statement of policy, my Noble Friend will take steps to ascertain what machinery would be most acceptable to Newfoundland public opinion and to devise means to enable it to be put into effect at an appropriate moment. . . . I would like to add that there is no desire on the part of the Government to impose any particular solution. The Government will be guided by the freely expressed views of the people. It is for Newfoundland to make the choice, and the Government, with the assent of Parliament, will be very ready to give effect to their wishes.[1]

In the House of Commons, on 11 December 1945, the Prime Minister, Mr Attlee, announced His Majesty's Government's plan for enabling the people of Newfoundland to consider and discuss their future status. He said:

In pursuance of the statement of policy made on behalf of the Coalition Government in December 1943, which they fully endorse, His Majesty's Government have decided to set up in Newfoundland next year, as early as climatic conditions permit, an elected National Convention of Newfoundlanders. Elections to the Convention will be held broadly on the basis of the former Parliamentary constituencies. All adults will be entitled to vote and candidates for election will be required to be *bona fide* residents in the districts they seek to represent. . . .

The Convention will be presided over by a Judge of the Supreme Court of Newfoundland, and its terms of reference will be as follows:

'To consider and discuss amongst themselves, as elected representatives of the Newfoundland people, the changes that have taken place in the financial and economic situation of the island since 1934 and, bearing in mind the extent to which the high revenues of recent years have been due to war-time conditions, to examine the position of the country and to make recommendations to His Majesty's Government as to possible forms of future government to be put before the people at a national referendum.

'In order to assist the Convention, His Majesty's Government will make available to it when it meets the services of an expert adviser who could give guidance on constitutional forms and procedure; and they will also prepare for use of the Convention a factual and objective statement of the island's financial and economic situation. This statement will be made available to Parliament at the same time. . . .

[1] ibid.

'The object of the procedure which His Majesty's Government proposes is to enable the people of the island to come to a free and informed decision as to their future form of government.'

Elections to the forty-five seats in the National Convention were held on 21 June 1946, there being 129 candidates. The Convention assembled in September.

The full details of the process of changing the status of Newfoundland cannot be related in this handbook. Two points may be selected for notice, however. First, 'the true position in law . . . after the 1933 Statute had been passed, was that the United Kingdom Parliament enjoyed complete sovereignty, unfettered sovereignty, over Newfoundland and that Newfoundland, although in name a Dominion, was in fact a colony.'[1] Second, Parliament would use its sovereign power in accordance with the wishes of the people of Newfoundland; and would establish procedural machinery for the people to express their wishes.

Section 146 of the British North America Act, 1867, provided a procedure for one of the possible choices the people of Newfoundland might make, union with Canada; but the conditions in which it could be used were not all present in 1946-9. First, it required an Address to the Crown from both the Canadian Federal Parliament and the Newfoundland Legislature; and the latter had ceased to exist in 1934. Second, 'the Prime Minister of Canada, Mr St Laurent . . . argued in his House of Commons [on 8 February 1949] that it [the procedure] is not appropriate to the present constitutional position of his country, because the King in respect of Canada now exercises his prerogative not on the advice of his Ministers in the United Kingdom but on the advice of his Ministers in Canada alone.'[2] Moreover, this procedure covered only one choice, and provision had to be made for others, as well as for their consideration before parliamentary action could be taken. As outlined in the statement of 11 December 1945, the United Kingdom Parliament arranged *ad hoc* for consultative procedure in Newfoundland; and, when in due course Canada became concerned, there was consultation between Canada, the United Kingdom, representatives of the Newfoundland Convention, and the Newfoundland Commission of Government.

---

[1] The Attorney-General, Sir Hartley Shawcross (*Hansard*, Commons, vol. 462, col. 1266). Both he, and the Secretary of State for Commonwealth Relations, Mr P. J. Noel-Baker, stated the related point that the sovereign Parliament of the United Kingdom had complete power to legislate even when an appeal to the Privy Council on issues concerned was pending and, in the case of the unheard Newfoundland appeal, would legislate 'in the public interest' (ibid. cols. 376-7, 1267-78).
[2] Mr P. J. Noel-Baker, in the second-reading debate on the British North America Act (2 March 1949, *Hansard* (Commons), vol. 462, col. 378).

Parliamentary action to give effect to the decisions arrived at after consultation was taken by the two sovereign Parliaments concerned, in Canada and the United Kingdom. The final legislative action was taken by the United Kingdom; in accordance in respect of Canada, with Sections 4 and 7 of the Statute of Westminster, and, in respect of Newfoundland, with the United Kingdom Parliament's sovereignty over the island.

It is clear from the terms of reference quoted on p. 22 above that the United Kingdom, in undertaking to carry out the people's wishes, had not confined itself to taking account only of the views of the National Convention, as expressed by majority vote, nor had it undertaken to be bound by the Convention's recommendations. The United Kingdom Government held that the size of the vote for confederation with Canada on 3 June 1948 justified a decision to put that choice on the referendum paper, despite the National Convention's vote against such a course. It also held that, although the vote only gave a majority of 6,686 out of 149,657 cast in the referendum of 22 July 1948, the fact that eighteen out of twenty-five electoral districts voted for union with Canada sufficiently fortified the result.[1] Moreover, 'consequent upon this result,' the United Kingdom Government consulted the Canadian Government and found that they, too, were willing to proceed with arrangements for union.[2]

Negotiations opened at Ottawa on 4 October 1948, and terms of union were agreed by 11 December. A Bill to approve the proposed terms of union was introduced in the Canadian Parliament on 7 February 1949, and received an unopposed second reading on 8 February. On 15 February the Canadian side of the preliminaries to union was completed by the passage, by 170 to 74, of a resolution embodying an Address from the Canadian Parliament to His Majesty, petitioning him to invite the United Kingdom Parliament to pass the legislation needed to give effect to the terms of union. These terms were approved by the Newfoundland Commission of Government on 21 February.

His Majesty's Government in the United Kingdom, in order to give effect to the petition in the Canadian Parliament's Address, introduced the British North America Bill, which received its second reading in the House of Commons on 2 March 1949. The Bill, which proposed that Newfoundland should confederate with Canada on 31 March 1949, passed through all its stages and received the Royal Assent on 23 March. Newfoundland became the tenth Province of Canada on 31 March.

[1] The relevant United Kingdom debates are: *Hansard* (Lords), vol. 160, cols. 627–53 and 937; vol. 161, cols. 309–49, and 586–7; *Hansard* (Commons), vol. 462, cols. 371–472, and 1259–95.
[2] *The Times*, 31 July 1948.

In the case of the decision of the Union of India to declare itself a republic, questions of procedure under the Statute of Westminster might have arisen, but in the event did not. The central issue was the matter of the consequences of the change of political character in its Commonwealth context; and the procedure employed to deal with it was arranged *ad hoc*. The procedure chosen was simple: direct consultation between the Prime Ministers of the United Kingdom, Australia, New Zealand, South Africa, India, Pakistan, and Ceylon, and (since the Prime Minister of Canada was unable to come) the Canadian Secretary of State for External Affairs. In preparation for the first full meeting on 22 April, the Prime Minister of the United Kingdom had individual talks with the visiting statesmen. The final full session (there were six in all) took place on 27 April, and the communique afterwards issued made fully clear the unanimous decisions of the meeting.

During the past week the Prime Ministers of the United Kingdom, Australia, New Zealand, South Africa, India, Pakistan, and Ceylon, and the Canadian Secretary of State for External Affairs have met in London to exchange views upon the important constitutional issues arising from India's decision to adopt a republican form of constitution and her desire to continue her membership of the Commonwealth.

The discussions have been concerned with the effects of such a development upon the existing structure of the Commonwealth and the constitutional relations between its members. They have been conducted in an atmosphere of good will and mutual understanding, and have had as their historical background the traditional capacity of the Commonwealth to strengthen its unity of purpose, while adapting its organization and procedures to changing circumstances.

After full discussion the representatives of the Governments of all the Commonwealth countries have agreed that the conclusions reached should be placed on record in the following declaration:

The Governments of the United Kingdom, Canada, Australia, New Zealand, South Africa, India, Pakistan and Ceylon, whose countries are united as Members of the British Commonwealth of Nations and owe a common allegiance to the Crown, which is also the symbol of their free association, have considered the impending constitutional changes in India.

The Government of India have informed the other Governments of the Commonwealth of the intention of the Indian people that under the new constitution which is about to be adopted India shall become a sovereign independent republic. The Government of India have, however, declared and affirmed India's desire to continue her full membership of the Commonwealth of Nations and her acceptance of the King as the symbol of the free association of its independent member nations, and as such the Head of the Commonwealth.

The Governments of the other countries of the Commonwealth, the basis of whose membership of the Commonwealth is not hereby changed, accept and recognize India's continuing membership in accordance with the terms of this declaration.

Accordingly the United Kingdom, Canada, Australia, New Zealand, South Africa, India, Pakistan and Ceylon hereby declare that they remain united as free and equal members of the Commonwealth of Nations, freely co-operating in the pursuit of peace, liberty and progress.

These constitutional questions have been the sole subject of discussion at the full meetings of Prime Ministers.

The following extracts are selected from the statements made subsequently by the participants in the meeting.

The Prime Minister of the Union of India, Pandit Nehru, broadcast in India on 10 May 1949. He said that the decisions of the meeting would be placed before the All-India Congress Committee, and before the Constituent Assembly for its approval.

Nothing has been done in secret and no commitments of any kind limiting our sovereignty in our internal or external policy have been made, whether in the political or economic or military spheres. . . . The Commonwealth is not a super-State in any sense of the term. We have agreed to consider the King as the symbolic Head of this free association. But the King has no function attached to that status in the Commonwealth. So far as the constitution of India is concerned, the King has no place and we shall owe no allegiance to him.

I have naturally looked to the interests of India for that is my first duty. I have always conceived that duty in terms of the larger good of the world. . . . Our Master taught us . . . to pursue the ways of peace and friendship. . . . I associated myself with the decisions taken in London . . . in the full belief that they were the right decisions for our country and for the world.[1]

Presenting the unanimous Declaration to the Constituent Assembly on 16 May, Pandit Nehru stressed the benefits of Commonwealth co-operation, which were recognized by India's desire to remain in the association, and by the desire of the other Members to retain India within it. 'At the same time, it is made perfectly clear that each country is completely free to go its own way', even to leaving the association. But, in a world full of disruptive forces, it was better 'to keep a co-operative association going which may do good'. The Constituent Assembly, after a two-day debate, ratified the Declaration with only one dissentient vote.

The Prime Minister of Pakistan, Mr Liaqat Ali Khan, made a press statement in London on 28 April 1949. 'India's unquali-

[1] *The Times*, 12 May 1949; *Statesman* (Calcutta), 11 May 1949.

fied affirmation of her desire to continue a full Member of the Commonwealth, and her willingness to accept the King as the symbol of the association of the Commonwealth, and, as such, Head of the Commonwealth, has enabled the other Members . . . to accept the continuation of India as a full Member.' While the relationship of other Members with the Crown remain unaffected, it had become obvious that allegiance no longer constituted an essential requirement of membership. Pakistan's position in the Commonwealth was unaffected, and it retained its full freedom to frame the constitution of its choice.[1]

The Prime Minister of Ceylon, Mr Senanayake, issued a press statement on 4 May 1949, on his return home. He welcomed the Conference decisions, and the continued membership of India, and stressed the mutual understanding and flexibility which characterized the Commonwealth. Regarding Ceylon's position, he said: 'Though we have, of course, full liberty to alter both our constitution and our relationship with the other independent nations of the Commonwealth, I think it is the consensus of opinion in Ceylon that they have been found to be satisfactory.'[2]

The Prime Minister of New Zealand, Mr Peter Fraser, told the press on his return that he ranked the London Declaration with the great landmarks of the past in Commonwealth relations, such as the Durham Report and the Balfour Declaration. He had always said that 'we in New Zealand regard membership of the British Commonwealth as not merely independence, but independence with something of great value added'. He had returned strengthened in his belief that the British Commonwealth stood more secure than ever. New Zealand's position in it was unchanged; he had made it clear 'that we would not be able to agree to any diminution whatsoever of our own bonds of allegiance to the Crown'.[3]

In South Africa the Prime Minister, Dr Malan, made a comprehensive statement, touching many aspects of policy, to the House of Assembly on 11 May. The sole question before the London Conference, he said, was whether India's expressed intention to become a republic was compatible, in the eyes of the other Commonwealth countries, with fulfilment of India's expressed desire to remain a Member of the Commonwealth; and under what arrangements. The possibility that India should occupy more or less the same position in which Ireland is placed to-day was eliminated because of India's desire to remain a Member of the Commonwealth.

[1] *The Times*, 29 April 1949; *Commonwealth Survey* (Central Office of Information, London), 14 May 1949, p. 7.
[2] *Commonwealth Survey*, 14 May 1949, p. 8.
[3] *New Zealand Herald*, 9 May 1949.

On the idea of a treaty basis of association, Dr Malan said:

I personally came to the conclusion that it would be wrong and dangerous, particularly for South Africa, to think for a moment of accepting ... that India would be associated with the Commonwealth on a treaty basis ... for this reason, that as soon as any country enters the Commonwealth on a treaty basis she is in a position where she is able to impose conditions and those conditions, in connexion with India's relations with us, could cause great difficulties, especially for South Africa. ...

[The South African view is] as long as the Commonwealth did not impose restrictions on the freedom and independence of its members or close the door to further constitutional development on the part of the separate members of the Commonwealth, so long would we in South Africa remain a member of this closer circle of sister nations known as the Commonwealth. ...

But there is yet another point of view which is important and which must not be overlooked ... the position of the Commonwealth in the world. In recent years, certain parts of the Commonwealth have broken away. ... India has declared her intention to become a republic. The impression may easily be created in the world that the Commonwealth is disintegrating, that it is no longer a powerful force in a world in which we are facing a dangerous situation. ... The decision ... to allow India to remain a member of the Commonwealth ... will give the world a different impression, and it will make the world realize that the Commonwealth is still a power in world affairs. ...

India, by becoming a republic, has broken her ties with the Crown. The link with the Crown in the case of the other members of the Commonwealth has not been broken. The question arises what the position of the Crown is in those circumstances?

The declaration by the Prime Ministers' Conference, said Dr Malan, was self-explanatory. India, although a republic, would remain a Member of the Commonwealth. No change would come about in the position of other Members of the Commonwealth.

The King will form part of the government of all the members of the Commonwealth, except in the case of India. In our own South Africa Act, the government of the country is described as consisting of the King, the Senate and the Assembly ...

The relationship of the individual members of the Commonwealth ... remains unchanged; [each] ... retains the freedom that it has enjoyed hitherto in practice; the individual member of the Commonwealth is not bound by any policy laid down at the Commonwealth Conference or Prime Ministers' Conference, or at the Imperial Conference as it was known before. They bind themselves to consult one another and, as far as possible, to co-operate with one another. ... To that extent they bind themselves morally. But nevertheless every member has the fullest right to differ from the other members and even to go so far as to oppose one another at international conferences. . . .

Dr Malan had certain objections to the words 'Head of the Commonwealth'. Describing the King as Head of the Commonwealth might give rise to misunderstanding, might create the impression that the Commonwealth was a super-State and that the individual members were to a certain extent at any rate in a subordinate position.

I explained to the conference that it was necessary, particularly in the case of South Africa, that there should be no misunderstanding. . . . I do not think there is anyone who is acquainted with the facts, who still maintains that there is a super-State or that we have not got the right to remain neutral or the right to secede. . . . I was pleasantly surprised to find at the Prime Ministers' Conference that there was not a single member at that Conference who still accepted that erroneous interpretation [of the Preamble to] the Statute of Westminster.
. . . Nevertheless, with a view to possible misunderstanding, I deemed it necessary to ask the Conference to put that interpretation in black and white. This resolution was then unanimously passed, that where the King as Head of the Commonwealth is used, it must not be interpreted to mean that it alters any of the existing rights of the various members of the Commonwealth, and that the King—although he is indicated as Head of the Commonwealth—fulfils no constitutional function as this.

The question was raised whether the declaration required legislation by the various Parliaments in order to validate it, but the legal advisers held that legislation was unnecessary. The declaration in the Preamble of the Statute of Westminster could be replaced by this new authoritative declaration:

The fact that the Commonwealth has again shown that it has the ability to adapt itself and has shown that it is not an organization but an organism, made it possible for it to exist and to remain in existence in the past; it makes it possible for it to remain in existence to-day. . . . What does that prove to us? The step that was taken at the Conference goes to show that what is described in the Preamble to the Statute of Westminster, namely, that the Commonwealth is based on a common allegiance, in other words, that all the members must—and in actual fact they do—recognize the Crown and form a link with the Crown, is not the only bond holding the Commonwealth together.
I go further and say that it is not even the most important bond holding the Commonwealth together. I do not want to detract in any way from the value of the bond of common allegiance in certain cases. . . . I also want to concede that the Kingship in the case of some other member countries of the Commonwealth is a unifying force. . . .

But there are other member countries of the Commonwealth that are in a different position. I take South Africa by way of example. . . . There are some of us who are republicans; there are others who believe in the maintenance of the link with the Crown, but I make bold to say . . . all sections in South Africa . . . agreed . . . that we want to remain in the Commonwealth if no restrictions are placed on our freedom; if our right of self-determination is not affected.[1]

The Canadian Secretary of State for External Affairs, Mr Lester Pearson, broadcast from London on 28 April 1949. He said the Declaration represented compromises and concessions— as it was bound to do—achieved by frankness and a common desire to reach agreement.

To Canada the Crown means no impairment of our freedom, but on the contrary symbolizes the continuity of our historical development and the depth and strength of our democratic roots. The King, however, stands for something more than this. He is the symbol of the free association of the Members of this Commonwealth of Nations. India joins with the rest of us in accepting the King as such a symbol and as the Head of our Commonwealth. The nations who compose it remain joined not by a written compact, but by other and stronger bonds; some by allegiance to the Crown, all by acceptance, in addition, of the symbolic position of the Crown as Head of the Commonwealth; all, too, by our common belief in . . . the bases on which the Commonwealth has been developed and on which it will grow stronger.[2]

The republican Constitution of India was adopted by the Constituent Assembly on 26 November 1949, and was proclaimed by India's last Governor-General, Mr Rajagopalachari, at New Delhi on 26 January 1950. The Preamble to the Constitution states: 'We, the people of India, having solemnly resolved to constitute India into a sovereign democratic republic . . .'

After the proclamation, the Chief Justice of India administered the oath of office to the first President of the new republic, Dr Rajendra Prasad. On 28 January the first Parliament met, and Members took the Oath of Allegiance to the Constitution.

As a result of the change in India's position within the Commonwealth association, certain changes in the law of the United Kingdom became necessary. These were effected by the India (Consequential Provision) Bill, which received its second reading in the House of Commons on 5 December 1949 without a division, passed through all its stages, and received the Royal Assent on 16 December. In moving the second reading, the Secretary of State for Commonwealth Relations, Mr P. J. Noel-Baker, said:

[1] Union of South Africa, Public Relations Office, *Dr Malan Defines South Africa's Position in the Commonwealth* (pamphlet, London, 1949).
[2] *Commonwealth Survey*, 30 April 1949, pp. 6–7.

Freedom is complete. It means sovereign independence in every facet of every Commonwealth country's life. It includes the right—that was implicit in the Statute of Westminster . . . to determine the form of constitution under which a Commonwealth country shall live. All parties in all Commonwealth countries have fully accepted that proposition for many years.

In pursuance of that right, and in fulfilment of principles which they declared before they came to power, India's leaders, with the support of their elected Parliament, have decided that India shall become a republic, with a President of its own, on 26 January 1950. . . . But Pandit Nehru, on behalf of his Government and people, also declared that India desired to remain a member of the Commonwealth.

These two decisions faced the other Governments of the Commonwealth with a new problem, something which they have never had to face before. Could a nation become a Republic, could its territory cease in law to be part of the dominions of the King, and could that nation yet remain a full member of the Commonwealth? That new question concerned not us alone, nor us and India alone; it concerned in equal measure every self-governing member of the Commonwealth. After lengthy preparatory consideration the Prime Ministers met to deal with it in April last, and everyone is familiar with their decision. . . .

They . . . agreed on a solemn declaration, unanimously accepted by all the other nations, whose relation with the Crown had not been changed, by which India remained a full and equal member of the Commonwealth, by which she accepted the King as the symbol of the free association of its independent members, and as such the Head of the Commonwealth.

'It was implicit in the historic decision,' the Minister continued, that the other links, of friendship, co-operation, and enjoyment of rights and privileges by Indians in United Kingdom and colonial law, should not be broken.

But if this is to happen there must be legislation by our Parliament. When India ceases to be in law part of His Majesty's dominions, innumerable provisions in our Statute Book will forthwith cease to apply to India and Indians unless something new is done. . . . We have sought to make [this Bill] comprehensive so that it shall cover all the many questions which may arise.[1]

By Clauses 1 (1) and (2) of the Act, existing United Kingdom and colonial law continued to apply to India, its commerce, its nationals and their property, without prejudice to the normal powers and rights to change the law. Sections 30 to 33 of the British Nationality Act, 1948 (which Act colonial legislatures have no powers to alter) continued applicable to India's citizens. Clause 1 (3) gave powers to deal by Order in Council with matters which

[1] *Hansard* (Commons), vol. 470, cols. 1542–3.

might in future arise through legislation in India which affected existing United Kingdom and colonial law.

Recent Legal Changes Affecting Dominion Constitutions

As has been noticed above, the Acts basic to the constitutions of Canada, Australia, and New Zealand were at their desire excepted from the operation of the Statute of Westminster, and under Section 4 of the Statute the position regarding amendment to the constitutions of these Members actually remained as agreed at the Imperial Conference of 1930.[1] Canada and New Zealand have, since the end of the War of 1939–45, both asked for legislation changing this position.

In the Speech from the Throne on 23 February 1944, it was announced that the New Zealand Government intended to adopt the Statute of Westminster. Four years later, in November 1947, the New Zealand Parliament passed the Statute of Westminster (Adoption) Act, which came into operation on 25 November 1947.[2] There were previously fifteen entrenched clauses in the New Zealand Constitution.

On 27 November the New Zealand Constitution (Amendment) Bill was introduced in the House of Lords, following a Request and Consent Act passed by the New Zealand Parliament shortly before. The Bill, which was designed to remove all the restrictions on constitutional amendment left by the New Zealand Constitution (Amendment) Act, 1857,[3] passed through all its stages without a division and received the Royal Assent on 10 December 1947.[4]

Moving the second reading of the Bill in the House of Commons, the Secretary of State for Commonwealth Relations, Mr P. J. Noel-Baker, explained its object as follows:

In 1852, Parliament conferred a Constitution on New Zealand, creating self-governing institutions. The Act limited the power of New Zealand to amend the Constitution. Another Act in 1857 made some changes, but left intact some of the limitations on this right to amend the Constitution. Those limitations were still retained at the desire of New Zealand by Section 8 of the Statute of Westminster. . . . The New Zealand Parliament now desire us to remove these limitations, and to give full power to amend their Constitution in any way they please. . . . In presenting their legislation [the Request and Consent Act] a little while ago, the New Zealand Government . . . said that the sole purpose . . . was to give them the full legislative capacity which every self-governing member of the British Commonwealth possessed . . . [and not] to lessen the tie between New Zealand and the Empire.[5]

---

[1] pp. 5 and 7 above.
[2] No. 38 of 1947.
[3] 21 & 22 Vict., c. 53.
[4] 11 & 12 Geo. vi, c. 4.
[5] *Hansard* (Commons), vol. 445, cols. 797–8.

In the House of Lords, Lord Addison pointed out that the saving to the New Zealand Constitution of 1857 by Section 8 of the Statute of Westminster was now being revoked as provided for by Section 10 (2) of the same Statute.[1]

Similar action to remove limitations on its powers was taken by the Canadian Parliament also during 1949. On 27 October the Canadian House of Commons passed a resolution (introduced by the Prime Minister, Mr St Laurent, on 17 October) petitioning His Majesty, in an Address, to invite the United Kingdom Parliament to amend Section 91 of the British North America Act, 1867. The purpose of the requested amendment was to give the Canadian Parliament power to amend the Constitution embodied in this Act: except in regard to 'rights and privileges by this or any other Constitutional Act granted or secured to the Legislature or the Government of a Province'.[2] Other matters excepted were: existing rights and privileges in the field of education; the use of the English and French languages; and extension of the term of a Canadian House of Commons beyond five years' duration (except in cases of war and emergency).

In accordance with the terms of the Address, the British North America (No. 2) Bill, 1949, was introduced in the House of Lords on 16 November, passed through all its stages without a division, and received the Royal Assent on 16 December. Moving the second reading, the Lord Privy Seal, Lord Addison, said:

It so happens that, when the Statute of Westminster was passed, at the express request of the Canadian Government an exception was made with regard to the British North America Act, with special reference to the division of powers between the Federal and Provincial authorities. . . . The Bill before you . . . will authorize the Canadian Parliament to amend the Canadian Constitution in relation to the matters which are solely within the jurisdiction of that Parliament. . . . I understand that early in the New Year there will be a conference between the Federal and Provincial authorities in Canada to consider matters which are semi-federal or semi-provincial in their character.[3]

In the House of Commons, the Secretary of State for Commonwealth Relations, Mr P. J. Noel-Baker, said:

In proposing the Address to His Majesty, the Canadian Prime Minister said in the Canadian House of Commons: 'It is our responsibility to see that the fundamentals of the Canadian Constitution are protected and preserved. It is a matter to be settled in Canada by Canadians and for Canadians. . . . It should not be left as a burden

---

[1] *Hansard* (Lords), vol. 152, col. 1018.
[2] Clause 1 of the British North America Act (No. 2) 1949.
[3] *Hansard* (Lords), vol. 165, cols. 809-10. The conference referred to opened on 10 January 1950.

on the Parliament of another nation.' I am sure that everyone in the United Kingdom will agree with what Mr St Laurent said. . . . The legislatures of the provinces of Canada can amend their own provincial constitutions. They have full powers in that regard.[1]

[1] *Hansard* (Commons), vol. 470, cols. 1458–62. The Canadian Parliament abolished the appeal to the Privy Council in civil cases in September 1949; see below, p. 127.

Part I

MACHINERY FOR CONSULTATION AND CO-OPERATION

CHAPTER II

THE CROWN AND THE GOVERNORS-GENERAL

THE Declaration of 27 April 1949 and its effect on the position of the Crown in relation to the Republic of India has been set out in the preceding chapters; as have also the modifications of the position of the Crown in relation to Eire before 1949, and the statements made and legislation enacted when Eire became a republic and its Commonwealth association ended. The changes in the Royal Style and Titles made in 1927 and 1947 have been noticed, and the change in the Succession in 1936. The position of Governors-General has only been briefly touched upon since this matter was fully dealt with in the first issue of this handbook.[1] Certain other matters remain to be noticed, and will be found below in chronological order.

The Status of the Union Act, 1934

In 1934, the Parliament of the Union of South Africa passed *An Act*[2] *to provide for the declaration of the Status of the Union of South Africa; for certain amendments of the South Africa Act, 1909, incidental thereto, and for the adoption of certain parts of the Statute of Westminster, 1931.* It was primarily an Act to declare status, and to adopt the Preamble, and sections relevant to the Union, of the Statute of Westminster, which 'shall be deemed to be an Act of the Parliament of the Union and shall be construed accordingly'; but it also defined the position of the Crown in the Union. Section 4 of the Act replaced a provision of the South Africa Act, 1909, which read: 'The Executive Government of the Union is vested in the King and shall be administered by His Majesty in person or by a Governor-General as his representative.' It declared:

'The Executive Government of the Union in regard to any aspect of its domestic or external affairs is vested in the King, acting on the advice of his Ministers of State for the Union, and may be administered by His Majesty in person or by a Governor-General as his representative.'

The Section went on to affirm that any reference to the King in the Act, or in the South Africa Act, 1909, intended the King acting on the advice of his Ministers in the Union, but qualified

---

[1] See pp. 6, 8-10, 30-2, and 231-38 (Appendix A); also, in the second issue, pp. 5-106.
[2] No. 69 of 1934.

this by the phrase 'save where otherwise stated'. Section 5 of the Status Act provided that the words 'heirs and successors' should be taken to mean 'His Majesty's heirs and successors in the sovereignty of the United Kingdom of Great Britain and Ireland as determined by the laws relating to the succession of the Crown of the United Kingdom of Great Britain and Ireland'. The power of the Governor-General to dismiss Ministers was expressly preserved. Reservation of Bills was abolished, save only in connexion with legislation relating to appeals to the Judicial Committee of the Privy Council or altering the conditions for the transfer to the Union of the High Commission Territories. The Oath of Allegiance was altered, the words 'of the United Kingdom of Great Britain and Ireland' being deleted.

The Royal Executive Functions and Seals Act, 1934[1]

This Act was supplementary to the Status Act. It provided for a separate Royal Great Seal and Signet for the Union. It authorized the Governor-General, acting on the advice of the Union Government, to dispense with His Majesty's Sign Manual 'whenever for any reason the King's Sign Manual cannot be obtained or whenever the delay involved in obtaining the King's signature to any instrument in the ordinary course would, in the opinion of the Governor-General-in-Council, either frustrate the object thereof, or unduly retard the dispatch of public business'.

The Abdication Enactments, 1936

On 10 December 1936 His Majesty King Edward VIII executed an Instrument of Abdication. By it, he renounced the Throne for himself and his descendants, and expressed his desire that immediate effect should be given to the Instrument. The Instrument has been held to be a personal act: it was witnessed by His Majesty's brothers, but not countersigned by any Minister.[2]

In the United Kingdom, Parliament passed His Majesty's Declaration of Abdication Act. This Act effected the change of monarch for Australia and New Zealand, which in 1936 had not adopted the Statute of Westminster, and for Newfoundland.[3] Their assent thereto was, however, formally recited in the Preamble to the Act. In accordance with Section 4 of the Statute, Canada (where Parliament was not at the time in session) assented by an Order-in-Council of 10 December 1936. The Preamble to the Abdication Act recited Canada's 'request and consent'. When

---

[1] No. 70 of 1934.
[2] A. Berriedale Keith, *The Constitution of England from Queen Victoria to George VI* (London, Macmillan, 1940) vol. I, p. 31.
[3] See p. 21, above.

the Canadian Parliament reassembled in January, it passed an Act expressing assent to the alteration in the law of Succession to the Throne set forth in the United Kingdom Act. The action taken by the Irish Free State was described in the preceding chapter.

The Preamble to the Abdication Act recited, at South Africa's desire, the Union's assent, although the Union's constitutional position, under the Status Act of 1934, was different, in that it did not rely on extensions of United Kingdom Acts, but required a statute of its own. The strict legal position regarding the abdication in respect of the Union has been variously argued. What actually happened was that the Union Government took the view that the abdication was legally effected by the monarch's act (i.e. by the execution of the Instrument of Abdication), on 10 December, but that the change in the succession (i.e. the exclusion of King Edward's possible issue) took effect with the passage of His Majesty King Edward VIII's Abdication Act by the Union Parliament in January 1937. The accession of King George VI was actually proclaimed at Pretoria on 11 December, the same day as it was proclaimed in London.

A companion Act, the Coronation Oath Act,[1] bound His Majesty to rule South Africans 'according to the Statutes agreed on in the Parliament of the Union and according to their other laws and customs'. This formula was substantially embodied in the collective oath taken by His Majesty King George VI at his coronation on 12 May 1937.

The Coronation Oath

Until the coronation of King George VI, the form of the Coronation Oath implied the full sovereignty of the United Kingdom only, referring to 'the statutes in Parliament agreed on' and 'the Dominions thereto belonging'. To bring the form into accord with the position under the Statute of Westminster, the oath taken in May 1937 ran: 'Will you solemnly promise and swear to govern the peoples of Great Britain, Ireland, Canada, Australia, New Zealand, and the Union of South Africa, of your possessions, and of the other territories to them belonging or pertaining and of your Empire of India, according to their respective laws and customs?' The alteration was not made by statute.[2]

---

[1] No. 7 of 1937.
[2] Keith, *Constitution of England*, p. 28; see also W. P. M. Kennedy, *The Constitution of Canada*, 2nd ed. (London, Oxford University Press, 1938), pp. 564–5.

The Regency Act, 1937

This Act was passed by the United Kingdom Parliament in March 1937, to provide for a regency 'in the event of a Sovereign being on his Accession under the age of eighteen years, and in the event of the incapacity of the Sovereign through illness, and for the performance of certain of the Royal functions in the name and on behalf of the Sovereign in certain other events'. By Section 2 it was provided that evidence to establish the total incapacity of the Sovereign must be given to the Privy Council and 'communicated to the Government of His Majesty's Dominions and the Government of India'. The Act did not extend to the Dominions.

We have kept the Dominion Governments informed of the proposals now before the House. The provisions as explained to the Dominion Prime Ministers [when they were in London in May 1935 for the celebration of King George V's Silver Jubilee] were found to be generally acceptable, but it was made clear that it was entirely a matter for each Dominion to decide whether any legislation of its own may be necessary.[1]

At the time of its passage, the Act was held to apply to Australia and New Zealand, which had not then adopted the Statute of Westminster, and to India and the Colonies. The 'other events' mentioned included the Sovereign's absence from the United Kingdom, in which case Counsellors of State, limited to members of the Royal Family, were to be appointed. Letters Patent under the Act were executed for the first time in May 1939, when Their Majesties visited Canada and the United States. The provision (by Letters Patent) made for this visit gave no power in respect of the Dominions.[2] Similar Letters Patent were issued on certain occasions after 1939, including the Royal visit to South Africa in 1947.

The Declarations of War, 1939–40

Proclamation of states of war and peace, and declarations of neutrality, are prerogative acts of the Crown acting on advice; and generally with the assent or confirmation of Parliament, although the constitutional usage has varied.

1. *Against Germany.* In the United Kingdom, a public notification of a state of war with Germany was issued by the Privy Council Office on 3 September 1939, and published in the *London Gazette* on that date; there was no Royal Proclamation. The Prime Minister, Mr Neville Chamberlain, broadcast to the nation

---

[1] The Home Secretary, Sir John Simon, *Hansard* (Commons), vol. 319, col. 1452.
[2] Keith, op. cit. p. 37.

at 11 a.m. and made a statement to the House of Commons at 12.6 p.m.[1]

The Prime Minister of Canada, Mr Mackenzie King, fulfilled his repeated previous pledges not to involve Canada in participation in war without the consent of Parliament. On 22 August he informed the Opposition leaders of the gravity of the situation; and they gave assurances of support. By various Canadian Orders-in-Council, the unrepealed War Measures Act of 1914 was brought into operation, and steps towards preparing the country for an emergency began. Parliament was summoned for 7 September. The Speech from the Throne put the issue of active participation before it, and was accepted without dissent by the House of Commons on 9 September. The Cabinet met that evening and with the concurrence of the Governor-General in Council, approved an Order-in-Council authorizing the Prime Minister to petition the King to declare a state of war between Canada and Germany from 10 September, by proclamation. Instructions to submit the petition to His Majesty were cabled to the Canadian High Commissioner in London, and his reply, conveying the King's approval, was received in Ottawa at 11.15 a.m. on 10 September. The proclamation was published in a special edition of *The Canada Gazette* at 12.40 p.m.[1]

The Australian Cabinet met on 3 September at 8 p.m. (Australian time—a few minutes after Mr Neville Chamberlain's broadcast at 11 a.m. B.S.T.) and approved the issue, by the Governor-General acting on the advice of the Federal Executive Council, of a proclamation of the existence of war as required under the Australian Defence Acts, 1903–39. The proclamation was immediately published in a special edition of the *Commonwealth Gazette*. At 9.15 p.m. the Prime Minister, Mr Menzies, broadcast on all Australian stations announcing to the people 'that in consequence of Germany's persistence in her invasion of Poland, Great Britain has declared war and, as a result, Australia is also at war'. As in the United Kingdom, Parliament, which was in session passed no *formal* motion of assent.[3]

In New Zealand the Governor-General announced that he had it in command from His Majesty to declare that a state of war existed between the United Kingdom and Germany from 9.30 p.m. (New Zealand time) on 3 September. The Government of New Zealand replied to 'the intimation just received' by associating themselves fully with the action of the United Kingdom. The telegram continued:

[1] *Hansard* (Commons), vol. 351, cols. 291–4.
[2] *Journal of the Parliaments of the Empire*, vol. 20, no. 4 (October 1939) pp. 891–906.
[3] ibid. pp. 929–33.

D

The existence of a state of war with Germany has accordingly been proclaimed in New Zealand and H.M. New Zealand Government would be grateful if H.M. Government in the United Kingdom would take any steps that may be necessary to indicate to the German Government that H.M. Government in New Zealand associate themselves with the action taken by H.M. Government in the United Kingdom.[1]

Parliament, which was in session, was not first consulted; on 5 September it unanimously adopted a resolution approving the Cabinet's action.

In South Africa Parliament was specially summoned to meet on 2 September. In a debate on a motion in favour of neutrality proposed by the Prime Minister of the Union, General Hertzog, on 4 September, the Government was defeated by 80 votes to 67. On being refused a dissolution by the Governor-General, General Hertzog resigned, and General Smuts was sent for, and formed a Government. On 6 September the Governor-General issued a proclamation declaring a state of war between the Union and Germany, dispensing with the Royal Sign Manual under the provision of the Royal Executive Functions and Seals Act, 1934, authorizing such a course on grounds of urgency.

The United Kingdom's action on 3 September was effective for the rest of His Majesty's dominions, including Newfoundland and India.

In Eire, Mr De Valera had made a press statement on 21 February 1939, affirming his intention to do all in his power to ensure his country's neutrality in the event of war in Europe. Parliament, which had adjourned, was summoned specially on 2 September, when Mr De Valera reaffirmed his intention as stated in February. He added:

On Thursday last [31 August] the German Minister called on me to find out what was likely to be the attitude of the Government in the event of a European war. I referred him to a statement which I had made back in February indicating what the aim of the Government policy was. The Minister said that the German attitude towards our country in case of war would be peaceful and that it would respect our neutrality. I replied that, as far as we were concerned, we wished to be at peace with Germany as well as with other States.[2]

Mr De Valera was speaking on a Bill to give the Government certain emergency powers, which passed through all its stages on the same day.

---

[1] *The Times*, 4 September 1939. Neither New Zealand nor Australia had diplomatic representation in Berlin.
[2] *Journal of the Parliaments of the Empire*, vol. 20, no. 4, p. 999.

2. *Against Other Countries*. Italy declared war against the United Kingdom on 10 June 1940. On the same day Mr Mackenzie King moved a resolution in the Canadian House of Commons:

Whereas Italy has declared her intention to enter the war on the side of Germany and against the Allied Powers; and

Whereas a state of war now exists between the United Kingdom and France on the one hand, and Italy on the other; and

Whereas at the outbreak of war the Parliament of Canada decided to stand at the side of the United Kingdom and France in their determined effort to resist aggression and preserve freedom;

It is expedient that the Houses of Parliament do approve the entry of Canada into a state of war with Italy, and that this House do approve the same.

He said that he had that day received a cable from the Secretary of State for Dominion Affairs reporting Italy's declaration of war. When the resolution had been passed, its adoption by both Houses would be followed by a submission to His Majesty from his Privy Council for Canada, with a view to the authorization by him of a Proclamation declaring the existence of a state of war between Canada and Italy.[1]

The resolution was adopted without dissent, and the Proclamation of a state of war was issued on 11 June 1940.

On the same day the Prime Minister, Mr Peter Fraser, told the New Zealand House of Representatives that the Government had sent a message to the United Kingdom Government asking them to inform the Italian Government that the Governor-General had, on that day, formally declared a state of war with Italy.[2] In Australia, a special issue of the *Gazette* announced the existence of a state of war with Italy as from 9 a.m. E.S.T. on 11 June.

In the South African Parliament, the Speech from the Throne on 26 August 1940 announced that: 'Within a few weeks of the termination of the last Session, Italy had entered the war, and a Proclamation was issued declaring the existence of a state of war between the Union and the Italian Empire.' On 29 August, in response to a peace resolution moved by the Opposition, the Prime Minister, General Smuts, moved a comprehensive amendment reaffirming the Union's intention to abide by its resolution of 4 September 1939 to enter the war; and approving the declaration of war on Italy made on 11 June 1940. The Government amendment was carried by 85 votes to 65.[3]

The declarations of war made by Australia on Finland,

[1] *Journal of the Parliaments of the Empire*, vol. 31, no. 3 (July 1940) pp. 474–5.
[2] ibid. p. 524.
[3] ibid. pp. 739, 741.

Roumania, Hungary, and Japan are instances of Commonwealth consultation as well as of procedure. Addressing the House of Representatives on 16 December 1941, the Minister for External Affairs, Dr H. V. Evatt, said that Australia's action in face of the Japanese attack of 7 December on Pearl Harbour and British territories was never in doubt, and the Cabinet meeting on 8 December had decided unanimously on a declaration of war, to be operative from 5 p.m. of that date. But the Cabinet meeting had originally been called for another purpose:

I expressed the view that it was a strange feature of the present struggle that while we were allies of Russia in her heroic struggle against Germany, we were still at peace with Finland, Hungary, and Roumania. We held that a refusal to accede to the request of Russia—that we declare war against Finland, Roumania, and Hungary—might well be disastrous to Russian morale and dangerous to our own. The Government's view, which was supported by all members of the Advisory War Council, was that the question of a declaration of war on these three countries should be submitted to Stalin, always a realist, and the decision of all the British nations should be determined by his attitude. Our suggestion was adopted by the Government of the United Kingdom. Stalin's attitude never wavered. Neither did the attitude of this country. Finally, ultimatums were addressed by the United Kingdom Government to the three Governments concerned. They were informed that unless by 5 December, they abandoned military operations against Russia, the existence of a state of war would be declared. The individuals for the time being constituting the Governments of Hungary and Roumania ignored the ultimatum. Finland gave a reply which plainly admitted that her troops were operating far beyond the original Russian frontiers, and that the British ultimatum would not be obeyed. . . .
It was to declare a state of war in the Commonwealth in relation to the three countries that the full Cabinet was summoned for 8 December last. As I have previously explained, authoritative declarations of Imperial Conferences show that this Commonwealth possesses full status in every aspect of its external relationships, as well as in all its internal affairs. It is a necessary consequence of that status that, in relation to Australia, the vital decision as to peace or war with any country should be determined exclusively by Commonwealth Ministers. I agree that facts are more important than forms. Still, there are some who will dispute the fact of power and status unless the form adopted corresponds to that fact. In this case we took special care to make the forms correspond to the facts.
As to the procedure adopted, there are three comments which should be made. First, it was important to avoid any legal controversy as to the power of the Governor-General to declare a state of war without specific authorization by His Majesty. I express no opinion whether specific authorization was necessary as a matter of strict law. Certainly the royal powers already exercisable under the Constitution

by the Governor-General as the King's representative are extremely wide. However, the matter was too important and too urgent to invite any legal controversy. We therefore decided to make it abundantly clear that there was an unbroken chain of prerogative authority extending from the King himself to the Governor-General. For that purpose we prepared a special instrument, the terms of which were graciously accepted by His Majesty. Reference to the documents in the white paper will show that His Majesty assigned to His Excellency, the Governor-General, the power of declaring a state of war, first with Finland, Roumania, and Hungary, and second, a state of war with Japan.

The second and more important matter involved no legal question but did involve the question of proper constitutional practice. The procedure adopted was in accordance with the practice that, in all matters affecting Australia, both the King and his representative will act exclusively upon the advice of the Prime Minister and Ministers responsible to this House. Accordingly, His Majesty was pleased to execute the instrument to which I have referred, upon the advice of the Commonwealth Executive Council. The instrument will, in due course, be countersigned by the Prime Minister of the Commonwealth. United Kingdom Ministers took no part in the arrangements which were made directly with the palace authorities by our High Commissioner in London. Similarly, the actual proclamations of a state of war were made by His Excellency the Governor-General on the advice of his Executive Council.

Thirdly, the history of the transactions illustrates the fact that separate action by the King's Governments is perfectly consistent with close co-operation in all matters affecting their common interests.[1]

In Canada, Mr Mackenzie King tabled copies, in the House of Commons on 21 January 1942, of a Proclamation of 7 December 1941 declaring war on Roumania, Hungary, and Finland, and a Proclamation of 8 December declaring war on Japan.[2]

Similar proclamations were issued in the Union of South Africa, as stated in the Speech from the Throne on 12 January 1942. After debate, resolutions of approval were passed in both Houses on 17 January and 2 February.[3]

Changes in the Letters Patent used in the Appointment of the Governor-General of Canada

Revised Letters Patent for Canada came into force on 1 October 1947. On 12 February 1948 the Secretary of State for External Affairs, Mr St Laurent, made a statement in the Canadian House

---

[1] Dr H. V. Evatt, *Foreign Policy of Australia: Speeches* (Sydney, Angus & Robertson, 1945) pp. 18–21.
[2] *Journal of the Parliaments of the Empire*, vol. 23, no. 2 (April 1942) p. 278.
[3] ibid. p. 327 ff.

of Commons. He quoted a previous press release issued by the Prime Minister, as follows:

New Letters Patent governing the office and appointment of the Governor-General of Canada had been signed by His Majesty the King on 8 September 1947, and countersigned by the Prime Minister. The new Letters Patent came into force on 1 October 1947, and will supersede on that date the existing Letters Patent of 1931 (as amended in 1935) and the Royal Instructions of 1931[1]. The Royal documents relating to the office of Governor-General had not undergone a careful revision since 1931. The Canadian Government accordingly recommended to His Majesty the issuance of new Letters Patent, consolidating the former documents and bringing them up to date.

Apart from textual alterations designed to bring the new Letters Patent into line with constitutional developments and practices in Canada and within the Commonwealth, the principal alterations may be summarized as follows:

(a) By the introductory words of Clause 2 of the new Letters Patent, the Governor-General is authorized to exercise, on the advice of Canadian Ministers, all of His Majesty's powers and prerogatives in respect of Canada. This does not limit the King's authorities. Nor does it necessitate any change in the present practice under which certain matters are submitted by the Canadian Government to the King personally. However, when the new Letters Patent come into force, it will be legally possible for the Governor-General, on the advice of Canadian Ministers, to exercise any of the powers and authorities of the Crown in respect of Canada, without the necessity of a submission being made to His Majesty. (These . . . include, among others, Royal full powers for the signing of treaties, ratification of treaties and the issuance of letters of credence for Ambassadors.) There will be no legal necessity to alter existing practices. However, the Government of Canada will be in a position to determine, in any prerogative matter affecting Canada, whether the submission should go to His Majesty or to the Governor-General.

(b) The new Letters Patent revoke and supersede the existing Letters Patent and the existing Royal Instructions. The Royal Instructions have been incorporated in the new Letters Patent, which have been issued under the Great Seal of Canada.

No new commission will be issued to Viscount Alexander, the former Letters Patent having been revoked without prejudice to anything having been done lawfully thereunder. Moreover, Viscount Alexander's present commission is a continuous one, expressed to be subject to the existing Letters Patent or any other substituted for the same.

In a further statement on 16 February, Mr St Laurent said that there had been no communication whatsoever from the King regarding the manner agreeable to him of dealing with Ambassadors' and Ministers' letters of credence since May 1947, and there had

[1] For texts, see the first issue of this handbook, pp. 234-5.

been no communication at any time which would amount to an intrusion by the United Kingdom Government in the foreign politics of Canada. Any suggestion that His Majesty had, in the course of the correspondence with the Canadian Prime Minister, acted on the advice of United Kingdom Ministers was 'fantastic'. The right to advise His Majesty in prerogative matters affecting Canada resided exclusively in the Government of Canada. The new Letters Patent represented a significant constitutional advance in line with the Statute of Westminster and current constitutional convention in the Commonwealth.[1]

The Appointments of Governors-General of the Union of India, and Pakistan, 1947

The exceptional circumstances affecting the appointment of the Governors-General of the newly created Dominions of India and Pakistan involved certain departures from normal procedures and powers. In the second-reading debate on the Indian Independence Bill on 10 July 1947, the Prime Minister of the United Kingdom, Mr Attlee, explained the situation as follows:

Clause 5 of the Bill provides for the appointment by the King of a Governor-General for each of the new Dominions, with the proviso, however, that until provision is made to the contrary by either of the new Dominions, the same person may be Governor-General of both. This is a pretty clear Clause. Normally, it would be both unnecessary and inexpedient for a Minister here to say anything more about it. The House is, of course, aware that the appointment of a Governor-General in the Dominions is made by the King on the advice of his Ministers in the Dominion concerned, and it would be wholly improper for His Majesty's Government in the United Kingdom to be in any way concerned with the matter. But, to-day, it is necessary for me to make some further comments, because the position in relation to the appointment of Governors-General of the new Dominion is exceptional.

In the first place, there is the matter of procedure. It is not possible to follow the normal procedure in this case. Under the Bill, Governors-General will have to be appointed as from 15 August. Although the two countries become Dominions as from that date, there can be no Ministers formally to advise the Crown until a Governor-General has been appointed and Ministers have taken office. In these circumstances it was agreed with the Indian leaders, and the King's approval was obtained, that the Viceroy should consult the recognized leaders of Congress and the Muslim League as to whom they would wish to recommend for appointment as Governors-General. Then their advice would be formally tendered to the King by His Majesty's Government in the United Kingdom. This procedure would, of course, only

[1] *Journal of the Parliaments of the Empire*, vol. 29, no. 1 (April 1948) pp. 129–30.

apply in the present case. I wish to emphasize the fact that, although the appointments would be made on the formal advice of Ministers here, they were, in fact, the recommendations of the Indian leaders themselves.

So much for the exceptional procedure in the present instance. But the Viceroy has represented that it would be in the interest of all if some statement could be made at an early date about the persons who are to be recommended for these posts. This, again, is a most unusual procedure. I should inform the House that I have received the King's specific authority for referring to the recommendations before him and to which assent cannot, of course, be given until the Bill has become law. It had been intimated to us that it would be most convenient to all concerned to have one Governor-General for both of these Dominions in the initial stages, and, for some time, we proceeded on this assumption. It has recently become clear, however, that the Muslim League was in favour of a separate Governor-General to be appointed for Pakistan.

It is obviously very desirable that this matter should be settled at the earliest possible opportunity in order that the position may be understood in India, and so that the new Governors-General can prepare themselves to take over on 15 August. Both Congress and the Muslim League, who have been recognized in the Bill as the successor authorities, have made recommendations which have been conveyed by His Majesty's Government to His Majesty. While formal announcement must await the passing of the Bill, His Majesty has intimated that he is prepared to accept these recommendations as soon as the Bill is passed. The recommendations are in favour of the present Viceroy as Governor-General of India, and of Mr Jinnah as Governor-General of Pakistan.[1]

It [the Government of India Act, 1935] contained many limitations on the powers of the Legislature, and gave, among other things, extensive powers to the Governor-General and to the Provincial Governors to act in their own discretion. The proviso in Clause 8 [of the Bill] in effect sweeps away all these special powers and is intended to place the Governor-General and the Provincial Governors in the position of Dominion Governors-General—that is to say, they act only on the advice of their Ministers.

I said that the Act of 1935 will be, in the first instance, until other action is taken, the basis of the new Constitution, with necessary adaptations. Clause 9 [of the Bill] sets out the machinery of adaptation. This is to be done by order of the Governor-General. If hon. Members will refer to Clause 19, the definition Clause, they will see that up to the appointed day, 15 August, the powers are exercisable by the Governor-General, within the meaning of the Act of 1935, that is to say, by Lord Mountbatten, but after that date, where the Order or Act affects only one Dominion, by the Governor-General of that Dominion; where it concerns both Dominions, by the two Governors-General acting jointly. I must admit that the powers given here are

---

[1] *Hansard* (Commons), vol. 439, cols. 2448–50.

very wide. That is inevitable in the nature of the case. The Governor-
General has to bring the Act into operation. He has to effect a division between the two Dominions, dividing the powers, rights, assets,
property, liabilities, etc.[1]

The Appointment of the Governor-General of Ceylon, 1948

The normal procedure for appointment could not be followed
in the case of the new Dominion of Ceylon because, as in India
and Pakistan, there could be no Dominion Ministers in office
formally to advise the Crown until a Governor-General had been
appointed. Under the 'Soulbury Constitution', a government
under Mr Senanayake as Prime Minister had taken office on 25
September 1947. On the advice of Mr Senanayake, His Majesty
appointed Sir Henry Monck-Mason Moore as first Governor-
General of Ceylon.

---

[1] ibid. cols. 2455–6.

CHAPTER III

NATIONALITY AND CITIZENSHIP

The Evolution of a Common Code

QUESTIONS of nationality and citizenship have for many years been matters of consultation and co-operative action. The reasons for this derive partly from history and partly from convenience. Historically, the concept of a natural-born British subject—'born within His Majesty's allegiance'—has its foundation, not on statute, but on the Common Law of England.[1] The Common Law and the prerogative were carried to the King's dominions beyond the seas by his subjects who colonized or conquered in his name. Here was the root of a common status, based on allegiance to His Majesty.

But in more modern times the condition of birth 'within His Majesty's allegiance' did not cover all situations and categories, especially those arising from the immigration of aliens into the United Kingdom, the Dominions and Colonies. Difficulties also arose over the status of British-born persons emigrating to foreign countries, particularly the United States. Many colonies had enacted local naturalization statutes, granting local status to aliens; but this was not an imperially valid status, although it could not, under the Colonial Laws Validity Act, 1865, be repugnant to the legislation of the Imperial Parliament. The same situation obtained after these Colonies became individually or unitedly to form Dominions. The first instances of Dominion naturalization legislation were the Canadian Act of 1886, and the New Zealand Aliens Act of the same year. Other Dominions also enacted legislation or adapted previous colonial statutes; but they were still only of local validity, and the United Kingdom Naturalization Act of 1870 was limited in its application to the United Kingdom and did not consolidate the position for the Empire. The result was anomalous and inconvenient; for example, 'an alien naturalized in Australia became an alien again the moment he crossed into New Zealand'.[2]

The evident necessity for clarification led to the setting-up of a Home Office Departmental Committee which reported in 1901 in favour of legislative action.[3] Since the desirable aim was a

---

[1] The basis is declared in the judgement in *Calvin's Case*, 1608.
[2] The Secretary of State for the Colonies, Viscount Harcourt, introducing the British Nationality & Status of Aliens Act, 1914 (*Hansard* (Commons), vol. 62, col. 1198).
[3] Cd. 723.

comprehensive code of nationality law based on agreed and de-
fined principles, the Committee's report was circulated by the
Secretary of State for the Colonies to the Governments of the
Empire, inviting their views. A draft Bill was submitted to the
Colonial Conference of 1907, but was not wholly acceptable; and
the Conference passed a resolution as follows:

That with a view to attaining uniformity so far as practicable, an
inquiry should be held, to consider further the question of naturalization, and in particular, to consider how far, and under what conditions,
naturalization in one part of His Majesty's dominions should be effective in other parts of these dominions. A subsidiary conference to be
held if necessary.[1]

In the interval between the 1907 and 1911 Conferences, an
inter-departmental committee sat in the United Kingdom, and
further communication was had with the overseas Governments.
A revised draft Bill was presented to the Imperial Conference of
1911, but again did not command complete approval. The Conference adopted a resolution based on the following points of
principle put forward by the Home Secretary, Mr Winston
Churchill:

(1) Imperial nationality should be world-wide and uniform, each
Dominion being free to grant local nationality in such terms as its
legislature should think fit.

(2) The Mother Country finds it necessary to maintain five years
as the qualifying period [for naturalization]. This is a safeguard to the
Dominions as well as to her, but five years anywhere in the Empire
should be as good as five years in the United Kingdom.

(3) The grant of Imperial nationality is in every case discretionary,
and this discretion should be exercised by those responsible in the
area in which the applicant has spent the last twelve months.

(4) The Imperial Act should be so framed as to enable each self-
governing Dominion to adopt it.

(5) Nothing now proposed would affect the validity of local laws
regulating immigration or the like, or differentiating between classes
of British subjects.[2]

These five points, which were not agreed without considerable
discussion, clearly distinguished between the status of British
subject, which must be imperially valid, and the right of the
Dominions to regulate by their own municipal law the various
categories of citizenship.[3] This had an obvious application to

---

[1] Cd. 3523 (1907). [2] Cd. 5745.
[3] 'There is a common law rule of long standing that within its general legislative competence the legislature of every self-governing colony can regulate the
incidents or consequences of the imperially valid status of British subjects, but not
the *status* itself. This is still law.' (R. T. E. Latham, writing in 1937, in *Survey
of British Commonwealth Affairs*, vol. I, p. 592.)

naturalization questions, for which a completely uniform law for all British territories had been shown by the discussions not to be practical politics; but differentiation between citizenship categories could also be applied to natural-born British subjects.

Before the Imperial Conference of 1911 dispersed, a redrafted Bill was circulated to its members. Further exchanges of views occupied the next two years, and by 1913 the countries of the Commonwealth had achieved unanimity on the terms of new legislation to be introduced into the Imperial Parliament.

The Act of 1914

This legislation was the British Nationality and Status of Aliens Act, 1914, which was the fundamental statute for more than thirty years. The only parts of the Act which created any controversy were those relating to the nationality of married women, inevitably a matter of great complexity in the extensive and varied territories of a maritime empire. The Act came into operation on 1 January 1915.

The Act is divided into three parts. Part I consists of one section, defining natural-born British subjects. Part II relates to the naturalization of aliens. Part III contains general provisions on the national status of married women and infant children, the loss of British nationality, and provisions relating to procedure and evidence. . . . The material point to notice is the application of the Act. Parts I and III were intended to apply to all territories which form part of the British Empire. Their application is, however, subject to the provisions of Section 26 of the Act. The effect of this section is to preserve the power of Colonial or Dominion Governments and legislatures to legislate on the subject of nationality, and to safeguard the validity of laws passed by them relative to the treatment of different classes of British subjects. The Section must now be read in the light of the Statute of Westminster, 1931, which enables Acts of the Imperial Parliament to be repealed or amended by the Dominions, in so far as they are part of the law of the Dominion. . . . As regards Part II of the Act, Section 9 provides that it shall not have effect within the Dominions specified in the First Schedule to the Act, unless the Legislature of the Dominion adopts that Part of the Act.[1]

Most of the Dominions re-enacted Parts I and III of the Act: and adopted or re-enacted Part II on the following dates: Canada, 1914; Newfoundland, 1916; Australia, 1920 and 1936; New Zealand, 1928; Union of South Africa, 1926.[2] At the time of the passage of the Act, Ireland was a part of the United Kingdom, and no adoption or re-enactment of any part of the Act

[1] J. Mervyn Jones, *British Nationality Law and Practice* (London, Oxford University Press, 1947), pp. 114–15.
[2] ibid.

was there required. Mention of subsequent developments in the Irish Free State and Eire appears later; in the immediately follow-ing paragraphs, the expressions 'Dominions' and 'Common-wealth' should be regarded as excluding Eire unless otherwise stated. Before 1933, Newfoundland had not adopted Sections 2 to 6 of the Statute of Westminster which, by its Section 10, did not apply to Newfoundland unless adopted. After the suspension of Dominion status in 1933, there was no body in Newfoundland legally capable of taking action under Section 10. The British Nationality Act therefore continued fully applicable to New-foundland from 1916 until the entry of Newfoundland into the Dominion of Canada as a province in 1949, and the immediately following paragraphs apply to Newfoundland for the period within those dates. In India, Pakistan, and Ceylon the British Nationality Act, 1914, continued to be part of the law of those Dominions by virtue of its original enactment by the Parliament of the United Kingdom until such time as their legislatures enact other measures,[1] since, under the Statute of Westminster and the Indian and Ceylon Independence Acts (1947), new legislation en-acted at Westminster in 1948 does not apply to the Dominions nor does it effect a repeal of the British Act of 1914 in so far as it applies to them. 'So far as the British Colonies are concerned . . . this legislation [the 1914 Act] is part of their law,'[2] and remained so until July 1948.

Modification of the 1914 Act

The content of the 1914 Act (and of subsequent amending Acts) is not the province of this handbook, which is concerned only with the part played by consultation in achieving agreement in principle on the substance of this and subsequent Acts (whether Acts of the United Kingdom or of Dominion Parliaments), and the part played by co-operation in making such agreement effec-tive. The thirteen years of discussion which preceded the 1914 Act, and the emergence of the Act as an agreed measure, suf-ficiently established the necessity for consultation and co-opera-tion. The Act itself gave statutory expression to the concept of common status—the status of natural-born British subject—in-digenous to the Common Law of England; and prescribed a code of rules governing the conditions under which the common status may arise, be lost, be regained, etc. The basis of the Common Law status was birth within His Majesty's allegiance; to this Section 1 (1) of the Act added the condition of being born

---

[1] Professor E. C. S. Wade, 'The British Nationality Act 1948', *Journal of Comparative Legislation and International Law*, November 1948, p. 69.
[2] Jones, op. cit. p. 232.

within His Majesty's dominions; the two conditions—place of birth and allegiance—taken together, being the most complete definition of a British subject. Not all persons could fulfil both conditions; therefore the Act proceeded to cover cases—so far as possible, for the variations are almost infinite—of persons fulfilling one condition. This coverage was subsequently developed by case law; and the practical tendency has generally been in marginal cases for the Common Law requirement of allegiance to have more force than the statutory requirement of place of birth.[1] In the matter of naturalization of aliens, a certificate of naturalization could not become effective until the oath of allegiance was taken, or an equivalent affirmation made (Section 2 (4) of the 1914 Act).

The Act of 1914 was amended by the United Kingdom Parliament in 1918, 1922, and 1933, and Section 2 (1) of the 1933 Act authorized the four Acts to be cited together as the British Nationality and Status of Aliens Acts, 1914–33. The 1918 amending Act was mainly concerned with the power to revoke certificates of naturalization, and therefore affected Part II of the 1914 Act and automatically extended to the Dominions which had adopted that Part. The 1918 amendment to Section 7 of the 1914 Act required that, under Sub-Section (5), the revocation by the Home Secretary in the United Kingdom of a certificate of naturalization granted by a Dominion or Colonial Government needed the 'concurrence' of the grantor Government. The amendments which became law in 1922 touched a vital matter; the transmission of British nationality by descent.

The question . . . was one in which the Dominions had to be consulted. The Home Office prepared a memorandum on the subject, which was considered by a special committee under the chairmanship of the Secretary of State for the Colonies. It reported in favour of an amendment, and the Imperial Conference in 1921 approved the terms of its report which were as follows:[2] 'The Committee having considered the memorandum prepared in the Home Office regarding the nationality of the children born abroad of British parents commends the principles of the proposals contained therein to the favourable consideration of the Governments of the Dominions and India.'[3]

Throughout the history of co-operation on nationality matters, the question of the nationality of married women has been particularly difficult. It was discussed at the Imperial Conference

[1] The conviction of 'Lord Haw-Haw' turned largely on this point: the correlation between protection and allegiance. On this relationship see Latham, op. cit. p. 520, and Jones, op. cit. p. 57.
[2] Cmd. 1474 (1921).
[3] Jones, op. cit. pp. 117–18.

of 1923, which concluded that no case for major change had been made out. The 1926 Imperial Conference failed to reach agreement on the matter. In 1930 the Hague Conference on the Codification of International Law agreed on a 'Convention concerning certain questions relating to the Conflict of Nationality Laws'.[1] The Convention made proposals for remedying the situation of women who lost their original nationality upon marriage without acquiring the nationality of their husbands and so became stateless; and the British amending Act of 1933 gave effect to these proposals. In the meanwhile, the Statute of Westminster had been passed, and the operation of the 1933 amending Act was confined to the United Kingdom and Colonies. The Dominions' legislation does not in all cases follow the 1933 Act; Australian, New Zealand, and South African legislation was, on the whole, on the same lines; the Irish Citizenship Act, 1935, was not; and Canada had passed legislation in 1931, before the United Kingdom Act.

The legal theory that the Imperial Parliament could legislate for the Dominions irrespective of their request and consent had been undermined by convention and usage long before 1931. Even the 1914 Act, which crystallized the concept of common status throughout the Empire, was preceded by thirteen years of consultation; and its Section 25 safeguarded considerable powers for the Dominions to legislate on nationality questions so long as they did not purport to regulate common status. The Statute of Westminster only made more clear in law something that was already established: that 'the maintenance of common status rested', not on an Imperial Act, but 'on parallel action in the legislatures of the United Kingdom and the Dominions; and had to be kept alive by agreement on policy'.[2]

Discussions at the Imperial Conference of 1930

The Imperial Conference of 1930, and the Conference on the Operation of Dominion Legislation and Merchant Shipping Legislation which preceded it, fully recognized this practical basis of common status. The latter Conference stated the matter as follows:

Under the new position, if any change is made in the requirements established by the existing legislation, reciprocal action will be necessary to attain this recognition [i.e. the recognition of the common status], the importance of which is manifest in view of the desirability

[1] The Convention came into force in 1937. Of Commonwealth countries, Australia, Canada, India, and the United Kingdom ratified it (League of Nations, *Official Journal*, Special Supplement 193, 1944).
[2] Jones, op. cit. p. 234.

of facilitating freedom of intercourse, and the mutual granting of privileges among the different parts of the Commonwealth. It is, of course, plain that no Member of the Commonwealth could or would contemplate seeking to confer on any person a status operative throughout the Commonwealth save in pursuance of legislation based upon common agreement, and it is fully recognized that this common status is in no way inconsistent with the recognition within and without the Commonwealth of the distinct nationality possessed by nationals of the individual States of the British Commonwealth.[1]

This statement was approved by all the Members of the Commonwealth (including the Irish Free State) by resolution of the Imperial Conference of 1930. The Conference also added its own three resolutions as follows:

(1) That, if any changes are desired in the existing requirements for the common status, provision should be made for the maintenance of the common status, and the changes should only be introduced (in accordance with present practice) after consultation and agreement among the several members of the Commonwealth.

(2) That it is for each member of the Commonwealth to define for itself its own nationals, but that so far as possible those nationals should be persons possessing the common status, though it is recognized that local conditions, or other special circumstances, may from time to time necessitate divergencies from this general principle.

(3) That the possession of the common status, in virtue of the law for the time being in force in any part of the Commonwealth, should carry with it the recognition of that status by the laws of every other part of the Commonwealth.[2]

The Status of British Subjects in Municipal Law

The net effect of these resolutions, and of the Statute of Westminster in the following year, was to place within the control of the legislatures of the Dominions all the consequences in municipal law of the status of British subject. Moreover, if Dominion legislation were so drafted as to erect serviceable categories of nationality in international law, as was done by Canada, South Africa, and the Irish Free State, the international law consequences of common status lay within the control of Dominion legislatures. This encroachment by statute—municipal law— upon status rendered the convention of co-operation more, and not less, important.[3]

Despite the progressive subordination of status to statute, and despite the fact that 'there is in the modern Commonwealth a welter of nationalities, citizenships, and unnamed personal

---

[1] Cmd. 3479 (1929), paras. 77–8.
[2] Cmd. 3717, pp. 21–2.
[3] Latham, *The Law and the Commonwealth*, pp. 594, 581, 584, 614.

statuses which exist for a multitude of purposes',[1] Commonwealth co-operation was on the whole effective in preserving the
economic, political, and legal advantages which ensued from
common status. This was perhaps specially true in matters of
external relations, wherein a member of the genus 'British subject', whatever his local species, fell heir to solid advantages, for
instance treaty and trading rights, many of which pre-dated by
varying periods the passage of the 1914 Act.[2] Divergencies,
however, within the limits imposed by the general agreement on
the advantages of common status, were numerous; and their importance should not be minimized, in that they symbolized
mental and emotional attitudes. Only in the United Kingdom
were British subjects from every part of the Commonwealth
accorded the same footing, irrespective of place of origin or race,
as persons born in the country.[3]

Canada in 1921 passed the Canadian Nationals Act.[4] The immediate reason for the passage of the Act was an international,
not a Commonwealth, problem. It was disputable under the
Court's statute whether two British subjects would be entitled
simultaneously to sit as judges on the Permanent Court of
International Justice, etc.,[5] and the Canadian Government
wished, by defining an internationally serviceable category of
Canadian nationals, to obviate any objections which might be
raised by foreign States. The Canadian Act did not affect the
concept of common status, but it did recognize two categories
within Canada: Canadian nationals and Canadian citizens. The
category of Canadian citizen had been defined by the Immigration Acts 1910–19; that of Canadian national was defined by the
1921 Act. The two were not co-extensive, since the latter was
wider. Certain practical difficulties resulted. For example, if a
Canadian citizen married abroad, his wife automatically became
a Canadian national, but not a Canadian citizen. She could,
therefore, even if a British subject, be excluded from Canada if
ineligible for entry under the Immigration Acts 1910–19. A
British subject who had lost his Canadian domicile as defined by
the Immigration Act of 1919, thereby also lost his Canadian
citizenship, and with it his Canadian nationality; and could, if
deported from elsewhere, be refused re-entry into Canada if ineligible under the Immigration Acts (and, as a deportee, he was

---

[1] ibid. p. 592.
[2] See pp. 334–5, below.
[3] Royal Institute of International Affairs, *The British Empire*, 2nd ed.
(London, Oxford University Press, 1938) p. 317.
[4] R.S.C. 1927, c. 21. A summary of the provisions of the Act may be found in
Jones, op. cit. pp. 262–4.
[5] See Chapter XII, below.

E

probably ineligible). Such British subjects were often deported to the United Kingdom instead.[1] These examples of difficulties arising under local nationality legislation do not amount to a breakdown of co-operation but illustrate its problems.

It may be noted in passing that in Canada neither the status of national nor that of citizen necessarily carried political rights; nor does the status of Union national in South Africa, which is dealt with below. Disfranchisement is an effect of electoral, not nationality, law in both countries. Thus, in Canada, 'East Indians', even though British subjects and Canadian nationals and citizens, were, until a few years ago, disfranchised by the law of the Province of British Columbia in both federal and provincial elections; in South Africa, native Africans and Coloureds are Union nationals, and so also are certain other non-Europeans, but they are not generally enfranchised.

The Union Nationality and Flags Act, 1927,[2] defined the nationals of the Union of South Africa. There was no separate category of 'citizens' as in Canada. British subjects entering the Union might acquire Union nationality by two years' continuous domicile; naturalized aliens required three years. 'The conception of Union nationality fits into the framework of British nationality law, and there is no separate naturalization of a Union national, though either local naturalization or Imperial naturalization (in either case as a British subject) may produce Union nationality.'[3] The possession of Union nationality was a condition for enfranchisement and for eligibility for membership of either House of Parliament; the latter also required five years' residence in the Union. 'In this respect there is a difference only in degree between Union nationality and an unnamed status in the other Dominions where immigrant white British subjects must satisfy residence requirements, similar to those on which the acquisition of Union nationality depends, before they are entitled to political rights.'[4]

In Canada such persons had normally to have a year's continuous residence; possession of Canadian nationality or citizenship was not a condition. Neither Australia nor New Zealand created a separate nationality by statute, as was done in Canada and South Africa. In New Zealand, immigrant British subjects required a year's continuous residence to qualify for political rights, and the franchise extended to British subjects irrespective of race. The qualifying period for white immigrant British sub-

[1] Jones, op. cit. p. 263.
[2] No. 4 of 1927. A convenient summary of the provisions may be found in Jones, op. cit. pp. 265-7.
[3] ibid. p. 266.
[4] *The British Empire*, p. 316.

jects in the Commonwealth of Australia was six months for the franchise, three years for eligibility for membership of either House of Parliament. 'The Commonwealth franchise is denied to aboriginal natives of Australia, Asia (except British India), Africa, and the islands of the Pacific (except New Zealand) unless they have become naturalized; and in Western Australia the State franchise is denied to Indians.'[1]

Immigration law and nationality law are separate matters, although there may be a connexion between them: as in Canada and South Africa, where part of the definition of a Canadian citizen, for instance, and a Union national was by reference to immigration legislation. All Members of the Commonwealth can regulate immigration, and where these regulations differentiate between classes of British subjects separate unnamed local statuses may be created. Differentiation by immigration law, like differentiation by electoral law, may create resentment in those who, although British subjects, feel themselves penalized; and may produce friction in the machinery of general Commonwealth co-operation on questions of nationality and citizenship. No Member country, however, is willing to forego its rights to regulate immigration or title to political rights, and therefore cannot expect other Members to do so; thus friction, although serious at times, never reached the point of bringing about a general breakdown of the principle of reciprocal action accepted by the Imperial Conference of 1930.

Discussions at the Imperial Conference of 1937

The Imperial Conference of 1937 considered the difficult question of the nationality of married women. Attention was drawn to the Hague Convention of 1930, and the steps taken by some Members of the Commonwealth to give legislative effect to its recommendations. The Australian and New Zealand delegates then drew attention to the more recent legislation passed in their countries, not affecting the common status but permitting a female British subject, on marriage to an alien, to retain on complying with certain procedures her rights and duties as a British subject within Australia and New Zealand. 'The possibility of securing reciprocal arrangements on the basis of the general adoption of legislation on the lines of the Australian and New Zealand referred to' was considered; and the discussion also went fully into the general question of the nationality of married women, both within the Commonwealth and in its international context.

[1] ibid. p. 317.

It was not found possible to arrive at an agreement in favour of any change in the existing law. While therefore the Committee [of the Conference which had been examining these questions under the chairmanship of Mr E. Lapointe, of Canada] was unable to put forward any recommendation, it was assumed that the matter would be the subject of further consideration by and consultation between the respective Governments.[1]

The Conference, and its Committee under Mr Lapointe, also considered the more important constitutional question of the common status and its relation to the particular status of nationals (whether so defined or not) of any Member country. In 1935 the Irish Free State had repealed the British Acts of 1914–18,[2] 'if and so far as they respectively are or ever were in force in Saorstát Eireann'. This, although it was of course without effect in the municipal law of other Commonwealth Members, was a breach in the co-operative preservation of common status. The Irish Free State was not represented at the 1937 Conference. General Hertzog, Prime Minister and leader of the South African delegation, proposed at the Conference that the British Nationality and Status of Aliens Acts 1914–33 be amended so as to confine the meaning of 'British subject' to 'subject of Great Britain'— an exclusive meaning which in fact it did not possess, and never had possessed. It was pointed out that members of the genus 'British subject' had each their special connexion with some part of the Commonwealth, and the Conference adopted the phrase 'member of the community' to express that connexion irrespective of whether a legislative definition thereof existed (as was the case in Canada and the Union) or not (as in the case of the other Members represented). A member of the community 'belonged' to a particular part of the Commonwealth 'for the purposes of civil and political rights and duties, immigration, deportation, diplomatic representation, or the exercise of extra-territorial jurisdiction'.[3] It was pointed out by the proponents of a change 'that in the absence of rules for determining the part of the Commonwealth with which any particular person has the connexion just referred to, practical difficulties arise, or might arise, with regard to such matters'.[4] There were also certain international aspects; for instance, in the election of judges to the Permanent Court of International Justice, to which the Canadian nationality legislation of 1921 had been directed.

The opponents of change pointed out various difficulties,

[1] Cmd. 5482 (1937), pp. 27–8.
[2] The 1922 Act was not mentioned in the Irish Free State Act.
[3] Cmd. 5482, p. 25.
[4] ibid. p. 24.

many being particularly serious in the case of the United Kingdom. In this case 'the wide difference existing between the large number of separate territories, legal jurisdictions and races for which the United Kingdom was responsible would render impracticable the adoption of any single classification which would be in any real sense analogous to that expressed by the terms 'national' or 'citizen' or 'member of the community' in the case of other Members of the Commonwealth.[1] The United Kingdom made no distinction between classes of British subjects for any purpose. Another, and more general, objection concerned the right of diplomatic and consular representation and protection, which could, as things stood, be claimed by a British subject from His Majesty's diplomatic and consular representative if his own 'community' was not represented in the particular foreign State, notwithstanding on which Commonwealth Government's advice His Majesty's representative had been appointed.

The above are particular, although forceful, arguments; but commentators have generally held that the crux of the matter, although it was not stated in the records of the Imperial Conference, was that common status was based on common allegiance, and that the abolition of the former might involve the abandonment of the latter, which was held to be a fundamental convention of the Commonwealth. In the event, the Conference found that all members were not disposed to introduce legislation in the sense proposed, and, in the absence of general agreement, no general change was advocated by the Conference. Short of general change, the Conference reached a degree of agreement which may be summarized as a recognition (a) of the practice of defining 'a member of the community' by legislation if 'the community' wished so to define it, and (b) of the desirability of securing, as far as possible, uniformity in principle in such definitions on account of the practical value and usefulness of such uniformity and the inconveniences which would arise in its absence. With special reference to migrant British subjects and their acquisition of 'membership of the community', it was recommended, since time had not permitted the Conference to consider all the criteria of 'membership', 'that any member of the Commonwealth passing a law on the membership of the community, should submit its proposals to the other members for comment if they desired. Members of the Commonwealth not wishing to define the members of their communities by legislation were invited to consider taking administrative action, on grounds of expediency, in order to preserve a degree of parallelism in practice.[2]

[1] ibid.
[2] The conclusions of the Conference are stated in Cmd. 5482, pp. 25–7.

Until 1946 nationality and citizenship questions in the Commonwealth remained as they were left by the 1937 Imperial Conference. As always, conditions of war, with the problems they raise regarding aliens, war refugees, oversea movements of persons, and multifarious hard cases, tested the comprehensiveness and flexibility of existing nationality legislation, and gave rise to many administrative orders and even to legislation; for example, the highly technical amendments to existing law introduced by the United Kingdom Act of 1943. On the whole, however, war-time action may be regarded as emergency action aimed generally at security and at meeting special circumstances, but not as affecting the principles of Commonwealth co-operation as they were left in 1937.

The Canadian Citizenship Act of 1946

The post-war years have produced more radical developments, some of which are still in progress at the time of writing. These actually started in Canada, with the passage of the Canadian Citizenship Act, 1946, which received the Royal Assent on 27 June and came into force on 1 January 1947. In the words of a French commentator: 'Il est curieux de constater que l'initiative ne vient plus toujours de la métropole, mais parfois des Dominions. L'inégalité fonctionnelle tend à disparaître.'[1] The new Act repealed the Canadian Nationality Act, 1921, and the Naturalization Act, 1914 (the latter Act was that which brought Canadian law into line with the United Kingdom Act of the same year) and did away with the inconveniences of definition by reference to the Immigration Acts which had been a complicating feature of the 1921 Act. The new Act gave a general definition of 'Canadian citizen', independent of reference to other legislation. The Act was based on three main principles:

(1) The definition of Canadian citizens;
(2) The provision that all Canadian citizens are British subjects;
(3) The provision that all persons who are British subjects under the law of any other Commonwealth country would be recognized by Canada as British subjects.

Part I of the Act defined natural-born Canadian citizens, covering also those qualified who were born before 1 January 1947. There was very little that was new in this part except that the immigrant brides of Canadian servicemen automatically became citizens. Part II dealt with those who acquire or had acquired Canadian citizenship, including persons already naturalized,

[1] P. F. Gonidec, 'Le Statut commun et les Citoyennetés locales dans l'Empire britannique', *Revue Juridique et Politique de l'Union Française*, 2nd year, no. 3 (July–September 1948) p. 342.

British subjects with five years' domicile and foreign-born wives of Canadian citizens who had been lawfully admitted to Canada (i.e. under the Immigration Acts) and had resided there for one year with their spouses. Naturalization requirements were almost exactly the same as under previous legislation, except that the residence requirement was reduced to one year for aliens who had served in the Canadian Forces. This, and the reduced residence period for foreign-born wives, were the main changes. British subjects who fulfil the five years' residence condition for citizenship after 1 January 1947 can apply for a certificate of citizenship, which did not exist under the old law; and aliens must take one out before taking the oath of allegiance on naturalization. British subjects qualified for citizenship by residence before 1 January 1947 did not need to take out a certificate.

Part III dealt with loss of citizenship. Here again the law was almost unchanged, except for the concession that it required six years'—instead of one year's—absence from Canada before citizenship was automatically lost; and that Canadian women citizens marrying aliens might make a declaration choosing their nationality. This concession to married women was in line with the pre-war Australian and New Zealand practice.

Part IV stated that 'Canadian citizens are British subjects' (Section 26). Commenting on this section Mr Colin Gibson stated that the common status was thus maintained, 'although for Canadian purposes the basic national status is Canadian citizenship'.

Parts V and VI dealt with the status of aliens and procedure and evidence, and made no change of consequence from the 1914 legislation.

The Second Schedule to the Act gave the terms of the oath of allegiance, which had been altered by adding 'and that I will faithfully observe the laws of Canada and fulfil any duties as a Canadian citizen' to the previous 'I swear that I will be faithful and bear true allegiance to His Majesty King George VI, his heirs and successors, according to law'.

Certain consequences flowed from the maintenance of common status by Section 26 in regard to political rights. The old right of British subjects, even though not Canadian citizens, to vote after one year's residence remained. A Canadian citizen who gets on the electoral register and votes in the United Kingdom, or acquires by residence the 'unnamed status' (see p. 58, above) of British subjects with electoral rights in other Dominions which have not defined their nationals, and votes there, does not thereby lose his Canadian citizenship. The description of the holder on passports issued in Canada to Canadian citizens became 'Canadian citizen' instead of 'British subject', but if a passport was issued in Canada to a British subject who was not a Canadian citizen the holder was described as 'British subject' as in the past.

The Evolution of the Citizenship Concept

Consultation before and after the Canadian Bill was introduced, and the effects of the legislation, are thus described in the official *Summary* which was issued with the subsequent United Kingdom Bill:[1]

In September 1945, Canada advised the United Kingdom and the other members of the Commonwealth that it found it desirable to introduce legislation to lay down the conditions for the acquisition and loss of Canadian citizenship, and in 1946 Canada passed the Canadian Citizenship Act. This Act in providing for the acquisition and loss of Canadian citizenship followed with certain modifications the principles of the former provisions relating to the acquisition and loss of British nationality. It also enacted that all Canadian citizens were British subjects and that all persons who were British subjects by the law of any other part of the Commonwealth should be recognized as British subjects in Canada. This Canadian Act thus continued to recognize the common status of British subjects while departing from the common code system.

It appeared to the United Kingdom Government that the question ought to be considered whether the citizenship principle introduced by the Canadian Act should be extended by agreement to the other Commonwealth countries. As a result of consultation with the Governments of these countries a conference of experts met in London in February 1947, at the invitation of the United Kingdom Government. At this conference there assembled expert representatives from the United Kingdom, Canada, Australia, New Zealand, South Africa, Eire, Newfoundland, Southern Rhodesia, Burma, and Ceylon. No representative of India attended, but arrangements were made to keep the Government of India informed of the course of the proceedings. At the conference agreement was reached as to a general scheme which the representatives of each country were prepared (subject to reservations as to certain details) to submit to their respective Governments for consideration.

The United Kingdom Government has subsequently been in correspondence with the Governments of Canada, Australia, New Zealand, South Africa, Eire, Newfoundland, India, Pakistan, Southern Rhodesia, and Ceylon, and subject to what is said below with regard to Eire it is believed that legislation on these lines of this Bill will be acceptable to the other self-governing countries of the Commonwealth, and is likely to be followed by legislation on similar lines in many of these countries.

The conference of experts referred to met from 3 to 26 Feb-

[1] British Nationality Bill, 1948, *Summary of Main Provisions*. Cmd. 7326 (1948), pp. 2–3.

ruary 1947, under the chairmanship of Sir Alexander Maxwell, Permanent Under-Secretary of the Home Office, and was at the official level. The objects sought by the conference and the Commonwealth Governments' agreement on the 'key clause' are set out in the *Summary*:[1]

A scheme of legislation which combines provisions defining the persons who are citizens of the several parts of the Commonwealth with provisions for maintaining the common status of British subjects throughout the Commonwealth has the advantage of giving a clear recognition to the separate identity of particular countries of the Commonwealth, of clarifying the position with regard to diplomatic protection, and of enabling a Government when making treaties with other countries to define with precision who are the persons belonging to its country and on whose behalf it is negotiating. Such a system also enables each country to make alterations in its nationality laws without having first, as under the common code system, to consult the other countries of the Commonwealth and to ascertain whether the alterations contemplated would impair the common status.

The essential features of such a system are that each of the countries shall by its legislation determine who are its citizens, shall declare those citizens to be British subjects, and shall recognize as British subjects the citizens of the other countries. For this last purpose there is need of a 'common clause', of which the substantial effect shall be the same in each country, to ensure that all persons recognized as British subjects in any part of the Commonwealth shall be so recognized throughout the Commonwealth. Clause 1 of the Bill, which is the key clause, has been agreed with all the countries named in it.

The United Kingdom Act of 1948

The first Commonwealth country to legislate after this conference was the United Kingdom, which passed the British Nationality Act, 1948. The 'key clause' appears as Section 1 (1) of this Act [2] as follows:

'Every person who under this Act is a citizen of the United Kingdom and Colonies or who under any enactment for the time being in force in any country mentioned in subsection (3) of this section is a citizen of that country shall by virtue of that citizenship have the status of a British subject.' The countries enumerated in subsection (3) are: Canada, Australia, New Zealand, the Union of South Africa, Newfoundland, India, Pakistan, Southern Rhodesia, and Ceylon. Subsection (2) of Section 1 reads:

(2) Any person having the status aforesaid [i.e. in subsection (1)] may be known either as a British subject or as a Commonwealth citizen; and accordingly in this Act and in any other enactment or instru-

[1] ibid. p. 3.
[2] 11 & 12 Geo. VI, c. 56: received the Royal Assent on 30 July 1948 and came into force on 1 January 1949.

ment whatever, whether passed or made before or after the commencement of this Act, the expression 'British subject' and the expression
'Commonwealth citizen' shall have the same meaning.

Dr Mervyn Jones says:

The scheme . . . is that each Commonwealth country will enact a
citizenship law containing the principle enunciated in Section I (1),
quoted above, by which mutual recognition as British subjects will be
given to the citizens of other Commonwealth countries. When all
these laws have been passed, British subjects, instead of being ascertained by reference to a common code, will simply be the sum-total
of the citizens of all the Commonwealth countries. This fact is emphasized by the provision in Section I (2) that British subjects have
the alternative title of 'Commonwealth citizens'. . . . The effect of all
the Commonwealth legislation when it is completed will be that for
the purposes of British (or Commonwealth) nationality there will, in
the United Kingdom and the other Commonwealth countries in future
be three classes of persons:

    (1) A citizen of the country.
    (2) Citizens of other Commonwealth countries (or of Eire).
    (3) Aliens.[1]

Since English Common Law and United Kingdom statute
had been the *fons et origo* of the previous common code, and since,
at the time of the passage of the United Kingdom Act, only one
other country of the Commonwealth—Canada—had legislated on
the new lines, provision had to be made in the United Kingdom
Act to obviate the legal difficulty that a potential 'Commonwealth citizen' might be left without defined status. There was
also the special case of Eire, already briefly mentioned (p. 53,
above), which will be dealt with later. Thirdly, the United Kingdom is or was responsible for territories, other than Crown
Colonies, having a variety of statuses (i.e. the Isle of Man and the
Channel Islands, protectorates, protected States, trust territories,
and the Indian Princely States), and the position of persons born
in or connected with these territories required to be regulated.
The United Kingdom Act was therefore extended and complicated by the need to provide for statuses and special cases which
did not arise, or arose only in a much less degree, in connexion
with the legislation enacted or contemplated by the other Commonwealth countries. These complexities are of interest to some
and often to all other Commonwealth countries; and the United
Kingdom Bill, although introduced into the House of Lords on
17 February 1948, was first debated only in May 1948, the delay
having given the Commonwealth countries the time required for

---

[1] 'The British Nationality Act, 1948', *British Year Book of International Law*,
1948 (London, Oxford University Press for R.I.I.A., 1949), pp. 160–1.

the scrutiny of its provisions, and for a certain amount of further consultation.[1]

The full details of the United Kingdom legislation are not relevant to this handbook, and a very brief account will suffice. The basic principle underlying the regulation of statuses which, until the completion of legislation by all the Members of the Commonwealth, might have been inconveniently indeterminate, is simple. It is: that no one having the status of British subject on 31 December 1948 should lose it; but its form may be modified pending the completion of legislation in all the Commonwealth countries. Thus, for example, potential citizens of a Commonwealth country which had not yet legislated became, under the transitional provisions of the United Kingdom Act, 'British subjects without citizenship', retaining generally the rights they have possessed up to 31 December 1948.[2] It may be that some individual British subjects may not, even when all the Commonwealth countries have legislated, have acquired a citizenship. In fulfilment of the basic principle, a citizenship 'gateway' to the permanent status of British subject had to be found, and 'any who still remain homeless and unhoused will become citizens of the United Kingdom and Colonies'.[3] British subjects (in the pre-1949 usage of the expression) born in a protectorate, protected State, or United Kingdom trust territory became citizens of the United Kingdom and Colonies. British protected persons, hitherto 'nationals of His Majesty' in international law but 'aliens' in United Kingdom municipal law, have been distinguished from aliens under the 1948 Act, are eligible for naturalization on more favourable terms than those extended to aliens under the Act, and are also exempt from certain disabilities imposed on such aliens. These changes do not apply to persons who are protected by reason of their connexion with another Commonwealth country; they remain aliens under United Kingdom municipal law. The status of these protected persons is a matter for legislation by the Commonwealth country affording the protection.

The 1948 Act made a new departure in British nationality law: the introduction of registration for the acquisition of citizenship. Dr Mervyn Jones says:

Registration is an entirely new and unique method of obtaining citizenship which does not exist outside the Commonwealth, and only applies in relation to citizens of Commonwealth countries. All that is

---

[1] 31 May 1948, *Hansard* (Lords), vol. 156, col. 9.

[2] J. Mervyn Jones, loc. cit. pp. 167-8, gives details of some four or five modifications of absolute retention of previous rights, and a few other cases of extension of rights (particularly in respect of minors, and of British women married to aliens).

[3] ibid. p. 163.

required under the law of the United Kingdom is that the applicant should be a citizen of a Commonwealth country, or a citizen of Eire, of full age and capacity, who *either* (*a*) is ordinarily resident in the United Kingdom, and has been so resident throughout a period of twelve months (or a shorter period in special circumstances at the discretion of the Secretary of State) immediately preceding the application; or (*b*) is in Crown Service under His Majesty's Government in the United Kingdom. If these requirements are satisfied the applicant has the *right* to be registered as a citizen of the United Kingdom and Colonies. Registration is therefore essentially different from naturalization, which is always discretionary. Although Section 19 allows for the voluntary renunciation of another Commonwealth citizenship, *registration* as a citizen does not involve the loss of any other Commonwealth citizenship. The possibility of dual citizenship within the Commonwealth was clearly contemplated and accepted.[1]

The occasion of the Act was taken to revise United Kingdom practice in regard to the vexed question of the nationality of married women in accordance with principles agreed with Canada, Australia, New Zealand, and South Africa. Except in so far as it may be necessary to apply the pre-1949 practice—mainly under the 'transitional provisions'—the Act of 1948 makes no distinction between the rights of a male citizen and a married woman. A female marrying an alien and thereby acquiring his citizenship no longer automatically loses her United Kingdom citizenship. This is in line with pre-war Australian and New Zealand practice, and with Canadian practice under the 1946 Act.[2]

The Special Case of Eire

With regard to the special case of Eire, it has been seen above (p. 60) that the Irish Free State Nationality and Citizenship Act, 1935, abolished in that country the common status of British subject; although Irish legislation could not affect the fact that citizens of Eire continued to be British subjects in the municipal law of the other Commonwealth countries. Eire (then still a member of the Commonwealth) was represented at the official conference on nationality law held in London in February 1947, and an understanding with the other Commonwealth countries on the status of Eire citizens was reached. As regards the United Kingdom, the

[1] ibid. p. 169. Canadian certificates of citizenship are mentioned on p. 63 above.
[2] The Home Secretary, Mr Chuter Ede: 'The principles accepted by the five Governments are that the law should provide in effect that a British woman on marriage to a foreigner, whether she does or does not acquire his nationality under the law of his country, shall not lose her British nationality unless she takes some active steps to renounce it; and that a foreign woman on marriage to a British subject shall not automatically acquire British nationality, but shall have the right to apply for it, subject to the exercise by the Minister concerned of a discretion as to the grant or refusal of the application'. (1 August 1946, *Hansard* (Commons), vol. 426, col. 1214)

understanding was embodied in the 1948 legislation, and remained unaffected by Eire's withdrawal from membership of the Commonwealth in 1949. Under Section 2 of the 1948 Act, citizens of Eire who were British subjects (in United Kingdom law) up to 31 December 1948, can at any time give notice to the Secretary of State claiming retention of this status on certain specified grounds (e.g. residence, Crown Service). This notice is essential; citizenship of Eire, or birth in Eire, does not of itself command the status of British subject in United Kingdom law. However, Eire citizens have a status in United Kingdom law by the mere fact of their citizenship; they are 'not aliens' under Section 32 (1) of the 1948 Act. The implications of this negative status have not yet been tested in international law. British subjects, however, are aliens under the law of Eire (unless they belong to the class of 'British subject by notice' who are also Eire citizens). As will be seen below, some other Commonwealth countries have taken action producing a like effect on Eire citizens, although the terms are not necessarily identical with those used in the United Kingdom.

The New Zealand Act of 1948

The next country to take legislative action was New Zealand, where the British Nationality and New Zealand Citizenship Bill was introduced in the House of Representatives on 17 August 1948, became law on 6 September, and came into force on 1 January 1949. The Minister for Internal Affairs, Mr W. E. Parry, introducing the measure, said that no initiative for change would have come from New Zealand, which regretted the passing of the common code; but the new system had the support of the majority of Commonwealth countries, so New Zealand was following its traditional policy of supporting the Commonwealth connexion. The title of the Bill, with 'British Nationality' coming first, represented the order of importance of its elements in New Zealanders' eyes. Its text, Mr Parry explained, followed the lines agreed at the conference of February 1947 and the main lines of the United Kingdom Act. In respect of naturalization, however, the Bill adopted two provisions of the Canadian Act of 1946: that an applicant should give at least twelve months' notice of intention to apply for naturalization, and should possess sufficient knowledge of the responsibilities and privileges of citizenship. New Zealand accepted dual citizenship within the Commonwealth, but only there: it did not accept dual nationality. It defined the status of New Zealand protected persons, and gave them specially easy conditions for naturalization as in the United Kingdom Act—the United Kingdom Government had, in fact, adopted the suggestions made to it by New Zealand. In general, commented the Minister, changes were being kept as slight as consonant with the change of principle accepted as a result of the Conference of February 1947. Immigration law would remain quite unchanged; and so would electoral law, which would still give British subjects the vote in New Zealand parliamentary and local government elections after twelve months' residence.

As under the United Kingdom Act, citizenship of Eire, or birth in Eire, does not of itself confer the status of British subject. Such persons do not become British subjects under Section 3 of the New Zealand Act. Other sections of the Act, however, relate to the status of Irish citizens in New Zealand law. Most Irish-born residents in New Zealand being British subjects until 1 January 1949 are New Zealand citizens (and therefore British subjects) by virtue of Section 16 (1) (c) of the Act whether or not they are also Irish citizens by virtue of the Irish Nationality and Citizenship Act, 1935. Such New Zealand citizens who are also Irish citizens can be treated on the same basis as the former. Unlike the United Kingdom Nationality Act 1948 and the corresponding Australian Act of that year, the New Zealand Act makes no provision for Irish citizens who have associations of various sorts with New Zealand, but make application to remain British subjects by virtue of Section 4 of the New Zealand Act. The status conferred by Section 2 of the United Kingdom Act or Section 8 of the Australian Act is recognized in New Zealand.

Under Section 8 of the New Zealand Act Irish citizens who are not British subjects may apply for registration as New Zealand citizens in the same manner as citizens of Commonwealth countries.

Finally, the Irish citizen who is not also a New Zealand citizen by virtue of the fact that he was a British subject until 1 January 1949, and who does not apply for New Zealand citizenship by registration, is nevertheless treated for the purpose of all legislation enacted prior to 1 January 1949 as though he were a British subject. This means in fact that the rights and privileges, but not the status of a British subject are conferred, and if an Irish citizen wishes to enjoy the status of New Zealand citizenship in addition to the rights, he must apply for citizenship by registration. In conformity with Section 23 of the Irish Nationality and Citizenship Act 1935, the New Zealand Citizen (Irish Citizenship Rights Order 1949) dated 1 January 1949, extends equivalent rights to New Zealand citizens in Ireland.

The Australian Act of 1948

The Australian Nationality and Citizenship Bill was introduced in the House of Representatives on 30 September 1948 by Mr Arthur A. Calwell, the Minister for Immigration, and received the Royal Assent on 21 December. The Bill made the changes required by the agreement based on the consultations at the conference of February 1947, and the 'key clause', Clause 7 (1), was identical with that in the United Kingdom Bill, with the substitution of the words 'Australian Citizen' for the words 'Citizen of the United Kingdom and Colonies'. As in New Zealand, British subjects resident in Australia retained all their previous privileges under Australian electoral law, and their right to enter the public service. Such British subjects could become Australian citizens by registration (though they did not lose these privileges if they did not choose to do so); and the Bill accepted the possibility of dual citizenship within the Commonwealth only. The provisions in the Bill (Section 8 (1)) covering the position of citizens of Eire were identical with those in the United Kingdom Bill.

The Act was proclaimed on Australia Day, 26 January 1949.

By Section 25 (6), (7) and (8), the new Act laid down that persons classed as prohibited immigrants could not become Australian citizens unless they had been granted permission by the Minister permanently to reside in Australian territory. This exclusion extended to persons who had been granted certificates of exemption under Section 4 of the Immigration Restriction Act, 1901, as amended and in force, and excluded considerable numbers of war-time refugees who had been given asylum in Australia on compassionate grounds. Owing to the numbers involved (there were said to be some 35,000 Europeans in Australia under exemption certificates, besides Asians) by a recent High Court judgement invalidating exemption certificates,[1] the administrative situation was difficult to clarify, and to remedy certain defects in the existing law revealed by the High Court proceedings, an Amending Bill to the 1901 Act was introduced by Mr Calwell in the House of Representatives on 8 June 1949. He said:

Australia's immigration policy is not based on any assumption of racial superiority. . . . The ideal underlying our policy is the preservation of the homogenous character of our population and avoidance of the friction that inevitably follows the influx of people having different standards, traditions, and national characteristics. . . . The Government will resolutely resist any attempt to whittle down our established immigration policy.[2]

The Bill validated existing exemption certificates and provided

[1] The case of Mrs Annie O'Keefe, Indonesian wife of an Australian, which came before the High Court on 2 March 1949.
[2] *The Times* and *Manchester Guardian*, 10 June 1949.

that, henceforth, certificates might be issued to persons liable to be subjected to a dictation test within five years of their arrival. A supplementary Bill authorized the deportation of Asian wartime refugees admitted on compassionate grounds and others who had entered irregularly. These Bills were passed through all their stages by 7 July 1949.

Action Taken by the Union of South Africa

To cover the situation in regard to Eire until such time as it should introduce new citizenship legislation, the Government of the Union of South Africa made the following statement at the end of November 1948. After welcoming the action of the United Kingdom, the statement continued:

> The Union Government are prepared also for their part to recognize the Republic of Eire, as such, when it comes into being, and to make concessions in regard to rights of citizenship on a reciprocal basis as may be mutually agreed, on the understanding that the existing position be maintained in the meantime. . . . The Union Government are prepared to regard the concessions which are to be negotiated on a reciprocal basis as a matter of exceptional arrangement, applicable solely in the special case of Eire, and as not in any respect affording a precedent which can be invoked in the case of any other nation outside the Commonwealth.

The mutual agreement with Eire, the Union Government hoped, would be speedily concluded.[1]

The South African Citizenship Bill was introduced in the House of Assembly on 25 May 1949, and received the Governor-General's signature on 30 June. It came into force on 2 September. In general, the South African Act followed the lines of the Canadian Act of 1946. In respect of citizens of Eire, it was in line with the United Kingdom and Australian Acts. But the preceding positions in the Union had not been the same in certain respects as in these countries, and also, as Dr Dönges, the Minister of the Interior, maintained in his second-reading speech, the Conference of Commonwealth Prime Ministers in London, in April 1949, had made changes in Commonwealth constitutional convention which, he held, necessarily affected the Bill. In two respects, therefore, the Government maintained, the Bill must differ from those already passed by other Commonwealth countries.

The first difference stemmed from the pre-existing position in regard to electoral rights.[2] 'Union nationality' was a condition of enfranchisement and that status could be obtained, under the

---

[1] Union of South Africa, *Weekly Newsletter* (Pretoria), 27 November 1948.
[2] See p. 58, above.

Union Nationality and Flags Act 1927, by British subjects ('old style') after two years' residence. Under the new Act the concept of 'Union nationality' disappeared, and that of South African citizenship replaced it; and the time needed for citizens of other Commonwealth countries to acquire citizenship was extended to five years' residence in the Union. The acquisition of citizenship also required the act of registration, whereas the acquisition of 'Union nationality' had been automatic. The simple fact that registration was required was in line with, for instance, the Canadian Act of 1946; but there were important differences from Canadian practice. In Canada, the immigrant British subject still retained his right to vote after a year's residence and, if he later wished to register as a Canadian citizen, his application for registration, once he had fulfilled the five years' residence qualification, was automatically accepted or (exceptionally) went before an ordinary court. In the Union the grant of registration was placed entirely within the discretion of the Minister, without right of appeal against refusal of registration; and registration as a citizen was a condition for the exercise of the franchise.

The second difference was that the Union Act repealed the Nationality and Flags Act, which had made use of the expression 'British subjects' and thus implied recognition of the common code and status. The new Act contained no reference to a common or Commonwealth status. Dr Dönges gave the Government's reasons as follows:

The recent Conference of Prime Ministers has written a new chapter in the history of the evolution of the Commonwealth from Empire to a community of States bound together by common interests. Constitutionally it is no longer possible to talk of a common status. It is only possible to do so when there is either a common allegiance to one King or a super-State, but since the common allegiance is no longer an essential condition of membership of the Commonwealth, there cannot be a common subjecthood, circumscribing common status, and since there is no question of a super-State, there cannot be a common citizenship. Constitutionally, therefore, there is no longer a Commonwealth status for citizens. There are now . . . only citizens of Commonwealth countries enjoying preferences within that community of States. . . . I want to make it perfectly clear that it is not this Bill which creates a new constitutional position. That is already there. The Bill merely gives expression to it.[1]

The opponents of the Bill replied that the communiqué issued by the Prime Ministers' Conference on 21 April 1949 had explicitly stated that no change had been made in the status of Commonwealth countries other than India, and accused the

[1] Quoted in *Commonwealth Survey*, 3 September 1949, pp. 6-7.

F

Government of unilateral repudiation of the agreements reached at the conferences of 1946 and 1947. Dr Malan, in debate, admitted that citizenship had not been discussed at the 1949 Conference; but Dr Dönges argued that the Government's view did not mean that the position of the citizens of other Commonwealth countries in South Africa would in practice be altered by the Bill.

By virtue of their citizenship of other Commonwealth countries, they still enjoy all the rights they could enjoy through a common status, and still receive preferential treatment in the acquisition of South African citizenship.[1] The only practical difference is that all are not known by the same term, viz. British subject or Commonwealth citizen. . . . It is the only way in which the South African Citizenship Act really differs from the recommendations of the conferences of 1946 and 1947 subsequently applied in the other Commonwealth countries. But . . . that legislation was, in most cases, passed in the other Commonwealth countries in 1948 and thus before the London Declaration of April 1949, which made that one essential difference juridically necessary.[2]

Legislation by Ceylon

The Ceylon Citizenship Act (No. 18 of 1948) received the Royal Assent on 21 September 1948. It created (Section 2) what had not previously existed: 'a status to be known as "the status of a citizen of Ceylon" ', by right of descent within the meaning of the Act (Part II) or by virtue of registration according to its provisions (Part III). People having a connexion with Ceylon had hitherto been British subjects under the United Kingdom Act of 1914; and the definition of Ceylon citizenship was a matter of importance to the new Dominion. Right of descent within the meaning of Part II of the Ceylon Citizenship Act is not strict racial descent, but rather hereditary connexion with the territory of Ceylon (i.e. through male progenitors born in Ceylon). This is of interest in relation to Section 2 of the Act, which appears to reject the *jus soli*. Section 2 of the Act states:

A person shall be or become entitled to the status of a citizen of Ceylon in one of the following ways only:
(a) by right of descent as provided by this Act;
(b) by virtue of registration as provided by this Act or by any other Act authorizing the grant of such status by registration in any special case of a specified description.

An exception would appear to be 'newly born deserted infants

---

[1] The residence qualification for aliens who apply for naturalization and registration as South African citizens is six years.
[2] *Commonwealth Survey*, 3 September 1949, p. 7.

of unknown and unascertainable parentage' found in Ceylon; these are 'deemed to have the status of a citizen of Ceylon by descent' (Section 7). But the degree to which 'descent' is used in the sense of 'hereditary connexion' tends to combine the concept of *jus soli* with that of *jus sanguinis*, rather than actually to reject the former.

The Act generally does not contemplate the existence of dual citizenship, but it is understood that further legislation is under consideration, and this might deal with the question whether dual Commonwealth citizenship may be allowed. Clearly dual citizenship involving a foreign country is excluded. Section 8 (Part II) provides that: 'No person who is a citizen of any other country under any law in force in that country shall have the status of a citizen of Ceylon by descent unless he renounces citizenship of that other country in accordance with that law'; and Section 14 (2) (Part III) similarly provides against dual citizenship by making previous renunciation of any other citizenship a condition for registration as a citizen of Ceylon.

All applicants for citizenship by registration must be: of full age and sound mind; ordinarily resident, and intending to continue to reside, in Ceylon. Apart from these requirements, applicants fall into two classes. (*a*) Under Section 11, application may be made, subject to stated periods of residence in Ceylon, by persons (i) descended from female citizens of Ceylon; (ii) spouse, widow or widower of a Ceylon citizen; (iii) who, having been Ceylon citizens, renounce any other citizenship obtained under Section 19 (quoted above). (*b*) Under Section 12, persons ineligible for registration under Section 11 may make application: (i) if they have rendered distinguished public service; (ii) if they had been granted (and had not since lost) naturalization in Ceylon under the British Nationality and Status of Aliens Act, 1914, or under the Ceylon Naturalization Ordinance of 1890. The granting of registration in both categories, (*a*) and (*b*), is at the Minister's discretion, and there is no appeal to any court; registrations in category (*b*) are limited to twenty-five in any one year. Under Section 17, an alien granted registration must take an oath of allegiance as well as an oath of citizenship, while a 'British subject' need only take the oath of citizenship; and in Section 26 (Part V, Miscellaneous) 'British subject' has the same meaning as in the law of the United Kingdom, and 'alien' means a person who is 'not a British subject'. Apart from these provisions, the Act does not recognize any difference between aliens and British subjects (or Commonwealth citizens), and gives the latter no privileges when applying for citizenship.

It will thus be seen that the present Ceylon Act deviates in certain particulars from the pattern generally common to the Canadian, United Kingdom, Australian, and New Zealand legislation. Further, throughout it makes no mention of 'Commonwealth citizen', except by reference in Section 26, which provides that ' "British subject" has the same meaning as in the law of the United Kingdom'. The Ceylon Act does not explicitly repeal the British Nationality and Status of Aliens Acts; but, by Section 27, Part V, it repeals the Ceylon Naturalization Ordinance. As mentioned above, however, it is understood at the time of writing that the Government of Ceylon is considering further legislation, following the recommendations of its experts who attended the 1947 conference in London (see p. 64, above).

The Ceylon Act recognizes no special position of citizens of Eire.

The Government of Ceylon also passed a new Immigrants and Emigrants Act (No. 20 of 1948), assented to on 6 October 1948. Apart from the usual provisions exempting from the operation of the Act diplomatic and other official missions, ships' crews in Ceylon territorial waters and persons entering the employment of the Ceylon Government, it also exempts the following categories of British subjects: members of His Majesty's Naval, Military, or Air Forces; their wives, dependent children, and official staff or household. Part III of the Act deals with *visas* and residence permits for persons entering Ceylon who are not citizens of Ceylon, Section 14 (3) (*a*) providing that no spouse, dependent child or other dependant of a citizen of Ceylon shall be refused a residence permit (so long as, in the case of 'other' dependants, maintenance is assured), and Section 14 (3) (*b*) providing that no 'British subject' who has resided in Ceylon during the immediately preceding five years shall be refused a temporary residence permit. The Act provides for the exclusion of the various types of undesirable immigrants usually listed in such legislation; but it does not exclude anyone on racial or religious grounds.

A further Act, the Indian and Pakistani Residents (Citizenship) Act (No. 3 of 1949), assented to on 28 February 1949, laid down in considerable detail (compared with the Ceylon Citizenship Act) the conditions governing application for registration for citizenship by Indians and Pakistanis having the stated residence qualifications. The main difference under this Act, which applies only to Indians and Pakistanis, would appear to be that it exempts them from the operation of Section 12 of the Citizenship Act which, as was mentioned above, limits the grants of Ceylon citizenship to twenty-five in any one year in the case of persons from overseas having no qualification through descent, marriage, or lapsed previous citizenship.

Nationality in the Union of India

Since the United Kingdom ceased to have any power to legislate for India after that country became a Dominion in August 1947, the repeal of the British Nationality and Status of Aliens Act, 1914, and its replacement by the British Nationality Act of 1948 was without effect in the municipal law of the Union of India. The 1914 Act continued in force until the new Dominion passed its own legislation. As an interim measure, the Government of India had issued the following statement in the spring of 1947:

The Government of India have decided to suspend naturalization in India of foreigners under both the British Nationality and Status of Aliens Act, 1914, and the Indian Naturalization Act, 1926, pending the enactment of an Indian Nationality Law which is at present under consideration. Foreigners who have already been declared *prima facie* eligible for naturalization are not affected by this decision and the further examination of their cases will proceed.[1]

Part II of the new Indian Constitution consists of the following provisions regarding citizenship:

5. At the date of commencement of this Constitution, every person who has his domicile in the territory of India and—

(*a*) who was born in the territory of India; or

(*b*) either of whose parents was born in the territory of India; or

(*c*) who has been ordinarily resident in the territory of India for not less than five years immediately preceding the date of such commencement,

shall be a citizen of India, provided that he has not voluntarily acquired the citizenship of any foreign State.

[The territory of India is defined in Article I of the Constitution, and includes the previous Princely States. In Part XV ('Miscellaneous Provisions'), a foreign State is defined as any State other than India; but exceptions may be made by notification, and such notification has in fact been given in the case of other Members of the British Commonwealth.]

5A. Notwithstanding anything contained in Article 5 of this Constitution, a person who has migrated to the territory of India from the territory now included in Pakistan shall be deemed to be a citizen of India at the date of the commencement of this Constitution if—

(*a*) he or either of his parents or any of his grandparents was born in India as defined in the Government of India Act, 1935 (as originally enacted); and

(*b*) (i) in the case where such a person has so migrated before the nineteenth day of July, 1948, he has ordinarily resided in the territory of India since the date of his migration, and

(ii) in the case where such person has so migrated on or after

---

[1] *Indian Trade Bulletin*, 16 March 1947, p. 37.

the nineteenth day of July 1948, he has been registered as a citizen of India by an officer appointed in this behalf by the Government of the Dominion of India on an application made by him therefor to such officer before the date of the commencement of this Constitution in the form prescribed by that Government:

Provided that no such registration shall be made unless the person making the application has resided in the territory of India for at least six months before the date of his application.

5AA. Notwithstanding anything contained in Articles 5 and 5A of this Constitution, a person who has after the first day of March 1947 migrated from the territory of India to the territory now included in Pakistan shall not be deemed to be a citizen of India:

Provided that nothing in this Article shall apply to a person who, after having so migrated to the territory now included in Pakistan, has returned to the territory of India under a permit for resettlement or permanent return issued by or under the authority of any law and every such person shall for the purposes of clause (b) of Article 5A of this Constitution be deemed to have migrated to the territory of India after the nineteenth day of July 1948.

5B. Notwithstanding anything contained in Articles 5 and 5A of this Constitution, any person who or either of whose parents or any of whose grandparents was born in India as defined in the Government of India Act, 1935 (as originally enacted) and who is ordinarily residing in any territory outside India as so defined shall be deemed to be a citizen of India if he has been registered as a citizen of India by the diplomatic or consular representative of India in the country where he is for the time being residing on an application made by him therefor to such diplomatic or consular representative, whether before or after the commencement of this Constitution, in the form prescribed for this purpose by the Government of the Dominion of India or the Government of India.

5C. Every person who is a citizen of India under any of the foregoing provisions of this Part shall, subject to the provisions of any law that may be made by Parliament, continue to be such a citizen.

6. Nothing in the foregoing provisions of this Part shall derogate from the power of Parliament to make any provision with respect to the acquisition and termination of citizenship and all other matters relating to citizenship.

In general, it will be observed that the provisions of the Constitution do not cover all questions of nationality: for example, naturalization, the nationality of married women, and various other matters which were subjects of discussion at the official conference in London in February 1947 (at which, it will be recalled, India was not represented, although the Government of India was kept fully informed). The exception by notification of Member countries of the Commonwealth from the category of foreign States permits the recognition of dual citizenship within the Commonwealth. The British Nationality and Status of Aliens Act, 1914, has not been expressly repealed: although, as was seen above, the naturalization of aliens under the Act was suspended in 1947. At the time of writing it is understood—as is indicated in the notice of suspension of naturalizations already quoted— that legislation comprehending all details of nationality matters is under consideration.

Nationality in Pakistan

At the time of writing, the Government of Pakistan had not passed any citizenship legislation.

CHAPTER IV

THE IMPERIAL CONFERENCE

History

THE Imperial Conference is the oldest intra-Commonwealth organ of consultation, at which the responsible statesmen of all the Member countries can meet for personal exchanges of views. In the constitutional field, in the course of its series of meetings from 1887 to 1937, it defined the major conventions governing the relations between Members. Executive action consequential upon the acceptance of the resolutions of the Conference was taken by the individual Governments in the Commonwealth, either severally or acting in concert, and led to a body of developments in law and Commonwealth co-operation in many different spheres which composed the main corpus of Commonwealth relations.

The first Conference in the series, the Colonial Conference of 1887, was held to mark the occasion of Queen Victoria's Golden Jubilee and its significance to imperial solidarity. Matters of common interest were discussed, but no arrangements were then made for another conference. In 1894 the Government of Canada convened a conference on imperial economic relations at Ottawa, and the continuation of the Ottawa discussions formed part of the business of the second Colonial Conference held in London in 1897, the Diamond Jubilee year. This conference, which was restricted to the self-governing Colonies and had a more concentrated agenda than in 1887, began to show the lines on which the series was in future to develop. In 1900 the Australian Colonies united to form the federal Commonwealth of Australia, so that one, instead of six, Australian delegates attended the next Colonial Conference held in 1902, on the occasion of the Coronation of King Edward VII.

The Resolutions of the 1907 Conference

The Colonial Conference of 1907 agreed upon the periodicity, character, and shape of future conferences in the following resolutions:

That it will be to the advantage of the Empire if a Conference, to be called the Imperial Conference is held every four years, at which questions of common interest may be discussed and considered as between His Majesty's Government and his Governments of the self-governing Dominions beyond the seas. The Prime Minister of the

United Kingdom will be *ex officio* President, and the Prime Ministers of the self-governing Dominions *ex officio* members of the Conference. The Secretary of State for the Colonies will be an *ex officio* member of the Conference, and will take the chair in the absence of the President, and will arrange for such Imperial Conferences after communication with the Prime Ministers of the respective Dominions.

Such other Ministers as the respective Governments may appoint will also be members of the Conference—it being understood that except by special permission of the Conference each discussion will be conducted by not more than two representatives from each Government and that each Government will have only one vote.

That it is desirable to establish a system by which the several Governments represented shall be kept informed during the periods between the Conferences in regard to matters which have been or may be subjects for discussion by means of a permanent secretarial staff, charged under the direction of the Secretary of State for the Colonies with the duty of obtaining information for the use of the Conference, of attending to its resolutions, and of conducting correspondence on matters relating to its affairs.

That upon matters of importance, requiring consultation between two or more Governments, which cannot conveniently be postponed until the next Conference, or involving subjects of a minor character or such as call for detailed consideration, subsidiary conferences should be held between representatives of the Governments concerned, specially chosen for the purpose.[1]

The above resolutions recognized the title 'Dominion' for the self-governing Colonies, and gave the name 'Imperial Conference' to future meetings in the series.

The Imperial Conference of 1911

The first conference under the new name was held in 1911, and the Union of South Africa, which had been proclaimed in 1910, was represented for the first time. The 1907 conference had not assigned a place in future conferences to the non-self-governing territory of India, but in 1911 the Secretary of State for India attended to represent its interests.

Developments During the War of 1914–18

The planned series was brusquely interrupted by the war of 1914–18, but in 1917 and 1918 Imperial War Conferences were held. The Secretary of State for the Colonies presided, and the two meetings were contemporaneous with meetings of the Imperial War Cabinet set up in 1917 and composed of representatives of the Governments of the Empire, including India, associated with the British War Cabinet in the common war effort. The

[1] Cd. 3523, pp. 82–94.

Imperial War Conference of 1917 provided for the future representation of India at Imperial Conferences by the following resolution moved by Sir Robert Borden (Canada):

The Imperial War Conference desires to place on record its view that the Resolution of the Imperial Conference of 20 April 1907, should be modified to permit of India being fully represented at all future Imperial Conferences and that necessary steps be taken to secure the assent of the various Governments in order that the next Imperial Conference may be summoned and constituted accordingly.[1]

At its meetings in 1917 and 1918, the Imperial War Cabinet had agreed that similar Cabinet meetings might be held annually after the war, but the proposal lapsed after 1918 and the Imperial Conference of 1921, although it was not formally so designated, was of the normal type, not associated with such a Cabinet meeting, and with the Prime Minister of the United Kingdom presiding.[2] The 1917 Imperial War Conference had proposed that a special Imperial Conference should meet after the war to consider the constitutional relations of the Empire, but the 1921 Imperial Conference negatived this as unnecessary, while affirming the desirability of frequent conferences. The next Imperial Conference met in 1923, and an Imperial Economic Conference was held concurrently. The Irish Free State, which had become a Member of the Commonwealth in 1922, was represented for the first time at this conference.

The Conferences of 1926 and 1930

The Imperial Conference of 1926 is perhaps the most famous in the series. At the instance of the Union of South Africa and the Irish Free State, it undertook the task of defining the relations of the countries of the Commonwealth on the basis of complete autonomy and equality combined with co-operation. It adopted the 'Balfour Report', drawn up by the Committee on Inter-Imperial Relations set up by the Conference under the chairmanship of the first Earl Balfour. Its definition of Dominion status, although convention and not law, was the motive principle of extensive subsequent developments in both convention and law. The Committee's report outlined the nature of a number of the developments which would be required, and was followed in 1929 by a technical Conference on the Operation of Dominion Legislation and Merchant Shipping Legislation, which undertook the detailed examination of the legal changes necessary to make

---

[1] Cd. 8566, p. 22.
[2] The title used was 'Conference of Prime Ministers and Representatives of the United Kingdom, the Dominions and India' (Cmd. 1474, 1921).

effective the principles of the Balfour Report. The results of this technical conference, which had been circulated in advance to the Governments of the Commonwealth, were before the 1930 Imperial Conference, which used them as the basis upon which to frame the terms of the enactment which, after discussion and some amendment by the Parliaments of the Commonwealth, was passed, at their request, by the United Kingdom Parliament in 1931 under the title of the 'Statute of Westminster'; and was subsequently adopted by each of the Dominions named therein except Newfoundland.[1]

The 'Ottawa Conference' of 1932

The severe impact of the economic depression which broke upon the world in 1929 led the Commonwealth countries to meet in an Imperial Economic Conference, convened by the Government of Canada, at Ottawa in 1932.[2] To this conference India, hitherto represented at Imperial Conferences by the Secretary of State, one Ruling Prince, and one public man from British India, sent a delegation of eight led by Sir Atul Chatterjee and including members of the Executive Council, the Legislative Council, and a State Government. Southern Rhodesia was represented by observers, and entered into trade agreements; and the Secretary of State for the Colonies in the United Kingdom Government represented the territories of the Dependent Empire in the negotiations for the Imperial preferential trading system which was the aim of the conference.

The Imperial Conference of 1937

The next Imperial Conference met in London in May 1937, on the occasion of the Coronation of King George VI. The innovation of 1932, of having a larger and therefore more representative Indian delegation, was maintained. Southern Rhodesia was represented by observers, as was also Burma, which had been administratively separated from India by the Government of Burma Act, 1935, which became operative on 1 April 1947. As the Dominion status of Newfoundland had been suspended in 1934, the island was not represented. The Irish Free State Government did not send representatives.

The War of 1939–45 interrupted the Imperial Conference series of meetings, and no post-war meeting has been summoned.

---

[1] See above, p. 20.
[2] The meeting was, strictly speaking, a resumption of the meetings of the adjourned Economic Section of the 1930 Imperial Conference; but was known as the Imperial Economic Conference (Dominion and Colonial Office List, 1940, p. xc).

CONSTITUTION AND CHARACTER

The constitution and functions of the Imperial Conference were not affected by the constitutional changes initiated by the 1926 conference, and, apart from the alterations in membership mentioned above, they continued on the footing laid down in 1907.

The character of the resolutions of Imperial Conferences has always been that of honourable undertakings on the part of those Governments which adopt them. Resolutions are thus not legally binding on any Government, and executive action lies solely with the individual Governments, each of which determines freely how soon and in what way it shall give effect to any resolution to which it has agreed. It may happen that a change of government in any country of the Commonwealth may lead to large changes of policy, and a new Government is not bound by any resolution agreed to by its predecessor if it is precluded by its political views from giving effect to it.

The functions of the Conference have been described thus by Mr Mackenzie King:

The task of an Imperial Conference has been well defined as that of considering whether the several Governments represented, while preserving their individual rights of decision and action, can co-ordinate their various policies in such a way as to assist one another to help forward the common cause of peace. Its function is not to formulate or declare policy. The value of an Imperial Conference lies mainly in the free exchange of information and opinion, and in furnishing the representatives of the several Governments with more adequate knowledge of the problems, difficulties and aspirations of the members of the British Commonwealth of Nations and in giving them the direct and immediate understanding of the national and personal factors of the situation, which cannot well be obtained by correspondence or indirect communication. With this further knowledge in their possession, the representatives of each Government, in consultation with their colleagues and their respective Parliaments, are in the best position to formulate policies where co-operation is required.[1]

Matters giving rise to friction between Commonwealth countries can also be freely ventilated in friendly discussion. The 1929 Conference on the Operation of Dominion Legislation made suggestions for 'determining differences and disputes between members of the British Commonwealth' by means, when occasion might arise, of an *ad hoc* Commonwealth tribunal with jurisdiction 'limited to justiciable issues arising between Governments'.

[1] Quoted in *Hansard* (Commons), 21 April 1944, vol. 399, col. 522.
[2] Cmd. 3479 (1930) p. 41.

The Imperial Conference of 1930 followed this up by recommendations as to the composition and competence which such an *ad hoc* arbitral tribunal might have;[1] but the machinery suggested has never in fact been used.

Proposals have from time to time been made for the creation of some form of permanent conference secretariat to ensure continuity, to act as the agency of the conference, and to prepare for the next conference in the intervals between conferences. Suggestions of this kind were made in 1905, 1911, 1924, and 1932; in 1932 the suggestion was for a permanent Commonwealth Economic Secretariat. Such proposals have invariably been rejected; partly from the fear that a permanent secretariat might acquire executive or other powers derogatory to the powers of the Governments and which would interfere with the principle of Cabinet responsibility; partly because, in the intervals between conferences, it would be difficult to define to whom or to what body the secretariat could be directly responsible; and partly because proposals for a secretariat have tended to be linked with proposals for altering or superseding some of the powers and functions of the conference itself, generally in the direction of a closer or even federal organization of the Commonwealth. Proposals of this last kind have never found general support; their character is discussed in the following subsection. The duties of the 'permanent secretarial staff' charged with carrying out minimum interim functions between conferences provided for in the 1907 Conference resolution quoted above, have been discharged by the staff of the appropriate Department of State in the United Kingdom: after 1907, the Colonial Office; after 1925, the Dominions Office; since 1947, the Commonwealth Relations Office.

Continuity is an essential practical requirement of Commonwealth relations, which the periodic meetings of Imperial Conferences could not fill. The permanent machinery of communication and consultation between the Governments of the Member nations meets the need for continuous mutual contact in face of the changing situations which policy has to meet. Some account of this permanent machinery will be found in the chapters which follow.

PAST PROPOSALS FOR MODIFICATION OF THE FUNCTIONS OF THE IMPERIAL CONFERENCE AND THE ANCILLARY MACHINERY OF CO-OPERATION

Imperial Federation Ideas, 1880–1905
When the Colonial Secretary, Mr Edward Stanhope, circu-

[1] Cmd. 3717, pp. 22-4.

larized the governors of Colonies under responsible government to summon them to the first Colonial Conference in 1887, he suggested for discussion various matters of common interest but deprecated discussion of 'subjects falling within the range of what is known as Political Federation'.[1] The idea of imperial federation was then some fifteen years old;[2] the Imperial Federation League had been formed in 1884. The main appeal of the federal idea lay in its apparently cogent logic, and this appeal survived the Colonial Secretary's deprecation. Federation provided too neat a solution of the dilemma of reconciling a strict view of sovereignty with the formal equality of the Dominions to be lightly discarded.

'Imperial federationist argument, therefore, was a constant background to the Imperial Conference.'[3] But it was also constantly suspect by those in all parts of the Commonwealth who distrust elaborate constitutional structures and the transfer of responsibility for their most vital interests to a supra-national body. This suspicion, as Professor Hancock points out, tended at times to hamper the consideration on their merits of proposals intended only to increase the efficiency of the conferences by providing ancillary machinery operating in the intervals between meetings.

In his opening address to the Conference of 1897, Mr Joseph Chamberlain offered 'as a personal suggestion that it might be feasible to create a great council of the Empire to which the Colonies would send representative plenipotentiaries'. Initially, he thought, it would be advisory, but 'it might slowly grow to that Federal Council to which we must always look forward as our ultimate ideal'. The colonial delegates, however, were more immediately interested in pressing for a measure of imperial preference and the Imperial Council proposal, although they discussed it, did not seem to them as urgent as persuading the United Kingdom to modify its free trade policy. They adopted the following resolution, New Zealand and Tasmania dissenting: 'The Prime Ministers here assembled are of opinion that the present political relations between the United Kingdom and the self-governing Colonies are generally satisfactory under the existing condition of things.'[4] In 1902 Mr Chamberlain returned to his Imperial Council proposal, which had in the interval become

---

[1] C. 5691 (1886). Letter of 25 November.
[2] C. E. Bodelsen in *Studies in Mid-Victorian Imperialism* (Copenhagen, 1924), traces its origins.
[3] Professor W. K. Hancock, *Survey of British Commonwealth Affairs* (London, Oxford University Press for the Royal Institute of International Affairs, 1937) vol. 1, p. 35.
[4] C. 8596 (1897), p. 15.

for him increasingly linked with his goal of some form of imperial *Zollverein*. But he was not able to press this view effectively because the United Kingdom Cabinet was already divided on the free trade issue, which finally split it in December 1905; and because the shock which the Empire had received over the South African war made defence questions appear more urgent to many of the participating statesmen.

Mr Lyttelton's Proposals for a Secretariat, 1905

In April 1905 Mr Alfred Lyttelton, Secretary of State for the Colonies, addressed a circular dispatch to the Governments in which he put forward proposals for an 'Imperial Council' and for an ancillary permanent 'Commission' with a secretariat. The dispatch purposely refrained from defining closely the functions of the proposed Council, and the idea was unfavourably received by Sir Wilfrid Laurier, whose chief concern was for the national autonomy of Canada; it was evidently feared that the Council might tend to acquire executive functions. In view largely of the attitude of Canada the proposal was finally dropped at the Conference of 1907, and the main features of the existing Imperial Conference system were laid down. As was natural, following the extensive study of federal problems in Australia prior to the union of the six States in a federal Commonwealth in 1900, Australian statesmen, both at Imperial Conferences and outside them, have taken a leading part in discussions on the subject. In 1907 Mr Deakin, the Australian Prime Minister, supported the idea, suggested in the Lyttelton Dispatch, of a permanent secretariat for the Imperial Conferences. His view of the secretariat was that it should be solely an agency of the conferences, to prepare their material, and carry out such instructions as they might give it. The reasons why the secretariat part of the proposal was rejected are given above (p. 85).

Sir Joseph Ward's 'Imperial Council' Proposal, 1911

A major discussion of the concept of an Imperial Council took place at the 1911 Conference. Sir Joseph Ward, the Prime Minister of New Zealand, introduced the following resolution: 'That the Empire has now reached a stage of imperial development which renders it expedient that there should be an Imperial Council of State, with representatives from all the self-governing parts of the Empire, in theory and in fact advisory to the Imperial Government on all questions affecting the interests of His Majesty's Dominions overseas'.[1] The background against which the discussion took place included the Dominions' objec-

[1] Cd. 5745 (1911), p. 46.

tion to the fact that Great Britain had ratified the Declaration of London (embodying the rules regarding sea-borne commerce in time of war agreed at the Hague Conference in 1907) without consulting them, and the threatening attitude of Germany (which reached its climax of the year with the Agadir incident in July, just after the Conference). Sir Joseph Ward, in addition to describing the changes produced by 'the rapid growth of the Dominions', related his proposal closely to the defence problem, especially naval defence, using the expressions 'an Imperial Parliament of Defence or a Defence Council' interchangeably with 'Imperial Council of State'. Sir Wilfrid Laurier objected: 'There is everything in the name',[1] and rejected the New Zealand resolution because it implied an imperial legislature, with power to create expenditure on defence, but without power to create revenue and therefore irresponsible. His points were elaborated by Mr Fisher (Australia) and General Botha (Union of South Africa), and Mr Asquith finally disposed of Sir Joseph Ward's plan by a restatement of the classic theory of imperial diplomatic unity: that the responsibility for foreign policy, war and peace, could not be shared but must remain with 'the Imperial Government, subject to its responsibility to the Imperial Parliament'.[2] Sir Joseph Ward by leave withdrew his resolution.

At the same conference Sir Joseph Ward introduced a group of six resolutions directed towards closer co-operation and improving the exchange of information. They included requests for the separation of its Dominions department from the rest of the Colonial Office, and the erection of the separated department into a distinct entity under its own permanent Under-Secretary. The secretariat of the Imperial Conference should go with the newly constituted department. Both it and the Colonial Office should be under the same Secretary of State, whose title should be changed to Secretary of State for Imperial Affairs.[3]

Mr Harcourt's Memorandum, 1911

The United Kingdom Government responded to these requests in a memorandum prepared by the Secretary of State for the Colonies, Mr L. Harcourt, suggesting the establishment of a Standing Committee of the Imperial Conference. It may be summarized as follows:

(i) The Standing Committee would in effect be a subsidiary Conference not limited to one subject, and meeting at more or less regular intervals for the transaction of the business referred to it by the Secretary of State for the Colonies with the assent of the Dominion Governments.[4]

[1] ibid. p. 56.   [2] ibid. p. 71.   [3] ibid. p. 76.   [4] Cd. 5746-1 (1911), p. 212.

Mr Harcourt also described it as a 'strengthening and enlarging of the secretariat in order to secure greater continuity and co-operation in the work between one conference and another and on any allied questions which may properly come up for consideration as conference questions.[1]

(ii) The Committee should be an advisory and not an executive body.

(iii) It should have the power to summon political or permanent heads of Government Departments to any of its meetings at which matters affecting them were being discussed.

(iv) Its personnel should comprise the Secretary of State and the political and permanent Under-Secretaries for the Colonies, together with representatives of each of the Dominions.

(v) It should deal only with matters of common concern to all members of the Imperial Conference and should undertake consideration of such matters only with the sanction of all the Governments.

(vi) There should be no voting.

(vii) Its members should not be members of the Imperial Conference when it met.

These proposals were very strongly urged on the Conference by Sir Joseph Ward, who was supported by Mr Fisher, Mr Harcourt making it clear that his memorandum had been prepared in deference to the wish of the New Zealand Government to raise the question, and not because of 'any conscious want on the part of the Home Government'.[2]

The discussion of Mr Harcourt's memorandum soon revealed difficulties, the chief of which were in relation to the position of the High Commissioners. In the original memorandum it was suggested that there should be on the Standing Committee 'the High Commissioners and other representatives' of the Dominions; specific mention of the individual High Commissioners was omitted since it was felt that it would be invidious if, in view of such mention, any High Commissioner failed to secure appointment to the Committee. Moreover, it was felt that there were several possible difficulties in the way of appointing High Commissioners: first, that it would mean extending the functions of the officer to those of a consultative authority, which might be unsatisfactory from the point of view of a Dominion Government that has to receive advice from an officer under its direction; secondly, that certain High Commissioners had business rather

---

[1] Cd. 5745 (1911), p. 173.   [2] ibid. p. 183.

G

than political qualifications; and thirdly, that it was undesirable to appoint Ministers and High Commissioners to the same Committee.

Sir Wilfrid Laurier expressed his real fears of the proposal when he said: 'If the body is to be anything at all, it will try to exercise its own views and impress its own views on the Governments.'[1] Despite, therefore, an urgent plea by Sir Joseph Ward for this 'bridge between the conferences', the opposition to the proposal caused it to be dropped.

The Imperial War Cabinet, 1917–18

Although the idea of a single imperial organ for foreign policy, war and peace, seemed to have been decisively rejected in 1911, the emergencies of the War of 1914–18 did lead to the creation, in March 1917, of a temporary Imperial executive in the form of the Imperial War Cabinet. Sir Robert Borden (Canada) described and commented upon it as follows:

> For the first time in the Empire's history there are sitting in London two Cabinets, both properly constituted and both exercising well-defined powers. Over each of them the Prime Minister of the United Kingdom presides. One of them is designated as the 'War Cabinet', which chiefly devotes itself to such questions touching the prosecution of the war as primarily concern the United Kingdom. The other is designated as the 'Imperial War Cabinet', which has a wider purpose, jurisdiction, and personnel. To its deliberations have been summoned representatives of all the Empire's self-governing Dominions. We meet there on terms of equality under the presidency of the First Minister of the United Kingdom; we meet there as equals; he is *primus inter pares*. Ministers from six nations sit around the Council Board, all of them responsible to their respective Parliaments and to the people of the countries which they represent. Each nation has its voice upon questions of common concern and highest importance as the deliberations proceed; each preserves unimpaired its perfect autonomy, its self-government, and the responsibility of its Ministers to their own electorate. For many years the thought of statesmen and students in every part of the Empire has centred around the question of future constitutional relations; it may be that now, as in the past, the necessity imposed by great events has given the answer.

The experiment appeared at the time so successful that in May 1917 the Imperial War Cabinet resolved on the holding of annual Imperial Cabinets in the future, and the hope was expressed that this would become 'an accepted convention of the British Constitution'.[2]

A second session was held from 11 June to 30 July 1918.

[1] Cd. 5745, p. 181.
[2] Mr Lloyd George in the House of Commons, 17 May 1917.

Australia, which in 1917 had been unable to be represented owing to a general election at home, sent its Prime Minister and the Minister of the Navy. An important change was made in the representation of India. In 1917 the Secretary of State for India (Mr Edwin Montagu) and three assessors attended; in 1918 the Secretary of State was supported by the Hon. S. P. Sinha, a member of the Executive Council of the Governor of Bengal, and the Maharajah of Patiala, representing the Princes. The machinery of the Imperial War Cabinet was extended and developed at this second session. It resolved that henceforward the Dominion Prime Ministers should have the right of direct communication, on matters of Cabinet importance, with the Prime Minister of the United Kingdom. It also resolved that each Dominion Prime Minister should have the right to nominate a resident or visiting Minister 'to represent him at meetings of the Imperial War Cabinet to be held regularly between plenary sessions'. The object of this second resolution was continuity of consultation, but victory had come before it could be put into effect. The right set out in the first resolution survives as an important part of Commonwealth consultative machinery.

The Imperial War Cabinet began its third plenary session on 25 November 1918, and addressed itself to the problems of the peace settlement. The Dominions, led by Canada, claimed the right as effective belligerents and autonomous States to be represented at the Peace Conference. The United Kingdom Cabinet recognized the claim, and the Imperial War Cabinet, including India's representatives, transferred itself to Paris as the British Empire delegation.[1]

Thereafter, the Imperial War Cabinet lapsed. It was not a true Cabinet on the accepted British model, with common responsibility to the elected representatives in Parliament of a people.[2] Neither was it truly federal. It was more in the nature of a reinforcement of the United Kingdom Cabinet for the common

---

[1] For further details, see Chapter XIV, below.

[2] 'In the Dominions as in the United Kingdom the term "Cabinet" carries with it, as a result of constant usage, the suggestion of a body of ministers who (1) owe a common responsibility to a single legislature; (2) are united by loyalty to a Prime Minister; and (3) are wont to decide policy by majority votes, the minority being bound to accept and faithfully execute majority decisions. None of these criteria apply to the Imperial Cabinet. There is no Imperial legislature to which it could be responsible. The British Prime Minister may preside, but only, as Sir Robert Borden insists, as *primus inter pares*. What is still more important, it cannot take a majority decision. . . . If a Dominion Premier dissents from a line of policy proposed by the majority of the Imperial Cabinet, the decision of the majority is null as regards his Dominion.' (A. Berriedale Keith, *Letters on Imperial Relations, Indian Reform, Constitutional and International Law*, 1916-35 (London, Oxford University Press, 1935) pp. 23-4. See also *Round Table*, vol. 11, no. 43 (June 1921) pp. 539-40.)

purposes of war—a council of allies. It was not continued for peace-time purposes, and as a war-time device it was not revived in 1939–45. Its constitutional significance was secondary, but its contribution to the political development of the Commonwealth was considerable.

The Influence of Developments in International Co-operation

It has been observed that the controversy about Imperial federation was constantly in the background of all proposals for change in or extension of the functions of the Imperial Conference during the previous twenty years and more. The theory and practice of the League of Nations and the obligations of membership formed as constant a background in the years after 1919. In the early days, when hopes of the League stood high, there was a feeling that the lesser good of Commonwealth co-operation would be merged in and superseded by the greater good of League co-operation. As hopes of the League faded and finally died, some who saw the best as the enemy of the good turned their attention to the Commonwealth field again. About this stage a new counter-argument appeared: the alleged incompatibility of closer Commonwealth co-operation with the requirements of loyalty to the aim of world co-operation. This theory of incompatibility is a curious feature of intra-Commonwealth controversy. As has been pointed out by various statesmen, it has never, by contrast, been put forward as an argument against closer Pan-American co-operation,[1] or against the Little Entente or the Balkan confederation.[2]

Proposals made between the wars for supplementing the Imperial Conference machinery may be roughly divided as: functional and specific, and general. Both types spring from a recurrent impulse to increase continuity and intimacy of contact between the statesmen in power in the Commonwealth countries; but the more functional and specific suggestions—which, however, cannot be clearly demarcated from the more general proposals—tended to be at the technical rather than the ministerial level, and were, therefore, less liable to reflect, in personnel and expert membership, changes of government. The more general proposals were concerned with continuity of contact in matters of high policy, and were therefore apt to be more controversial. It is noticeable throughout the history of the Imperial Conference

[1] An admirable *exposé* of the controversy, which strikes the reader in 1950 mainly by its unreality, is to be found in British Commonwealth Relations Conference, 1933, *Proceedings of the First Unofficial Conference at Toronto*, ed. by A. J. Toynbee (London, Oxford University Press, for the Royal Institute of International Affairs, 1934), see especially pp. 35–52 and 184–95.

[2] See, e.g. Lord Bruce of Melbourne, *Hansard* (Lords), vol. 153, col. 1112.

how frequently even functional proposals were not followed up.

Resident Ministers and Cognate Proposals

The proposal to have Resident Ministers from the Dominions appointed to London was discussed in 1911 and 1912, both at the Imperial Conference and at the Committee of Imperial Defence, and on 10 December 1912 Mr Harcourt, Secretary of State for the Colonies, addressed a dispatch[1] on the subject to the Governors-General of Australia and South Africa, and the Governors of New Zealand and Newfoundland. The dispatch stated that the question of representation of the Dominions on the Committee of Imperial Defence had recently been discussed with Mr (later Sir) Robert Borden during his visit to London, and that he was in favour of appointing a Minister to spend some months annually in London for this purpose.

The dispatch further stated that there was general agreement both at the Imperial Conference of 1911 and at subsequent meetings of the Committee of Imperial Defence that the Dominions should not be represented on the Committee by their High Commissioners, but that Ministers would be most welcome to attend any meetings at which questions affecting the Dominions were under discussion. Finally, the dispatch invited Dominions to send Ministers to London annually for attendance at the Committee and for personal consultations with British Ministers on matters of defence and foreign policy, and pointed out that this would provide opportunities of close consultation without raising any of the difficult problems of Imperial Federation, since the Committee was a purely advisory body without executive authority or power to make decisions on policy, these functions resting with the individual Cabinets and Parliaments.

In 1914 Canada appointed Sir George Perley, Minister without portfolio, to London with the status of Acting High Commissioner. He had the authority of the Canadian Government to attend meetings of the Committee of Imperial Defence. He became High Commissioner in 1917.

The special circumstances of the War of 1914–18 led to the application of the system on a large scale by the formation of the Imperial War Cabinet; and during the Imperial War Conference of 1918 Mr W. F. Massey, the Prime Minister of New Zealand, expressed his conviction that the appointment of Resident Ministers in London after the war was the only solution of the difficulty of enabling the Dominions to play an adequate part in the conduct of the affairs of the Commonwealth.

After the termination of the Ottawa Conference Mr Bruce, who

[1] Cd. 7347.

was then an Honorary Minister of the Australian Cabinet, came to London as Minister representing the Commonwealth. Mr Bruce remained a member of the Australian Cabinet and combined with his new duties those of the High Commissioner, which office had fallen vacant in June 1932. On 7 October 1933 he resigned from the Cabinet and was appointed High Commissioner for Australia in the United Kingdom.

Visits of Dominion Statesmen, 1939–44

After Mr Bruce resigned in 1933, no Dominion had a Minister resident in London until the outbreak of the War of 1939–45. The question then naturally arose whether an Imperial War Cabinet on the 1917–18 model should again be established. Very shortly after the outbreak of hostilities the United Kingdom Government inquired whether the other Governments of the Commonwealth already engaged in the war would be willing to send a Cabinet Minister to London to confer with Ministers there and with each other for the co-ordination to the best advantage of the contribution each could make to the common task. The suggestion was welcomed and in October 1939 missions were arriving from all the Dominions, neutral Eire of course excepted. India applied for representation and this was at once conceded. She nominated Sir Muhammad Zafrullah Khan, a member of the Governor-General's Executive Council. Canada sent a full mission headed by Mr Thomas A. Crerar, the Minister of Mines, who had with him representatives of the defence services and the departments of trade and agriculture. Australia nominated Mr R. G. Casey, at that time Minister for Supply; South Africa, Colonel Deneys Reitz, then Minister of Native Affairs; and Mr Peter Fraser, then Deputy Prime Minister and Minister of Education, Health, and Marine came from New Zealand. This gathering of missions was not an Imperial War Cabinet.

Thereafter various Dominion Ministers visited London and sat with the War Cabinet.[1] Mr Menzies, Prime Minister of Australia, was the first of the Dominion Prime Ministers to come to London. The Australian Government and Opposition both strongly desired direct and permanent representation for Australia in the War Cabinet in London. Hence Mr Menzies accepted a special invitation from the War Cabinet in London to join their counsels. He arrived on 21 February 1941, and, by agreement with his colleagues in Australia, remained till May. On 29 August he resigned the premiership in favour of his former deputy, Mr Fadden, and accepted instead the portfolio for

[1] Similarly, Mr Churchill, when visiting Canada during the war, was invited to sit with the Dominion Cabinet.

Defence Co-ordination. Subsequent to this exchange of responsibilities, Sir Earle Page, Minister of Commerce and leader of the Country Party, was chosen for London. He was on his way there when the Fadden Government, after defeat on the Budget, resigned office and a Labour Ministry was formed by Mr John Curtin. The new Cabinet did not, however, recall Sir Earle Page. Instead, it asked him to continue his journey to London and serve as Australia's Envoy Extraordinary in the War Cabinet. On his arrival Sir Earl Page defined his mission thus:

My function will be to establish personal Cabinet liaison between the Governments. I am still directly responsible to the Australian Parliament and people. The primary purpose of my mission will be the presentation of the Australian point of view on certain major problems and immediate strategy in the war situation. The second purpose will be to arrange the best mechanics for maintaining the system of direct Cabinet representation in London.

The question of the formation of an Imperial War Council had also been raised at Westminster. In reply to a question in the House of Lords on 2 February 1941, Lord Cranborne, Secretary of State for Dominion Affairs, said that such a Council was not at the time practicable, and that the existing channels of communication provided full and complete liaison with the Dominion Governments. On 11 June 1941 the Prime Minister, Mr Churchill, stated in reply to a question that there had been no formal request from the Dominions for the formation of an Imperial War Cabinet; and, while the United Kingdom Government was ready to welcome any meeting with the Dominion Prime Ministers, their tasks at home might make it impossible for them all to come at the same time. On 24 June he told the House of Commons that the exigencies of their work at home would prevent General Smuts and Mr Mackenzie King from coming, and announced that Mr Fraser had arrived four days previously.

As stated, in the meantime Mr Fraser had returned to London, this time as Prime Minister of New Zealand, having succeeded to the premiership on the death of Mr M. J. Savage in April 1940. Mr Fraser reached London on 21 June 1941, about a month after Mr Menzies had left, and became a member of the War Cabinet during his stay, which continued till late summer.[1]

[1] Mr Winston Churchill, after paying tribute to Mr Menzies's participation in the work of the War Cabinet ,said: 'He [Mr Menzies] had not been satisfied with the organization of the [War] Cabinet or with my exercise of such wide powers in the conduct of the war. He raised both points with me on several occasions, and I gave him my reasons for not agreeing with him. He desired the formation of an Imperial War Cabinet containing representatives of each of the four self-governing Dominions. On his homeward journey through Canada Mr Menzies formally submitted his proposals in writing to Mr Mackenzie King.

Mr Mackenzie King arrived from Canada on 20 August; Mr Fraser had by then departed for New Zealand, so that once again a single Dominion Prime Minister was sitting with the British War Cabinet. Mr Mackenzie King, immediately after his arrival, said: 'With regard to an Imperial Cabinet we have in actual practice the most perfect continuous conference of Cabinets that any group of nations could possibly have. I cannot conceive of more effective means of communication than we have at present.' In his first comment after reaching home in September, Mr Fraser said that it was impossible for a New Zealand Prime Minister to be a permanent member of an Imperial War Cabinet because his place was clearly in his own country, and that that would apply to a still greater extent if trouble developed in the Pacific.

In Australia, however, the outbreak of war with Japan and the growing menace of the Japanese advance intensified the call for closer association with the central direction of the war. Sir Earle Page was not a member of the Cabinet with the standing of Mr Menzies and the other visiting Prime Ministers: he attended and took part only when matters directly appertaining to Australia were under consideration. Broadcasting to Australia on 14 January 1942, he said: 'Any political make-up of War Cabinets, Imperial Conferences and so on—because of the immense distances and urgent domestic problems—is necessarily spasmodic and in and out in quality. We must build up an administrative foundation, the scaffolding of which is permanent and the quality of which will be standard.'

Australian attention was also turned in another direction. In a New Year message from Canberra on 27 December 1941, Mr Curtin stressed the importance of American help to Australia in the war in the Pacific and pointed out that strategic considerations made Australia look to the United States in that theatre of war. 'Summed up,' he said, 'Australian external policy will be shaped towards obtaining Russian aid, and working out, with the United States as the major factor, a plan of Pacific strategy along with British, Chinese, and Dutch forces.'[1] The logical conclusion would be representation on an inter-Allied body concerned with the war in the Pacific.

On 25 January 1942 Mr F. M. Forde, Deputy Prime Minister of Australia, told Parliament at Canberra that he had received a

General Smuts, and Mr Fraser. None of them was, however, in favour of the change, and Mr Mackenzie King in particular deployed formidable constitutional arguments against Canada's being committed by her representative to the decisions of a council in London.' (*Second World War* (London, Cassell, 1950), vol. 3, p. 409. Mr Churchill's own minute on constitutional difficulties may be found on pp. 844–6 of the same volume.)

[1] *Sydney Morning Herald*, 29 December 1941.

message from Mr Churchill saying that the United Kingdom Government was giving immediate consideration to the Australian Cabinet's request for the creation of an Allied War Council for the Pacific and an Empire War Council. On 27 January Mr Churchill told the House of Commons that additional means of associating the Australian, New Zealand, and Netherlands Governments with the conduct of the war in the Pacific had been among the important questions considered at his conference with President Roosevelt in Washington from 22 December 1941 to 14 January 1942. He said:

> In order to wage the war effectively against Japan, it was agreed that I should propose to those concerned the setting up of a Pacific Council in London, on the ministerial plane, comprising Great Britain, Australia, New Zealand, and the Dutch Government. . . . The united view of the British Commonwealth and the Dutch would be transmitted, at first, to the Combined Chiefs of the Staff Committee sitting at Washington. In the event of differences between the members of the Pacific Council in London, dissentient opinions would also be transmitted. In the event of differences between the London and Washington bodies, it would be necessary for the President and me to reach an agreement. I must point out that it is necessary for everybody to reach an agreement for nobody can compel anybody else.

This arrangement might have satisfied the Dutch Government, but 'the Australian Government desired and the New Zealand Government preferred that this Council of the Pacific should be in Washington, where it would work alongside of the Combined Chiefs of the Staff Committee. I have therefore transmitted the views of these two Dominions to the President.' There had not yet been time to receive his reply. In the British Commonwealth itself, the United Kingdom had always been ready to form an Imperial War Cabinet if desired, and now the Australian Government had specifically requested that its representative should have the right to be heard in the War Cabinet. New Zealand had since made a similar request; and the 'same facilities' would be available to Canada and the Union of South Africa.

The formation of a Pacific War Council 'on the ministerial plane' in London was announced on 9 February, and it met for the first time on the following day. Its membership was as foreshadowed by Mr Churchill on 27 January.[1] On 12 February it was officially announced in Delhi that His Majesty's Government in the United Kingdom were anxious that India should have similar facilities for representation on the Pacific Council and the War Cabinet in London, and that the Viceroy had invited the

---

[1] It was officially announced on 24 February 1942 that the Government of China had accepted an invitation to be represented.

Government of India to arrange such representation if it so desired.

The President of the United States had meanwhile accepted the idea of a Pacific War Council sitting in Washington, and it met for the first time on 20 March 1942. The formal announcement of its establishment was made on 31 March by the Office of the Secretary to the President. The composition of the Council in Washington was the same as that in London, and Canadian representation was shortly added to both. The question of Canadian representation had been raised in the House of Commons on 28 and 30 January, and on 16 February the Prime Minister, Mr Mackenzie King, said that he had subsequently been in communication with Mr Churchill. The Council was concerned with the actual zone of Japanese hostilities, and the countries represented on it were those in that zone. If future strategic developments made it necessary to enlarge the scope of the Council, then Canada would be represented.[1] On 21 April the Prime Minister stated that Canada would be represented on the Council in Washington by the Canadian Minister to Washington, and on its counterpart in London by the High Commissioner.[2]

Commenting on the Pacific Council in the House of Lords on 22 April 1942, the Minister of Economic Warfare, Lord Selborne, explained that it was one organ among several in the arrangements by which the Governments concerned in the Pacific war made known their wishes. It sat both in London and Washington for the same reason as the Combined Chiefs of Staff organization existed in both capitals: because parts of common decisions—depending on their nature—might have to be carried out in either Great Britain or the United States.[3]

The Australian Government was initially represented on the Pacific Council in London by Sir Earle Page, who was also their representative in the War Cabinet.[4] During Sir Earle Page's indisposition Dr Evatt was temporarily in London and sat in his place in the War Cabinet. On 5 June 1942 Mr S. M. Bruce, Australia's High Commissioner in London, on being specifically and permanently appointed to succeed Sir Earle Page as the Australian representative in the War Cabinet, delegated a major portion of his functions as High Commissioner to a deputy, Mr J. S. Duncan, so that he might devote himself mainly to this Cabinet duty. An office and staff for this purpose was established on the War Cabinet premises, the precedent by which

[1] *Hansard* (Commons), vol. 377, cols. 611–12, and 614.
[2] *Journal of the Parliaments of the Empire*, vol. 23, no. 2, pp. 267, 282.
[3] *Hansard* (Lords), vol. 122, col. 697.
[4] *J. P. E.*, vol. 23, No. 3, p. 496.

the Australian liaison office was set up within the British Foreign Office being largely followed. New Zealand had an equal right to representation on the War Cabinet but did not make any specific appointment, though she nominated her High Commissioner (Mr W. J. Jordan) as her representative on the Pacific War Council in London. Mr Walter Nash, when in London as a member of the New Zealand Cabinet, sat with the British War Cabinet.

It was not until October 1942 that Field-Marshal Smuts was able to come to London. 'I have felt', he said on his arrival, 'that my best service to the Commonwealth could be rendered in South Africa and by occasional visits farther north in the African continent. The position in that respect has considerably eased in South Africa and my talks with Mr Churchill in Egypt last August made it clear to me there might be some advantage in further talks in London.' Field-Marshal Smuts spent five weeks in London and sat during that time as a full member of the British War Cabinet. Almost exactly a year later he was in London again, staying from 5 October to 11 December 1943, and again taking part in the War Cabinet's deliberations. The Australian Office in the War Cabinet building was maintained until early in 1946, but no other Dominion availed itself of its right to request similar facilities. When Mr Beasley came to London in January 1946, he came as Resident Minister, retaining his seat in the Australian Cabinet; but he ceased to hold that position in August 1946, when he assumed office of High Commissioner for Australia in London. On 16 February 1950 Mr Eric Harrison, Minister for for Defence in the Menzies Cabinet, was appointed Resident Minister, while retaining his office in the Government. It was announced that his appointment in London would terminate in May 1951.

Proposals for Some Form of Imperial Executive

The other general proposal which reappeared at intervals for nearly fifty years, in one form or another, was that of some kind of Empire Council. As the discussion at the 1911 Imperial Conference showed, the idea was apt to take different names, and to vary in form. Its most usual proponents have been the Pacific Dominions; its most usual opponents, Canada and South Africa. Since the War of 1914–18 its proponents have discarded the remnants of 'federationist' thought; its opponents have combined remnants of 'anti-federationism' with the newer objection, mentioned above, of incompatibility with due loyalty to the world organization. The 'Empire Council' idea went into abeyance for long periods, but never quite disappeared.

In April 1921 Mr W. F. Massey, Prime Minister of New Zealand, proposed an imperial executive, meeting every two years, and responsible to the Parliaments of the United Kingdom and the Dominions. His formulation was not very explicit, and received a uniformly bad press in the Commonwealth countries, New Zealand included. Nothing further was heard of it, and no mention of it appeared in the record of the Conference of 1921.[1]

After 1921, the Empire Council idea virtually disappeared from official correspondence and ministerial pronouncements for many years, though it continued to be canvassed in unofficial discussion. But the Commonwealth was occupied in digesting and formulating the changes and developments which led up to and flowed from the passage of the Statute of Westminster, to the exclusion of more theoretical concepts. The next revival of the discussion at the ministerial level was again initiated by a Pacific Dominion.

Mr John Curtin's Proposals, 1943

Mr Curtin, Prime Minister of the Commonwealth of Australia, put forward proposals—in outline in a speech at Adelaide on 14 August 1943, in more detail at a press interview on 6 September —for improving and extending post-war British Commonwealth co-operation in the light of war-time experience. Especially in the spheres of defensive security and economics, he said, all phases of Empire Government after the war would call for constant association between the best minds in Britain and the Dominions. He envisaged an Empire Council, which would be a permanent body with a standing expert secretariat, modelled on the lines of the Pacific War Council. This Empire Council would meet regularly for inter-Commonwealth consultation between High Commissioners and representatives of the United Kingdom Government, but Dominion Ministers would, when appropriate and convenient, sit instead of the High Commissioners. In this connexion, part of Mr Curtin's plan was the holding of meetings in capitals of the Dominions and not only in London: this, he held, would be in line with all that was now inherent in Dominion status, and 'would go far towards achieving the maximum benefit from it [the proposed Council] for the constituent members.'[2]

Mr Curtin's proposals had a good press in Australia, and the

---

[1] Cmd. 1474 (1921). For comment see *Round Table*, vol. 11, pp. 968–9; also, p. 542: 'How the orthodox believer of to-day is to worship the diversity in unity and the unity in diversity of the British Commonwealth, neither confounding the persons by undue centralization nor dividing the substance to the point of the complete independence of its parts, is a question which awaits solution by some Athanasius of Empire, who has not yet appeared and would probably find himself *contra mundum* if he did.'

[2] *The Times*, 7 September 1943.

Prime Minister of New Zealand promised his Government's careful and friendly examination. Opposition spokesmen in Australia stressed that the proposals were in no way new, and compared them with Mr Alfred Deakin's scheme of thirty-six years earlier. The South African press, which was unenthusiastic, took a similar line. In the United Kingdom the proposals were the subject of a debate in the House of Lords on 2 November 1943, on a motion of Lord Elibank, who, in welcoming Mr Curtin's proposals, expressly divorced them from any implication of imperial federation, which he considered impracticable and unacceptable. Several peers, including Lord Bennett, the former Canadian Prime Minister, supported the proposals. The Secretary of State for Dominion Affairs, Lord Cranborne, replying, described the existing consultative machinery in detail and felt that Mr Curtin's plan ought rather to be discussed by an Imperial Conference or Dominion Prime Ministers' meeting. The same line was taken for the Government in the debate on the Address in the House of Commons on 2 December, and also, earlier, in a reply to a question.[1] In a speech at Guildhall on 23 November Lord Cranborne, repeating that future consultative machinery should be discussed with the Dominion Prime Ministers as soon as practicable, also made the suggestion that there might be annual meetings between the Commonwealth Ministers of External Affairs.

At the federal conference of the Australian Labour Party in December 1943, Mr Curtin further defined his plan, embracing various previous proposals, such as exchanges of staff between corresponding Departments in the Commonwealth countries, and linking it with the possibility of regional organizations between countries of the United Nations specially interested in given areas. He emphasized that, for the Commonwealth, nothing could effectively replace the meetings of Prime Ministers, as only they could speak for the Governments of the sovereign Member Nations; but he held that ancillary machinery such as he proposed would usefully supplement these top-level meetings. Contemporaneously with the Australian Labour Party's discussions, Mr Vincent Massey, High Commissioner for Canada in the United Kingdom, emphasized the value of the British Commonwealth's existing co-operative machinery and suggested that the Commonwealth might provide the model and even the nucleus for wider international collaboration.

[1] Question to the Prime Minister: whether 'he will state the views and intentions of His Majesty's Government' regarding Mr Curtin's speech. Mr Churchill replied: 'Such spacious issues would be appropriate for an Imperial Conference or for a meeting of Dominion Prime Ministers whenever either of these becomes possible.' (22 September 1943, *Hansard* (Commons), vol. 392, col. 207).

The Australian Labour Party conference unanimously adopted a resolution moved by Mr Curtin, as follows:

This conference affirms that Australia should collaborate with other peace-loving nations in accordance with the provisions of the Atlantic Charter to establish a peace conferring on all nations the means of dwelling in safety within their own boundaries, and affording the assurance that all may live their lives in freedom from fear and from want. To this resolution I annex two positives: (1) that the evolution of the British Commonwealth has exemplified the manner in which autonomous nations can co-operate in matters of mutual interest; (2) that participation in further development of co-operation among the members of the British Commonwealth, the nations of the world at large, and the Pacific nations in particular should be subject to the sovereign control of the policy of Australia by her own people, Parliament, and Government.

Emphasis, as may be observed from the terms of the motion, had shifted from Commonwealth co-operation, as such, to the prospects of a world organization and the contribution which British Commonwealth experience might make towards it. Mr Curtin discussed his proposals with the other Commonwealth Prime Ministers at their meeting in May 1944,[1] but no mention of this was made in the communiqué issued at the end of the meeting. Since Mr John Curtin's death in July 1945, there has not been much discussion of the details of his Empire Council concept.

Imperial Consultative Machinery in an International Setting

But, though detailed consideration of the late Australian Prime Minister's proposal went no further, the fact that discussion had shifted during his lifetime from the Commonwealth angle to the world angle was notable, and possibly related to developments within the Commonwealth countries themselves. Nearly twenty years previously *The Times*, in a series of special articles on Commonwealth co-operation, had said: 'But the greatest obstacle [to formulating policy] is . . . more subtle. It is the result of the wide gulf . . . between the long experience and constant contact of Great Britain, and the comparatively small experience and absence of contact of the Dominions, with the international world.'[2] By 1944, the range of the Dominions' contact had greatly increased. Mr Curtin's proposal touched off a series of speeches and discussions which carried the consideration of Commonwealth co-operation into an international context.

[1] As mentioned by Mr Chifley; see extracts from his speech on p. 214, below.
[2] *The Times*, 5 February 1925.

Field-Marshal Smuts's Speech, 1943

On 25 November 1943, Field-Marshal Smuts made a speech to a private meeting of the Empire Parliamentary Association in London, of which the text was released for publication on 3 December. In his speech, which he expressly described as 'explosive', he sketched his idea of the post-war world and of the role the Commonwealth would play. Idealism, he said, was not enough, and peace not backed by power remained a dream. The post-war power units would be three: the United States, the great extra-European Power; Russia, the 'new colossus' bestriding the Eurasian continent—for France, Italy, Germany and Japan were no longer effective Great Powers; and the United Kingdom, greatest in prestige and honour, but small beside the other two in strength and resources. Rejecting an 'Anglo-American power axis' as provocative, he advocated a Power 'trinity' to safeguard peace. But the United Kingdom's position would be too unequal in that trinity. For this he had two simultaneous remedies: intimate co-operation between the United Kingdom and the western European democracies, which could maintain their un-impaired sovereignty in co-operation as the Commonwealth countries had found the way to do; and the extension of Common-wealth co-operation by regional groups of colonies, associated with both the United Kingdom and an adjacent Dominion.

It would be possible to bring these new groups closer to a neigh-bouring Dominion and thereby interest the Dominion in the colonial group. You will create fresh links between the Empire and the Com-monwealth and create a new interest and life in the system as a whole. . . . You will create better co-operation. Not only Great Britain and London, but the Dominions also should by loose consulta-tive arrangement have a hand in this new colonial pattern. . . . Perhaps the new link could best be introduced by means of a system of regional conferences, which would include both the local Dominion and the regional colonial group of the area concerned.[1]

This regional pattern of co-operation would decrease the exces-sive centralization of colonial affairs in London, sometimes irk-some to local sentiment, and would ease problems of racial rela-tions. In the world political picture, the working relation between the United Kingdom and western Europe would reinforce and be reinforced by the extra-European co-operation of the proposed regional groups in the Commonwealth, and the resultant power unit would not unbalance the Great Power 'trinity'.

As the Field-Marshal's speech had been made at a private

[1] *Manchester Guardian, Chicago Daily News*, 3 December 1943; *New York Times*, 12 December 1943.

gathering, and was not an expression of policy,[1] it was not the subject of official comment; but it aroused much interest and comment in the press, both in Commonwealth and in foreign countries.

Lord Halifax's 'Toronto' Speech

On 24 January 1944 Lord Halifax, United Kingdom Ambassador at Washington, made a speech at the centenary dinner of the Toronto Board of Trade which was widely linked, in press comment, with Field-Marshal Smuts's speech of the previous November. Lord Halifax took the view that in the post-war world there would be four Great Powers: the United States, the U.S.S.R., the United Kingdom, and China; and that in the company of the three 'Titans' the United Kingdom would be an unequal partner. 'Not Great Britain only, but the British Commonwealth and Empire must be the fourth Power in that group on which, under Providence, the peace of the world will henceforth depend.' Having described how the Dominions, confronted in 1939 by the dilemma of either breaking up the Commonwealth or confirming a policy in the framing of which they had had only a partial share, had demonstrated their essential unity of ideal by declaring war, he said:

It is plainly loss if, with our essential unity of ideal, the responsibility for action which represents that unity is not visibly shared by all. It is an immeasurable gain if on vital issues we can achieve a common foreign policy, expressed not by a single voice but by the unison of many. So, too, in the field of defence, while there must be individual responsibility, there must also be unity of policy.

This did not mean, he emphasized strongly, any retreat from the position of complete independence assured by the Statute of Westminster. The Commonwealth countries were free to choose isolation, although he personally felt that in the field of common interest 'we should leave nothing undone to bring our people into closer unity of thought and action'. How this might be achieved was a question admitting of 'no easy answer'. It might be by extending and adapting the 'war-time procedure of planning and consultation which itself adapted and extended the methods practised in time of peace'. Whatever the answer, it should be one of the first problems before the Ministers of the

---

[1] Field-Marshal Smuts at a Press Conference at Pretoria, 13 December 1943; and Mr Attlee in reply to questions in the House of Commons on 7 December 1943 (*Hansard*, vol. 395, col. 773–5): 'As Field-Marshal Smuts himself made clear, it does not, and never was intended, to constitute a statement of Government policy.'

Commonwealth countries when they could again meet together.[1]

At a press conference two days subsequently, Lord Halifax made clear: that he had no concrete proposals for the reorganization of Commonwealth machinery; that he was not propounding a new line of United Kingdom policy; and that he was interested mainly in providing food for thought and stimulating discussion of the problems of co-operation. Nevertheless the reaction of hostility and suspicion to his speech in the Canadian press was so marked that both the Prime Minister of the United Kingdom, Mr Churchill,[2] and the Prime Minister of Canada, Mr Mackenzie King, considered it advisable officially to reiterate Lord Halifax's statement of his position and intentions. Elsewhere in the Commonwealth the speech elicited no significant support. In Australia and South Africa it was criticized mainly on the practical grounds that the fundamental problem of co-operative organization was left vague; in New Zealand Mr Peter Fraser, the Prime Minister, referred to the accepted Commonwealth principle of maintaining constant consultation, and quoted the Canberra Agreement between Australia and New Zealand as an example of regional machinery which in no way conflicted with either sovereign responsibility or international obligations, but was an effective extension of co-operation.

What had come to be called the 'Smuts-Halifax proposals' were finally rejected on Canada's behalf by Mr Mackenzie King in the Canadian House of Commons on 31 January 1944; thereafter the controversy died down. After stating that Lord Halifax's speech had been somewhat misunderstood, and had been intended mainly to provoke thought and discussion, Mr Mackenzie King continued:

Behind the conception expressed by Lord Halifax and Field-Marshal Smuts there lurks the idea of inevitable rivalry between the Great Powers. Could Canada, situated as she is geographically between the United States and the Soviet Union, and at the same time a member of the British Commonwealth, for one moment support such an idea? . . . What would seem to be suggested is . . . a common policy to be framed and executed by all the Governments of the Commonwealth. I maintain that, apart from all questions as to how that common policy is to be reached or enforced, such a conception runs counter to the establishment of effective world security and therefore is opposed to the true interests of the Commonwealth itself.[3]

[1] The Times, Daily Telegraph, Manchester Guardian, New York Times, 25 January 1944.
[2] 'Lord Halifax in his recent speech at Toronto . . . was not making any pronouncement on behalf of His Majesty's Government.' (1 February 1914, Hansard (Commons), vol. 396, cols. 1136–7.)
[3] New York Times, 1 February 1944 (verbatim report).

The Debate on Mr Shinwell's Motion, 1944

On 20 April 1944 Mr Shinwell proposed the following motion in the House of Commons: 'The United Kingdom should do its utmost by close co-operation and regard for the different points of views of nations of the Commonwealth to preserve in time of peace the unity of purpose and sentiment which has held them together in time of war.'[1] In the two-day debate which followed, members supported the motion irrespective of party, and discussion ranged over every aspect of Commonwealth affairs. The motion was agreed to without a division. In view of the imminence of the meeting of Commonwealth Prime Ministers, Government speakers confined themselves to noting the value of the debate as a preliminary to that meeting. But the Prime Minister, Mr Churchill, at the close of his speech, attacked the assumption

that there must be some inherent antagonism between a world order to keep the peace and vast national or federal organizations. . . . I have never conceived that a fraternal association with the United States would militate in any way against the unity of the British Commonwealth and Empire, or breed ill feeling with our great Russian ally. . . . There will be room for all generous, free associations of a special character so long as they are not disloyal to the world cause nor seek to bar the forward march of mankind.[2]

Australian Views

A feature of the debate was the warm approval by several members of the principle of regional co-operation as expressed in the terms of the Australian-New Zealand Pact of 1944.[3] While some theories of regional co-operation were criticized, this concrete case was welcomed as providing a model which could with advantage be adapted for other Commonwealth purposes and interests. It has been noted above how frequently the Pacific Dominions have initiated discussion about the Commonwealth co-operative machine. Dr Evatt, the Australian Minister for External Affairs, speaking in Parliament on 13 March 1946, drew some conclusions from developments since the Australian-New Zealand Pact of 1944. He said:

An entirely new concept in British Commonwealth relations is now emerging [which] . . . tends to reconcile full Dominion autonomy with full British co-operation. The same principle involves the possibility of a Dominion acting in certain regions or for certain purposes on behalf of the other members of the British Commonwealth, including the United Kingdom itself. This is evidence that the machinery of co-

[1] *Hansard* (Commons), vol. 399, col. 390.
[2] ibid. col. 586.
[3] See p. 38, below.

operation between nations of the British Commonwealth has now reached a stage where a common policy can be carried out through a chosen Dominion instrumentality in an area or in relation to a subject matter which is of primary concern to that Dominion. This principle is capable of extension and suggests the possible integration of British Commonwealth policy at a higher level by a new procedure.[1]

Australia, for instance, represented certain other British Commonwealth countries on an Advisory Council in Japan and in 1947 convened a meeting in Canberra at which all the Member Nations of the Commonwealth had discussed issues arising over the preparation of a peace treaty with Japan. An Australian general commanded the British Commonwealth contingent with the occupation forces in Japan, and an Australian judge was president of the Allied Tribunal for the trial of Japanese war criminals.

The Debate on Lord Bruce's Motion, 1948

A debate on Commonwealth relations took place in the House of Lords on 17 February 1948, initiated by Viscount Bruce of Melbourne. Moving the resolution 'that this House is of the opinion that the closest relations within the Commonwealth and Empire are essential', Lord Bruce said that he saw three possibilities in world relations: full international co-operation and the complete realization of the aims of the United Nations; groupings of nations on a regional or other basis, with partial success for the United Nations ideal; breakdown of the attempt at genuine co-operation and a return to unbridled power politics. If the first and best hope were realized, the British Commonwealth could make a great contribution to it; in the second event, it would form a natural group; in the third and worst possibility, the British people's need to co-operate would be vital to their future.

Reviewing existing co-operative and consultative machinery, Lord Bruce said that information went out from the United Kingdom to the Dominions 'in an almost unlimited flow', but that the return flow was not more than 10 per cent, and exchanges between the Dominions were negligible. Even the stream from the United Kingdom was 'purely factual' and gave no indication of 'policy on any great question during the formulative period'. This meant plenty of information, but no real consultation.

Lord Bruce then reminded the House of Mr Curtin's proposals in 1944, the rejection of which he regretted, and put forward his own, which

[1] Quoted by Professor Douglas Copland in an article of much interest on 'Australia's Attitude to British Commonwealth Relations' in *International Journal*, Winter 1947-8, pp. 39-48 (Toronto Canadian Institute of International Affairs).

do not differ in conception very greatly. . . . We require a Council of British Nations—and I quite deliberately leave out any 'Imperial Council' or anything of that sort . . . a Council of British Nations, a meeting of Governments which are self-governing inside the great British Commonwealth, . . . based on the Prime Ministers of the great self-governing parts of the Empire. . . .

The Council would have a secretariat, recruited from all the Member countries, for administrative work, liaison, report, organization of research, experts' meetings and non-ministerial meetings. The Council would normally meet monthly, but special meetings could be called whenever most convenient. Normally the High Commissioners would represent the Dominions, but visiting Ministers would attend. The United Kingdom Prime Minister would preside at the regular meetings. Plenary sessions of all the Prime Ministers would be held as required; these would replace the old Imperial Conferences. Lord Bruce stressed that he was not suggesting 'a blueprint for a magnificent secretariat of the Empire' or 'a sealed pattern for consultation and co-operation'. He wanted maximum flexibility, suitable to the different circumstances of the Members but consonant with continuity of consultation and with effective action. He firmly rejected the idea that intra-Commonwealth co-operation could be derogatory to international co-operation.

. . . All the British nations [Lord Bruce continued] now accept the secretariat of the United Nations and their vast organization; they all contribute towards the very heavy expense. . . . Yet the moment one talks of British co-operation, somebody seems to think there is something mysteriously vicious about it. . . . Take the case of the Little Entente and the Balkan Confederation [which] were . . . regarded as contributing to the great ideals for which the League stood. . . . It cannot be that by co-operating together we would do something . . . contrary to the spirit of the United Nations Charter. Indeed I say that we would be doing something that was completely and absolutely in line with it.[1]

Viscount Addison, replying for the Government, held that Lord Bruce had underrated the extent and effectiveness of existing machinery. He also welcomed the recent Canberra Conference summoned by Australia to discuss the issues arising in connexion with the Japanese peace treaty as a new and potentially fruitful departure in methods of Commonwealth consultation.[2]

The various general proposals for improving the machinery of the Imperial Conference which have been described above were spread over a period of some fifty years; yet they bear a certain

[1] *Hansard* (Lords), vol. 153, cols. 1107-12.
[2] ibid., col. 1156.

family resemblance. So, too, does the response to them. On practically every occasion, they have produced official statements, whether made by a Conference or by individual statesmen, which emphasize, on the one hand, the dangers of rigidity and, on the other, the speakers' satisfaction with the suitability, effectiveness, and capacity for development of the existing machinery. Typical of this response is the statement issued at the end of the Prime Ministers' meeting in 1946, which is quoted in full below, on p. 115, or, more briefly, Field-Marshal Smuts's comment on Lord Bruce's motion: 'The more machinery we have, the more friction there will be.'[1]

'Functional' Proposals for Supplementing Conference Consultation

Functional proposals connected with the Imperial Conference, directed towards improving Commonwealth consultative and cooperative machinery, have generally been concerned with an Imperial Conference secretariat in some form, or with a specialized or *ad hoc* secretariat or research unit for some more specific subject or circumstance. They have as often as not been ancillary to proposals for changes in the Imperial Conference machine itself, and some account of them has therefore been given in the description of the more general proposals.

The 1924 Proposals

In 1924 the United Kingdom Government initiated a general discussion with the Governments of the Dominions 'as to the adequacy of the present system of consultation with the other self-governing parts of the Empire on matters of foreign policy and general Imperial interest'. While the United Kingdom Government fully accepted the necessity for effective consultation, and the recognized constitutional principles governing the action which each Commonwealth country might take as a result of consultation, they felt—the initial telegram continued—that the system in practice had two main deficiencies.

First, it renders immediate action extremely difficult, more especially between Conferences on occasions when such action is imperatively needed, particularly in the sphere of foreign policy.

Secondly, when matters under discussion are subjects of political controversy, economic or otherwise, conclusions reached at or between Imperial Conferences are liable to be reversed through changes of government.

Such a state of affairs inevitably leads to ineffectiveness; it also causes disappointment, and doubts are thrown on [the] utility of the whole Imperial Conference system.[2]

[1] In the Union House of Assembly, 18 February 1948.
[2] Cmd. 2301 (1925), p. 5.

With regard to the first difficulty Mr Ramsay MacDonald, Prime Minister of the United Kingdom, suggested the desirability of a further examination of the Treaties Resolution of the Imperial Conference of 1923. With regard to the second, he stated the growing need for the creation of some workable machinery by which the public opinion of the Commonwealth as a whole might be brought to bear upon the formulation of any policy which concerned the Commonwealth as a whole.

He also touched upon various remedies which had been suggested in the past. One such suggestion was that representation at Imperial Conferences should include members of all political parties; another was that each Government should 'obtain from its own Parliament beforehand a general approval, within sufficiently wide limits, of the attitude to be taken up by its representatives'.[1] He expressed his own doubts as to the feasibility of either, but invited the Dominions to express their views.

Mr Ramsay MacDonald's telegram was coldly received,[2] especially the suggestion that representatives of all political parties might attend Imperial Conferences. But the Government of Australia submitted, in its reply, some suggestions for functional developments. Questions of urgent foreign policy, they submitted, are in an entirely different category from other matters upon which common policy may have been determined at Imperial Conferences, because they must be dealt with according to the circumstances in which they arise. While no alteration to the principle of consultation is practicable, its machinery of operation could be improved. They suggested: (a) closer liaison between the Foreign Office and Dominion Governments by the creation of a Foreign Office Branch in the Dominion High Commissioners Offices under an officer with adequate standing to enjoy Foreign Office confidence; (b) fuller and more regular advice on foreign affairs than at present; (c) greater efforts to anticipate, and to obtain Dominion views upon, questions likely to arise and to require urgent decision.

With regard to questions other than foreign policy, my Government is of opinion that the establishment of a permanent Imperial secretariat responsible to the Prime Ministers of all the self-governing parts of the Empire whose task would be to prepare for the Imperial Conferences, carry out all secretarial work during the sittings of such Conferences, follow up all resolutions and decisions arrived at, and keep the Dominions constantly informed of developments between the Conferences, would go a long way towards solving the problem of effective and continuous consultation. . . . At the present time the

[1] ibid. p. 6.
[2] The replies and subsequent exchanges are printed in Cmd. 2301 (1925).

secretariat for Imperial Conferences is provided by the British Government, together with representatives of the Dominions concerned, but immediately the Conference is over the secretariat is broken up, and no effective machinery exists for keeping the Dominions continuously informed as to developments or alterations necessitated by changed circumstances. In the opinion of my Government a great improvement would be effected by the establishment of a permanent Imperial secretariat.[1]

A change of Government in the United Kingdom intervened, and neither the general proposals which Mr Ramsay MacDonald had made, nor the functional proposals of the Australian Government, were then pursued. A general review of the situation was, however, made *inter alia* at the important Imperial Conference held in 1926.

On 27 March 1924 Mr Bruce, speaking in the Australian House of Representatives, made some criticism of the slowness with which the existing machinery of Commonwealth consultation operated, and the lack of continuity between Imperial Conferences. To remedy the second defect, he suggested the establishment of a permanent secretariat on the model of the War Graves Commission. Under the present system the secretariat was responsible to the Conference as a whole, and also to a British Department. This placed the Dominion Governments in a wrong position; the secretariat should be responsible to the whole of the self-governing parts of the Empire, drawing its finances and personnel from them all. The type of secretariat proposed would be quite a small body, consisting probably of one representative from each Dominion. Mr Bruce also announced that Mr Leeper had been lent to Australia by the Foreign Office for six months to put the Foreign Office branch of the Prime Minister's Department on the best possible basis. He thought the number of Australians in the Foreign Office should be increased.[2]

Mr Coates's Proposals, 1928

Mr J. G. Coates, speaking in the New Zealand House of Representatives on 24 August 1928, outlined some suggestions for the gradual development of a permanent staff for foreign and Empire affairs.

He proposed that in course of time officers should be appointed to London to act as liaison officers in close touch with the Foreign Office and other Government Departments, that such officers

[1] Cmd. 2301, pp. 9–10.
[2] Australia, House of Representatives, *Debates*, 2nd Session, 1924, no. 1, pp. 35–42.

would, in the course of years, work round to different parts of the Empire, and become part of an organization

through which all parts of the Empire could depend upon getting almost at first hand the outlook of the various Dominions; and the representatives of the Dominions in Great Britain could gain a knowledge that would be of great value as to the point of view of the whole Empire . . . and make it a much more simple matter to express the opinion of the Empire on any questions which arose. The system would not bind the Dominions in any way, but it would give the Imperial authorities a much clearer idea of the way in which the people of New Zealand, for instance, looked upon the various international questions that came up for discussion.

The Imperial Government and the New Zealand Government in conjunction were also considering a scheme whereby a number of New Zealand men from the New Zealand University . . . would be selected for employment in the Imperial Colonial Services. . . . It was desired to secure a permanent staff fully acquainted with every part of the Empire and with a knowledge of Foreign Office procedure.[1]

The Commonwealth Economic Secretariat Proposal, 1932

In 1930 the Trades Union Congress agreed with the Federation of British Industries on certain proposals which they embodied in a memorandum and presented to the British Government. The object of the proposals is stated as being 'to promote as full a development as possible of economic relations between the constituent parts of the British Commonwealth'. In February 1932 the General Council of the Trades Union Congress decided to put forward their proposals again; and on 2 March Mr Thomas received a deputation of their representatives who urged that: 'A permanent Commonwealth Economic Secretariat should be set up with the duty of investigating economic questions and problems affecting the Commonwealth and preparing the Agenda for economic questions at Imperial Conferences.'

During the Ottawa Conference all the existing intra-Imperial bodies were reviewed by the Committee on 'Methods of Economic Co-operation'. As a result the Conference adopted a resolution that a further Committee should be formed

to consider the means of facilitating economic consultation and cooperation between the several Governments of the Commonwealth, including a survey of the functions, organization, and financial bases of the (existing) agencies . . . and an examination of what alterations and modifications, if any, in the existing machinery for such co-operation within the Commonwealth are desirable.[2]

[1] *Journal of the Parliaments of the Empire*, vol. 10, no. 1, pp. 115–16.
[2] Cmd. 4714 (1932), p. 14.

The South African and Irish Free State delegations made reservations to this resolution as follows:

SOUTH AFRICA [Mr Havenga]: While not wishing to object to the acceptance of the Report of the Committee on Methods of Economic Co-operation, I desire, in order to remove any ground for misapprehension, to record the following reservations on behalf of the Union of South Africa:

1. While not generally averse to the institution of *ad hoc* bodies for economic investigation and preparation, the Union Government will not associate itself with any scheme for the erection of any organization in the nature of a permanent secretariat or preparatory committee to Commonwealth Conferences, whether economic or otherwise.

2. That portion of the report which introduces the draft resolutions relating to the appointment of a Committee to consider the means of facilitating economic consultation and co-operation must not be read in the sense that the Union Government is committed in principle to give financial support to Commonwealth economic organizations.

IRISH FREE STATE [Mr Lemass]: I do not object to the adoption of this report and the accompanying resolutions, but I wish it to be made perfectly clear in the published records of the Conference that the Government of the Irish Free State are not prepared to contemplate the setting up of an Imperial Economic Secretariat or of any similar organ of centralization.[1]

The above account is mainly chronological. In so far as the proposals reviewed in it have led to action, details will be found under the appropriate headings in the other parts of this handbook.

[1] ibid. pp. 14-15.

CHAPTER V

MEETINGS OF PRIME MINISTERS

THE meetings of Commonwealth Prime Ministers, or their deputies, held in London in 1944, 1946, 1948, 1949, and 1951, were quite distinct from the formal series of Imperial Conferences, which were held at intervals between 1911 and 1937, and which conducted discussions based on a formal agenda and issued joint statements. The meetings of Commonwealth Prime Ministers were informal, with no formal agenda or joint statements other than a final communiqué. The title under which these meetings are known has not yet been formalized.

The Prime Ministers of the United Kingdom and the then Dominions, together with representatives of British India and Southern Rhodesia, met in London between 1 and 17 May 1944, to review the course of the war and the general plans for the conduct of hostilities. They also examined the principles 'which determine our foreign policies and their application to current problems',[1] and affirmed their adherence to the idea of a strong world organization. The final communiqué was signed by Mr Churchill, Mr Mackenzie King, Mr Curtin, Mr Fraser, and Field-Marshal Smuts.

The Commonwealth Prime Ministers met again in 1946. This meeting fell into three stages. In the first week the representatives of Australia and New Zealand, Mr Chifley, Dr Evatt and Mr Nash, and the United Kingdom representatives were present. Field-Marshal Smuts joined them in the second week. The third stage was marked by the arrival of Mr Mackenzie King from Canada in the middle of May, by which date Mr Chifley had returned to Australia. At the end of their Conference, the following statement was issued from 10 Downing Street; it was unsigned. It indicated both the kind of discussion taking place at the Prime Ministers' meetings, and the participants' views on Commonwealth methods of consultation:

In the course of the last five weeks the Prime Minister of the United Kingdom, the Right Hon. C. R. Attlee, and several of his Cabinet colleagues, the Prime Minister of Canada, the Right Hon. W. L. Mackenzie King; the Prime Minister of Australia, the Right Hon. J. B. Chifley, and the Australian Minister of External Affairs, the Right Hon. H. V. Evatt, the Deputy Prime Minister of New Zealand, the Right Hon. W. Nash, and the Prime Minister of South Africa, Field-

[1] *The Times*, 18 May 1944.

Marshal the Right Hon. J. C. Smuts, have engaged in informal consultations on a number of questions arising in connexion with the post-war settlements.

The representatives of Canada, Australia, New Zealand, and South Africa desire to place on record their sincere thanks to the Prime Minister of the United Kingdom for presiding over the meetings and for his constant and valuable help.

The discussions have been in the nature of an informal exchange of views. They have covered a broad field and have contributed greatly to the elucidation of many problems and to a mutual understanding of the issues involved. Among the subjects on which views were exchanged were the draft peace treaties with Italy, Roumania, Bulgaria, Hungary, and Finland; the future of Germany; security responsibilities and arrangements for liaison between British Commonwealth Governments on military affairs; and economic and welfare co-operation in the South Pacific and South-East Asia.

The opportunity was taken for consultations on other current issues and matters of mutual interest, including separate consultations between individual United Kingdom and Dominion Ministers on questions specially affecting one or two countries only.

At the conclusion of the meetings the assembled representatives of the United Kingdom, Canada, Australia, New Zealand, and South Africa place on record their appreciation of the value of this series of consultations, which exemplify the system of free discussion and exchange of views that characterizes the relations of the countries of the British Commonwealth.

The existing methods of consultation have proved their worth. They include a continuous exchange of information and comment between the different members of the Commonwealth. They are flexible and can be used to meet a variety of situations and needs, both those where the responsibility is on one member alone and where the responsibility may have to be shared.

They are peculiarly appropriate to the character of the British Commonwealth, with its independent members, who have shown by their sacrifices in the common cause their devotion to kindred ideals and their community of outlook. While all are willing to consider and adopt practical proposals for developing the existing system, it is agreed that the methods now practised are preferable to any rigid centralized machinery. In their view such centralized machinery would not facilitate, and might even hamper, the combination of autonomy and unity which is characteristic of the British Commonwealth and is one of their great achievements.

They reaffirm their belief in the efficiency of free and constant consultation and co-operation, not only within the British Commonwealth but also in the wider international sphere. They are determined to do everything in their power to maintain in time of peace the historic co-operation achieved by the Allies in time of war. They look forward to the steady development throughout the whole world of closer international co-operation based on increasing mutual con-

fidence and devoted to the raising of standards of living and the promotion of democratic liberty. Their Governments and peoples are
determined to give the fullest support to the United Nations organization, not only as a foundation of peace and security, but also as a
means for promoting economic progress and social welfare.[1]

After this meeting Field-Marshal Smuts declared that in his
opinion it had been 'more useful in many ways and more effective
and helpful than the old formal Imperial Conferences'. He
described these informal conferences as 'a meeting for exchange
of views and establishing contacts and getting to know each
other's affairs'.

At the Conference which took place between 10 and 22 October
1948, the Prime Ministers of India, Pakistan, and Ceylon were
present for the first time. Mr Mackenzie King was unable to
attend, having been taken ill after his arrival in London. Mr
Norman Robertson, the High Commissioner for Canada in London, deputized for him until Mr St Laurent, the Minister of
External Affairs, arrived by air from Canada. The Conference
discussed the general political and economic situation, and 'recommendations for improving Commonwealth consultation on foreign
affairs, economic affairs, and defence were submitted to the
Governments for consideration and decision'.[2] The final communiqué, which was unsigned, also stated that: 'The purpose of
these informal meetings of Commonwealth Prime Ministers is to
provide opportunities for a free exchange of views on matters of
common concern.' In economic affairs, 'the Conference reaffirmed
the desirability for all the Commonwealth Governments, in formulating their policies, to consult with one another so far as practicable so that each can co-operate by taking into account the
needs and policies of the others'. In regard to the association of
the United Kingdom, under the Brussels Treaty, with her western
European neighbours, 'there was general agreement that this . . .
was in accordance with the interests of the other members of the
Commonwealth, the United Nations, and the promotion of world
peace. It was agreed that the other Commonwealth Governments
should be kept in close touch with the progress of this co-operation with western Europe.' The meeting also 'recorded its support for Ceylon's application for membership of the United
Nations'.

In a speech of welcome to the Prime Ministers and other
representatives of the Commonwealth at the 1948 meeting, His
Majesty the King said: 'I hope that opportunity will be found

---

[1] *The Times*, 24 May 1946.
[2] ibid. 23 October 1948.

from time to time to hold some of our meetings in other Commonwealth capitals.'[1]

The next meeting was opened on 21 April 1949, and was attended by the Prime Ministers of the United Kingdom, Australia, New Zealand, South Africa, India, Pakistan, and Ceylon and the Canadian Secretary of State for External Affairs. In the words of the final communiqué, issued on 27 April, 'the important constitutional issues arising from India's decision to adopt a republican form of Constitution and her desire to continue her membership of the Commonwealth' were 'the sole subject of discussion at the full meetings of Prime Ministers'. After full discussion the assembled representatives of all the Commonwealth countries agreed upon and recorded the declaration already quoted on p. 25, above.

The next Commonwealth Prime Ministers' meeting was held in London from 4–12 January 1951. As Dr Malan was prevented by illness from coming, Dr T. E. Dönges, Minister of the Interior, attended from South Africa. The other Commonwealth countries were represented by their Prime Ministers. Mr Liaqat Ali Khan was not present on 4–5 January, but arrived in London in time to attend the sessions from 8 January onwards. Southern Rhodesia was represented by its Prime Minister, Sir Godfrey Huggins. On 4 January the King held a Privy Council, unique in that it was attended by six Prime Ministers, at which the Prime Ministers of Ceylon and New Zealand, Mr Senanayake and Mr Holland, were sworn in; they had been appointed Privy Councillors in January and April respectively.

The official communiqué, issued at the end of the meeting, stated that its main purpose had been to review the international situation and consider what further positive action could be taken to secure and preserve peace. The meeting kept the progress of the United Nations Assembly's discussions under daily review, together with the instructions given to Commonwealth representatives taking part. The Prime Ministers discussed the possible terms of a peace treaty with Japan, which they regarded as urgently needed. They reviewed the situation in the Middle East, and in Europe; and those whose countries were signatories of the North Atlantic Treaty explained their obligations under it, and the measures being taken to meet them. They agreed to strengthen Commonwealth consultation on measures to meet the problems arising from current raw material shortages.

The participants in the meeting also issued a separate declaration on 12 January. Desiring, they said, 'to state in simple terms some of the great principles' inspiring their meeting, they re-

[1] *The Times*, 14 October 1948.

affirmed that the Commonwealth countries are, jointly and severally, pledged to peace. To this end they would not cease to pursue the aim of mutual understanding as well with those nations from whom they differ as with those with whom they are in harmony. 'We think it proper to declare once more that the Commonwealth countries, though they have a special and precious association which they value profoundly, do not regard themselves as some sort of exclusive body. They welcome co-operation with other nations.' They reject any intention to interfere in the affairs of any country, but are determined to retain the mastery of their own. They regretfully face the necessity for strengthening their defences against aggression, and declare again their support of the United Nations and their intention to promote, through the Colombo Plan and by other means, the economic and social development of under-developed countries. They affirm their 'faith in the existence of a purpose of justice in this world', and recognize their 'duty to forward it by everything we do', and to uphold the rule of law, whatever sacrifices these aims might entail.

Commonwealth Finance Ministers' Conference

Commonwealth Finance Ministers met in London from 13–18 July 1949, to discuss positive steps to prevent the continuing heavy drain on the central reserves of gold and dollars of the sterling area and to consider the long-term problem of securing a stable relationship between the sterling and dollar areas. The Conference was attended by the Finance Ministers of the United Kingdom, Canada, Australia, New Zealand, South Africa, India, Pakistan, Ceylon, and Southern Rhodesia. The Conference was opened by the United Kingdom Prime Minister, Mr Attlee, who said that the broad problem they had to face was one which concerned the whole Commonwealth, indeed the whole world.

The communiqué[1] issued at the conclusion of the Conference recorded the agreement by the Ministers concerned to recommend to their Governments action comparable to that already decided upon by the United Kingdom to check the drain on the central reserves of the sterling area. The Ministers further agreed that their Governments would consider measures designed to establish conditions in which the dollar and non-dollar countries could operate together within one single multilateral system.

The representatives of the sterling-area countries expressed their pleasure that Canada was represented at the Conference, although not a member of the sterling area.

The need for close and continuing consultation between

[1] *The Times*, 19 July 1949.

Governments was recognized and the Ministers made recommendations for the necessary action to meet this need.

The Colombo Conference of Foreign Ministers

At the meeting of Commonwealth Prime Ministers in October 1948, it was contemplated that, apart from the meetings of the Prime Ministers, other Commonwealth meetings should be held at ministerial level, as occasion required, on such subjects as foreign policy and economic affairs. The first such Conference on foreign affairs was held at Colombo, Ceylon, in January 1950, at the invitation of the Government of Ceylon. Mr Senanayake, the Prime Minister of Ceylon, presided at the meetings.

The greater part of the time of the Conference was spent in a comprehensive review of the current problems of South-East Asia, both political and economic. The most significant result of the Conference was the adoption of a plan, proposed by Mr Spender, the Australian Minister for External Affairs, for establishing a system of mutual aid among all Commonwealth countries willing to join and eventually open to other countries also. In the first place the plan would be directed towards helping the countries of South-East Asia, but it could also be used, if need be, to help India, Pakistan, and Ceylon.

The official statement[1] issued at the end of the Conference records the main conclusions:

Executive decisions are not taken at Commonwealth meetings of this kind but, as a result of the valuable exchange of views which has taken place, recommendations for the furtherance of economic development in South and South-East Asia will be submitted to the Commonwealth Governments for their consideration. These recommendations include a proposal for the establishment of a consultative committee representing the Commonwealth Governments. The Australian delegation proposed that the first meeting of this committee, when set up, should be held in Australia. . . .

They reconsidered in the light of subsequent developments the provisional conclusions reached at the Commonwealth Conference held in Canberra in 1947 on the conditions of a peace settlement with Japan. On this subject, the Ministers attending the Conference will submit recommendations to their Governments. . . .

Commonwealth officials concerned with economic affairs have held a separate series of meetings throughout the week. Their primary purpose has been to exchange information on developments since the Commonwealth Finance Ministers met in London in July [1949]. These meetings have afforded a valuable opportunity for the joint survey of the sterling area's current and prospective balance-of-payments position and for the discussion of economic problems that face

[1] The Times, 16 January 1950.

the Commonwealth. Particular attention was given to the recent trend of, and future prospects for, dollar exports of the sterling area.

The proposed Commonwealth Consultative Committee on South-East Asia met for the first time in Sydney from 15–19 May 1950, at the invitation of the Australian Government, which was represented by Mr Spender, who presided. Great Britain, Canada, New Zealand, Pakistan, and Ceylon were represented by Ministers, and India by Sir Ramaswami Mudaliar. The United Kingdom's Commissioner-General in South-East Asia, Mr Malcolm MacDonald, was also present. The Colombo precedent of a simultaneous meeting at the official level of financial experts was followed. The ministerial meeting agreed to recommend to the Governments: a six-year development plan to be based on economic reports from each participating Government (requested for 1 September 1950); the inauguration of a scheme to organize technical assistance between the Governments; the establishment of a co-ordinating bureau at Colombo; a formal approach to non-Commonwealth Governments in the area, informing them of the Commonwealth's plans and inviting them to be associated therewith.

The next conference of the Commonwealth Consultative Committee opened in London on 25 September 1950. It was preceded by discussions at the official level, begun on 6 September, of the economic reports sent in by the participating Governments. The United Kingdom Minister of State for Economic Affairs, Mr Hugh Gaitskell, presided at the ministerial meeting. Mr Malcolm MacDonald again participated, and Dato Onn bin Jaafar and Mr C. C. Tan represented the Federation of Malaya and Singapore respectively. On 2 October the Commonwealth representatives welcomed delegations from Siam and the Associated States of Indo-China, who joined in the discussions. The ambassadors in London of Burma and Indonesia attended as observers on behalf of their Governments. South Africa, not a member of the Committee, has at its own request been kept informed of progress.

The Committee recommended to Governments the adoption of a constitution for the council for technical co-operation which had been proposed at the Sydney Conference. The constitution had been drafted by a standing committee meeting in Colombo during July and August. Secondly, the Committee unanimously adopted the draft economic report prepared by the preceding official meeting, and recommended it to the Governments for approval and subsequent publication. The Colombo Plan[1] (as this report has come to be called) presented detailed schemes for

[1] *The Colombo Plan for Co-operative Economic Development in South and South-East Asia*, Cmd. 8080, 28 November 1950.

agricultural development, irrigation and hydro-electric works, industrial and mining development, and improvement of transport, to cost £1,868 millions over six years. Of this, £1,084 million represented external finance required for imports of goods and services, beyond what could be supplied by the home capital markets of the countries in the area. Commonwealth Governments outside the area subsequently considered what contribution they could make to this external financing. £8 million for technical assistance was earmarked for the council for technical co-operation.

CHAPTER VI

THE JUDICIAL COMMITTEE OF THE PRIVY COUNCIL

THE Privy Council was originally the chief advisory body of the Crown, and exercised both its administrative and its judicial functions in the supervision of the 'colonies'. These functions were separated by Acts of 1833 and 1844: the Act of 1833 constituted the Judicial Committee of the Privy Council, and the Judicial Committee Act of 1844 made its jurisdiction statutory, giving it the right to hear appeals from all courts in the Colonies.

Appeals come to the Judicial Committee in two ways: as of right, and by special leave. Appeals as of right still lie from the courts of the Australian States, and from New Zealand; and normally appeals from the Colonies come as of right. The right of appeal is ordinarily only from High Courts, although the Judicial Committee can admit appeals from lower courts, and exists only where it has been expressly created, i.e. by statute, Order in Council, letters patent, etc. The lower courts concerned are usually entrusted, by the same instrument which lays down the right of appeal, with the duty of granting or refusing appeal in the manner laid down. If such appeal as of right is refused by the lower court, special leave to appeal may be sought from the Judicial Committee itself by the applicant. Such special leave may be granted on purely legal grounds—i.e. that the refusal was wrong—or of discretion, on the ground that the matter ought to be determined by His Majesty in Council. Special leave to appeal may also be sought when there is no appeal as of right from the court below. The Judicial Committee also retains odds and ends of jurisdiction within the United Kingdom (including appeals from the Channel Islands and the Isle of Man), and in respect of copyright; and decides matters referred to it by Order in Council of the United Kingdom. The Labrador boundary question between Canada and Newfoundland was so referred to it in 1927.

The Judicial Committee consists of: the Lord President of the Council and ex-Lords President; the Lord Chancellor and ex-Lords Chancellor; such Privy Councillors as shall from time to time hold or have held 'High Judicial Office' within the meaning of the Apellate Jurisdiction Acts, 1876 and 1887 (i.e. who are, or have been, Lords of Appeal in Ordinary, Lords Justices of Appeal or Judges of the Supreme Courts of England or Northern Ireland, or Judges of the Scottish Court of Session; Privy Councillors who are or have been Judges of the Supreme Courts of Canada, South Africa, and Newfoundland, or Judges of the High Court of Australia, or of the Superior Courts in New Zealand, the Canadian Provinces, and the Australian States; or Chief Justices or Judges of a High Court in India). Under the Appellate Jurisdiction Act, 1929, two persons specially appointed for their experience in Indian cases might be added.

In addition to English barristers and Scottish advocates, members of the Bar of any tribunal from which appeals lie have the right of audience.

Historically, the Acts of 1833 and 1844, by constituting a Committee of the Privy Council to hear all petitions to His Majesty in Council which are in the nature of judicial appeals, did not alter the source of the Privy Council's jurisdiction, which is still the royal prerogative and coextensive with the sovereignty of the Crown. This jurisdiction can technically not be altered except under powers conferred by Act of the Imperial Parliament. Thus the right of an applicant to the Committee for special leave to appeal, which leave can be granted by the Judicial Committee itself at discretion even in cases where a subsidiary court has refused leave to appeal as of right, survived with certain exceptions[1] until the passage of the Statute of Westminster; and Dominion and Colonial legislation prohibiting application for special leave to appeal was invalid unless enacted under powers expressly given by an Imperial Act.

The practice by which the Judicial Committee had tended to become more a tribunal for the argument of refined points of law than an instrument for the protection of the royal prerogative was recognized by the Imperial Conference of 1926 when it declared that 'it was no part of the policy of His Majesty's Government in Great Britain that questions affecting judicial appeals should be determined otherwise than in accordance with the wishes of the part of the Empire primarily affected'.[2]

To the convention declared by the 1926 Conference, the Statute of Westminster, 1931, added a large measure of legal confirmation, which has since been endorsed and liberally interpreted in at least three major constitutional cases brought to the Judicial Committee: *Moore* v. *Attorney-General for the Irish Free State* (1935), *British Coal Corporation* v. *R.* (1935), and *Attorney-General of Ontario and others* v. *Attorney-General of Canada and others, Attorney-General of Quebec, Intervener*.[3] Matters arising from these cases can most conveniently be considered below,

---

[1] See under 'Australia' and 'Union of South Africa', below.
[2] Cmds. 2758–9 (1926).
[3] [1947] A.C. 127.

where the situation in respect of each Commonwealth country is outlined.

The Statute of Westminster did not deal directly with the right of appeal: the portions of the Statute having a general bearing on Privy Council jurisdiction are paragraph 3 of the Preamble and Sections 2 and 4.[1] Paragraph 3 and Section 2 abolished the doctrine of repugnancy and disallowance which was incompatible with the equality of status of the Dominions with the United Kingdom; and Section 4 was a formal declaration by the Imperial Parliament of renunciation of its power to legislate for the Dominions except by consent. The Dominion Parliaments were thus—subject to certain reservations made at the request of the Dominions concerned and examined below—free to pass legislation abolishing appeals in any circumstances to the Judicial Committee.

Concentration of attention on constitutional issues has caused the advisory functions of the Judicial Committee to be somewhat overlooked. In fact, all its judgements are tendered as advice. 'A judgement of the Judicial Committee is in form a statement of the grounds on which the Committee will advise His Majesty to give effect to their decision, and becomes binding only when it is embodied in an Order of the King in Council. . . . The Committee submit a single joint opinion, dissent from which is not recorded.'[2] In this latter respect, procedure is based on an Order of 1627, and is unique in the practice of superior courts in His Majesty's dominions (except the English Court of Criminal Appeal). The Committee advises the Crown on matters specially referred to it. It 'has been called upon for advice on several occasions in recent years. . . . The procedure is for the Crown to refer a set of questions, agreed upon beforehand by the parties to the dispute, to the Judicial Committee, which thereupon examines the evidence and hears the arguments of counsel and finally gives its decision in the form of advice to the Crown.'[3]

The present extent in law of appeals from the Dominions to the Privy Council is set out below.

Canada

Until the Judicial Committee's decision in the case of *British Coal Corporation* v. *R.* in 1935, appeals lay from the Supreme Court of Canada and from the Superior Courts of the Provinces in constitutional, criminal, and civil matters; but only from the

---

[1] For text of the Statute, see Appendix.
[2] Royal Institute of International Affairs, *The British Empire*, 2nd ed. (London, Oxford University Press, 1938), p. 197.
[3] ibid. pp. 202–3.

Provinces as of right. The exclusive powers of the Dominion are set out in Section 91 of the British North America Act, 1867, and the particular powers of the Provinces in Section 92. Criminal law is assigned to the Dominion in Section 91. The British Coal Corporation petitioned for special leave to appeal against a conviction under the Canadian Criminal Code. The Privy Council barred the petition, upholding, under its interpretation of Section 2, 3, and 7 of the Statute of Westminster, the provisions of Section 17 of Canadian Act 23–4 Geo. V (an Act to amend the Criminal Code), which is as follows:

Subsection (4) of Section 10 of the said Act [the Criminal Code] is repealed and hereby re-enacted as follows:
(4) Notwithstanding any royal prerogative, or anything contained in the Interpretation Act or in the Supreme Court Act, no appeal shall be brought in any criminal case from any judgement or order of any Court in Canada to any Court of Appeal or authority in which in the United Kingdom appeals or petitions to His Majesty may be heard.

Since Section 91 of the British North America Act had already assigned criminal matters to the Dominion Parliament, Section 17 of the amending Act quoted above was valid under Section 7 (3) of the Statute of Westminster.

Their Lordships added that they had 'in this judgement been dealing only with the legal position in Canada in regard to this type of appeal in criminal matters', and that it was 'here neither necessary nor desirable to touch on the position as regards civil cases'.

The appeal to the Privy Council in criminal matters was thus validly abolished by Section 17 of 23–4 Geo. V, and, in so far as criminal cases might involve constitutional issues, the final decision in such issues would remain with the Supreme Court of Canada. A group of appeals concerning labour legislation came to the Privy Council in January 1937; and the judgements ruled that the legislation was *ultra vires*. The main grounds of appeal against the legislation were that it was not a valid contention that the legislation—which implemented certain International Labour Organization recommendations—arose 'under Treaties between the Empire and Foreign Countries' (British North America Act, Section 132) and so was within the area of the federal power; and that it invaded the area of 'property and civil rights' which is No. 13 of the Provincial powers enumerated in Section 92 of the Act. The Judicial Committee upheld these grounds of appeal, stating *inter alia* that 'For the purposes of . . . the distribution of legislative powers between the Dominion and the Provinces, there is no such thing as treaty legislation as such. . . . As a treaty deals with a particular class of subjects, so will the legislative power of performing it be ascertained.'[1]

This group of decisions was criticized, both in the United Kingdom and in Canada, as excessively legalistic and a retreat, in favour of Provincial powers, from the view put forward by Lord Sankey in 1930 that the British North America Act 'planted in Canada a living tree' which should not be cut back by literalist interpretation of the Act.[2] The Dominion Parliament grasped the nettle when Mr C. H. Cahan introduced Bill No. 9 of 23 January 1939, which read:

Section 54 of the Supreme Court Act, C.35, R.S.C., 1927, is repealed and the following substituted therefor:

54. (1) The Supreme Court shall have hold, and exercise exclusive ultimate appellate civil and criminal jurisdiction within and for Canada; and the judgement of the Court shall, in all cases, be final and conclusive.

(2) Notwithstanding any Royal prerogative or anything contained in any Act of Parliament of the United Kingdom or any Act of the Parliament of Canada or any Act of the Legislature of any Province of Canada or any other statute of law, no appeal shall lie or be brought from any Court now or hereafter established within Canada to any Court of Appeal, tribunal or authority by which, in the United Kingdom, appeals or petitions to His Majesty in Council may be ordered to be heard.

The Bill received a first reading, but the debate on the second reading was adjourned for it to be referred to the Supreme Court. The Court decided by a majority that the Bill was *intra vires*, and leave to appeal against this decision was granted by the Judicial Committee in 1940; but owing to the war it was agreed to postpone the hearing. The appeal was heard on 13 January 1947, and their Lordships upheld the majority judgement of the Canadian Supreme Court. Their grounds were the powers given by the Statute of Westminster and Section 101 of the British North America Act ('The Parliament of Canada may, notwithstanding anything in this Act, from time to time provide for the constitution, maintenance, and organization of a General Court of Appeal for Canada and for the establishment of any additional Courts for the better administration of the laws of Canada.') The Lord Chancellor said:

The power vested in the Dominion Parliament by Section 101 of the British North America Act to establish a general Court of Appeal for Canada was necessarily subject to the prerogative right of His

---

[1] *In re Weekly Rest in Industrial Undertakings Act*, 28 January 1937.
[2] *Edwards* v. *Attorney-General for Canada*, A.C. 124, 1930.

Majesty, since that right was not expressly or by necessary intendment excluded, and this limitation was recognized in the first words of Section 54 of the Supreme Court Act. But that was a restriction or fetter on the legislative power of the Dominion, which could be removed, and has been removed by an Act of the Imperial Parliament, and, since it has been removed, it must be within the power of the Dominion Parliament to enact that the jurisdiction of its Supreme Court shall be ultimate. No other solution is consonant with the status of a self-governing Dominion. . . .

They would emphasize that Section 101 confers a legislative power on the Dominion Parliament which by its terms overrides any power conferred by Section 92 on the Provinces or preserved by Section 129; 'Notwithstanding anything in this Act' are words in Section 101 which cannot be ignored. They vest in the Dominion a plenary authority to legislate in regard to appellate jurisdiction, which is qualified only by that which lies outside the Act—namely, the sovereign power of the Imperial Parliament.

The latter part of the quotation disposed of the doubt whether the Dominion power in this matter overrides, even though it may conflict with, Provincial power under Section 92 of the British North America Act—a doubt which had been debated by such authoritative commentators as Latham and Wheare.[1]

A fresh Bill to abolish the appeal in civil cases was introduced on 19 September 1949, passed through all its stages without a division, and received the Royal Assent on 10 December. The Minister of Justice, Mr Garson, said the purpose of the Bill was 'to create in the Supreme Court of Canada exclusive, ultimate, appellate civil and criminal jurisdiction within and for Canada by abolishing appeals to the Privy Council and by making the judgement of the Supreme Court in all cases final and conclusive'. It would remove one of the two remaining 'badges of colonialism' (the other being the exception of the Canadian Constitution from the operation of the Statute of Westminster). The number of Supreme Court Judges from Quebec Province would be increased from two to three, and the total number from seven to nine. Mr Garson referred to the 'massive judicial services' which the Judicial Committee of the Privy Council had rendered to Canada in the past.[2]

Australia

Australia adopted the Statute of Westminster in 1943, with effect from 3 September 1939, but has since then introduced no

[1] Latham, *The Law and the Commonwealth*, p. 550; Wheare, *The Statute of Westminster* (2nd ed.), pp. 199–200.
[2] *Montreal Gazette, Winnipeg Free Press*, 21 September 1949; *Commonwealth Survey*, 4 February 1950, p. 5.

legislation affecting appeals. Appeals still lie as of right from the courts of the Australian States, but not from the High Court of Australia. As regards appeals by special leave, there is an important limitation on these in Section 74 of the Commonwealth Constitution, which provides *inter alia* that there shall be no appeal

upon any question, however arising, as to the limits *inter se* of the constitutional powers of the Commonwealth and those of any State or States, or as to the limits *inter se* of the constitutional powers of any two or more States, unless the High Court shall certify that the question ought to be determined by Her Majesty in Council.

The High Court has only once, in 1914,[1] granted a certificate and is, in fact, virtually the final interpreter of the Constitution. The Commonwealth Parliament may legislate to limit appeals, but has not used this power; it is subject to reservation of the legislation for the Royal Assent (Constitution, Section 74). Professor Wheare has pointed out that assent would not be withheld on the advice of His Majesty's Government in the United Kingdom, since the constitutional convention agreed upon at the Imperial Conference of 1930 covered this matter.[2] The Judiciary Act 1903-7, Sections 39, 39B, 40, 40A, limited constitutional appeals direct from State Courts by making the investment of State Courts with jurisdiction in certain matters conditional upon there being no appeal save to the High Court; the Commonwealth possessed power to do this under Section 77 (2) of the Constitution.

The provisions of the Statute of Westminster bearing generally on the right of appeal are circumscribed, in the case of Australia, by Sections 8, 9 (1) and (2) of the Statute. There seems to be general concurrence among authorities that the Statute's effect on appeals from Australia is negligible.[3]

[1] *Attorney-General for Australia* v. *Colonial Sugar Refining Co.*, A.C. 237. In 1949 the Commonwealth Government appealed against a decision of the High Court, which had ruled that an Act providing for the absorption of the Australian trading banks into the Commonwealth Bank was *ultra vires*. The Government's application for special leave to appeal was opposed by the banks, on the ground that the litigation involved matters which, under Section 74 of the Australian Constitution, could not come to the Privy Council without a High Court certificate. The Government did not apply for a certificate and argued, on several grounds, that the appeal could be validly heard. The Privy Council then granted leave, but subject to the right of the respondents to shew that leave had been wrongly granted. In July 1949, after argument at great length, the Privy Council decided that leave had been wrongly granted in the absence of a High Court certificate, and dismissed the Commonwealth Government's appeal. Their Lordships gave their reasons, and their views on the internal constitutional questions involved.

[2] Wheare, op. cit. pp. 130, 222.

[3] W. Ivor Jennings and C. M. Young, *Constitutional Laws of the British Empire* (Oxford, Clarendon Press, 1938) p. 221; Latham, op. cit. p. 551; Wheare, op cit. p. 222.

New Zealand

In New Zealand, a Bill for the adoption of the Statute of Westminster was passed at the end of November 1947, together with a Bill requesting the United Kingdom Parliament to pass legislation relieving New Zealand of the restrictions surviving, under an Imperial Act of 1857, on the Dominion's powers to amend its own Constitution. Introducing the New Zealand Constitution (Amendment) Bill in the House of Lords on 2 December 1947, Lord Addison said:

My Lords, I am sure the House will grant me the second reading of this Bill. It is interesting to note that the Dominion of New Zealand, since 1857, has not required any intervention by this House and its Constitution was set up only in 1852. There are certain limitations of the power of the New Zealand Government as so constituted. The Statute of Westminster, in Section 8 provides that:

'Nothing in this Act shall be deemed to confer any power to repeal or alter the Constitution . . . of the Commonwealth of Australia or . . . New Zealand otherwise than in accordance with the law existing before the commencement of this Act.'

That would be the law of 1857. The Statute goes on to say, in Section 10 (2):

'The Parliament of any such Dominion as aforesaid may at any time revoke the adoption of any section referred to in subsection (1) of this section.'

And New Zealand is mentioned as one of the Dominions so entitled.

This Bill seeks to remove the limitations imposed hitherto on the Government of New Zealand and gives them complete freedom, which is only logical and reasonable, to amend their Constitution according to their own wishes.[1]

Before the adoption of the Statute of Westminster, the New Zealand Parliament had power to bar appeals as of right. It now has powers to abolish appeals both of right and by special leave, although it has not yet exercised them. Pending legislation, appeals in both categories still lie.

Union of South Africa

Up to February 1949 appeals as of right from any South African Court were precluded by Section 106 of the South Africa Act, 1909. Appeals by special leave were permissible only from the Appellate Division of the Supreme Court, and were very rare. Section 106 gave power to abolish or limit such appeals by Bill subject to reservation (cf. Australia, above), subject to the proviso that the right of appeal under the Colonial Courts of Admiralty Act, 1890, should not be affected. Since Section 106

[1] *Hansard* (Lords), vol. 152, cols. 1018-19.

was expressly saved by the Status of the Union Act, 1934, the position remained unchanged. By Chapter VI of the South Africa Act, 1909, the various existing High Courts in South Africa became divisions of the Supreme Court, and, by Section 103, appeals to the Privy Council from the High Court of Southern Rhodesia might only come via the Appellate Division of the Supreme Court by special leave.

A Bill to abolish appeals was introduced into the Union Parliament in 1947, but was rejected. In 1950 a fresh Bill was introduced. Moving the second reading on 8 February, Mr Swart, the Minister of Justice, said that the intention of the Constitution had always been to limit appeals. There had in fact been ten appeals, and a number of applications had been refused. It no longer befitted the sovereignty of the Union to permit appeals to an external body, over the appointment of whose members the Union had no control. The Union's own appeal court was the most suitable and competent to hear South African appeals. Another consideration in favour of abolition was the expense involved by appeals to the Privy Council.[1]

This Bill, enacted as the Privy Council Appeals Act, 1950, repealed Section 106 of the South Africa Act only. Its phraseology confined its application to 'appeals from any judgement or order of the Appellate Division of the Supreme Court of South Africa given on appeal from any court in the Union or the territory of South West Africa; or from any judgement or order of any court in the Union or the said territory, other than such Appellate Division'.

Newfoundland

In Newfoundland the position in regard to appeals was generally the same as in New Zealand, but, with the entry of Newfoundland as a Province into the Dominion of Canada in 1949, the position became as described under Canada above.

India before 1947

Until 15 August 1947 the constitutional position regarding appeals from British India was that the Federal provisions in general of the Government of India Act, 1935, had not come into force but 'the Federal Court, which by the Act of 1935 . . . has jurisdiction on issues of legal right between the Federation and one or more of its component units *inter se* and . . . appellate jurisdiction on appeal from the High Courts, was brought into being [by Order in Council] on 1 October 1937, with the same jurisdiction between the Central and Provincial Governments as

[1] *Weekly Newsletter* (Pretoria), 11 February 1950, p. 2.

it would have exercised on a federal basis if the whole of the Act had come into force'.[1] An Indian authority described the situation regarding Privy Council appeals as follows:

An appeal will lie to the King in Council from a decision of the Federal Court passed by the Federal Court in its original jurisdiction, in cases involving issues of the constitutional rights of the Federation and its constituent units, or of the units *inter se*. Such an appeal lies of right; in all other cases appeals will be by leave of the Federal Court or of the Privy Council.[2] But there is no right of appeal, whether by special leave or otherwise, direct to the Privy Council from any decision of the High Courts in cases where, under the provisions of [the] Act, an appeal lies to the Federal Court.[3]

The Federal Court had exclusive appellate jurisdiction in matters affecting the interpretation of the Act of 1935 or Orders in Council made thereunder (with certain exceptions mainly affecting the Indian States and therefore inoperative in the absence of federation,[4] or the interpretation of rights and obligations arising thereunder (i.e. in the field of its original jurisdiction); outside this area of exclusive appellate jurisdiction, appeals still lay from the High Courts to His Majesty in Council.

The Republic of India

By the new Constitution of the Republic of India (proclaimed on 26 January 1949), Sections 103–122A, the Supreme Court of the Republic has final appellate jurisdiction in all matters, civil and criminal; and appeals to the Privy Council are therefore abolished. The occasion was marked by a message on 6 February from the Indian Government to the Judicial Committee:

Now that the Judicial Committee of the Privy Council has finished hearing its last appeal from India, the Government of India take this opportunity to place on record their deepest appreciation of the valuable services rendered by the Privy Council to India over a period of more than two centuries. During their long connexion with Britain and British institutions, nothing has impressed the people of India more than the high sense of detachment, independence and impartiality which has invariably governed the deliberations and decisions of the Privy Council.

The Committee, through the Lord Chancellor, Lord Jowitt,

[1] Sir Reginald Coupland, *Indian Politics* 1936–42, part 2 (London, Oxford University Press, 1943) p. 233.

[2] Section 208 of the Government of India Act, 1935.

[3] S. M. Bose, *The Working Constitution of India* (Calcutta, Oxford University Press, 1939) p. 350.

[4] Section 204 of the Government of India Act, 1935; and Sections 131–3, etc.

replied expressing their warm appreciation of the message and the spirit in which it had been sent.[1]

Pakistan

The Pakistan Constituent Assembly, on 28 December 1949, passed the Federal Court (Enlargement of Jurisdiction) Act, which abolished all appeals direct from the High Courts to the Privy Council, save in pending cases or cases in which special leave to appeal had already been granted.

On 12 April 1950 the Constituent Assembly finally abolished the right of appeal, with effect from 1 May. The Government of Pakistan, in a message to the Lord Chancellor marking the cessation of the Privy Council's jurisdiction in relation to Pakistan, said that the extent and value of the influence exercised and the services rendered by their Lordships of the Judicial Committee could not be overestimated. 'They have set a standard which it will be the best endeavour of the Courts of Pakistan to maintain.' The Government took the opportunity to express their deep sense of obligation for these services.

Ceylon

The Ceylon Independence Act, which came into force on 4 February 1948, together with the Ceylon Independence Order-in-Council of 19 December 1947, revoked all limitations which had survived in the 1946 Constitution[2] upon the right of the Dominion of Ceylon to alter its Constitution; with the sole exception that any alteration in the constitutional provision (Section 29 of the 1946 Order-in-Council) safeguarding religious minorities against discriminatory legislation shall require a two-thirds majority of all members (whether voting or not) of the House of Representatives. Neither the 1946 Order, nor the Independence Act, nor the 1947 amending Order, dealt with appeals to the Judicial Committee; but the Dominion Parliament has the right to abolish appeals, on general grounds of the assimilation of the terms of the Independence Act to those of the Statute of Westminster and because the right of reservation of legislation touching the Royal Prerogative in Sub-section (2) of Section 37 of the 1946 Order is abolished. Until such time as the Dominion shall decide to legislate, appeals continue to lie to the Judicial Committee in both civil and criminal cases.

Eire

The Irish Free State Parliament in 1933 passed the Constitu-

---

[1] *Commonwealth Survey*, 17 February 1950, pp. 5–6.
[2] Ceylon (Constitution) Order-in-Council, 1946.

tion (Amendment No. 22) Act abolishing appeals, and the Judicial Committee, in the case of *Moore* v. *Attorney-General for the Irish Free State*, 1935, held that all appeals to it from the Irish Free State were thereby validly abolished under the powers given by the Statute of Westminster. Their Lordships did not base their argument on the analogy with Canada expressly made in Article 2 of the Anglo-Irish Treaty of 1921, but on a liberal interpretation of Section 2 (2) of the Statute of Westminster.

There was no mention of the Commonwealth connexion in the Irish Constitution of 1937, and the Supreme Court was given final and exclusive appellate jurisdiction (Article 34). Eire's membership of the Commonwealth terminated on 18 April 1949.

CHAPTER VII

MISCELLANEOUS OFFICIAL ORGANS FOR COMMONWEALTH CO-OPERATION

A NUMBER of intra-Commonwealth organizations have been established from time to time for the purpose of co-operation in particular spheres. Generally these organizations have originated as the result of recommendations made by Imperial Conferences or by imperial economic or agricultural conferences. Most are permanent, but a few were set up for *ad hoc* purposes and lapsed when their purpose was fulfilled.[1]

The organizations are constituted in varying ways and cover a wide range of topics. They are composed sometimes of officials and sometimes of politicians, depending on the nature of what they are discussing, who are representatives of the several Governments and the Colonial Empire. Some are supported by grants from the participating Governments and some are financed entirely by the Government of the United Kingdom, with representatives of the Commonwealth countries participating in their management. Their work consists chiefly of collecting and disseminating information, though in some cases they may advise Commonwealth Governments on policy.

Principles Governing Imperial Organizations

On the recommendation of the Imperial Agricultural Research Conference held in London in 1927, the Governments of the Commonwealth approved the formation of eight bureaux, to act as clearing houses for the interchange of information between research workers in eight branches of agricultural science throughout the Commonwealth. These bureaux were to be supported co-operatively by all Governments and were placed in charge of an autonomous body, known as the Executive Council of the Imperial Agricultural Bureaux, representative of the contributing Governments. In its final form, duties, and methods of work, this Council marked a new development in intra-Commonwealth organization, in that the membership of the Council was on a basis of equality of representation and the Council was responsible, through its constituent members, to all the participating Governments. The staff engaged by the Council for the work of the bureaux were the servants of all the Governments and not of any one particular Government.

[1] See below, p. 161, for Empire Marketing Board, Empire Timbers Committee, Oversea Mechanical Transport Council.

Although many of the organizations described below were already constituted at this time, the Executive Council of the Imperial Agricultural Bureaux was the first to work out an effective system of intra-Imperial co-operation for specialist bodies. Speaking at the British Commonwealth Scientific Conference in London in 1936 Mr Walter Elliott, then Minister of Agriculture in the United Kingdom, warmly approved of the Executive Council's 'pioneer work in a field of intra-Imperial effort'.

By 1932 there was a considerable number of specialist organizations, and at the Imperial Economic Conference held at Ottawa in that year it was decided to set up a committee to consider methods of economic consultation and co-operation and to propose alterations, if such were considered desirable, in the existing machinery. The Committee met in London in 1933 under the chairmanship of Dr O. D. Skelton of Canada. In its report,[1] the Committee surveyed the functions, organizations, and financial bases of existing agencies, and made certain recommendations, many of which were subsequently put into effect. The recommendations were concerned rather with the organization and finance of existing bodies than with the scope of their activities.

The general recommendations of the report are as follows:

We recommend that the following principles should be observed in regard to the organization of agencies for inter-Imperial consultation and co-operation:

(a) The complete constitutional equality of the participating Governments should be recognized in the method of appointment to, and composition and organization of, each agency.

(b) The formal instrument appointing persons as members of inter-Imperial agencies should be issued by each Government concerned.

(c) Adequate financial provision should be forthcoming. This implies not only sufficient funds but also a reasonable certainty of income over a definite period of years.

(d) At the same time, there should be careful and periodical examination of the various institutions at Empire conferences suitable for the purpose, as without this assurance Governments could hardly be expected to provide financial support as visualized in (c) above.

(e) The managing bodies of inter-Imperial agencies should in no way be subject to financial control by the Finance Department of any one Government of the Commonwealth, but over and above regular scrutiny by a suitably constituted finance committee, they should be free to take advantage of the experience of such departments.

(f) Each inter-Imperial agency should approach the participating

[1] Cmd. 4335.

Governments directly through the appropriate channel. We anticipate that such communications would normally take one or other of two main forms. On formal questions, such as the presentation of estimates, communications would be addressed by the secretary of the agency concerned to the Governments concerned. . . . On more important questions of policy we assume that the representatives on the agency concerned would themselves take steps to obtain the views of their respective Governments.

(g) As a general rule to which, however, exceptions may at times be necessary, Imperial organizations should serve only those members of the Commonwealth that subscribe to their funds, or pay for such services on a fee basis.

Some, but not all, of the organizations described below have made adjustments in their constitutions in order to meet the recommendations of the Skelton Committee.

A further step in the development of intra-Commonwealth organization was taken at the British Commonwealth Scientific Conference in London in 1946, when a resolution was passed recommending that the several Governments should set up Scientific Liaison Offices.[1] The offices are grouped together in one building under the general title of British Commonwealth of Nations Scientific Liaison Offices and share clerical and other services, but they operate as independent, autonomous units, responsible only to the authorities of their respective Governments.

The various agencies appear below in alphabetical order of their subject matter.

The Executive Council of the Commonwealth Agricultural Bureaux
(Farnham House, Farnham Royal, Nr. Slough)

Origin and Composition

The Executive Council of the Commonwealth Agricultural Bureaux is an intra-Commonwealth body set up in 1929 as a result of recommendations made by the Imperial Agricultural Research Conference in 1927. It is supported co-operatively by all the participating Governments and membership is on a basis of equality of representation. The Council is not responsible to any one Minister or Government, but, through its constituent members, is responsible to all Governments.

The Council supervises the work of the eleven Commonwealth agricultural bureaux, eight of which were set up at the start in

[1] See p. 150, below.

1929, two others being added subsequently. The eleventh, the Bureau of Biological Control, was, until 1946, the Imperial Parasite Service and has not the same functions as the other ten bureaux. Originally a branch of the Institute of Entomology, it was transferred to Canada from the United Kingdom in 1940.

The Imperial Committee on Economic Consultation and Co-operation (1933) reviewed and approved the system of organization and work and extended the duties of the Council by making it responsible for the supervision of the Imperial Institute of Entomology and of the Imperial Mycological Institute, which were placed in the same relation to it as the bureaux.

From 1 January 1948 the name of the organization was changed from Executive Council of the Imperial Agricultural Bureaux to Executive Council of the Commonwealth Agricultural Bureaux. The titles of the institutes and bureaux were similarly changed from 'Imperial' to 'Commonwealth'.

Finance

The income of the Council is derived from contributions from the several Commonwealth Governments and from receipts from sales of its publications. The contributions are made by the several Governments in proportions agreed among them. There is a single fund for the ten bureaux in Great Britain. The Bureau of Biological Control and the Institutes are separately funded. The total income of the fourteen bodies amounted in 1948-9 to approximately £150,000, of which £126,000 is provided by the contributions.

Organization

The Council is an autonomous body. It elects its own chairman and vice-chairman and appoints its own secretary and officers. A liaison officer appointed by the appropriate department in each participating country keeps in touch with the headquarters of the bureaux and with the bureaux administration generally, and in each country for each bureau a scientific officer is nominated as official correspondent of that bureau in that country.

The ten bureaux act as clearing houses of information on research in ten specialized fields of agricultural science. Each is attached to, but is not a part of, a research institute well known for its work in that branch. Each bureau abstracts information on its own subject and circulates it to research workers on that subject throughout the Commonwealth.

The heads of the several institutes at which bureaux are located act as Consultant Directors of the bureaux, thus giving the Coun-

K

cil and bureaux the benefit of their wide experience and scientific knowledge.

The work of the Bureau of Biological Control is quite different from that of the other bureaux. It is primarily engaged in field and laboratory operations.

The work of the bureaux is subject to careful and periodical examination at Commonwealth conferences suitable for the purpose.

The bureaux under the administration of the Executive Council are:

Commonwealth Bureau of Agricultural Parasitology (Helminthology):
 Winches Farm Drive, Hatfield Road, St. Albans, Hertfordshire.
Commonwealth Bureau of Animal Breeding and Genetics:
 Institute of Genetics, West Mains Road, Edinburgh.
Commonwealth Bureau of Animal Health:
 Veterinary Laboratory, New Haw, Weybridge, Surrey.
Commonwealth Bureau of Animal Nutrition:
 Rowett Research Institute, Bucksburn, Aberdeen.
Commonwealth Bureau of Biological Control:
 Science Buildings, Carling Avenue, Ottawa.
Commonwealth Bureau of Dairy Science:
 National Institute for Research in Dairying, Shinfield, Reading, Berkshire.
Commonwealth Forestry Bureau:
 Imperial Forestry Institute, South Parks Road, Oxford.
Commonwealth Bureau of Horticulture and Plantation Crops:
 East Malling Research Station, East Malling, Kent.
Commonwealth Bureau of Pastures and Field Crops:
 Agricultural Research Building, Penglais, Aberystwyth.
Commonwealth Bureau of Plant Breeding and Genetics:
 School of Agriculture, Cambridge.
Commonwealth Bureau of Soil Science:
 Rothamsted Experimental Station, Harpenden, Hertfordshire.

COMMONWEALTH INSTITUTE OF ENTOMOLOGY
(British Museum (Natural History), Cromwell Road, London, S.W.7)

Origin

The origin of the Institute goes back to 1910, when an Entomological Research Committee was appointed by the Colonial Office to deal with entomological problems in tropical Africa. Of the funds originally required, i.e. £2,000 per annum, one-half was provided by the Governments of the African Dependencies concerned and the other half by the Government of the United Kingdom. As a result of discussions at the Imperial Conference of 1911 it was decided to form an Imperial Bureau of Entomology whose function it would be to cover all parts of the Empire. The bureau came into existence in 1913 and developed rapidly. In 1930 its title was changed to Imperial Institute of Entomology. In 1933 it was placed under the control of the Executive Council of the Commonwealth Agricultural Bureaux in accordance with the recommendations of the Imperial Committee on Economic Consultation and Co-operation (1933).

Constitution

From 1910 until 1933 the management of the Institute was undertaken by the former Entomological Research Committee. Subsequent to 1933 this function has been assumed by the Executive Council of the Commonwealth Agricultural Bureaux. This Council consists of one representative from the United Kingdom, one from each of the Dominions and Southern Rhodesia, and one member representing the Colonies.

A Commonwealth entomological conference is normally held every five years. Prior to 1933 the finance and activities of the Institute were reviewed at these quinquennial conferences. Since the Institute came within the Commonwealth Agricultural Bureaux organization the finances and administration have been reviewed at the Commonwealth Bureaux Review conferences, the last of which was held in 1946. The technical activities of the Institute continue to be reviewed at the Commonwealth Entomological conferences, of which the last was held in July 1948.

Functions

The Institute is essentially a centre for the collection and co-ordination of all information bearing upon injurious or useful insects and for the dissemination of such information to those interested throughout the world. As a centre of information its activities fall under three main headings:

(1) *Publications.* The *Review of Applied Entomology* published monthly in two series—one agricultural, the other medical and veterinary—comprises abstracts of the world literature in all languages on economic entomology. Its primary object is to give a summary of the latest information on insects and other arthropods that are of economic importance.

The *Bulletin of Entomological Research*, published quarterly, consists of original articles on economic entomology.

The *Insecta* part of the *Zoological Record*, published annually, contains as complete a record as possible of the entomological literature, chiefly systematic, of the previous year.

A few special publications dealing with entomological subjects of major importance have been issued at various times.

(2) *Identification Service*. Insects of direct or indirect economic importance are identified on behalf of the entomologists of the various countries of the Commonwealth and large quantities of insect material are handled annually.

(3) *Information*. Apart from the information service provided through the medium of (1) and (2) above, the Institute supplies information in a variety of other ways. A very extensive library of works dealing with economic entomology in particular has been built up and is much used by entomologists resident in the British Isles or on leave from overseas. Photostat and, to a limited extent, microfilm copies of works in the library are supplied to entomologists overseas at cost price. A very large number of requests for information is received and dealt with on a wide range of matters pertaining to the field of economic entomology and on a variety of specific problems often involving a review of the literature, much of which is not available to the entomologist abroad.

Finance

Contributions towards the maintenance of the Institute, amounting in 1948 to £20,800, are made in agreed proportions by the United Kingdom and Commonwealth Governments, by the Colonies, Southern Rhodesia, and the Sudan.

COMMONWEALTH MYCOLOGICAL INSTITUTE
(Ferry Lane, Kew)

Origin and Constitution

The Institute came into being in 1920 as the result of a decision taken by the Imperial Conference of 1918. It was modelled on a plan similar to that of the Institute (then known as Bureau) of Entomology and, like it, has since the Skelton Committee reported come under the supervision of the Executive Council of the Commonwealth Agricultural Bureaux.

Functions

The Institute has two main functions:

(i) The collection and dissemination of information.

(ii) The identification and study of fungi of economic importance.

The first of these is performed through the publication of the *Review of Applied Mycology*, containing abstracts of all papers on plant pathology and applied mycology published in any part of the world. The second consists in the examination and determination of material received from plant pathologists and others throughout the Commonwealth and Colonies in connexion with investigations in regard to the diseases of crop plants and forest trees, soil fungi, fungi attacking textiles, etc.

The Institute also publishes maps showing the world distribution of major plant diseases.

In addition it issues at six-monthly intervals an *Index of Fungi*, published since the beginning of 1940, as well as a series of *Mycological Papers* dealing with systematic mycology.

An *Annotated Bibliography of Medical Mycology* is published annually and a *Bibliography of Systematic Mycology* has been issued in mimeographed form for 1943–6, 1947, 1948, and 1949.

A culture collection of fungi (excluding medical fungi, yeasts, and timber-rotting fungi) is maintained and cultures are available to all clients.

No parallel institution exists in any part of the world, and close co-operation is maintained not only with mycologists in the Commonwealth but also with those in the United States and other foreign mycological departments.

Finance

Finance is provided in the same manner as for the Commonwealth Institute of Entomology, although the amounts subscribed by the different Governments are neither the same in the two cases nor are they in the same proportions. The present contributions to the Institute amount to approximately £13,200 per annum.

COMMONWEALTH AIR TRANSPORT COUNCIL
(Ariel House, Theobalds Road, W.C.1)

Origin

The formation of the Commonwealth Air Transport Council was formally announced in the House of Lords by Lord Swinton (then Minister of Civil Aviation) on 16 January 1945.[1]

The Council was set up as a result of informal Commonwealth conversations held in Montreal in October 1944 and continued in London in December of the same year, when a resolution was passed in favour of constituting a Council of a consultative character to discuss matters affecting civil aviation of common interest to the Commonwealth countries.

[1] *Hansard* (Lords), vol. 134, cols. 581–3.

Terms of Reference

The terms of reference of CATC are as follows:

(i) To keep under review progress and development of Commonwealth civil air communications.

(ii) To serve as a medium for exchange of views and information between Commonwealth countries on civil air transport matters.

(iii) To consider and advise on such civil aviation matters as the Commonwealth Governments may agree to refer to the Council.

The Minister of Civil Aviation in the United Kingdom is the permanent chairman of the Council.

Secretariat and Organization

A permanent CATC secretariat housed in and staffed by the United Kingdom Ministry of Civil Aviation was set up in accordance with the recommendations of the first meeting of the Council with the following terms of reference:

(i) (*a*) To act as the secretariat of the Council before, during and after its periodic meetings.

(*b*) To obtain information as to the action taken on Council recommendations.

(ii) To maintain contact with various Commonwealth countries through their High Commissioners about civil aviation policy and air transport agreements.

(iii) To serve as a medium for exchange of information of general interest about any aspect of air transport or civil aviation, including statistics.

A quarterly News Letter, which serves as a medium for the collection and exchange of information between the countries of the Commonwealth on civil air transport matters, is issued by the secretariat.

Meetings of the Council are held from time to time, as they are required, to consider current developments in civil aviation. The level of representation at particular meetings of the Council is determined by the Governments concerned and may be either ministerial or official as considered appropriate.

At the first meeting of the Council held in London in July 1945 the development of air communications and provision of ground facilities along Commonwealth routes were considered, and the formation of a standing technical committee concerned with operational planning on the Commonwealth trunk routes, to be called the Committee for Air Navigation and Ground Organization (CANGO), was recommended. It was also recommended that this Committee and the existing Commonwealth and Empire

Radio for Civil Aviation (CERCA) Central Office should be incorporated, as subordinate technical sections, in the CATC secretariat.

Affiliated Bodies

Ancillary to the main Council and performing similar functions to the parent body but on a regional basis are the South Pacific Air Transport Council set up in March 1946 and the Southern Africa Air Transport Council set up in March 1945. These bodies maintain separate and independent secretariats in Australia and the Union of South Africa respectively and work in close liaison with the secretariat of the main Council.

COMMITTEE FOR AIR NAVIGATION AND GROUND ORGANIZATION

The Committee for Air Navigation and Ground Organization (CANGO) although established under the aegis of CATC does not constitute a Committee of the Council itself. It has no official terms of reference, but functions on lines broadly similar to those of CERCA. It has no executive powers; individual Governments working through their Departments of Civil Aviation take the necessary action upon any joint recommendation made by the Committee.

CANGO met for the first time in July 1945 and its functions and purpose were then defined. It was agreed that its first task should be to determine the services and facilities which would be required at each of the staging posts which had been selected for use on the Commonwealth trunk air routes.

A permanent secretariat forming part of the main CATC secretariat is maintained in London.

COMMONWEALTH AND EMPIRE RADIO FOR CIVIL AVIATION (CERCA)
(Ariel House, Theobalds Road, W.C.1)

Origin

As a result of British Commonwealth conversations held in London in October 1943 Sir Stafford Cripps, then Chairman of the Radio Board of the War Cabinet, was invited to consider the technical aspects of radio for civil aviation, first from the point of view of the United Kingdom and then on a Commonwealth and Empire basis. The Radio Board agreed to this course of action and invitations to attend a Commonwealth Conference on Radio for Civil Aviation were issued to and accepted by the Dominion Governments and the Secretary of State for the Colonies. This meeting held in London in February 1944 constituted the first CERCA Conference, and out of it the CERCA organization was born.

Functions

The original aim of the CERCA organization was to formulate within the Commonwealth and Empire tentative conclusions on all matters relating to the immediate and ultimate international standardization of radio aids to civil aviation. During the war years it was the policy of CERCA at all stages of its proceedings, as and when security considerations permitted, to have informal discussions with other allied nations, in order to ensure that at the first appropriate international conference their tentative conclusions had a maximum probability of acceptance.

Since the end of the war in 1945 and consequent upon the formation of the International Civil Aviation Organization the initial aims of CERCA have to a large extent been fulfilled. It is worthy of note that the recommendations of the third CERCA Conference did in fact form the basis of discussion at the first meeting of the Communications Division of ICAO and that certain of them were adopted by ICAO *in toto*.

CERCA has also aimed at the provision of a technical information service between the Radio Research Establishments of the Commonwealth and Empire. It was agreed at the Second Meeting of the Commonwealth Air Transport Council that this service had proved of great value and the Council recommended that it should be continued.

Conferences of CERCA are held from time to time to exchange views and information on technical matters relating to civil aviation.

Secretariat

At the second CERCA Conference, held in Ottawa in November 1944, it was agreed that it would be desirable to establish a CERCA central office with a full-time permanent secretariat which, at the request of the Conference, the United Kingdom undertook to set up and maintain.

The terms of reference of the CERCA Central Office are as follows:

(i) To provide a recognized centre and mechanism for the exchange of technical information, and the integration of ideas among those concerned with civil aviation radio services for the Commonwealth and Empire countries.

(ii) To maintain and ensure liaison with all bodies within the Commonwealth and Empire dealing with tele-communications in relation to civil aviation.

(iii) To encourage and promote by its initiative the exchange of views on radio matters among countries of the Commonwealth and Empire.

(iv) To ensure that all documents of potential interest to civil aviation radio authorities within the Commonwealth and Empire be made available as soon as their security classification permits.

(v) To arrange for the provision of a conference secretariat at future Commonwealth and Empire Conferences.

The secretariat issues two quarterly News Letters known as the *CERCA News Letter* and the *Ministry of Civil Aviation Radio News Letter*. Circulation of the *CERCA News Letter*, with which copies of technical documents of current interest are issued as appendices, is restricted to Government Departments within the Commonwealth. The *Ministry of Civil Aviation Radio News Letter* is an unclassified document and is circulated internationally.

Relationship to the Commonwealth Air Transport Council

At the second meeting of the Commonwealth Air Transport Council held in Montreal in May 1947 it was agreed that CERCA should continue to operate within the organization of the Commonwealth Air Transport Council as a part of the technical section of the Council. It was further agreed that CANGO and CERCA should together deal with such problems of ground organization, radio, airworthiness, and other technical matters as might come within the scope of CATC.

The Council recommended that the combined secretariats should continue to be provided and accommodated by the United Kingdom Ministry of Civil Aviation.

COMMONWEALTH ECONOMIC COMMITTEE[1]
(2 Queen Anne's Gate Buildings, London, S.W.1)

Origin and Constitution

This Committee, which was first projected at the Imperial Economic Conference of 1923, took shape in March 1925, since when its terms of reference have been gradually extended by subsequent decisions of Imperial Conferences. It is purely advisory in character, its present functions having been determined by the Imperial Conference of 1930.

[1] Formerly styled 'Imperial Economic Committee'.

The Committee originally had the following terms of reference:

To consider the possibility of improving the methods of preparing for market and marketing within the United Kingdom the food products of the overseas parts of the Empire with a view to increasing the consumption of such products in the United Kingdom in preference to imports from foreign countries and to promote the interests both of producers and consumers.

The Imperial Conferences of 1926 and 1930 extended these terms of reference to cover a wider range of economic subjects of special interest within the Empire.

In 1933 the Governments of the British Commonwealth and Empire established the Committee as an official co-operative agency conforming to the conditions laid down in the report of the Imperial Committee on Economic Consultation and Co-operation (the 'Skelton Committee'). According to those conditions, each co-operating Government appoints directly its own representatives (usually two for each Government) to the Committee. The Committee is responsible to all the co-operating Governments jointly. It elects its own Chairman from among its own members.

The work of the Committee is reviewed and its future financial requirements determined by agreement among member Governments. Subject to these reviews the Committee has full control over its staff and finance.

Finance

Until 1 October 1933, all the expenses of the Committee were borne by the United Kingdom. The Skelton Committee recommended that henceforth the Committee should be financed by contributions on an agreed basis from the participating Governments. The annual income amounted in 1949-50 to approximately £30,000.

Functions

The work of the Committee is discharged through two main channels:

  (i) *Reports to Governments.* These reports are specially prepared by the Committee at the request of the various Commonwealth Governments. They deal with particular subjects and are submitted to all Commonwealth Governments jointly. By 1939 their scope had become general so as to cover most raw materials in addition to the 'food products' originally assigned and also to allow the Committee 'to examine and report on any economic question which the Governments of the Commonwealth may agree to refer to the Committee'.

Reports of this kind issued since the war are *A Review of Commonwealth Trade* (1949) and *A Survey of the Trade in Fertilizers* (1950).

(ii) *Intelligence Services*. These services include the periodical collection and publication, weekly, monthly, or annually, of current economic information on production, trade, and marketing of particular commodities which are of direct importance to the countries of the Commonwealth. The subjects dealt with are mainly connected with agricultural products used either for food or industry.

The services are of three kinds: (*a*) World studies or surveys of the production of and trade in particular commodities. These appear from time to time as required. Since the war companion volumes on wool production and wool consumption have been issued; (*b*) the 'Commodity Series', which is a regular part of the Committee's arrangements for publicizing economic intelligence and bringing together, in a comparative and convenient form, information on the production of and trade in groups of closely allied commodities. This series has been reissued with figures covering the war and post-war years; (*c*) the periodical intelligence services, which deal with current up-to-date economic information on a particular subject of interest to Commonwealth countries. These have also started again since the war with 'Wool Intelligence' (monthly); a general monthly 'Intelligence Bulletin', chiefly concerned with dairy produce, meat and fruit; and the quarterly, 'Tobacco Intelligence'.

This intelligence work does not duplicate the work of any Government department or international authority or of any commercial intelligence service, for, while the information is collected on a world scale, the object is to place in the foreground information of particular significance to the co-operating Commonwealth countries.

THE COMMONWEALTH LIAISON COMMITTEE

The Commonwealth Liaison Committee was set up in 1948 to supplement the existing inter-governmental channels for keeping Commonwealth countries fully informed on matters connected with the European Recovery Programme. In 1949 its functions were expanded so as to cover discussion of financial and economic problems of general interest to Commonwealth countries. It does not formulate policy, but provides a useful forum for the exchange of information on economic affairs. It meets at frequent intervals. Representatives of the United Kingdom Government Departments most closely concerned with the subjects under discussion and members of all High Commissioners' Offices in London attend its meetings.

STANDING COMMITTEE ON BRITISH COMMONWEALTH FORESTRY
(25 Savile Row, London, W.1)

Origin

The Committee originated in a resolution of the second Empire Forestry Conference held in Canada in 1923. It is intended to serve as a link between, and to prepare agenda for, Empire Forestry Conferences,[1] dealing with the scientific, technical, and economic aspects of the production and disposal of timber, and assisting and advising Governments in the formulation of a progressive policy of forest conservation.

Composition

The Committee consists of the Chairman of the British Commonwealth Forestry Conference, the Technical Commissioner of the British Forestry Commission, the Director of the Imperial Forestry Institute, a member of Council of the British Empire Forestry Association, and one representative from each of the following: Colonial Office; unit of Empire in which the last Conference was held; unit of Empire in which the next Conference is to be held. The Committee have power to add to their number.

Functions

The first function of the Committee is to promote the implementation of resolutions passed at the previous Empire Forestry Conference. On technical matters it corresponds with the forest authorities in the several parts of the Empire, and on financial questions through the appropriate United Kingdom Government department.

The second function of the Committee is to prepare agenda for the next Conference in consultation with Forestry Depart-

---

[1] Resolution xii of the 1947 Conference recommended that the title be changed to British Commonwealth Forestry Conference. After consultation with all the Commonwealth Governments, this change was made; and the name of the Standing Committee was correspondingly altered.

ments in the Dominions and Colonies, also to guide the various Empire Governments in the preparation of statistics for submission to the conference.

A further important function of the Committee is to direct and co-ordinate the work of technical committees set up on the instructions of the Conference, such as the committees on aerial survey of forests and on forest products research.

Finance

The expenses of the Standing Committee are practically nil. Incidental expenses incurred at the Conference have hitherto been defrayed by the Government in whose territory it was held. The expenses of the committee on aerial survey of forests are at present met by contributions from the Forestry Commission and the Colonial Office.

IMPERIAL FORESTRY INSTITUTE
(Oxford)

Origin and Functions

The Imperial Forestry Institute was established in 1924 as a result of resolutions passed by the Empire Forestry Conferences of 1920 and 1923. It was intended to serve both Dominions and Colonies as a centre of:

(i) Undergraduate and post-graduate training in forestry.
(ii) Research on biological and economic problems bearing on forestry.
(iii) Refresher courses for forest officers of the Empire and others.
(iv) Structural examination and identification of woods and the identification of trees.

Administration

The Institute has now been combined with the University of Oxford Department of Forestry under the Professor of Forestry. It is supervised by a University Committee which includes representatives of the non-University interests. The permanent staff consists of the Professor and a number of lecturers and research workers.

Finance

The Institute is financed jointly by grants from the Colonial Governments, the Forestry Commission and the University, together with smaller contributions from other Commonwealth Governments. Its income in 1949 was approximately £40,000.

IMPERIAL COLLEGE OF SCIENCE AND TECHNOLOGY
(Prince Consort Road, London, S.W.7)

The College was founded by Royal Charter in 1907 for the purpose of giving the highest specialized instruction and providing the fullest equipment for the most advanced training and research in various branches of science, especially in its application to industry.

The Imperial College is a School of London University in Science and Engineering, and it includes as integral parts the Royal College of Science, the Royal School of Mines and the City and Guilds College.

The administration of the College is vested in a Governing Body consisting of 50 members representing the Crown, the Dominions,[1] the Minister of Education, the University of London, the London County Council, the City and Guilds of London Institute, the Royal Commissioners for the Exhibition of 1851, the Royal Society, the teaching Staff of the Imperial College and learned societies concerned with industries. The Beit Fellowships for post-graduate research are open to men and women under 25 years of age holding a degree or approved diploma from any Commonwealth or approved university.

BRITISH COMMONWEALTH OF NATIONS SCIENTIFIC LIAISON OFFICES (B.C.S.O.) (LONDON)
(Africa House, Kingsway, London, W.C.2)

Origin and Functions

The British Commonwealth Scientific Official Conference, convened by His Majesty's Government in the United Kingdom, was held in London in 1946. Its terms of reference were 'to consider the best means of ensuring the fullest possible collaboration between civil government scientific organizations of the Commonwealth and to make formal recommendations for the approval of the Governments represented'.[2]

Before the War of 1939–45 there was no central Commonwealth organization for promoting collaborative scientific work. In 1944 the British Central Scientific Office in Washington, D.C., originally set up in 1941 to facilitate exchange of scientific information between the United Kingdom and the United States,

---

[1] The Canadian Government has not exercised its right of representation on the Governing Body since 1931.

[2] Cmd. 6970.

developed into the British Commonwealth Scientific Office through the housing of the other Commonwealth Scientific Offices in the same premises. In London there was no similar organization but Scientific Liaison Officers were attached to the offices of the several High Commissioners.

The 1946 Conference recommended that a common office, similar to the one in Washington, should be established in London 'by housing the several scientific liaison offices of the various parts of the Commonwealth, including suitable United Kingdom representation, under one roof'. Experience in Washington had shown that propinquity led to a substantial measure of co-operation between the offices in the conduct of their liaison work. There should also be co-operation in clerical and other services, but each of the offices would remain completely autonomous and the officer in charge of each office should be responsible only to the authorities of his own Government.

Following on these recommendations the British Commonwealth of Nations Scientific Liaison Offices in London were opened in April 1948, in Africa House, Kingsway, where most Commonwealth Scientific Liaison Offices now have their headquarters. The Overseas Liaison Division of the United Kingdom Department of Scientific and Industrial Research is also accommodated in Africa House, and the Commonwealth Agricultural Bureaux are represented.

As in Washington, the Commonwealth Scientific Liaison Offices in London have continued to operate as independent autonomous units, although grouped together in one building under the general title of British Commonwealth of Nations Scientific Liaison Offices.

The functions of the individual London Offices differ somewhat from those of the corresponding ones in B.C.S.O. Washington (now re-named B.C.S.O. North America) and include the following:

    (i) To assist scientific visitors from Commonwealth countries.

   (ii) To maintain close personal contact with United Kingdom Government, university, and other research institutions.

  (iii) To obtain answers to questions on scientific and technical subjects asked by their home departments.

  (iv) To stimulate and maintain the exchange of scientific and technical reports between Commonwealth countries.

   (v) To keep their home governments informed of new developments in scientific matters in Great Britain, and

conversely, to bring to the notice of the United Kingdom authorities details of similar developments in their
own countries.

There is in addition a small Common Services Section, operating under the control of the B.C.S.O. (London) Committee,
whose main functions are as follows:

(i) To provide the secretariat of the Standing Committee and Working Party set up by the 1946 British
Commonwealth Scientific Official Conference.

(ii) To undertake certain Commonwealth projects assigned
to B.C.S.O. (London) by the 1946 Conference or subsequent Specialist Conferences, of which the following
are examples:

(*a*) Preparation of lists of post-graduate scholarships
available for scientific study within the Commonwealth.

(*b*) Preparation of a directory and catalogues of culture
collections of micro-organisms.

(*c*) Organization of machinery to ensure that there is
within each co-operating country a list of transla-
tions of scientific papers in languages other than
English made or contemplated throughout the
Commonwealth.

(*d*) Preparation of a report on methods for promoting
the utilization of non-patentable scientific and technical results.

(iii) To provide certain common office services, and facilities
(secretarial, duplicating, etc.).

Finance

The salaries and expenses of scientific and attached personal
staffs are to be borne directly by the Governments concerned.
The cost of the various specified common services, including
accommodation, are to be shared in agreed proportions by the
Governments permanently represented in the Office.

*Standing Committee of the British Commonwealth
Scientific Conference*

During the British Commonwealth Scientific Conference in
London in 1946 the question of providing suitable machinery for
initiating action for the calling of specialist conferences and for
following up the recommendations of the Conference after it
dispersed was discussed, and the Conference adopted a resolution
establishing a Standing Committee, with a secretariat and a working party to be located in London. The Standing Committee was

to consist of the executive heads of Government organizations for scientific, industrial, agricultural, and medical research in the Commonwealth countries, together with three scientific representatives nominated by the Colonial Office. It should have power to co-opt other members as might seem desirable. Its terms of reference are 'to consider the best means of ensuring the fullest possible collaboration between the Government scientific organizations of the Commonwealth and Empire'.

Through the Standing Committee and Working Party set up by the 1946 Conference discussions are taking place regarding plans for the next Commonwealth Scientific Conference to be held in Australia in February 1952, for which invitations have been issued by the Australian Government. This Conference will review action taken to implement the recommendations of the 1946 Conference and will also consider new proposals for collaboration in research.

BRITISH COMMONWEALTH SCIENTIFIC OFFICE NORTH AMERICA[1]

The British Central Scientific Office was established in Washington in 1941 to continue the work of a technical mission from the United Kingdom which had visited the United States in 1940 to arrange for the interchange of scientific and technical information between the two countries. Australia and New Zealand also established Scientific Liaison Offices in Washington in 1941, attached to the Australian Legation and the New Zealand Supply Mission respectively, and in 1944 the three offices, by mutual agreement, associated themselves with the newly arrived Mission from South Africa and with the Scientific Liaison Office of the National Research Council of Canada to form the British Commonwealth Scientific Office. The original Central Scientific Office was thereupon re-named the United Kingdom Scientific Mission.

One of the main functions of the B.C.S.O. (North America) is to transmit detailed information on technical research and development between the United States and the British Commonwealth. Economy of time and labour is achieved by a joint approach to the United States authorities on many questions of common interest to some or all of the Members of the Commonwealth.

In all routine matters, such as a central index, a comprehensive library of technical reports, duplicating, the distribution of

[1] Formerly British Commonwealth Scientific Office, Washington.

documents, the purchase of books and apparatus, etc., a common service is provided. In addition to the economy and efficiency thereby achieved, the Office is able to increase the scope of work of each of its units by the principle of common representation on scientific matters.

COMMONWEALTH SHIPPING COMMITTEE[1]
(Berkeley Square House, Berkeley Square, London, W.1)

Origin and Constitution

This Committee, which is concerned with the development of inter-Imperial sea communications, originated in a resolution passed by the Imperial War Conference of 1918, and was first appointed in June 1920. The Committee derives its authority from, and is responsible to, the Governments represented at the Imperial Conference. It consists of sixteen members, of whom the Governments of the United Kingdom, Canada, Australia, South Africa, Southern Rhodesia, India, Pakistan, and Ceylon each nominate one; one is nominated by the Secretary of State for the Colonies and five are co-opted by the Committee and, in accordance with usual practice, include two ship-owners, one ship-builder, one industrialist, and one merchant. The Committee maintains a close liaison with the Commonwealth Air Transport Council.

Finance

The normal[2] annual income of the Committee is about £2,000 and the whole of this amount was originally contributed by the United Kingdom Government. In 1933, however, the Committee on Economic Consultation and Co-operation recommended that as from 1 October 1933 each member Government should agree to contribute to the Committee on a scale based on general trade exports from each part of the Empire. The recommendation was adopted and contributions have continued on this basis up to the present time.

Terms of Reference and Functions

The Imperial War Conference of 1918 passed the following resolution:

[1] On 5 January 1948 it was agreed by all the Governments represented on the Imperial Shipping Committee that the Committee should be known in future as the Commonwealth Shipping Committee.

[2] The reference to 'normal' income is explained by the fact that few expenses were incurred during the war and the early post-war period, resulting in the accumulation of a reserve. It was therefore agreed that during the years 1948–9 to 1952–3 contributions to the Committee by member Governments should be at one-half the normal rates.

(i) That in order to maintain satisfactorily the connexions and at the same time encourage commercial and industrial relations between the different countries of the British Empire, this Conference is of opinion that shipping on the principal routes, especially between the heart of the Empire and the Overseas Dominions, including India, should be brought under review by an inter-Imperial Board on which the United Kingdom and the British Dominions and Dependencies should be represented.

(ii) That for this purpose an Imperial Investigation Board, representing the various parts of the Empire, be appointed, with power to inquire into and report on all matters connected with ocean freights and facilities, and on all matters connected with the development and improvement of the sea communications between the different parts of the Empire, with special reference to the size and type of ships, and the capacities of harbours; the Board to include, in addition to representatives of the Governments concerned, persons with expert knowledge of the problems involved, including representatives of the shipping and trading interests.

At the 1930 Imperial Conference, in Section III of the Report of the Committee on Economic Co-operation, the work of the Imperial Shipping Committee was commended and its maintenance advocated. Further, the Conference amended the terms of reference of the Committee, which now are:

(i) To inquire into complaints from persons and bodies interested with regard to ocean freights, facilities and conditions in the inter-Imperial trade, or questions of a similar nature referred to them by any of the nominating authorities, and to report their conclusions to the Governments concerned.

(ii) To survey the facilities for maritime transport on such routes as appear to them to be necessary for trade within the Empire, and to make recommendations to the proper authority for the co-ordination and improvement of such facilities with regard to the type, size, and speed of ships, depth of water in docks and channels, construction of harbour works, and similar matters; and in doing so to take into account facilities for air transport on the routes in question.

The Committee considers questions referred to it by Commonwealth and Colonial Governments and by private bodies such as Chambers of Shipping.

STERLING AREA STATISTICAL COMMITTEE

The Sterling Area Statistical Committee was set up by the Treasury in 1947 to serve as a forum in which representatives of the Commonwealth self-governing sterling area countries could give and seek information on financial developments affecting their countries.

The Chairman and secretariat are provided by the United Kingdom; and representatives of all the High Commissioners' Offices in London and of United Kingdom Government departments and the Bank of England attend meetings. Canada, not being a member of the sterling area, is represented by an observer.

The Committee meets normally every month. Its work consists mainly of consideration and discussion of the sterling area gold and dollar position based on regular documentation provided by the Bank of England; and of the financial aspects of past, present, and pending bilateral negotiations; but discussion also covers a wide variety of points raised by members.

The main purpose of the Committee is to provide members with as much information as possible on current financial problems and negotiations; and, by encouraging an exchange of views on any question of interest to their Governments, to promote co-operation between sterling-area countries. This applies in particular to bilateral negotiations which, although often indirectly affecting Commonwealth countries, have of necessity to be conducted between the United Kingdom and the country concerned.

COMMONWEALTH TELECOMMUNICATIONS BOARD

Origin

The Commonwealth Telecommunications Board was incorporated by the Commonwealth Telegraphs Act, 1949. It was established in pursuance of a recommendation of the Commonwealth Telecommunications Conference, 1945 (Cmd. 6805), which reached the unanimous conclusion that in order to secure the desired strengthening and better ordering of the Commonwealth telecommunications system, a fundamental change in the existing organization was essential. The 1945 Conference had recommended: firstly, that the private shareholder interest in the overseas telecommunications services of the United Kingdom, the Dominions, and India should be eliminated; secondly, that the respective Governments should acquire the interest of Cable and Wireless Limited in the Dominion and Indian companies; thirdly, that the new national organizations should, if possible, be uniform as among all Commonwealth countries; fourthly, that a Commonwealth Telecommunications Board should be established in place of the Commonwealth Communications Council, with functions mainly advisory in character, but substantially wider. The latter body had itself superseded, in 1944, the Imperial Communications Advisory Committee, set up in 1929, as a result of the Imperial Wireless and Cable Conference 1928 (Cmd. 3163).

Constitution and Functions

The constitution and functions of the Board are fully described in the Second Schedule to the Commonwealth Telegraphs Agreement 1948 (Cmd. 7582), signed by the Governments of the United Kingdom, Canada, Australia, New Zealand, South Africa, India, and Southern Rhodesia. (The signatories are known as the Partner Governments. The Agreement provides that they may admit the Government of any other part of the British Commonwealth and Empire as a Partner Government on agreed terms.)

The Chairman is appointed jointly by the Partner Governments. He does not represent any government. Each of the Partner Governments separately appoints one member. In addition to its own member the United Kingdom Government also appoints a member to represent British Commonwealth and Empire territories not directly represented by other members. Pakistan and Ceylon have appointed observers.

The functions of the Board are:

(1) To make recommendations to the Partner Governments and to National Bodies[1] on the following matters relating to their external telecommunication systems:

(a) The formulation and execution of the joint telecommunication policy of the Partner Governments, including the fixing of rates (terminal transit and parcours proportions).

(b) Co-ordination of the development of the cable and wireless systems of the British Commonwealth and Empire.

(c) Extensions to and alterations of the Telecommunication systems of the British Commonwealth and Empire.

(d) The provision and, where appropriate, the apportionment among National Bodies, of capital expenditure on projects.

(e) Co-ordination with the appropriate authorities on telecommunication matters affecting the defence of the British Commonwealth and Empire or any part thereof.

(f) Co-ordination of reasearch in telecommunication matters conducted by National Bodies.

[1] 'National Bodies' means the nationalized telecommunications undertakings in the territories of the Partner Governments.

(*g*) The exchange of personnel between the Board and National Bodies.

(*h*) Any other telecommunication matter which may be referred to the Board by any of the Partner Governments or by any National Body.

(2) At the request of the Partner Governments or National Bodies to conduct negotiations with foreign telecommunication interests on their behalf.

(3) To promote and conduct research in telecommunication matters.

(4) To purchase or otherwise acquire and turn to account in any manner that may be thought fit any Letters Patent or patent rights or any interest in any Letters Patent or patent rights, *brevets d'invention*, licences, concessions, and the like conferring an exclusive or non-exclusive or limited right to use any secret or other information as to any invention in relation to any device or machine serving or calculated to serve any useful purpose in connexion with any of the functions of the Board or with the business of any National Body.

General

(1) It is laid down that meetings shall normally be held in London in the United Kingdom but that from time to time as may be found convenient meetings shall also be held in the territories of the other Partner Governments or elsewhere as the Board may determine.

(2) The Board must treat persons domiciled in any of the territories of the Partner Governments as equally eligible for appointment to the Board's staff.

(3) The Board must at all times observe the provisions of any International Conventions relating to telecommunications to which the Partner Governments have subscribed.

Finance

The Board's expenses are financed by the Partner Governments on an agreed basis.

IMPERIAL WAR GRAVES COMMISSION
(32 Grosvenor Gardens, London, S.W.1, and Wooburn House, Wooburn Green, High Wycombe, Bucks.)

The Imperial War Graves Commission[1] was appointed by Royal Charter of 21 May 1917. The Charter was drawn up and

[1] Imperial Conference Reports, 1917, 1918, 1923, 1930: Cmds. 8566, 9177, 1987, 3717.

revised after discussion at the Imperial War Conference of 1917.
The powers of the Commission were extended by supplementary
Charters in 1921, 1923, 1931, 1940, 1941, 1944 and 1948.

The Commission was originally constituted as follows:

President: H.R.H. the Prince of Wales.

Chairman: The Secretary of State for War.

The Secretary of State for the Colonies.

The Secretary of State for India.

The First Commissioner of the Office of Works,
and persons appointed by the Governments of
Canada, Australia, New Zealand, South Africa,
and Newfoundland and eight other persons as
may from time to time be appointed by Royal
Warrant, from among whom the Commission
select their Vice-Chairman.

Subsequent Charters introduced modifications into the composition of the Commission, which is now as follows:

President: H.R.H. the Duke of Gloucester.

Chairman: The Secretary of State for War.

The Secretary of State for the Colonies.

The Minister of Works.

Persons (in practice the High Commissioners)
appointed by the Governments of Canada,[1]
Australia, New Zealand, South Africa, India,
Pakistan, and nine other persons appointed by
Royal Warrant (including the Vice-Chairman).

The Charter of Incorporation of 1917 created the Imperial
War Graves Commission for the purpose of permanently com-
memorating those members of His Majesty's Forces who died in
the War of 1914–18. The Fourth Supplemental Charter of 1940
extended the Commission's powers to provide for the permanent
commemoration of those dying in the War of 1939–45. The fifth
Supplemental Charter empowered the Commission to compile
records relating to civilian war dead, and also laid down that the
term 'Military Forces' wherever used in former Charters,
should be deemed to have included, and to include, a reference
to Air Forces.

The Commission is granted power under the Charters to enable it to purchase land, establish and maintain cemeteries, and
perform all other operations for that object; also to operate super-
annuation, pensions, and insurance schemes. It also has power to
appoint sub-committees.

The Commission has been described as 'the first truly autonomous Imperial Administrative Organization'. Common finan-

[1] Newfoundland was separately represented from 1917–49.

cial control was achieved by means of a fund which was formed to meet the general expenditure. In each year a demand is made upon the several Parliaments, and each Parliament votes its share by way of a grant to the Commission. The share or quota of each member country is based upon the proportion which the number of the graves of its dead bears to the total graves of the whole Commonwealth. The Commission reports, and accounts, to all the member countries directly and in the same terms.

An endowment fund of £6 million was completed in 1940. The income from this is being used to meet as far as possible the cost of maintenance in perpetuity of the 1914–18 cemeteries and memorials created by the Commission all over the world. The capital fund is vested in three trustees incorporated under Act of Parliament and the expenditure of the income is accounted for by the Commission on the general principles mentioned above.

IMPERIAL WAR MUSEUM
(Lambeth Road, London, S.E.1)

The Museum was founded by the War Cabinet in March 1917 and established by Act of Parliament in 1920 as a memorial of the effort and sacrifice made by the men and women of the Empire during the War of 1914–18, and to provide a record and a place for the study of that period. On the outbreak of the Second World War in 1939 the Trustees were authorized to collect exhibits and records of this war on similar lines.

The exhibition galleries contain specimens, models, weapons, uniforms, badges, and medals, and record the achievements of the three fighting services and the war effort and experience of the home front. A reference library contains the important books dealing with all aspects of the military, social, political, and economic history of the two wars, and files of service journals and other periodicals published during those periods. The photographic department contains all the official war photographs and the official cinematograph films of the two wars. Prints of the photographs may be purchased. The art department contains all the paintings, drawings, and sculpture produced by the official war artists and many other works by contemporary artists during the two wars. These are recognized as forming one of the most important collections in the country of British art of the period.

The High Commissioners for the Commonwealth countries are among the Trustees of the Museum.

The annual budget for 1950–1 was estimated at £29,821.

AGENCIES WHICH HAVE CEASED TO EXIST

The following agencies, described in the first issue of this handbook, have ceased to exist:

Empire Marketing Board. In 1926 the United Kingdom Government established the Empire Marketing Board, with a grant of £1 million per annum, for the purpose of financing schemes to promote the sale of Empire produce in the United Kingdom. It was estimated that this sum represented the equivalent cash value of the advantages which would have accrued to the Empire if the preferential duties promised by the United Kingdom Government at the Imperial Conference of 1923 had been carried into effect. As a result of the new fiscal policy adopted by the United Kingdom and its extension·of preferences to Empire products the original motive for the creation of the Board was removed, and it ceased its activities in 1933. Certain of its functions were transferred to the Imperial Economic Committee and others to the Executive Council of the Imperial Agricultural Bureaux, while some lapsed altogether.

Empire Timbers Committee. This committee was appointed in 1929 by the Department of Scientific and Industrial Research for testing Empire timbers. It consisted of representatives of the Dominions, technicians, and trade representatives. It was dissolved in 1934 by decision of the Department of Scientific and Industrial Research when the funds provided by the Empire Marketing Board for the testing of Empire timbers were exhausted.

The Oversea Mechanical Transport Council was established to conduct experiments in regard to the use of mechanical transport in undeveloped territories where the construction of a branch railway would not be economically justified. The Council was closed down in 1937.

UNCLASSIFIED 'AD HOC' CO-OPERATIVE AGENCIES
United Kingdom-Dominion Wool Disposals Limited

Origin and Functions

On the outbreak of war in 1939, agreements were made with the Australian and New Zealand Governments for the purchase of their exportable surpluses of wool for the period of the war and one wool year thereafter. These agreements were made in the light of the experience of the last war, their purpose being to ensure to the United Kingdom and its Allies supplies of wool required for military and civilian purposes at reasonable prices, and to the wool-producing Commonwealth countries concerned a stable market for their wool under war conditions. In August 1940 an agreement on similar lines was made with the Government of the Union of South Africa.

It was not expected originally that any burdensome surplus would be left in the hands of the United Kingdom at the end of the war, having regard to the military requirements of France and Britain. But the long duration of the war, the disappearance of important continental markets from 1940 to 1945, and the reduction of civilian wool consumption in the United Kingdom, increased the size of the accumulated stocks and accentuated the marketing problem.

At the end of June 1945 the stocks owned by the United Kingdom amounted to about 3,250 million pounds, the cost of which was about £170 million.

It was evident that the disposal of a stock of wool of this magnitude together with the annual wool clips of the Commonwealth countries created a serious marketing problem. The four Governments therefore agreed that a Conference at the official and expert level should be held to examine the situation and make recommendations. The report and recommendations of this Conference, which met in London in April–May 1945, were accepted by the four Governments, and as a result the Joint Organization and its subsidiaries in Australia, New Zealand, and South Africa was set up in July 1946.[1]

The functions of this company were primarily to buy, hold, and sell wool as agent for the four Governments and generally to administer the scheme agreed upon between them. The operation of the scheme was to be reviewed by the four Governments at the end of five years.

In the event the disposal of the stocks handed over to the Joint Organization in 1945 has proved a somewhat easier task than was originally thought likely. World consumption of wool since 1945 has been consistently higher than the available new supplies from each season's clips and it is anticipated that the stocks of the Joint Organization will all have been sold by June 1951.

Organization

The United Kingdom-Dominion Wool Disposals Limited (Joint Organization) is a private limited company in which the shareholders are nominees of the respective Governments. Four shares are held by the United Kingdom Government, two by the Australian Government and one each by the New Zealand and

[1] Cmd. 6855.

Union Governments. The operations of the principal company in each of the Commonwealth countries are conducted by a subsidiary. These are: the Australian Wool Realization Commission, the New Zealand Wool Disposal Commission, and the South African Wool Disposals Organization. The directors consist of an independent chairman, appointed by the four Governments in agreement; four directors appointed by the United Kingdom Government, two by the Australian Government, and one each by the Governments of New Zealand and South Africa. In addition the chairmen of the three subsidiaries in Australia, New Zealand, and South Africa are *ex officio* directors of the principal company without additional voting power. Not more than two Australian directors, one New Zealand director, and one South African director may vote on any resolution.

The International Wool Textile Organization nominates representatives to form, with the addition of representatives from major consuming countries, a Committee to act in a consultative capacity to the Board of the company. Further, in order to facilitate and expand the consumption of wool, the Joint Organization maintains close contact with the appropriate bodies interested in such matters as the rehabilitation of the wool-textile industry in consuming countries.

Finance

The operating expenses arising from holding and selling the wool will be met half by the Joint Organization from the proceeds of sales, and half will be paid by the Governments of the three wool-producing Commonwealth countries primarily from a contributory charge on the industry on sales of new clip wool.

The ultimate balance of profit or loss arising from the transactions of the Joint Organization in the wool of any participating Commonwealth country was to be shared equally between the United Kingdom and the Government of the other Commonwealth country concerned.

United Kingdom–Canada Continuing Committee on Trade and Economic Affairs

This Committee was set up after a visit by Sir Stafford Cripps, Chancellor of the Exchequer in the United Kingdom, to Ottawa in September 1948 for consultation with Canadian Cabinet Ministers. In an announcement on 10 October, it was stated that

it had been agreed to recommend to the two Governments the establishment of a Continuing Committee of representatives of the two countries. The Committee will meet periodically, consult together and report to their respective Governments on commercial and economic matters of mutual concern and especially on measures which both countries might take to ensure the greatest possible trade between them. In the course of further discussions, the two Governments have agreed that the Committee will meet alternately in Ottawa and London. The functions of the Committee will, of course, be purely advisory to the Governments.

The Committee held its first meeting in London on 25 January 1949 under the chairmanship of the High Commissioner for Canada. The other Canadian representatives were: the Deputy Minister for Trade and Commerce, the Deputy Minister for Agriculture, and the Director of International Economic Relations, Department of Finance. The United Kingdom representatives were: the Permanent Secretary to the Board of Trade, the Permanent Secretary to the Commonwealth Relations Office, the Second Secretary for Overseas Finance in the Treasury, and the Permanent Secretary to the Ministry of Food.

CHAPTER VIII

STANDING MACHINERY OF COMMUNICATION

THE machinery of communication between the Member nations of the Commonwealth has developed over many years, but its main period of growth has been in the last quarter of a century. The principle governing its development is, in the words of the Balfour Committee's report to the 1926 Imperial Conference, that 'equality of status so far as Great Britain and the Dominions are concerned is . . . the root principle governing our inter-Imperial relations'. This principle has dictated the forms of Commonwealth machinery, in that the function of executive action agreed as the result of communication rests with the Governments of the Member countries and not with the machinery except in so far as Governments by express decision may choose to delegate some small part of their executive power to this or that accepted agency when convenient for the carrying out of a line of policy on which the Cabinets have reached agreement. Secondly, the growth of the power of the Dominions has been reflected in the growth both of Commonwealth machinery for communication and consultation and of the share of the Dominions in it. In 1926 it was true that equality of status did not mean equality of stature; since then, the growth of Commonwealth machinery has reflected the increasing approximation between the two.

Commonwealth machinery does not lend itself to tidy classification. It may be classified by subject-matter: but foreign policy, defence, and economic questions, for instance, are not the exclusive concern of separate agencies. Or it may be classified as machinery for consultation and machinery for communication: but one body or official may have both functions. Again, it may be classified by the status of the participants: whether politicians or officials (including, in the latter, officers of the services). This third classification does roughly correspond to the division between standing and other machinery—between, for example, the intermittent machinery of Imperial Conferences or Commonwealth Prime Ministers' meetings on the one hand, and High Commissioners' Offices or Commonwealth committees on special subjects on the other.

The 'intermittent' machinery is dealt with in the sections of Imperial Conferences, Prime Ministers' meetings, international conferences and organizations, and regional bodies (although, strictly speaking, the last may be 'standing' in a number of cases). More permanent machinery which is also more readily classifiable by subject-matter (such as scientific liaison or defence) may be found under 'Defence' and 'Miscellaneous Official Organs for Co-operation'. There remains a number of channels of communication and consultation which may be classified as 'standing', although some are used more intermittently and others very regularly. The more regular forms tend to be at the official level.

The first of these channels is direct communication between Prime Ministers. The arrangement that Prime Ministers should communicate directly with one another was made in 1918. It was the first modification of the old system of communication effected and was established in consideration of the view of Dominion Governments that their channel of communication with the United Kingdom should be more direct than previously.

The Imperial War Conference of 1918 invited the Imperial War Cabinet to consider this question, and as a result the Cabinet passed the following resolutions (30 July 1918):

(1) The Prime Ministers of the Dominions, as members of the Imperial War Cabinet, have the right of direct communication with the Prime Minister of the United Kingdom, and *vice versa*.
(2) Such communications should be confined to matters of Cabinet importance. The Prime Ministers themselves are judges of such questions.
(3) Telegraphic communications[1] between the Prime Ministers should, as a rule, be conducted through the Colonial Office machinery, but this will not exclude the addition of more direct means of communication in exceptional circumstances.[2]

In fact, this system has proved of less importance than was anticipated when it was established, despite the development of long-distance telephones; in practice, the usual means employed is communication by cable. In view of the accepted principle of Cabinet responsibility, this form of communication usually amounts, in practice, to consultations between Cabinets; but there are exceptions. For instance, between 27 November and 1 December 1936, Mr Baldwin requested the Dominion Prime Ministers to advise him of their views, and their assessment of public opinion in their countries, on the question of King Edward VIII's wish to marry Mrs Simpson, and the Prime Ministers of Australia, South Africa, and Canada replied without prior consultation with their Cabinets. About 5 December, Mr Baldwin suggested that the Dominion Governments might wish

---

[1] Communications can now also be made by telephone.
[2] Cd. 9177, p. 165.

formally to advise His Majesty direct; and the Cabinets of the same three countries then did so.[1]

The bulk of daily communications is between the Commonwealth Relations Office in London and the Departments of External Affairs in the Dominions. In the case of Canada, the High Commissioners have, of recent years, acted increasingly as intermediaries. Intercommunication between the Dominion Departments of External Affairs, while the same in principle, is far less in quantity. Lord Bruce of Melbourne estimated that the outward flow from London represented over 90 per cent of the total. As long as the Dominions had very few missions abroad, while the United Kingdom was represented in every capital, this was inevitable; but with increasing Dominion representation abroad, the pattern is being modified and the contribution of the Dominions is increasing.

Every day the Commonwealth Relations Office issues 'sheaves of telegrams'[2] to the other Commonwealth countries. In the special case of foreign policy, the Commonwealth Relations Office works in close association with a department of the Foreign Office known as the 'Commonwealth Liaison Department'. This department, which has access to virtually all the material which passes through the Foreign Office, is responsible for ensuring that the Commonwealth Relations Office is supplied with all the material necessary to enable it to keep the Commonwealth Governments fully informed on all aspects of foreign affairs, either direct or through the United Kingdom High Commissioners in Commonwealth capitals.

Much of this material, especially in relation to foreign affairs, is for background information rather than for action or comment. It is the general practice of the United Kingdom Government to keep other Members of the Commonwealth fully and continuously informed of all matters which the United Kingdom Government are called upon to decide but which may affect Commonwealth interests. The object is to give them an opportunity of expressing their views in confidence, if they so desire. These views are fully taken into account, but the decision must rest with the United Kingdom Government. The other Governments are not asked to share responsibility for it, and are not regarded as sharing the responsibility, even if they have expressed their agreement with the United Kingdom Government's course

---

[1] For details, see the Appendix to vol. I of Professor W. Hancock's *Survey of British Commonwealth Affairs*, especially pp. 624–5.

[2] Lord Cranborne's phrase, in a speech of 19 February 1945, quoted in *British Commonwealth Relations Conference*, 1945, ed. by R. Frost (London, Oxford University Press for the Royal Institute of International Affairs, 1947).

of action. The same applies in cases where the decision as to any course of action is that of one of the other Governments.

In some cases, where the matter is of special concern to one or more of the other Governments, their comments are specifically invited and, if the matter were one which in any way involved action or responsibility of the other Governments, they would be formally consulted. The general principles and practice in this matter have been described in reports of successive meetings of the Imperial Conference and by the Prime Minister of the United Kingdom in the debate upon the revision of the Anglo-Egyptian Treaty in 1946.[1]

The exchange of written information is supplemented by personal contacts. These are mainly between the High Commissioners (and their staffs) and the Departments of State in the Dominion capitals and London. Thus, in London, the Commonwealth High Commissioners meet fortnightly with the Secretary of State for Commonwealth Relations and a Minister representing the Foreign Service on foreign affairs. During the War of 1939–45, the Secretary of State met the High Commissioners in this way virtually every day. Now the regular fortnightly meetings are supplemented by additional *ad hoc* meetings arranged as required, attended by the Secretary of State for Commonwealth Relations and such other Ministers as the nature of the business recommends. The High Commissioners may also consult individually with United Kingdom Ministers between meetings if they desire. It was agreed at the Commonwealth Prime Ministers' meeting of October 1948 that the High Commissioners and their staffs in London should have the right of direct access to the Secretary of State for Foreign Affairs and to Foreign Office officials.

The organization of High Commissioners' Offices includes such sections or officials with specialized knowledge as may be required. These specialized officials are in frequent touch with the appropriate Departments of State in the capital to which they are posted, and form an additional line of personal contact. As a result of the now general exchange of High Commissioners between all Commonwealth countries, there is a more or less parallel system of contacts in all the capitals. In the Dominion capitals, the High Commissioners and their staffs form the principal channel of intercommunication; in London, the system is rather more complex. In the past it was difficult to define precisely the office of High Commissioner; now, his functions are virtually ambassadorial, and this was recognized in 1948 by an alteration in formal diplomatic precedence.

[1] *Hansard* (Commons), vol. 423, cols. 789–90.

As described in the section on defence, below, the disappearance of the Committee of Imperial Defence emphasized the need for developing alternative channels of communication, and a system of defence liaison officers was suggested at the 1948 Commonwealth Prime Ministers' meeting. A number of these liaison officers, generally Service personnel with the equivalent rank of Brigadier, has been appointed. This channel of personal contact is mainly for the exchange of technical information, an exchange which is now highly organized. It is supplemented by exchanges and visits of General Staff personnel and technical specialists, by Dominion officers taking courses at the Imperial Defence College, by the seconding of officers to courses and manœuvres overseas, etc. The long-standing Commonwealth practice of promoting identity of training manuals, standardization of weapons, etc., facilitates these exchanges.

The Status of High Commissioners

The position of High Commissioners was discussed at the Commonwealth Prime Ministers' Conference held in London in October 1948. There was general agreement that some modification was needed and that Commonwealth representatives should acquire a status and precedence equivalent to that of ambassadors, although under an appropriate designation. A committee was set up to make proposals. It was announced very shortly afterwards (23 October 1948) that precedence among High Commissioners would be ruled according to the date of appointment, and not, as formerly, that the High Commissioner for the United Kingdom should take precedence in Dominion capitals, while in London the High Commissioner for Canada should do the same.

The further results of the committee's work were embodied in a notice in the *London Gazette* of 24 December 1948, in which the King directed

that on all ceremonial occasions the High Commissioners in the United Kingdom for Canada, Australia, New Zealand, the Union of South Africa, Eire, India, Pakistan, and Ceylon, together with Ambassadors of Foreign States, should rank immediately after the Lord Privy Seal in a common order of seniority based on their respective dates of arrival in the United Kingdom for the purpose of assuming their official duties and that the High Commissioners be accorded the style of 'Excellency'.

The position of the High Commissioner of a Commonwealth country in relation to a Minister of the Crown visiting the United Kingdom from that country will remain unaltered; and a Minister of the Crown from a Commonwealth country visiting the United Kingdom will normally be given precedence before the High Commissioner of that country.

M

During December the Governments of Canada, India, South Africa, Australia, and New Zealand also announced an alteration in the precedence of High Commissioners when they decided that High Commissioners of Commonwealth countries in their capitals should rank with ambassadors according to the date of their arrival there. They would rank among themselves according to the date of their arrival and not, as formerly, according to the seniority of Commonwealth countries. Similar action has since been taken by Pakistan and Ceylon.

The Commonwealth Relations Office

In 1907 a special Dominions Division of the Colonial Office was formed following on the expression of views by certain Dominion statesmen who favoured some modification in the organization of the Colonial Office in recognition of the constitutional and political developments within the Dominions which differentiated them from the Crown Colonies. By 1925 the Government of the United Kingdom had ascertained that the ideas of establishing a separate Dominions Office and of creating a new Secretaryship of State were acceptable to the Dominion Governments. In announcing this change the Prime Minister (Mr Baldwin) said in answer to a question in the House of Commons on 11 June 1925:

The Government have come to the conclusion that the existing organization of the Colonial Office is no longer in correspondence with the actual constitutional position in the Empire, and is inadequate to the extent and variety of the work thrown upon it. It fails, more particularly, to give sufficiently clear recognition to the profound difference between the work of communication and consultation with the self-governing partner nations of the British Commonwealth and the administrative work of controlling and developing the Colonies and Protectorates for whose welfare this House is directly responsible. The following changes are, therefore, proposed:
(1) The conduct of affairs with the Dominions will be under a separate new Secretaryship of State for Dominion Affairs, with its own Parliamentary Under-Secretary of State, who will also act as Chairman of the Oversea Settlement Committee, and Permanent Under-Secretary of State.
(2) For reasons of practical convenience, the new Secretaryship of State will continue to be vested in the same person as the holder of the Secretaryship of State for Colonies, and the Department of Dominion Affairs will continue to be housed in the Colonial Office.[1]

This arrangement continued until 1930, when Dominion

[1] *Hansard* (Commons), vol. 184, col. 2239.

affairs became the entire charge of a principal Secretary of State.

By 1947 it was felt that a change of title was necessary, for reasons which were stated by the Prime Minister (Mr Attlee) in the House of Commons on 2 July 1947. He said:

> It has for some time past been clear that in certain quarters, both here and oversea, the view has been taken that the titles of the Secretary of State for Dominion Affairs and the Dominions Office are no longer entirely appropriate, and are liable to convey a misleading impression of the relations between the United Kingdom and the other members of the Commonwealth. His Majesty's Government in the United Kingdom have accordingly reached the conclusion that it is desirable that these titles should now be changed, and steps are accordingly being taken for the issue of an Order in Council . . . to alter the titles to Secretary for Commonwealth Relations and Commonwealth Relations Office respectively.[1]

As from 15 August 1947 (the date of the coming into force of the Indian Independence Act) the Secretary of State for Commonwealth Relations assumed responsibility for relations with the new Dominions of India and Pakistan, and as from 4 February 1948 (the date of Ceylon's independence) for relations with the Dominion of Ceylon. After the passage of the Newfoundland Act, 1933, and the consequent issue of Letters Patent establishing Government by Commission, the Governor of Newfoundland in Commission was responsible to the Secretary of State, and, through him, to Parliament at Westminster. The Commonwealth Relations Office was responsible for the correspondence concerning Newfoundland from the time of the establishment of Government by Commission until 1 April 1949, when Newfoundland became a Province of the Dominion of Canada. The South African High Commission territories are under the control of the United Kingdom Government, and come administratively under the Commonwealth Relations Office.[2] The Office has continued (1951) to be the Department responsible for relations with the Republic of Ireland.

Functions

The Commonwealth Relations Office is the Department concerned with the relations of the United Kingdom Government with Commonwealth countries, and its functions are of a diplomatic, rather than an administrative, character. It acts as a channel for negotiation, and for the exchange of views and of information with the Commonwealth countries. In the debate on the creation of the separate Secretaryship of State for Dominion

---

[1] ibid. vol. 439, col. 1320.
[2] For details of the High Commission territories, see below, pp. 177–8.

Affairs in the House of Commons on 27 July 1925, Mr Walter Runciman called it 'a Foreign Office with a family feeling'.[1]

The Overseas Settlement Department of the Dominions Office was concerned with carrying out the emigration policy embodied in the Empire Settlement Act, 1922. In 1935, as a result of recommendations made by the Inter-Departmental Committee on Migration Policy,[2] the Overseas Settlement Board, a small official, policy-making body, was appointed to prepare migration schemes. Both the Department and the Board have now lapsed and migration is dealt with by the Commonwealth Relations Office. It is assisted by the Society for the Oversea Settlement of British Women, which acts in migration matters as the Women's Branch of the Commonwealth Relations Office.[3]

Organization

Besides a Secretary of State and a Parliamentary Under-Secretary of State the Commonwealth Relations Office has a Permanent Under-Secretary of State, a Deputy Under-Secretary of State and five Assistant Under-Secretaries of State.

The work and staff of the office are organized into five divisions each consisting of two or more departments under Assistant Secretaries. These divisions are: (1) Establishment and Organization Division; (2) Finance and General Division; (3) Foreign Affairs Division; (4) Economic Division; (5) Constitutional and Political Division. Each division is under the charge of an Assistant Under-Secretary of State.

The Commonwealth Liaison Department of the Foreign Office

The functions of this department of the Foreign Office have been described on p. 167 above.

The Information and External Relations Department of the Ministry of Education

This branch advises on the selection of teachers for appointments overseas, arranges for the secondment of teachers for overseas services, for periods of 3 to 5 years, and for the exchange of teachers between the United Kingdom and overseas, thus linking both the teachers and the schools; it arranges for overseas teachers to visit educational establishments in this country and its experts are available to co-operate with and act in an advisory capacity to any Dominion or Colony seeking guidance in educational matters. Guidance is also given to those in the United

---

[1] *Hansard* (Commons), vol. 187, col. 65 ff.
[3] Cmd. 4689.
[3] *Commonwealth Relations Office List*, 1951 (London, H.M.S.O.) p. 34.

Kingdom teaching Empire subjects by the preparation and circulation of bibliographies.

Board of Trade; Commercial Relations and Exports Department

The Commercial Relations and Exports Department of the Board of Trade supplies information to United Kingdom manufacturers who are interested in exporting their goods overseas, whether to foreign countries or to the Commonwealth. In this work the Division is served by a network of official representatives, who are stationed in the important centres of industry and commerce abroad. In the Commonwealth the representatives are the Trade Commissioners, appointed by the Board of Trade.

The Trade Commissioner Service is an important source of local information for the Board of Trade and, through that department, for United Kingdom manufacturers and exporters about opportunities for furthering United Kingdom trade in the Commonwealth countries, including the Colonies. Apart from providing assistance in individual cases, Trade Commissioners are responsible for furnishing general information about local economic, industrial, and commercial conditions, such as shipping and banking facilities, labour disputes, rates of wages, cost of living, customs tariffs, development of local industry, opportunities to tender, new openings for United Kingdom trade, etc.

In addition, the Senior Trade Commissioners, and the Trade Commissioner at Colombo, act as Economic Advisers to United Kingdom High Commissioners. The Trade Commissioner at Dublin acted as Economic Adviser to the United Kingdom Representative in Eire.

The Division was formerly a division of the Department of Overseas Trade and was carried over to the Export Promotion Department of the Board of Trade in 1946 when that department took the place of the Department of Overseas Trade. The Export Promotion Department and the Commercial Relations and Treaties Department were merged in 1948 to form the Commercial Relations and Exports Department.

High Commissioners for the United Kingdom

The express assimilation, by the declaration of the 1926 Imperial Conference, of the position of the Governor-General in a Dominion to that of His Majesty in the United Kingdom left His Majesty's Government in the United Kingdom without any formal agency in the Dominions; for it was made clear by the discussions at the Conference that in future the Governor-General should be solely the representative of the King and not in any respect an agent of the United Kingdom Government or of any

Department of State. The Inter-Imperial Relations Committee of the Conference (the 'Balfour Committee') drew attention to the gap thus created in the machinery of inter-Commonwealth consultation in its report:

We reviewed the position now reached . . . with special reference to the desirability of arranging that closer personal touch be established between Great Britain and the Dominions, and the Dominions *inter se*. . . . A special aspect of the question of consultation which we considered was that concerning the representation of Great Britain in the Dominions. By reason of his constitutional position as explained in Section IV (*b*) of this Report, the Governor-General is no longer the representative of His Majesty's Government in Great Britain. There is no one, therefore, in the Dominion capitals in a position to represent with authority the views of His Majesty's Government in Great Britain.

We summed up our conclusions in the following resolution, which is submitted for the consideration of the Conference:

The Governments represented at the Imperial Conference are impressed with the desirability of developing a system of personal contact, both in London and in the Dominion capitals, to supplement the present system of inter-communication and the reciprocal supply of information on affairs requiring joint consideration. The manner in which any new system is to be worked out is a matter for consideration and settlement between His Majesty's Governments in Great Britain and the Dominions, with due regard to the circumstances of each particular part of the Empire, it being understood that any new arrangements should be supplementary to, and not in replacement of, the system of direct communication from Government to Government and the special arrangements which have been in force since 1918 for communications between Prime Ministers.[1]

To fill the gap, the United Kingdom Government adapted the system of High Commissioners which had long been employed by certain of the Dominions for their representation in London.[2] The functions formerly exercised by the Governor-General in his character as representative of the United Kingdom Government were transferred to a High Commissioner for the United Kingdom. On the initiation of the system by an appointment to Canada, Mr L. S. Amery, then Secretary of State for Dominion Affairs, stated on 21 May 1928 that it was not at present possible to define the functions of the High Commissioner in detail, but that their general character was indicated in the Balfour Report.[3] In fact the functions of the office have developed into something very similar to, and certainly no less responsible than, the tasks per-

[1] Cmd. 2768, p. 27.
[2] By Canada since 1880.
[3] *Hansard* (Commons), vol. 217, col. 1500.

formed by ambassadors and their commercial counsellors in foreign States.

The High Commissioners are under the authority of the Secretary of State for Commonwealth Relations. As in the case of Dominion High Commissioners in London, their position is not assimilated to that of representatives of foreign countries to the degree of according them diplomatic immunity; although their position—again like that of their Dominion[1] counterparts—in respect of exemption from general and local taxation is on the basis of placing them personally in a position not less favourable than that of foreign Heads of Missions. The alteration in precedence, which further assimilates the position of all High Commissioners to that of ambassadors, has already been described.

The High Commissioner in Canada for His Majesty's Government in the United Kingdom

This was the first High Commissioner's post to be established under the new conditions produced by the declarations of the 1926 Imperial Conference, and the first holder, Sir William Clark, took up his duties in September 1928. Speaking of the new office in the Canadian House of Commons on 28 May 1928 the Prime Minister of Canada said:

'I believe that the opportunity for personal conference with a representative of the British Government on many matters that arise between that Government and our own will prove an effective means of avoiding possibilities of misunderstanding that occur so frequently when communications are conducted in writing.'[2]

The High Commissioner's headquarters are at Ottawa.

The High Commissioner in the Commonwealth of Australia for His Majesty's Government in the United Kingdom

The creation of this post was announced in May 1931; pending an appointment, the existing United Kingdom migration representative would carry out the duties, with the title of United Kingdom Representative in the Commonwealth of Australia. This interim arrangement was continued during the period of financial stringency of the early nineteen-thirties, but it was announced in August 1935 that Sir Geoffrey Whiskard had been appointed High Commissioner and would take up his duties in September.

The High Commissioner's headquarters are at Canberra.

---

[1] Under Section 26 of the United Kingdom Finance Act, 1925, and by administrative action.
[2] *Journal of the Parliaments of the Empire*, vol. 9, no. 3 (July 1928) p. 654.

The High Commissioner in New Zealand for His Majesty's Government in the United Kingdom

The Government of New Zealand did not until 1939 fully implement the agreement reached at the Imperial Conference of 1926 limiting the functions of the Governor-General. The Governor-General of New Zealand was therefore the representative of His Majesty the King and the official channel of communication between the two governments. In 1928, however, arrangements were made to supplement the channels of consultation, particularly on foreign affairs. At the request of the Prime Minister of New Zealand, an officer from the Foreign Office in London was seconded for attachment to the Prime Minister's Department in Wellington for purposes of information and consultation.

New Zealand finally adopted the new system in 1939. In July 1938, it was announced that His Majesty's Government in the United Kingdom would appoint a High Commissioner in New Zealand and that Sir Harry Batterbee, the first holder of the post, would take up his duties early in 1939. The High Commissioner's headquarters are at Wellington.

The High Commissioner in the Union of South Africa for His Majesty's Government in the United Kingdom

In the Union of South Africa, the Governor-General had since 1910 been also the High Commissioner for South Africa, an office vested in him by separate Commission and which included, until 1923 and 1924 respectively, the discharge of certain functions in regard to Southern and Northern Rhodesia, as well as the administration of Basutoland, Bechuanaland Protectorate, and Swaziland.[1] After the limitation of the Governor-General's functions in 1926, therefore, there was a double set of duties to be reallocated. Arrangements were made from 1927 until 1930 by which the Imperial Secretary to the Office of High Commissioner for South Africa acted as a supplementary channel of communication between His Majesty's Government in the United Kingdom and the Union. On 21 November 1930 the office of High Commissioner in the Union for the United Kingdom was established, its first holder being Sir Herbert Stanley; and the duties of the High Commissioner for South Africa in regard to the three native territories were discharged by the officer appointed to the new post. Although still held by one officer, the two High Commissionerships remain distinct. The holder is appointed to what has, since 1934, been entitled the High Commissionership for Basutoland, the Bechuanaland Protectorate, and Swaziland by His

[1] See under following sub-head.

Majesty's Commission; to the High Commissionership in the Union of South Africa by letter from the Secretary of State for Commonwealth Relations. The two offices have different precedence, uniform, and staffs. The emoluments for both are provided under the vote for the High Commissioner for the United Kingdom in the Union.

His Majesty's High Commissioner in Basutoland, the Bechuanaland Protectorate, and Swaziland

This office was vested, by separate Commission, in the Governors-General of the Union of South Africa from 1910 to 1930. The title of the post was then 'High Commissioner for South Africa', and derived historically from a Commission vested in the Governor of Cape Colony in 1846. In 1930 His Majesty's Government established the post of High Commissioner for the United Kingdom in the Union of South Africa, and its holder also held the older Commission. By Order-in-Council of 20 December 1934, which came into operation on 7 January 1935, the title 'High Commissioner for South Africa' was changed to 'High Commissioner for Basutoland, the Bechuanaland Protectorate, and Swaziland'. Prior to the grant of responsible government to the colony in October 1923, the duties of the office included the exercise of certain powers over the administration of Southern Rhodesia, and until 1937 certain powers and functions in respect of native administration there still attached to the High Commissionership; the latter were terminated in that year by the Southern Rhodesia Constitution (Amendment) Letters Patent. Functions in regard to Northern Rhodesia which were exercised by the High Commissioner lapsed on the appointment of the first Governor in April 1924, when the British South Africa Company's administration was transferred to the Crown.

His Majesty's High Commissioner conducts the administration of Basutoland, Swaziland, and the Bechuanaland Protectorate through Resident Commissioners. He legislates by proclamation, and is responsible to the Secretary of State for Commonwealth Relations. In Basutoland there is an annual session of the Native National Council, a body of an advisory character. There is also a Native Advisory Council in the Bechuanaland Protectorate. In addition to native courts there are High Courts in each territory, whence certain appeals lie to the Judicial Committee of the Privy Council. The territories are under the control of the United Kingdom Government, and members of the civil services of the territories are recruited in the same way as for the British Colonial Service. Under a dormant commission, the Judge of the High Court of the territories, or in his absence the Chief Secretary in the High Commissioner's Office, discharges the functions of the High Commissioner for the territories if the holder of the office is on leave.

High Commissioners for the United Kingdom in India, Pakistan, and Ceylon

By the time when the Union of India, Pakistan, and Ceylon attained full Dominion status, all the previously existing Dominions had accepted the appointment of High Commissioners from the United Kingdom, and in no case did any relic of the system by which the Governor-General acted as a channel of inter-Governmental communication survive (New Zealand, as has been mentioned above, having been the last Dominion to use any part of the older practice). The appointment of High Commissioners to the new Asian Dominions was therefore automatic.

Union of India. The appointment of a United Kingdom High Commissioner to this Dominion actually preceded the effective date of the Indian Independence Act, Sir Terence Shone having been appointed in 1946. His tenure of the post was continued after 15 August 1947 until November 1948, when he was succeeded by Lieutenant-General Sir Archibald Nye.

The High Commissioner's headquarters are at Delhi, and there are branch offices at Bombay, Calcutta, and Madras.

Pakistan. The appointment of Sir Laurence Grafftey-Smith as the first United Kingdom High Commissioner to Pakistan was announced on 21 July 1947, to become effective on 15 August. Headquarters are at Karachi, and Deputy High Commissioners are in charge of branches at Lahore, Dacca, and Peshawar.

Ceylon. The Commonwealth Relations Office announced on 11 December 1947 the appointment of Mr W. C. Hankinson as first United Kingdom High Commissioner in Ceylon. The Maldive Islands, a Sultanate under the protection of His Majesty and in special relations with the United Kingdom Government, conducts these relations through the High Commissioner.

United Kingdom Representative to Eire

No post corresponding to the High Commissionerships for the United Kingdom established in the other Dominions was created after 1926 in the Irish Free State, with which relations were conducted direct. But in September 1939, to meet the special problems created by the war, the United Kingdom Government and the Government of Eire agreed that the usual channels of communication should be supplemented by the appointment of a

United Kingdom Representative to Eire. Sir John Maffey (afterwards Lord Rugby) was the first holder of the post, and was succeeded early in 1949 by Sir Gilbert Laithwaite.

Following the transition of Eire to statutory Republican status, it was announced on 24 July 1950 that the title of the United Kingdom's representative would be altered to ambassador.

Dominion High Commissioners in London and Interchange of High Commissioners Between the Dominions
Some information will be found below, in the accounts of the Dominion Departments of External Affairs.

CANADA

Department of External Affairs
Up to 1909 Canada's negotiations with foreign Powers on such matters as trade and boundaries were conducted through the British Foreign Office, with Canadian Ministers or officials taking part on occasion.[1] Dealings with other parts of the Empire proceeded through the Colonial Office.

By 1909 it had become evident that a single office for receiving and examining all communications from other countries was a practical necessity, because confusion was resulting from the use of various different channels of communication with the Canadian Government. The Department of External Affairs was therefore established in that year. It was attached to the office of the Secretary of State, but in 1912 the new department was given a Minister of its own, when the Secretaryship of State for External Affairs was joined by statute to the office of Prime Minister. In 1946 the External Affairs Act was amended to enable any Minister of the Crown to be Secretary of State for External Affairs, and Mr St Laurent was then appointed to this office.

It was not until after the War of 1914–18 that Canada was fully recognized as a sovereign independent State when she obtained the right to separate signature of the Treaty of Versailles and separate membership of the League of Nations.[2] This development was opposed at the time in Canada by a section of opinion which feared that separate representation might impair imperial diplomatic unity. Nevertheless, Canada's representation abroad and her separate participation in international conferences was assured and expanded—slowly between the wars and rapidly during the War of 1939–45.

Organization. The Cabinet Minister responsible for the department is the Secretary of State for External Affairs. The adminis-

[1] See Chapter XIV, below.   [2] See Chapter XII, below.

trative head of the department is the Under-Secretary of State for External Affairs. He has two Assistant Under-Secretaries.

The department is organized in twelve divisions: the Administrative, American and Far Eastern, Commonwealth, Consular, Defence Liaison, Economic, European, Information, Legal, Personnel, Protocol, and United Nations. Department services such as Records, Communications (code and cipher), and Supplies form part of the Administrative Division, which is also concerned with finance. The Passport Office is a part of the Consular Division. The Library and the Clipping Service form part of the Information Division.

Appointment to the department is usually on the basis of an open competitive examination, publicly announced and conducted at intervals according to the need for new personnel. Qualifications include graduation from a university of recognized standing, and command of at least one modern language other than English or French is desirable. During the War of 1939–45, when both the department and its representation abroad were expanding rapidly, the problem of personnel was partly met by recruiting from the universities and elsewhere a number of temporary assistants.

Functions. The department is the central and directing part of the whole External Service. Questions of policy are decided by the Secretary of State for External Affairs and instructions conveyed to the various offices abroad. Among other things it is the duty of the department:

> (a) to carry on or supervise communications with other British and foreign governments,
>
> (b) to prepare material in connexion with international and Commonwealth conferences and to arrange for Canadian representation at such conferences,
>
> (c) to draft, so far as Canada is concerned, treaties and conventions, and
>
> (d) to deal with the International Joint Commission, set up under the Boundary Waters Treaty of 1909 with the United States, and other international tribunals.

These duties are carried out in co-operation with the other government departments interested in the question at issue: e.g. the Fisheries Department regarding the Sockeye Salmon Treaty, the Interior Department regarding Niagara Falls waterpower matters. Until recently the Department of External Affairs handled all requests of the Canadian Government to provide technical assistance to international agencies. With the expansion of the United Nations programme of technical assistance, and the launching of the 'Colombo Plan', such requests have very greatly increased. In January 1951 a Technical Assistance Service, situated in the Department of Trade and Commerce, began operations. Its purpose is to co-ordinate all Canadian participation in international and intra-Commonwealth technical assistance programmes, and to meet requests for assistance from other governments. Its director reports to an inter-departmental committee under the chairmanship of an officer of the Department of External Affairs.[1]

Representation in the United Nations

Canada is a member of the Economic and Social Council of the United Nations, and in 1946 was elected one of the six non-permanent members of the Security Council for a two-year term till 31 December 1949. Canada is also a member of the Atomic Energy Commission of the United Nations, established by the General Assembly in 1946. This Commission consisted of the eleven members of the Security Council, and Canada.

Canada has a Permanent Delegate to the United Nations, with headquarters in New York, and a Deputy Permanent Delegate with headquarters in Geneva.

Representation Abroad

The work of the department abroad is carried on by the embassies, legations, and other offices, which form an integral part of the department itself, being under its direction both as to policy and as to administration.

(i) In countries of the British Commonwealth. With the Federation of the Provinces of British North America in 1867, a new political entity which could not avail itself of the services of the provincial agents was brought into existence. To supplement the ordinary method of communication between the Canadian and United Kingdom Governments (which at that time was by correspondence between the Governor-General and the Secretary of State for the Colonies, and now is between the Secretary of State for External Affairs of Canada and the Secretary of State for Commonwealth Relations in Great Britain), the position of High Commissioner for Canada in London was created in 1880. (This office is more fully described below.)

On 10 September 1939, the day of the proclamation of war between Canada and Germany, it was announced that the Government would send High Commissioners to Australia, New Zealand, South Africa, and Eire; these appointments were designed to develop closer co-operation between the Members of the Commonwealth.

[1] *External Affairs Bulletin*, vol. 3, no. 1, p. 19. (Ottawa, King's Printer.)

The appointment of a High Commissioner to Newfoundland in July 1941 was a recognition of the strategic importance of Newfoundland for the defence of Canada. This office came to an end in 1949 when Newfoundland entered confederation with Canada.

In December 1946 Canada appointed its first High Commissioner to India.

(ii) *In Foreign Countries.* Canada's first diplomatic representation abroad was in Washington. During the War of 1914–18 a Canadian War Mission had been established in Washington to deal with the numerous problems of the war that affected the relations of the two countries. The success of this mission convinced Sir Robert Borden (then Prime Minister of Canada) that it would be in the best interests both of the United Kingdom and of Canada for the Canadian Government to have separate representation in Washington. Accordingly it was announced in 1920 that the King would appoint a Minister Plenipotentiary to the United States, acting under instructions from and reporting directly to the Canadian Government, but it was not until 1926 that an appointment was made, when the Hon. Vincent Massey was designated Envoy and Minister Plenipotentiary in Washington. In 1943 the Minister in Washington was elevated to the rank of ambassador.

In 1924 Dr W. A. Riddell was appointed to take charge of the Canadian Advisory Office established in Geneva, his duties being to keep the Government informed of developments in the League of Nations and the International Labour Organization and to represent Canada at international conferences. In 1938 the title was changed to Permanent Delegate to the League of Nations in accordance with the usual practice in Geneva. This office was maintained until the events of May 1940 necessitated the withdrawal of Canadian representation.

Canadian Ministers to France and to Japan were appointed in 1928 and 1929 respectively, and in 1939 there was an exchange of Ministers with Belgium and with the Netherlands. These last transferred to London in the spring of 1940, but the liberation of Brussels in 1944 made possible the re-establishment of the Canadian mission as an Embassy, and in 1945 the Canadian Legation in the Netherlands was reopened. With the object of encouraging the growing trade with Latin America and establishing direct channels of political intercourse with its leading states, the Government in 1941 set up legations (which shortly afterwards were designated embassies) in Brazil, Argentina, and Chile, and in 1944 embassies in Mexico and Peru.

In 1942 the increasing magnitude of Canada's war effort and the desire to emphasize the concept of the United Nations by gestures of co-operation resulted in unusually rapid expansion in the exchange of diplomatic missions. In November Ministers were appointed to the U.S.S.R. and to China, and in 1943 these missions were elevated to embassy rank on a reciprocal basis. The same policy also found expression in 1942 in the appointment of a Minister to the Allied Governments in exile in London of Belgium, the Netherlands, Czechoslovakia, Greece, Norway, Poland, and Yugoslavia.

Relations with the Vichy Government, which had been maintained since 1940, were terminated after the Allied Forces landed in North Africa in 1942, and the Minister to the Allied European Governments in London was then authorized to consult with representatives of the French National Committee in London on matters of mutual interest relating to the conduct of the war. Subsequently, when the French Committee established its headquarters in Algiers, the Minister was sent there with the personal rank of ambassador and he returned to Paris as ambassador in 1944.

The war with its imperative demands for improved representation in foreign countries was responsible for this large-scale development, within a very few years, of the Canadian diplomatic service. This growth is maintained and Canada is represented, in addition to those countries already mentioned, in Cuba, Denmark, Finland, Italy, Luxembourg, Sweden, Switzerland, and Turkey.

(*iii*) *In the Consular Service.* The emergence of a separate Canadian consular service has also been largely the product of the war. Hitherto consular duties were carried out either by trade commissioners or by British consuls and commercial representatives, under an arrangement with the United Kingdom Foreign Office. Canada's advancing status combined with new war-time needs led to the establishment of her first permanent consulate in 1943 in New York City. Consulates were later set up in Portland, Me., in Venezuela, and in Lisbon.

Temporary consulates were established in Greenland in 1940 and in St Pierre and Miquelon in 1941. Both were set up for defence reasons and for furthering transatlantic air navigation, and were not maintained after the war.

(*iv*) *In the War of* 1939–45. The very great number of joint committees for the co-ordination of the war effort led to increased duties in the London High Commissioner's office and to an even greater extent in the Canadian Legation in Washington. Representatives of departments other than the Department of External Affairs were attached to the Washington Legation to deal with special and urgent needs as they arose, and they served to relieve the diplomatic mission of the responsibility for handling matters for which the normal staff was not equipped. In London and Washington the Canadian Department of Munitions and Supply, for example, maintained its own mission, and with other non-diplomatic missions communicated directly with the responsible department in Canada without recourse to normal diplomatic channels. At the same time there was close and informal contact between these missions and their opposite numbers in London and Washington, and such direct contact frequently supplanted the more circuitous methods of normal inter-governmental communication.

The High Commissioner for Canada in the United Kingdom

The position of High Commissioner for Canada in the United Kingdom was created in 1880 to supplement the ordinary method of communication between the Canadian and United Kingdom Governments, which at that time was by correspondence between the Governor-General and the Secretary of State for the Colonies.

The duties of the office were defined as follows:

The High Commissioner shall
(a) act as representative and resident agent of Canada in Great Britain, and in that capacity execute such powers and perform such duties as are, from time to time, conferred upon and assigned to him by the Governor in Council;
(b) take the charge, supervision, and control of the immigration offices and agencies in Great Britain, under the Minister of Immigration and Colonization;
(c) carry out such instructions as he, from time to time, receives from the Governor in Council respecting the commercial, financial, and general interests of Canada in Great Britain and elsewhere.

Sir Alexander Galt was the first Canadian High Commissioner, holding office from 1880 to 1883. When Sir George Perley came to London as Canadian representative in 1914, his position was that of Acting High Commissioner and a member of the Canadian Government.[1] This position was maintained until 1917, when he ceased to be a member of the Canadian Government and was given the title of High Commissioner.

Before and during the War of 1914–18 the Canadian representative was relied upon more and more to handle important negotiations with the British Government on Canada's behalf,

---

[1] Statement by Sir Robert Borden on 9 April 1915 in the Canadian House of Commons. In 1916–17 Sir George Perley held, concurrently with the appointment of Acting High Commissioner, the post of Minister of the Overseas Military Forces. In 1917 Sir Edward Kemp was appointed to the latter post.

and became the most important link between the Governments, apart from direct contacts between the Prime Ministers. Speaking in 1927 Mr Mackenzie King noted that the post had been

from the outset in part diplomatic and in part commercial, at the very outset more commercial than diplomatic perhaps, but the number of questions of a quasi-diplomatic character have increased with the passage of years, especially during the war. To-day the British Government gladly concedes to our High Commissioner the right to call upon any Ministers of the Crown and interview him in regard to departmental matters of concern to our country without first going through the formality of being accredited by the Secretary of State for Dominion Affairs. As a consequence the position of High Commissioner has become increasingly significant as a diplomatic post, and within the empire between Canada and Great Britain his position does correspond to the position an ambassador would hold between nations.

This change of emphasis in the High Commissioner's duties is expressed in the revised statute of 1938, which says that the High Commissioner shall:

(a) act as representative and resident agent of Canada in the United Kingdom, and in that capacity, execute such powers and perform such duties as are, from time to time, conferred upon and assigned to him by the Governor in Council;

(b) carry out such instructions as he, from time to time, receives from the Secretary of State for External Affairs respecting the general interests of Canada in the United Kingdom;

(c) subject to the provisions of the preceding paragraphs, supervise the official activities of the various agencies of the Canadian Government in the United Kingdom.[1]

The High Commissioner, with his staff, performs duties for almost all departments of the Canadian Government and supervises the official activities of those departments in England, including the emigration and commercial agencies. He acts as the agent of the Canadian Government in its financial relations with the British and other Governments and with private firms. He handles requests and inquiries made by government departments in Ottawa and by business men and tourists in England, as well as by the Canadian community resident in England. He supplies information in answer to British official and private inquires concerning Canadian legislation, passports, naturalization, customs and special duties, sales and excise taxes, business conditions and opportunities in Canada, and so on. Through the Press Officer information is circulated to business houses, Chambers of Commerce, and other institutions.

[1] *Statutes of Canada*, 1938, 2 Geo. VI, c. 30.

N

The office reports to the Canadian Government on political and economic developments in the United Kingdom. It also provides Canadian representatives to international conferences and to meetings of intra-Commonwealth committees, such as the Imperial War Graves Commission, the Commonwealth Economic Committee, the Commonwealth Shipping Committee, etc.

Agents-General in the United Kingdom for Individual Provinces

The Provinces of Alberta, Ontario, British Columbia, and Saskatchewan adhere to the former practice of Provincial representation in London by Agents-General. These officials are appointed by the Legislatures of the Provinces under general authority given in the British North America Act, and act for the Provincial Governments in matters which, under the Canadian Constitution, are within their competence. Thus their duties are mainly of a business rather than a diplomatic nature.

AUSTRALIA

Department of External Affairs

A Department of External Affairs, the earliest of Dominion departments to bear that name, was set up in 1901, immediately after federation, to handle matters such as immigration, the administration of Papua, etc. It later became part of the Prime Minister's office, but was separated from that department in 1935–6, when the growing volume of work in connexion with international and League of Nations affairs made a separate department essential. Its functions include communications with Commonwealth and foreign diplomatic missions and consulates on political matters, foreign affairs, treaties and international agreements, etc. Since the Australian-New Zealand Agreement of 1944[1] the contact with the New Zealand Department of External Affairs has been particularly close. In order to discharge the provisions of the Agreement a small secretariat is maintained within each External Affairs Department. The Australian Department of External Affairs also carried out much of the preliminary work required for preparing the South Seas Conference and for setting up the South Pacific Commission.[2]

Australia was one of the original non-permanent members of the Security Council of the United Nations, her two-year term ending on 31 December 1947. She is also a member of the United Nations Economic Commission for Asia and the Far East. Since the United Nations adopted the trusteeship agreement for New

[1] See p. 381, below.   [2] See p. 384, below.

Guinea, Australia, which administers this trust territory, automatically became a member of the United Nations Trusteeship Council. Australia was elected a member of the Economic and Social Council of the United Nations for a three-year term, beginning on 1 January 1948. The department is responsible for all United Nations matters, and for representation at United Nations conferences. Australia is also responsible for the administration of Nauru Island, Papua and Norfolk Island, which are not trust territories. Until 1941 the Prime Minister's Department administered these territories, but in that year the Department of External Territories was created for this purpose.

In 1936 the Department of External Affairs started publication of a periodical on matters of international interest, entitled *Current Notes on International Affairs*. It was originally intended for the use of Members of Parliament, but is now circulated as well to institutions of many kinds interested in international affairs.

Organization. There is a Secretary of the Department of External Affairs (with two Assistant Secretaries), and an Administrative Secretary, who is in charge of the work of the department. Since 1943 the department has been organized on the basis of regional sections, dealing with the Far East and the Pacific, including the Australian-New Zealand secretariat; the British Commonwealth; Europe and the Middle East; and America. Other sections deal with United Nations matters, international economic problems, and with legal, administrative, and consular matters.

In January 1943 the Minister for External Affairs, Dr H. V. Evatt, announced the setting up of a diplomatic staff cadet system to train men and women for permanent appointment to the department and to posts abroad. Because of the growth of Australia's foreign interests, particularly in the Pacific area, and because of the growing number of diplomatic missions abroad the staff of the department had become seriously depleted. The new system was devised to enable selected candidates to enter upon a course of intensive study in preparation for work in the department or abroad. Applicants for this training must be British subjects aged not less than seventeen years, and are required to possess a general aptitude for understanding international affairs from the Australian aspect, a competent knowledge of a foreign language, and a capacity for English composition. Applicants are required to have at least one university degree. Women are eligible for appointment equally with men.

Representation Abroad

In 1924, when the question arose as to the policy to be adopted by Australia with regard to information and consultation relating to external affairs, the Commonwealth Government decided that they would not appoint diplomatic representatives abroad but would continue to obtain information and to conduct negotiations through the Foreign Office of the United Kingdom and the existing British diplomatic representatives. This necessitated a closer liaison between the Foreign Office and the Commonwealth Government, which was effected by the establishment of an External Affairs Branch in the High Commissioner's Office in London under the control of an officer of such standing as to enjoy the confidence of the Foreign Office. A League of Nations Officer in London was also appointed to look after League matters other than those of a political nature.

Although Australia now has several diplomatic missions abroad and no longer has the same need for the services of the Foreign Office, the Department of External Affairs is still represented by a Counsellor in the High Commissioner's Office, and for purposes of consultation on Commonwealth and foreign affairs he communicates, on behalf of the High Commissioner, direct with the Department of External Affairs. He has several assistants for political work.

The High Commissioner for the Commonwealth of Australia in the United Kingdom

The office of the High Commissioner of the Australian Commonwealth in the United Kingdom was created by the High Commissioner Act of the Federal Parliament in December 1909, and the first High Commissioner took up his duties in February 1910. In September 1932 the Rt Hon. S. M. Bruce, after attending the Imperial Conference at Ottawa, arrived in London and, in addition to his duties as Minister without portfolio, took over the powers and functions of the High Commissioner, pursuant to the provisions of the High Commissioner Act of 1932. The operation of this Act, by which a Minister might be authorized to exercise the powers of the High Commissioner, was limited to two years. It was not intended to make a permanent change in the status of the High Commissioner. The presence of a Minister in London was opportune for the conduct of important financial operations, but, upon their completion, Mr Bruce resigned from the Cabinet, and was appointed High Commissioner from 1933 for the usual term of five years. In 1945 Mr Beasley was appointed Resident Minister. He resigned from the Cabinet in 1946, and was then appointed High Commissioner for the usual five-year term.

The High Commissioner is assisted by a secretarial and technical staff under the control of the Deputy High Commissioner and Official Secretary. In addition, officers are appointed to assist the High Commissioner in matters relating to the Naval, Military and Air Forces of Australia, and these officers were required to keep in close touch with the Admiralty, War Office, and Air Ministry in the United Kingdom. On matters of routine they communicate directly with their departments in Australia.

Many of the departments of the Australian Government are now represented in London by senior officers who advise the High Commissioner and carry out administrative responsibilities on behalf of their departments, for example, Senior Trade Commissioner, Chief Migration Officer, Director of the News and Information Bureau, etc.

The functions of the High Commissioner may be summarized as follows:

(i) While the normal official channel of communication between the Commonwealth Government and the Government of the United Kingdom is through the Australian Minister for External Affairs to the Secretary of State for Commonwealth Relations, the services of the High Commissioner are constantly utilized in negotiations between those Governments, and the tendency is to increase this personal consultation.

(ii) The High Commissioner acts as Agent for the Commonwealth in negotiating loans and in arranging for their repayment, which is actually effected by the Commonwealth Bank.

(iii) The High Commissioner's Office gives information in answer to inquiries regarding Australian natural and industrial resources and Commonwealth matters generally, and provides information and advice to Australian business men who have trade relations with or contemplate opening up business with the United Kingdom.

(iv) It supplies the Commonwealth Government with reports regarding market conditions in the United Kingdom and generally assists in furthering the export business of Australia.

The experiment of appointing an officer of the Department of External Affairs in London attached to the High Commissioner's staff was fully justified and was extended, in 1937, by the appointment of an Australian Counsellor to the British Embassy in Washington.

On the outbreak of war in 1939 Canada appointed a High Commissioner to Canberra, and this was followed by a reciprocal appointment in March 1940 of an Australian High Commissioner to Canada. In 1943 High Commissioners were exchanged between Australia and New Zealand. Thereafter a rapid expansion took place, as Australian High Commissioners were appointed to India (1944), Eire (1946), Union of South Africa (1946), and Pakistan (1948). An Australian Commissioner was appointed to Ceylon in 1947 and his status was raised to that of High Commissioner in February 1948.

The first full diplomatic appointment by Australia was that of Australian Minister to Washington in 1940, and at the same time a United States Legation was established at Canberra. These appointments reflected the common interest of both countries in the problems of the Pacific and of East Asia. The new office was also concerned to a considerable extent with business arising from Australian war purchases in the United States.

The status of the Australian Legation in Washington and of the United States Legation in Canberra was changed to that of Embassy in 1946 (and in 1945 the Australian Government established Consulates-General in New York and San Francisco).

In an attempt to place Japanese-Australian relations on a firmer footing an Australian Minister was appointed to Tokyo in 1940. The Legation was closed on the outbreak of war in December 1941. A Political Observer was appointed in 1945 and an Australian Mission established in 1947. Since the establishment of the Allied Council for Japan in 1946, an Australian has represented the United Kingdom, India, and New Zealand, as well as Australia.

In addition to the above, representatives of Australia have been appointed to Brazil (Minister), Chile (Minister), China (Ambassador), France (Ambassador), Germany (Australian Military Mission), Malaya (Commissioner), the Netherlands (Minister), and the U.S.S.R. (Ambassador).

After the French collapse in June 1940 the population of New Caledonia favoured continuing in the war as an active ally of the British Commonwealth. In order to encourage the Colony and also with a view to solving the many difficult problems with which it was confronted, the Prime Minister of Australia offered to send a representative to New Caledonia. This offer was accepted and an Official Commonwealth Representative in the Colony arrived in August 1940, and remained there until the liberation of France. The status was changed to that of Consul in 1945. Australia is also represented by a Consul-General at Bangkok, Manila, and Batavia, and by a Consul at Dili, Timor.

Agents-General in the United Kingdom for the Individual States of the Commonwealth

When the office of High Commissioner for the Commonwealth was established in 1909, the framers of the Act expected that in due course the new office would eliminate the need for separate State representation in London.[1] This has not in fact happened, however, and the governments of six constituent States (New South Wales, South Australia, Tasmania, Victoria, Queensland, and Western Australia) are still separately represented in London.

NEW ZEALAND

Department of External Affairs

The External Affairs Act, 1919, as amended by the External Affairs Amendment Act, 1920, provided for the appointment of a Minister of External Affairs, a Secretary for External Affairs and a staff for the department. Its functions were limited to the administration of New Zealand's island territories. Foreign and imperial affairs were handled by the Prime Minister's Department and the Prime Minister was also Minister of External Affairs.

In 1926 the Imperial Affairs Section of the Prime Minister's Department was established to deal with the ever-increasing volume of work consequent on the recognition of New Zealand's international status, such as the responsibilities involved in New Zealand's membership of the League of Nations and her election to the Council of the League in 1936. In 1943 the existing Department of External Affairs was given a new name—Department of Island Territories—which more accurately described its functions, and a new Department (the present Department of External Affairs) was set up under the provisions of the External Affairs Act, 1943, to co-ordinate and conduct New Zealand's relations with the other Members of the Commonwealth, with foreign Governments, and with international organizations.

It is not possible to make a clear distinction between the Prime Minister's Department and the Department of External Affairs. Since the Prime Minister is also Minister of External Affairs the two departments are run as a unit. The Secretary of External Affairs is also the permanent head of the Prime Minister's Department; the Assistant Secretary is Secretary to the Cabinet and to the Council of Defence. The staff of the two departments is held in common, and, though some officers are engaged on work peculiar to one department, the work of the majority involves both. The staff has been deliberately kept small and built up

[1] See High Commissioner Act, 1909, Section 5.

slowly and carefully. Of the total staff of the Prime Minister's and External Affairs Departments fewer than twenty are actually engaged in working upon the problems of external affairs.

Functions. To ensure co-ordination in New Zealand's external relations the Department of External Affairs is used as the channel of communication between the New Zealand Government and overseas governments or organizations and between the Government and its diplomatic Ministers, High Commissioners, and Consuls overseas. The department is thus a clearing-house and co-ordinating centre for a wide range of material, which in certain cases is passed on for detailed action to other appropriate departments. The department ensures that New Zealand's representatives abroad are adequately informed of the Government's actions or expressed opinions upon questions of external affairs. During 1949–50 the department's work increased in volume and diversity, and, to meet this increase, its sections were regrouped as follows: Western Political (Europe, the Middle East, Africa, America); Eastern Political (the Far East, South and South-East Asia); Pacific (also covering Antarctica, and trusteeship questions); United Nations and International Organizations; and two small sections, Economic and Legal.[1]

The New Zealand Government and its representatives abroad participate fully in intra-Commonwealth consultation upon a wide range of topics, of which the most important are foreign policy, economic policy and defence policy. Particularly close are the ties with Australia, whose interests in external affairs are practically identical with those of New Zealand. The Australian-New Zealand agreement of January 1944 provided for the establishment of machinery for continuous consultation between the Governments on matters of mutual concern and this is furnished by secretariats in each country within their respective Departments of External Affairs.

As a result of the adoption by the United Nations of the trusteeship agreement for western Samoa, New Zealand, which administers this trust territory, automatically became a permanent member of the Trusteeship Council. New Zealand is also responsible, under Chapter XI of the United Nations Charter, for the administration of the non-self-governing territories of Tokelau and Cook Island. The Department of External Affairs and the Department of Island Territories work closely together.

In June 1946 New Zealand was elected a member of the Economic and Social Council of the United Nations for a three-year term, beginning on 1 January 1947. New Zealand is also a mem-

---

[1] New Zealand, Department of External Affairs, *Annual Report for the Year ended* 31 *March* 1950 (Wellington, Government Printer, 1950) p. 7.

ber of the United Nations Economic Commission for Asia and the Far East. For these and for other international organizations and conferences the department prepares material and arranges for representation.

Although certain duties connected with international civil aviation, formerly carried out by the Department of External Affairs, have been transferred to the Civil Aviation Branch of the Air Department, it still remains essential, in view of the considerable impact of international civil aviation on the political and economic life of New Zealand, for the External Affairs Department to maintain an active interest in this field and to keep a close watch on trends and developments.

Representation Abroad

Until 1942 New Zealand had no permanent representation abroad other than the High Commissioner in London. New Zealand's relations with foreign governments were conducted through the Foreign or Dominions Office or her own High Commissioner in London. From 1942 onwards, however, an increasing number of diplomatic appointments have been made, although up to the present New Zealand posts have been established only in Commonwealth countries and in countries which are situated in, or have important interests in, the Pacific area.

Office of the High Commissioner for New Zealand in the United Kingdom

The duties of the High Commissioner are to

(a) Act as representative of New Zealand in the United Kingdom and to exercise such powers and perform such duties as are conferred upon and assigned to him by the Governor-General.

(b) Carry out such instructions as he receives from the Government respecting the commercial and financial and general interests of New Zealand in the United Kingdom and elsewhere.

He is assisted in this work by the following: the Official Secretary, Private Secretary, Finance Officer, External Affairs Liaison Officer, Military Liaison Officer, Air Liaison Officer, and Naval Affairs Officer. The total staff of the office in 1948-9 was approximately 243.

The example of Australia was followed by New Zealand in 1937, when a New Zealand Liaison Officer for External Affairs was appointed to the High Commissioner's Office. The functions of this officer correspond to those of the Australian External Affairs Liaison Officer.

Close contact is maintained by the High Commissioner and the External Affairs Liaison Officer with the Foreign Office and the Commonwealth Relations Office. The Joint Service Liaison staff is an efficient link between Chiefs of Staff in New Zealand and the United Kingdom Ministry of Defence. The High Commissioner's Office also deals with a wide variety of inquiries from prospective emigrants and visitors. It includes an Information Section and a Publicity Branch.

The representatives of certain New Zealand Government Departments at the High Commissioner's Office—namely, the Industries and Commerce, Customs, Tourist and Health Resorts, Scientific and Industrial Research, Marketing, and Agricultural Departments—whose duties in London are carried out under the general supervision of the High Commissioner, are most valuable, both from the point of view of facilitating the conduct of business between commercial and governmental organizations in the United Kingdom and Departments in New Zealand, and that of releasing members of the High Commissioner's staff for other duties.

New Zealand High Commissioners were appointed to Canada and to Australia in 1943; both appointments were the result of war-time co-operation.

New Zealand's first representative in a foreign country was the Envoy Extraordinary and Minister Plenipotentiary appointed to Washington in 1942, and at the same time the United States established a legation at Wellington. The staff of the New Zealand legation in Washington had frequently to represent New Zealand at the many United Nations meetings in the United States, until in 1947 a permanent delegate to the United Nations was appointed (see below). In 1948 the New Zealand Legation in Washington was raised to the status of Embassy. New Zealand has Consulates-General in New York and San Francisco.

A New Zealand legation was established in the U.S.S.R. in 1944, and in 1945 Ministers came to New Zealand from the U.S.S.R. and from France, though in the latter case no reciprocal appointment could be made until 1950. The New Zealand legation in Moscow was closed in June 1950, owing to the financial difficulty created by the raising of the rate of rouble exchange. During 1947 three more diplomatic missions, from the Netherlands, Belgium, and Denmark,[1] came to New Zealand. The Governments of these countries accepted the position that certain material circumstances, including the need to assemble and train properly qualified staff, would prevent New Zealand from fol-

[1] The Minister from Denmark was accredited both to Australia and to New Zealand and had his headquarters and residence in Canberra.

lowing the normal practice of making the exchange of missions immediately reciprocal.

In February 1948 the office of the New Zealand delegation to the Economic and Social Council of the United Nations was merged into a newly constituted Permanent Delegation of New Zealand to the United Nations. The establishment of this Permanent Delegation brings New Zealand practice into line with that of almost all members of the United Nations. In view of the expansion of the work of the United Nations and its ramifications through the whole field of governmental activity it was essential to have at the seat of the organization a branch of the Department of External Affairs whose officers might keep in touch with the United Nations Secretariat and see that New Zealand was adequately supplied with United Nations documents and with information on the activities of the organization. The position of permanent delegate to the United Nations is at present held by the Ambassador at Washington and his staff consists of the Secretary-General, Second Secretary and two Third Secretaries.

SOUTH AFRICA

Department of External Affairs[1]

The Ministry of External Affairs was first constituted on 1 June 1927 and the first holder of the new office, the Hon. J. B. M. Hertzog, was also Prime Minister of the Union at the time. The Department of External Affairs is quickly expanding, with the growth of the Union's activity in intra-Commonwealth and international affairs.

Organization. In 1949 the personnel of the department consisted of: the Prime Minister and Minister of External Affairs; Secretary to the Prime Minister and Secretary for External Affairs; Under-Secretary to the Prime Minister and Under-Secretary for External Affairs.

The department operated in two divisions—the Political and Protocol Division and the Economic, Trade and General Division. Each division was in charge of a Counsellor.

The main difficulty that hampered expansion in the department and increased representation abroad was the shortage of trained personnel, which accounted for the fact that some Commonwealth and foreign countries represented in South Africa did not in turn receive representatives from South Africa. In order

---

[1] An account of the history and functions of the Department is given in Eric Rosenthal's pamphlet, *South African Diplomats Abroad* (South African Institute of International Affairs, 1949).

to meet this difficulty a scheme for cadet training was introduced in 1945. Candidates for this training were selected in the first instance from ex-service men wishing to enter the department. When this source of supply was exhausted preference was given to candidates with a university degree in law or economics. Candidates must be bi-lingual. They serve a probationary period of three years and if satisfactory are then permanently posted, either in the department or with a mission abroad.

Representation Abroad

The post of High Commissioner for the Union of South Africa in the United Kingdom was created by Act No. 3 of 1911, and its functions are divided broadly between political affairs, trade, publicity, and general administration. Principal sub-officers include: Secretary, Political Secretary, Senior Trade Commissioner and Commercial Adviser, Director of Information, Accountant. Service liaison officers are attached to the Office; and also an immigration adviser who is responsible direct to the Department of the Interior in South Africa.

The Office was established for the representation of the Government of the Union in the United Kingdom and to do service as an agency of the Union in London for financial, commercial, and other purposes.

On the outbreak of war in September 1939 Canada appointed High Commissioners in each of the Commonwealth countries, and in May 1940 the Union of South Africa appointed a High Commissioner to Canada.

On 26 July 1948 the Prime Minister, who is also Minister of External Affairs, announced a new appointment, that of Mr Charles te Water as Ambassador Extraordinary 'accredited to all governments which it, the Union Government, felt should be advised on the policy of the Union Government'. In speaking of his appointment Mr te Water said: 'I am charged with the duty of strengthening our relations with other governments and peoples and of inviting their understanding of our problems, of trying to resolve misapprehensions and misunderstandings regarding the policies of our Government, and of seeking their friendship.' The period of duration of the appointment was not announced, and the appointment has since lapsed.

In November 1948 the Prime Minister announced his intention of appointing ambassadors to several countries abroad and of promoting South Africa's representatives in Commonwealth countries to ambassadorial rank. In making this announcement he further said that 'this step will confirm the fact that South Africa has reached her full status of freedom and independence'.

During 1929 legations were established in the Netherlands, Italy, and the United States, and during 1934 in Germany, Sweden, France, Portugal, and Belgium. In the same year South Africa, like many States members, appointed an Accredited Representative to the League of Nations, with an office in Geneva, mainly concerned with matters arising from South Africa's position as Mandatory Power for South West Africa. This office was closed shortly after the outbreak of war in 1939. Since South Africa continued to administer South West Africa in the spirit of the mandate, the Union did not enter into a Trusteeship Agreement with the United Nations.

At the outbreak of war in 1939 the legations in Berlin and Rome were closed, and in 1940 the Union's diplomatic representatives in the Hague, Brussels, and Paris were transferred to London.

In 1948 the consulates-general in three South American countries, Argentina, Brazil, and Chile, were changed to legations. Legations were also established in 1948 in Egypt and Greece.

The Union appointed a permanent delegate to the United Nations with an office in New York, and there was a military mission in Germany. A Commissioner represented the Union in Nairobi.

The Soviet Union has had a Consulate-General in the Union for a number of years, but the Union has not so far established diplomatic representation in Moscow.

Consulates of the Union are established in New York, in Lourenço Marques, in Leopoldville and Elizabethville, and in Madagascar.

The following official statement on the precedence of High Commissioners was issued on 24 December 1948:

Changes in Diplomatic Representation
In pursuance of the recommendations which were adopted at the recent Commonwealth Conference in London, the Union Government have decided to accord High Commissioners the same precedence as ambassadors in the Union. The senior ambassador will, however, be recognized as the doyen of the Diplomatic Corps even though his period of service in the Union may be less than that of the senior High Commissioner.

Ambassadors will derive their seniority from the date on which they present their credentials to His Excellency the Governor-General. The seniority of High Commissioners will be determined by the date on which they are received by the Prime Minister.[1] The new arrangement came into force on 1 January 1949.

---

[1] *Weekly Newsletter* (Pretoria), 25 December 1948.

INDIA

Ministry of External Affairs and Commonwealth Relations
According to memoranda submitted to the Simon Commission
in 1930:

Before 1919 the Government in India were not permitted, with
certain exceptions, to communicate with authorities elsewhere otherwise than through the India Office. They now (1930) have greater
latitude, but the Secretary of State is still, generally speaking, the
prescribed channel for correspondence on important issues of policy
and for communications addressed to the League of Nations and the
International Labour Office, except those on routine matters or re-
ing to the supply of information.[1]

After the Government of India Act, 1919, India began to
exercise some of the national functions already exercised by the
self-governing Dominions. Like them, India had her own representatives in the Imperial War Cabinet and in the Imperial Conference during and after the War of 1914–18. Under the Act a
High Commissioner for India in the United Kingdom was appointed for the first time. India signed the Treaty of Versailles
and became a separate member of the League of Nations and the
International Labour Office. As one of the eight leading industrial
countries she obtained a permanent seat on the Council of the
I.L.O. and an Indian was elected Chairman of the Council in
1933.

Although in all these cases her representatives were appointed
by the Government of India or the Secretary of State for India,
and were not responsible to the Indian Legislature, the international footing thus accorded to India was a step in the direction
of India's full and equal partnership in the Commonwealth.

Up to 1937 the Foreign and Political Department of the
Government of India was directly under the Governor-General
and the personnel of the two sides was interchangeable. It dealt
with the Indian States on its political side under a Political Secretary, and on its foreign side with, in particular, India's relations
with adjacent countries and the tribal areas, under a Foreign
Secretary. The handling of questions arising from India's membership of the League of Nations and her relations with other
Members of the Commonwealth (and indeed in some respects
with foreign countries other than those adjacent to India) rested
with the departments of the Government of India responsible for
the subject matter, and was not canalized through the foreign side
of the Foreign and Political Department, which was not concerned

[1] Indian Statutory Commission, *Report* (Simon Report), vol. 5, p. 1647.

unless the question was directly political in character. For example, Indians overseas were dealt with in the Education, Health, and Lands Department; disarmament in the Defence Department; and commercial treaties in the Commerce Department.

On the coming into force in April 1937 of the Government of India Act, 1935, the organization was revised. The functions of the Foreign and Political Department were divided between the External Affairs Department (which was under the Governor-General) and the Crown Representative's Office, which dealt with the Indian States and was under the Viceroy in his capacity as Crown Representative.

The Department of Indians Overseas was created in 1941 when it ceased to be a division of the Department of Education, Health, and Lands, and became a separate department concerned with the regulation of emigration from India to other parts of the British Commonwealth, the interests of Indians in the Dominions and Colonies, the Pilgrimage, and repatriation. Its name was changed to the Department of Commonwealth Relations in 1944. The portfolio was not held by the Governor-General but by a member of his Council.

When the Interim Government was set up on 1 September 1946, Pandit Nehru took the portfolios of both the External Affairs Department and the Commonwealth Relations Department. The two departments were later amalgamated into one department, designated the Department of External Affairs and Commonwealth Relations, with effect from 1 June 1947. Each side of the new department retained its own Secretary.

At the transfer of power in August 1947, the new department was carried over unchanged, the only difference being that it was re-designated a Ministry. The Prime Minister, Pandit Nehru, continued to hold the portfolio, and a Secretary-General directly responsible to Pandit Nehru was put in charge of both parts of the department. The transfer of power very greatly increased the size and responsibilities of the department and at the same time there was a rapid growth in India's Foreign Service. In March 1949 the two wings were amalgamated into one Ministry, designated the Ministry of External Affairs.

On the partition of India the department was divided both as regards staff and records in the same way as other departments of the old Government of India; namely, the records were divided and those members of the staff who opted for Pakistan were transferred to the Government of Pakistan.

India and the United Nations

India was an original member of the United Nations and her

membership was not affected by the Indian Independence Act, 1947. She is a member of the Economic and Social Council and of the Economic Commission for Asia and the Far East, and of other United Nations agencies.

High Commissioner for India in the United Kingdom

The Government of India Act, 1919, authorized the Governor-General of India in Council with the approval of the Secretary of State in Council to appoint from time to time some person to be High Commissioner for India in the United Kingdom. In the Government of India Act, 1935, it is laid down that 'the High Commissioner shall perform on behalf of the Federation such functions in connexion with the business of the Federation, and, in particular, in relation to the making of contracts as the Governor-General may from time to time decide'. After the transfer of power in August 1947 the High Commissioner became the representative of the new Government of India and most of the agency functions which were previously being performed by the Secretary of State for India on behalf of the Government of India automatically devolved on him. A separate High Commissioner was appointed by the Government of Pakistan.

High Commissioner for India in the Union of South Africa

The office of the Agent of the Government of India was established in 1927 as a result of a Conference at Cape Town between representatives of the Union and the Indian Governments, which met to consider the whole position of Indians in the Union. The Agent was appointed to secure continuous and effective co-operation between the two governments. The designation of the Agent was changed to 'Agent General' in 1935, and in 1941 the status of the Agent General was raised to that of High Commissioner.

In May 1946 the then High Commissioner for India in South Africa was recalled to India for consultation as a protest against the Asiatic Land Tenure and Indian Representation Bill, 1946. He resigned in 1947 and no successor was appointed, the Secretary to the High Commissioner for India in the Union being in charge of the office.

India has appointed High Commissioners to Australia, Canada, Ceylon, and Pakistan.

Representation in Foreign Countries

In 1941 there was attached to the United Kingdom Embassy in Washington an Agent-General for India who held the local diplomatic rank of Minister. As a reciprocal arrangement a United

States Commissioner was appointed to New Delhi. In 1946, after the Interim Government in India had taken office, these two representatives were accorded the status of fully accredited ambassadors. By the end of 1950 the Republic of India was represented by an ambassador in sixteen foreign States, and by ministers or chargés d'affaires in fifteen States.

PAKISTAN

Ministry of Foreign Affairs and Commonwealth Relations
The Dominion of Pakistan was constituted under the Indian Independence Act, 1947.[1] Pending the adoption of a Constitution the affairs of the Dominion remained in the hands of a Governor-General and a Provisional Government. Sir Muhammad Zafrullah Khan was the first Minister for Foreign Affairs and Commonwealth Relations.

The creation and organization of a new nation is a complicated and lengthy task, and in the domain of external affairs the new dominion had no past experience or trained personnel on which to build a department. Nevertheless, the international position of Pakistan is assured by its membership of the United Nations and by the steady expansion of the *corps diplomatique* at Karachi.

In December 1948, it was announced that the Government was about to create a new service, to be known as the Pakistan Foreign Service, consisting initially of 120 persons. All Pakistan diplomatic and consular posts, together with those in the Ministry of Foreign Affairs and Commonwealth Relations, would normally be filled from this source, though the Government reserved the right to fill some posts from public life, especially until career officers of the Pakistan Foreign Service could acquire the necessary experience and seniority. Recruitments were to be by means of a competitive examination, and successful candidates would be given a substantial period of training as probationers before being appointed to the Foreign Service.

Between 1947 and 1950 Pakistan appointed High Commissioners to the United Kingdom, Australia, Canada, and India, and these appointments have been reciprocated. By January 1951 Pakistan had appointed diplomatic representatives abroad as follows: Ambassadors to Afghanistan, Burma, Egypt, France, Indonesia, Persia, Turkey, the United States, and the U.S.S.R.; Ministers to Saudi Arabia, Iraq, Jordan, the Lebanon, and Syria.

Foreign representatives in Karachi at that date included the

[1] See p. 17, above.

o

Ambassadors of Afghanistan, Burma, Egypt, France, Persia, Turkey, the United States, and the U.S.S.R.

Pakistan and the United Nations

In September 1947, the General Assembly of the United Nations, acting upon a recommendation of the Security Council, agreed to admit Pakistan to membership of the United Nations, and Pakistan participated in the work of the Assembly for the remainder of the Session. The voting was 53—1, Afghanistan casting the one negative vote. This vote was later withdrawn in view of the progress made in negotiations relating to the boundary between Afghanistan and Pakistan.

In the First Committee of the Assembly, during discussion relating to the admission of Pakistan, the legal problem was raised as to what rules should apply in future in the cases of States coming into being as the result of the division of a Member State. The Sixth (Legal) Committee stated in its report to the First Committee that when a new State is created—no matter what may be the territory and the populations which it comprises and whether or not they formed part of a State member of the United Nations—that new State cannot claim the status of a member unless it has been formally admitted in conformity with the provisions of the Charter.

Pakistan has appointed a permanent representative at the headquarters of the United Nations, and is a member of the Economic and Social Council and of several of the specialized agencies.

CEYLON

Department of External Affairs

Under the Ceylon (Constitution) Order in Council, 1946, which came into operation in 1947, Ceylon had complete self-government in internal matters and a large measure of responsibility in external affairs and defence, but in relation to these latter functions the Government of the United Kingdom retained overriding powers. In August 1947 a general election was held under the Constitution and resulted in the return of the United National Party, of which Mr D. S. Senanayake was leader, as the largest party in the House of Representatives. Mr Senanayake was invited to form a Government and, in accordance with the Constitution, became at once Prime Minister and Minister of Defence and External Affairs. Meanwhile negotiations to confer Dominion status upon Ceylon were in progress, and three agreements were successfully concluded in November 1947 (p. 19).

In accordance with the intention of these agreements, the provisions of the 1946 Constitution which gave the United Kingdom Government controlling powers over defence and external affairs were revoked by the Ceylon (Independence) Order in Council, 1947.

Meanwhile a Department of Defence and External Affairs had been established as soon as the new Government was formed in October 1947. It took over the functions of the former Chief Secretary's office in relation to immigration, passports, the Ceylon Defence Force, and external relations generally. On the attainment of independence in February 1948 it also took over from the Governor's office all responsibility for communications with the United Kingdom and other countries, which now pass to and from the Prime Minister as Minister of External Affairs.

The provisions of the External Affairs Agreement signed on 11 November 1947 were as follows:

(1) The Government of Ceylon declares the readiness of Ceylon to adopt and follow the resolutions of past Imperial conferences.

(2) In regard to external affairs generally, and in particular to the communication of information and consultation, the Government of the United Kingdom will, in relation to Ceylon, observe the principles and practice now observed by the members of the Commonwealth, and the Ceylon Government will for its part observe these same principles and practice.

(3) The Ceylon Government will be represented in London by a High Commissioner for Ceylon and the Government of the United Kingdom will be represented in Colombo by a High Commissioner for the United Kingdom.

(4) If the Government of Ceylon so requests, the Government of the United Kingdom will communicate to the Governments of the foreign countries with which Ceylon wishes to exchange diplomatic representatives proposals for such exchange. In any foreign country where Ceylon has no diplomatic representative the Government of the United Kingdom will, if so requested by the Government of Ceylon, arrange for its representative to act on behalf of Ceylon.

(5) The Government of the United Kingdom will lend its full support to any application by Ceylon for membership of the United Nations, or of any specialized international agency as described in Article 57 of the United Nations Charter.

(6) All obligations and responsibilities heretofore devolving on the Government of the United Kingdom which arise from any valid international instrument shall henceforth in so far as such instrument may be held to have application to Ceylon devolve

upon the Government of Ceylon. The reciprocal rights and benefits heretofore enjoyed by the Government of the United Kingdom in virtue of the application of any such international instrument to Ceylon shall henceforth be enjoyed by the Government of Ceylon.

Even before 1947 the Ceylon Government had trade representatives in the United Kingdom and India and had exchanged 'Government representatives' with India. High Commissioners have now[1] been exchanged with the United Kingdom, India, and Australia. Ceylon has appointed a High Commissioner in Pakistan.

Most of the larger countries had had consular representatives in Colombo before 1947, and the United States had a Consul-General. After independence the United States and Ceylon exchanged ambassadors, while an agreement was made with France for a similar exchange and a French Minister Plenipotentiary was appointed in December 1948. Burma and Ceylon have exchanged ministers.

Ceylon applied for membership of the United Nations in May 1948 and again in October 1948. On both occasions the application was strongly supported by the other Members of the British Commonwealth but was defeated in the Security Council because one of the two negative votes was cast by a permanent member (U.S.S.R.). Ceylon has, however, become a member of several Agencies, including FAO, WHO, UNESCO, ICAO, and the ILO.

[1] January 1950.

Part II

DEFENCE

CHAPTER IX

COLLECTIVE DEFENCE

IMPERIAL CONFERENCES, since the inception of the series, and, since 1944, the conferences of Commonwealth Prime Ministers, have discussed defence policy in broad outline and general principle, while detail has been delegated to specially constituted bodies. But policy itself is conditioned by basic factors over which conferences can have little or no control, and which are fundamental to the conference discussions of policy. They are: (a) The facts of geography; (b) The legacy of history; (c) The progress of science and technology in its application to weapons of offence and defence, to means of transport and communication, and to industrial war potential; (d) The external policy of foreign States. The effects of the first three can be mitigated or adapted by policy; the fourth can be influenced by policy; but none of the four lies within the control of the Members of the Commonwealth. Nor can they be considered in purely military terms: military considerations are constantly subject to the impact and mutability of politics—internal, intra-Commonwealth, and external—which may ease or aggravate the purely military problem.

The Views of the Imperial Conference of 1923

It is against the background of these fundamental factors and their political mutations that successive Imperial Conferences considered the principles of imperial defence. Up to 1937, the declared basis remained the defence resolution of the Imperial Conference of 1923.[1] Prominence was given to four principles: recognition of the 'paramount importance of providing for the safety and integrity of all parts of the Empire', i.e. recognition that the problem of imperial defence was a single problem; the vital necessity for safeguarding adequately the maritime communications (and, later to an increasing degree, for ensuring and protecting the air communications) of all British territories; express recognition that 'it is for the Parliaments of the several parts of the Empire, upon the recommendations of their respective governments, to decide the nature and extent of any action that should be taken by them';[2] and that the primary responsibility

---

[1] Imperial Conference, London, 1923, *Summary of Proceedings*, Cmd. 1987, pp. 16–17 (quoted in full in the first issue of this handbook, pp. 82–3).
[2] ibid.

of each Dominion is for its own local defence. Implied in the last principle was the additional point: that the Dominions accepted responsibility for their own defence until such time as reinforcements could reach them. Regarded historically, it was natural that the main burden of imperial defence should lie on the United Kingdom, and constitutionally it remained responsible for the defence of British colonial territories; while, militarily, it was the strategic heart of the body of imperial defence.[1]

Defence Discussions at the Imperial Conference of 1937

The Imperial Conference of 1937, at which Eire was not represented, met after the Italian aggression against Ethiopia and under the shadow of Hitlerite Germany; and saw a change of emphasis. The special interest of the Pacific Dominions and India, set out in 1923,[2] in the sea route to the Far East and in secure maritime communications in eastern waters was extended to the Pacific Ocean region, and linked with the idea of a regional pact for the area; and the terms in which the conference expressed the individual defence responsibilities of members were widened by references to their international obligations. The conference stated, in the section of its report given to foreign affairs:

'While no attempt was made to formulate commitments, which in any event could not be made effective until approved and confirmed by the respective Parliaments, the representatives of the Governments concerned found themselves in close agreement upon a number of general propositions which they thought it desirable to set out in the present statement.' They agreed that their first objective was peace, and the substitution of joint inquiry and conciliation for recourse to force in disagreements between nations; and were 'unanimous in declaring that their respective armaments will never be used for purposes of aggression or for any purpose inconsistent' with the League Covenant and the Pact of Paris. They welcomed the principle of 'regional agreements of friendship and collaboration' consistent with these instruments, and noted the Australian representative's statement that his Government would welcome and promote such a regional understanding in the Pacific area.

They all desired earnestly to see as wide a measure of disarmament as could be obtained. At the same time they were agreed that the several

---

[1] ''The conception that the defence forces of one member should be available for the defence of the other parts of the Commonwealth is more highly developed in some places than in others. Only in the case of Great Britain is it taken completely for granted that the forces of the United Kingdom shall be available for the defence of the Empire as a whole.' (H. Duncan Hall, *The British Commonwealth at War* (New York, Knopf, 1943) p. 60.)

[2] Cmd. 1987, pp. 16–17.

Governments of which they are the representatives are bound to adopt such measures of defence as they may deem essential for their security, as well as for the fulfilment of such international obligations as they may respectively have assumed.[1]

Proceeding to report on defence, the conference stated its 'deep concern that, since the session of 1930, international tension had increased in a marked degree. . . . They recognized with regret that', despite some recent success in the limitation of naval armaments, 'international conditions were not at the moment favourable to further progress in the direction of disarmament', and took note of the United Kingdom representative's statement on his country's rearmament programme and the events which led up to its adoption.

Attention was also drawn to the important progress made in recent years in the standardization by the Governments concerned of the training and equipment of the defence forces in different parts of the Empire, as well as in uniformity of administrative practice in defence matters. Reference was made to the increasing importance of the industrial side of defence owing to the progress of technical development in armaments, and emphasis was placed on the advantages attending co-operation in the production and supply of munitions and raw materials as well as of food and feeding stuffs to meet the several requirements of the United Kingdom, the Dominions and India, and the Colonial Empire.[2]

The conference then heard full accounts, from the representatives of each Dominion and of India, of the defence programmes of their countries. The report continues:

The Conference took note of the measures recently adopted by the various countries represented at the Conference, often at a heavy cost, and recognized that the increased programmes of armaments were no more than sufficient for the defence of their territories and trade and the fulfilment of such obligations as each might have assumed.

The report went on to note the vital importance of maritime communications, naval bases and fuelling and repair bases, and the steps that had been taken to safeguard them, 'and in particular that substantial progress has been made towards the completion of the naval base at Singapore, with the aid of the generous financial assistance received from various parts of the Empire'.[3] The conference noted with satisfaction the important measures of active and passive air defence taken by the United Kingdom to

[1] Imperial Conference, London, 1937, *Summary of Proceedings*. Cmd. 5482, pp. 14-15.
[2] ibid. pp. 16-17.
[3] ibid. p. 19.

protect itself 'against attack by the strongest air force which may be at any time within striking distance. . . . The Conference also recorded the progress made by the several Governments in creating and maintaining an adequate chain of air bases and re-fuelling stations along the lines of communications between the different parts of the Empire.'[1]

Turning to more detailed questions of organization:

The Conference noted with satisfaction that in accordance with recommendations of previous conferences a common system of organization and training and the use of uniform manuals, patterns of arms, equipment, and stores had been adopted, as far as practicable, for the naval, military, and air forces of their several countries. Each of them would thus be enabled to ensure more effectively its own security and, if it so desired, to co-operate with other countries of the Commonwealth with the least possible delay. The interchange of individual officers of the naval, military, and air forces of the countries was recognized as conducing to the dissemination of the experience acquired by the officers concerned under the widely different conditions existing in various parts of the Empire. Defence Councils or Committees have been established in the Dominions. Considerable advantage has been taken by the Governments represented at the Conference of the facilities afforded by the Imperial Defence College in London for the education of officers in the broader aspects of strategy.

The Conference gave careful attention to the question of munitions and supplies required for defence both by the United Kingdom and other parts of the Commonwealth, and also to the question of the supply of food and feeding stuffs in time of emergency. The Conference was impressed with the value of the free interchange of detailed technical information and recommended that it should be continued between the technical officers of the Governments concerned, it being understood that any questions of policy arising in connexion with any such technical exchange and discussion would be submitted to the respective Governments for decision and that each Government reserved to itself complete freedom of decision and action.

In the course of the discussions, the Conference found general agreement among its members that the security of each of their countries can be increased by co-operation in such matters as the free interchange of information concerning the state of their naval, military, and air forces, the continuance of the arrangements already initiated by some of them for concerting the scale of the defences of ports, and measures for co-operation in the defence of communications and other common interests. At the same time the Conference recognized that it is the sole responsibility of the several Parliaments of the British Commonwealth to decide the nature and scope of their own defence policy.

[1] ibid. p. 20.

The War of 1939–45

Within little more than two years, the countries which had conferred in 1937 had to meet the impact of total war. As might be expected during actual hostilities, under conditions requiring the maximum of operational secrecy, declarations of principle on military questions were limited to expressions of determination to achieve victory in association with the Allies. Thus the communiqué issued after the Commonwealth Prime Ministers' meeting in May 1944 states:

> We shall not turn from the conflict till . . . our comrades in every country still in the grip of the enemy . . . are restored to freedom. We have examined the part which the British Empire and Commonwealth of Nations should bear against Germany and Japan, in harmony with our allies. We are in cordial agreement with the general plans which have been laid before us. . . . We affirm our inflexible and unwearying resolve to continue in the general war with the utmost of our strength until the defeat and downfall of our cruel, barbarous foes has been accomplished.[1]

The Commonwealth Ministers' Meeting, Spring 1946

The next meeting of Commonwealth statesmen was held between 23 April and 23 May 1946, and the Australian and New Zealand representatives were the first to arrive in London for the discussions. On 28 April Field-Marshal Smuts arrived; Mr Chifley left on 3 May; and Mr Mackenzie King joined the discussions during their final week. The text of the communiqué issued on 23 May made no reference to defence matters except to say that 'security responsibilities and arrangements for liaison between British Commonwealth Governments on military affairs' were among the subjects discussed. It also affirmed strongly the value of the existing general system of consultation and declared it 'preferable to any rigid centralized machinery'.[2]

On his return home, however, the Australian Prime Minister, Mr Chifley, in his report on the conference made to Parliament on 19 June 1946, gave more details of the views which he had presented on Australia's behalf, and of the actual proposals discussed by the Commonwealth Prime Ministers. He said:

'When the Conference was arranged, the Prime Minister of the United Kingdom suggested, and it was agreed, that the main subject for discussion should be matters pertaining to the Pacific, but that the consultations should afford an opportunity for conversations on other subjects of common concern.' After repeating the reaffirmation by the Conference that 'the fundamental basis of the foreign policy of the British Commonwealth' is support of

[1] *The Times,* 18 May 1944.   [2] Full text of communiqué on pp. 114–19.

the United Nations, and that the effective operation of the United Nations depends upon the co-operation of the major Powers, Mr Chifley continued:

I could not but feel disturbed at the burden of armaments resting upon the British Commonwealth, and on the United Kingdom in particular, after a war which had resulted in the complete victory of the United Nations. . . . It is a challenge to all . . . to make the United Nations an effective organization, and the principles of its Charter a predominant influence in national policies. . . .

The security of the British Commonwealth as a whole, or of any of its members, rests on the following factors, which are blended and interrelated:

(i) The forces placed at the disposal of the United Nations for the maintenance of international peace and security in accordance with Articles 43 and 45 of the Charter, including regional arrangements under Article 52.

(ii) The forces to be maintained by each member of the British Commonwealth under arrangements for co-operation in Empire defence in accordance with the inherent right of collective self-defence under Article 51.

(iii) The forces to be maintained by each member of the British Commonwealth to provide for the inherent right of individual self-defence under Article 51.

(iv) The provision of adequate machinery for co-operation in Empire defence, without infringing the determination and sovereign control of its policy by each member.

As the Conference was convened primarily to discuss matters pertaining to the Pacific, the security of this region was naturally the predominant subject. The Australian Government accordingly submitted proposals relating to regional security and Empire co-operation which were based on the four factors which I have mentioned. These proposals must also be viewed as part of the wider concepts of world and British Commonwealth security, the principles being of equal relevance to arrangements for regional defence and Empire co-operation in any other area. Proposals by the United Kingdom Government, which were essentially in agreement with those of the Australian Government, emphasized this wider aspect.

Embedded in the matter of regional security in the South-West Pacific is the use by the United States of bases on territory controlled by the Australian Government. The policy of the Government was stated to the House by the Minister for External Affairs on 13 March last. We welcome an arrangement for the joint use of bases on the principle of reciprocity, but the provision of bases is only a part of the whole military plan for the defence of the region, and must be related to an overall plan for the maintenance of security in this area.

On the aspect of policy and principle, Article 52 of the Charter not only permits but also encourages regional arrangements for peace and security, provided they are consistent with the purposes and principles of the United Nations. In relation to our resources, Australia played a notable and worthy part in the war, which proved the importance of Australia, with its manpower and material resources, as a strategic base for the maintenance of security in the South-West Pacific. If an overall plan can be prepared in accordance with the principles of the Charter, it would indicate the nature and strength of the forces, and the facilities and resources to be provided by each of the parties to the arrangement. This has a vital influence on our future defence organization and the basis of our planning.

As a principal Power and a member of the British Commonwealth in the Pacific, Australia must be prepared to shoulder greater responsibilities for the defence of that area, including the upkeep of our bases which are essential to the strategy plan.

Earlier I referred to the heavy burden of military commitments being borne by the people of the United Kingdom, who poured out blood and treasure without stint, to save the world. Therefore I told the Conference—and I am quite certain that I expressed the sentiment of both sides of this House and of the people of Australia—that it was recognized that Australia must in future make a larger contribution towards the defence of the British Commonwealth, that this could best be done in the Pacific, and that the approach to a common scheme of defence for this area should be by agreement between the United Kingdom, Australia, and New Zealand, and thereafter with the United States of America, and later with other nations with possessions in this area. These views met with the full endorsement of the United Kingdom and New Zealand. I shall not develop the matter further, in view of impending discussions between the Minister for External Affairs and the United States authorities on the subject of bases.[1]

[Although] the Australian proposals . . . primarily related to the Pacific, . . . the principles had equal relevance to arrangements for regional defence and Empire co-operation in any other area.

This wider view was emphasized in a proposal prepared by the United Kingdom that each member of the British Commonwealth should accept responsibility for the development and defence of its own area and the strategic zone around it, and should agree to the principle of joint responsibility for the protection of lines of communication between their areas. . . . It is interesting to note, however, that, in principle, it is in broad agreement with the Australian Government's proposal relating to regional security in the South-West Pacific and the assumption of a greater responsibility for British Commonwealth defence than before the war . . . and is in accordance with the principle of responsibility for local defence accepted by the self-governing Dominions at the Imperial Conference of 1923.

In regard to responsibility for the development and defence of surrounding strategic zones and the protection of lines of communication, I pointed out that, whilst the primary responsibility for the defence of Australia naturally falls on the Commonwealth Government, the proposal to extend this responsibility to include the development and defence of the strategic zone around it requires careful examination.

[1] See p. 260, below.

The method of approach should be through a regional arrangement along the lines already suggested, and to the Australian Government machinery, with United Kingdom and New Zealand representation, should be assigned the responsibility of developing the defence aspect of matters relating to regional security in the Pacific in which the United Kingdom, Australia, and New Zealand are concerned. It was agreed that this matter should be examined by the Governments concerned, in conjunction with their advisers.[1]

After referring to the late Mr John Curtin's proposals for improved machinery for Commonwealth co-operation in general made at the 1944 Prime Ministers' meeting,[2] Mr Chifley, reverting to his account of the 1946 meeting, continued:

In the statement submitted by the Australian Government on this occasion, the following proposals were made:
  (i) It is fundamental to future arrangements for co-operation in defence that appropriate machinery should be created to provide for an effective voice by the governments concerned in policy and in the higher control of planning on the official level.
  (ii) There should be assigned to the Australian Government machinery responsibility for the development of the defence aspect of matters relating to regional security in the Pacific, in which the United Kingdom, Australia, and New Zealand are concerned, and provision should be made for the representation of the United Kingdom and New Zealand at the appropriate levels of such machinery.
  (iii) Corresponding provision would also be necessary for Dominion representation on any parallel machinery in the United Kingdom. On the official level, the Australian Government contemplates the strengthening of its Joint Service Staff in London, as a counterpart to the Defence Committee in Australia, and to provide an agency for advice to the Resident Minister in London on defence matters.
  (iv) Consideration is also being given to the Australian Joint Service Staff requirements in Washington and at the seat of the United Nations. Development in this direction would depend on any arrangement reached with the United States of America, and machinery which may be created for the purpose of implementing any agreement.
The proposal of the United Kingdom was that each member of the British Commonwealth should maintain Service missions in London. These missions would receive their instructions from the appropriate body in their respective Governments. The United Kingdom would maintain similar missions in each Dominion, and these missions would, in their particular case, receive their instructions

[1] *Current Notes on International Affairs*, vol. 17, no. 6 (Department of External Affairs, Canberra, June 1946) pp. 333-5.
[2] See above, Chapter IV.

from the United Kingdom Chiefs of Staff after consultation as necessary with the United Kingdom Government. There would be an inter-
Dominion exchange of missions as required. The system would be
based on the national defence organizations to be maintained in the
United Kingdom and in each Dominion.

It will be noted that the United Kingdom proposal, which states
a general principle relating to the whole of the British Commonwealth,
is in broad harmony with the views of the Australian Government.
These were necessarily limited to co-operation between the United
Kingdom, Australia and New Zealand, with whom a special defence
relationship has been established owing to common commitments
which have been accepted.

The Conference agreed that the proposals be referred to the
Governments for consideration in conjunction with their advisers.[1]

Mr Chifley then emphasized the obligations for both general
and regional security undertaken under the Charter by members
of the United Nations (Articles 43, 45, and 52), and the unim-
paired right of self-defence recognized by Article 51; as well as
the imperative duty of the Commonwealth countries to maintain
adequate forces and war potential to meet its obligations, and
provide for its defence needs 'until the security system is developed and firmly established'. The Imperial Conference of
1937, he said, had laid down certain principles relating to strategic
decentralization of British Commonwealth defence resources, and
during the war Australia had done much to give effect to these
principles. Scientific developments had underlined their paramount importance. He continued:

Britain's proximity to Europe has made her more vulnerable than
ever, but she cannot contract out of European affairs. The United
Kingdom, with its population of 45 million and industrial resources,
is the hard core of Empire defence, and will remain so for a long time.
A greater contribution by us to Empire defence will doubly strengthen
the security of the British Commonwealth: first, by enabling Britain
to provide for its own regional defence and overseas commitments,
and secondly, by spreading the aggregate strength of the British Commonwealth over a wider area. . . . I explained that it is [Australia's]
policy to develop in peace resources for the manufacture of munitions
as well as the supply of raw material, in order to make the Commonwealth as self-supporting as possible in armaments and munitions of
war, including aircraft and shipbuilding. I stated that with the development of government factories and the fostering of commercial industries, Australia is seeking to provide the widest possible base for a
supply structure for the needs of the Empire in the Pacific.

The United Kingdom submitted to the Conference the following

[1] *Current Notes on International Affairs*, vol. 17, no 6, pp. 336-7.

general suggestions regarding the development and distribution of resources:

(i) The development of heavy industry, and in particular the shipbuilding and aircraft industries, in the Dominions, is a task to which British Commonwealth countries should give the highest priority which economic conditions will allow.

(ii) On strategic grounds, it is desirable to spread man-power more evenly throughout the British Commonwealth. The importance in this connexion of facilitating emigration within the British Commonwealth is obvious.

[Mr Chifley said these two points were entirely in harmony with Australia's policy.]

(iii) The vulnerability of the United Kingdom makes it undesirable to hold there the main concentration of supplies and materials for a British Commonwealth war effort.

I said that [this] was in keeping with the general view on the dispersion of resources. Arrangements for the production and storage of stocks was a matter for examination in regard to the details of specific proposals.

(iv) The Dominions to maintain their own Service training establishments on such a basis that they could expand quickly and easily to receive and train United Kingdom man-power in the event of war.

I stated that this was a matter for consideration in relation to other defence requirements, and for examination in regard to the basis on which any such arrangements would be made.

(v) The necessity for formally correlating research in all matters concerning defence.

I mentioned that we had established a Defence Scientific Advisory Committee, the function of which is to maintain a general survey of the scientific field. We were also creating a New Weapons and Equipment Development Committee, and had sent to the Defence Science Conference in London a strong delegation of Service and scientific advisers.[1]

(vi) Joint Intelligence Bureaux to be established in Australia, Canada, and the United Kingdom.

I stated that the Government is at present considering the establishment of a Joint Intelligence Bureau for the Pacific area, in accordance with the principle of Australia accepting a greater responsibility for British Commonwealth defence.

These proposals are being examined by the Government's advisers, and, after Government consideration, will be taken up through the proposed improved machinery for Empire co-operation.[2]

The Main Lines of the Post-War Defence Problem

Mr Chifley's review brings out the nature of the defence problems discussed at the 1946 meeting in the light of war experience,

---

[1] See below, pp. 225–7 2nd 259.
[2] *Current Notes on International Affairs*, vol. 17, no. 6, pp. 338–9.

and their interrelation. The Member countries of the British Commonwealth had each to carry out certain post-war tasks in the organization of their military resources. First, they had to fulfil their obligations, as members of the United Nations, under its Charter and under any regional agreements within its framework to which they might become parties. The nature of this series of obligations was contingent, and they did not readily lend themselves to definition in exact terms of military resources, particularly in the absence of 'the establishment of a system for the regulation of armaments' contemplated under Article 26 of the Charter and pending the conclusion of agreements, between individual members and the Security Council, regarding 'the numbers and types of forces, their degree of readiness and general location, and the nature of the facilities and assistance' to be made available to the Security Council for the maintenance of international peace and security under Article 43. Second, they had to take adequate measures for the organization of their own national defence, and the fulfilment of their right of self-defence recognized by Article 51 of the Charter. In the case of the United Kingdom, the defence of British Colonial territory was included. Third, they had to agree upon the measures and degree of co-operation which they might desire to establish among themselves as Members of the British Commonwealth, for the security of the whole and of its parts in the event of aggression.

The Work of the Committee of Imperial Defence

These three classes of defence obligations had clearly existed before 1939, when obligations under the Covenant of the League of Nations corresponded to those under the United Nations Charter in the post-war period. Measures for Commonwealth co-operation were agreed at Imperial Conferences, and worked out in greater detail through the usual channels of communication, particularly by correspondence between the Defence Ministries of the Dominions and by means of the defence liaison staff attached to the Dominions' High Commissioners' offices in London. Further inter-service contact was provided by the Imperial Defence College, set up in 1927 to supplement the separate services' Staff Colleges, and providing courses attended by officers from the armed services of all the Commonwealth countries.

In addition, an important organ of defence consultation and co-operation was located in London: the Committee of Imperial Defence, with its Overseas Defence Sub-Committee and some fifty other sub-committees for detailed work. The Committee of Imperial Defence, set up under a Treasury Minute of 4 May

P

1904, and considerably developed after the report of the Salisbury Committee in 1924,[1] was a purely advisory body, without any executive powers, but so constituted that its advice carried great weight. By a resolution of the Imperial Conference of 1911, the Dominions were accorded the right of sending representatives by invitation to meetings of the Committee when matters affecting them were under discussion.[2] The establishment and constitution of the Committee, which were fully described in the first issue of this handbook,[3] reflected the predominant part played in imperial defence by the United Kingdom, while its advisory character was designed so as not to infringe Cabinet responsibility—executive action in pursuance of its advice being taken by the United Kingdom and Dominion Governments as appropriate and upon those Governments' decision to accept the advice.[4]

Participation of Dominion representatives in the deliberations of the Committee of Imperial Defence, which had actually occurred before the 1911 Resolution, was freely used thereafter. Before the War of 1914–18:

> Our defensive arrangements were communicated to the Dominions and they, of their own volition, prepared war books somewhat on the same lines. . . . [Between 1918 and 1930] many important matters affecting the Dominions, notably the revision of their coast defences, were referred by the Dominions themselves and dealt with by the Committee of Imperial Defence and its sub-committees, often with Dominion representation. Exchanges of documents increased and we had many useful suggestions on our reports from the Dominions. The Statute of Westminster of 1931 did not interrupt this steady evolution of co-operation on the lines I am describing, and in the 1930s, as the international situation became threatening and Imperial Conferences were less frequent because all Governments were so busy, the pace was increased. . . . At the Imperial Conference in 1926, Mr Baldwin had invited each Dominion to use the facilities of the Committee to whatever extent and in whatever manner they considered appropriate.

---

[1] Cmd. 2029 (1924).

[2] Cmd. 7347, p. 5.

[3] pp. 107–14.

[4] 'The founders of the Committee of Imperial Defence were concerned to design a mechanism which would not run counter to current conceptions of Cabinet government, and would not interfere with the collective and individual responsibility of Ministers to Parliament. The Committee of Imperial Defence was therefore established as an advisory body; but in order that its recommendations should carry due weight the Prime Minister was made the Chairman and only permanent member. He was given absolute discretion in the selection of persons, whether Ministers, officials, or experts, to attend its meetings. This arrangement secured to the new body both authority and flexibility. A small permanent secretariat was established to arrange the business and keep the records of the Committee and thus to provide continuity in its proceedings.' (*Central Organization for Defence*, Cmd. 6923 of 1946, para. 3.)

That is just what they did. The more distant Dominions made 100 per cent use of this right of representation by sending their High Commissioners to a high proportion of the meetings of the full Committee, while sub-committees were attended by Dominion liaison officers. . . . There was a tremendous transmission of documents by the Dominions Office, which included those of the Imperial Defence Committee; and all the Dominions had *mutatis mutandis* some central council, committee, or department for co-ordination of defence. The result was that in matters of defence policy and preparation, all the Dominions were fully informed on what we were doing at all levels to meet the growing threat to peace, and in the case of most of them that knowledge was enlightened by the comments of a representative —Mr Bruce, for example—who had taken part in the proceedings and could cross the t's and dot the i's and draw his Government's attention to points of importance.

I only wish I were free to indicate some of the really outstanding results. . . . The Dominions had influenced us and we had influenced the Dominions. . . . They did not know the detailed, intimate, secret plans, perhaps, but they knew the appreciation, and they knew that because of this system. . . . They made [their contributions to defence] because they knew: they had been in those consultations and they had made their own representations. They knew, as I say, everything except the absolutely secret plans. I was there and I kept a record.[1]

As before 1914, the United Kingdom, the Dominions (except Eire), and India had their 'War Books' in readiness to be opened at any time if the precautionary stage telegram required by the United Kingdom War Book were dispatched to all parts of the British Empire warning them that war was likely to break out, and thus enabling them to take their preliminary dispositions.[2] At the time of the Munich crisis of September 1938, the Chamberlain-Hitler conversations led to postponement of hostilities, and the telegram was not sent. But the Dominion Governments were fully informed, through the usual channels, of the continuing serious situation in the year that elapsed before the actual declaration of war in 1939.

Other Defence Arrangements, 1936–45

The Committee of Imperial Defence was not intended or designed to take executive control in time of war. In the course of the War of 1914–18 it was superseded by the Imperial War Cabinet. In 1939 a United Kingdom War Cabinet was immediately established, and this took over with little alteration, from the Committee of Imperial Defence, its organization of the Chiefs of Staff Committee and other committees and sub-committees.

[1] Lord Hankey, 16 October 1946, *Hansard* (Lords), vol. 143, cols. 308-11.
[2] H. Duncan Hall, *The British Commonwealth at War*, pp. 10-11.

There had been created by the United Kingdom Government, in 1936, the post of Minister for the Co-ordination of Defence, the holder of which acted as Deputy-Chairman of the Committee of Imperial Defence, had special duties in regard to the oversee-ing of the United Kingdom's rearmament programme, and acted in certain circumstances as Chairman of the Chiefs of Staff Com-mittee.[1]

The Minister for the Co-ordination of Defence . . . at first remained in office as a member of the War Cabinet, but his position was anoma-lous. He could not control the mobilization and direction of the whole resources of the nation for total war, a task which of necessity falls to the Prime Minister, nor had he any specific responsibility for knitting together the activities of the three Services. The post was abolished in April 1940. . . . [In May 1940] when Mr Churchill became Prime Minister he assumed the additional title of Minister of Defence.[2]

No Imperial War Cabinet corresponding to that set up in 1917 was established during the War of 1939–45, but Dominion Prime Ministers, and some other visiting Ministers, when in London, attended meetings of the United Kingdom War Cabinet.[3]

POST-WAR DEVELOPMENTS IN THE ORGANIZATION OF COLLECTIVE DEFENCE

After 1945 the United Kingdom, in common with the other Member Nations of the Commonwealth, was confronted with the task of setting its defence organization upon a post-war footing consonant with its international obligations and its national security. Mr Chifley's speech quoted above indicates the line of thought which emerged during the meetings of Commonwealth statesmen in April and May 1946. It was after these discussions that the United Kingdom Government produced its proposals for its reorganization of the country's defence in the White Paper *Central Organization for Defence* (Cmd. 6923) presented to Par-liament in October 1946.

Owing to the predominant position so long held by the United Kingdom in the structure of imperial defence, and to the nature and development of the Committee of Imperial Defence, the United Kingdom's post-war proposals affect the defence co-operation of the Commonwealth in a special degree. Therefore, although those proposals are dealt with in detail below in the

[1] Cmd. 6923 (1946), p. 3; Lord Chatfield in the debate on Cmd. 6923, 16 October 1946, *Hansard* (Lords), vol. 143, col. 279.
[2] Cmd. 6923 (1946), p. 3.
[3] See above, Chapter IV.

section on 'United Kingdom Defence', some mention requires to be made here of salient points.

The Defence Committee of the United Kingdom Cabinet

First, the Committee of Imperial Defence was not re-established. Its functions as an advisory body were taken over by a Defence Committee of the United Kingdom Cabinet, under the chairmanship of the Prime Minister; but added to those functions was responsibility 'for co-ordinating departmental action in preparation for war'.[1] The new committee 'will have powers of decision to the extent to which authority is devolved upon it' by the Cabinet.[2] The post of Minister of Defence was created by the Ministry of Defence Act, 1946, which received the Royal Assent on 19 December 1946. The Minister of Defence is Deputy Chairman of the Defence Committee, and presides over the Chiefs of Staff Committee whenever he or they may so desire. The Minister is responsible to Parliament for certain stated subjects.

Section V (paragraphs 35–40) of Cmd. 6923 was entitled 'Organization for Collective Defence'. In paragraph 35 it said: 'Our defence problems cannot . . . be viewed in isolation. We must be ready to play our part in any measures of collective defence which may be organized under the aegis of the United Nations; and we must maintain and develop our machinery for collaboration in the defence of the British Commonwealth and Empire.' The White Paper went on to state that the principles embodied in the Statute of Westminster govern the methods of Commonwealth collaboration. For many years before its enactment the Member Nations had neither desired, nor regarded as practicable, the establishment of a central defence authority for the Commonwealth. But practical, flexible, and close co-operation on defence matters had operated effectively without centralized machinery; and the general effectiveness of the existing system of Commonwealth consultation and co-operation was endorsed in the communiqué issued after the Prime Ministers' meeting of April–May 1946.[3] The White Paper continued:

The natural starting-point for future progress in Commonwealth defence has been the idea of regional association. Geography largely decides which problems most directly concern the separate members of the Commonwealth, and it is the aim of the various Governments to recognize and take advantage of this fact by arranging that regional

[1] Cmd. 6923 (1946), p. 6.
[2] Mr Attlee, in the debate on Cmd. 6923, 30 October 1946, *Hansard* (Commons), vol. 428, col. 622.
[3] See Chapter V, above.

questions shall in the first place be studied in the appropriate regional centre. His Majesty's Government in the United Kingdom have proposed that there should be established in the capital of each of the Dominions United Kingdom liaison officers who could join with the Dominion Chiefs of Staff in studying regional security problems. Similarly they have proposed that Dominion Governments should appoint liaison officers in London. It has been suggested that by this means regional studies can be directed by the Government most immediately concerned with the help of a team of joint advisers. The fruits of these studies can be made available in London, and in the other Dominion capitals, and in this way that measure of co-ordination which is necessary can be secured. The exact method of organizing the interchange of liaison officers will depend upon the varying constitutional practice in the different parts of the Commonwealth.

These proposals were well received as providing a means of effective consultation and collaboration, and as likely to fit in with any future regional security arrangements under the United Nations; while at the same time giving full play to the independence of the individual Commonwealth countries.

Colonial Defence. For the defence of the Colonial Empire His Majesty's Government in the United Kingdom is directly responsible. The two main objects to be achieved in this field are first the security of the Colonies themselves from external attack, and secondly the development of the full resources of the Colonies in the event of war. The security of the Colonies rests mainly upon the maintenance by the Imperial forces of command of the sea and air approaches and of the freedom of the lines of communication between the different parts of the Empire. Plans and preparations for Colonial Defence thus fall (apart from any arrangements for Regional Defence which may be made with the Dominions) within the general scope of the defence measures for which the United Kingdom Government is primarily responsible. It is proposed to revive the Overseas Defence Committee as a sub-committee of the Defence Committee in London, and this body will be charged, as it was before the war, with surveying the whole field of defence preparations in the Colonies, and their correlation with the general picture of Imperial Defence. It will also be the duty of this Committee to make sure that full account is taken in Imperial plans of the contribution in men, materials, and facilities which each Colony is capable of making to the general pool in time of war.[1]

The Commonwealth Aspect of the 1946 Defence Arrangements
In the debates on the White Paper in both Houses, Section V

[1] Paragraphs 38–40. By the Colonial Naval Defence Bill, introduced into the House of Lords on 6 December 1948, powers supplementary to those under the Colonial Naval Defence Act, 1931, were taken to enable a Colony to join with other Colonies to raise a naval force for their defence within the territorial waters of all or any of them, etc.

was criticized on the grounds that it reduced, rather than developed, Commonwealth means of defence co-operation from the level reached in 1939. Another point of criticism was that the Secretary of State for Commonwealth Relations was not a permanent member of the new Defence Committee. Government speakers replied to these points and developed others arising out of Section V.

In the House of Lords, on 16 October 1946, the Secretary of State for Dominion Affairs, Viscount Addison, said:

I would remind the noble Lords of one or two points with regard to the Committee of Imperial Defence. When it was established in 1904, the state of the British Commonwealth was very different from what it is now, and our general outlook was clearly very different. . . . The central control, or the measure of central control in these matters which might have been possible or acceptable in 1904, has for long been out of the question in the way the British Commonwealth has developed.[1]

The United Kingdom Government, Lord Addison continued, had had to face the problem of remedying certain defects in the overall preparation for national defence which the crisis of 1939 had made manifest. This was to be done by a development in Cabinet government: the creation of a Defence Committee of the Cabinet with certain executive powers, and of the post of Minister of Defence with specific responsibilities to Parliament.

Here . . . is a very substantial and vital difference between this organization and the Committee of Imperial Defence. This is a body which is intimately concerned with plans affecting the whole life of the nation and with a Minister responsible to Parliament for certain functions which are set out. . . . That is clearly something much beyond, and entirely different from, the original conception of the Committee of Imperial Defence, which . . . was an advisory body with no executive powers at all. . . .
Arrangements will be made no doubt from time to time as necessity arises, to take into counsel members from other Parties and to receive visitors from our Dominions. . . . I think it is fair to say that the statement in the [White] Paper, in paragraph 37, . . . was put out deliberately by the meeting of Commonwealth Prime Ministers after the most careful scrutiny. . . . They came to the conclusion . . . that the methods now practised are preferable to any rigid centralized machinery. The Dominions and their point of view are in a different world from that in which they were in 1904. . . . We do not say that this is the last word. . . . We deliberately say that it is being developed, and I can assure your Lordships that we are now busy and anxious developing on the widest possible scale, and in the most intimate possible manner, the consultation and co-operation with the Dominions.[2]

[1] *Hansard* (Lords), vol. 143, col. 328.　　　[2] ibid. cols. 335–6.

Lord Addison then gave three specific examples of means of consultation and liaison employed; and continued:

Then there are the regional problems which have developed completely differently since 1904. . . . I am not going into details, for it is not desirable that I should do so. But we are well aware of them and are doing all we can to deal with them in the most intimate and practical fashion. . . . These liaison officers . . . [mentioned in paragraph 38 of the White Paper] will be officers of high standing and it will be their function to promote daily contact between Staff officers from the Dominions here and our Staff officers as a vital part of that close consultation and co-operation which we are developing. . . . I am sure that the present scheme—recognizing as it does that the British Commonwealth is made up of a number of independent nations—is well adapted to the changes of our time and the interests of the Commonwealth.[1]

In the debate in the House of Commons on 30 October 1946, the Prime Minister, Mr Attlee, said that although the Dominions Secretary was not included among the nucleus of permanent members of the new Defence Committee, he 'will, of course, be kept in closest possible touch . . . and will attend all meetings and discussions which involve the defence of the Commonwealth as a whole or in any way affect the interests of any part of the Commonwealth'.[2]

Winding up for the Government on 31 October, the Minister without portfolio, Mr A. V. Alexander, said:

The term 'collective defence' . . . was used simply and solely because this section of the White Paper deals not only with Colonial defence and with contacts on defence matters with the Dominions, but it must deal with any measure of collective defence which may be organized under the aegis of the United Nations. [Regarding defence co-operation with the Dominions]: If we approach the general consideration of this matter from a recognition of their complete freedom and of the way they have helped us in the past, we shall make better progress. . . . The intention of the Government is to increase and not to diminish any opportunities which were previously available for the exchange of information and views with the Dominion Governments on matters of defence. What is required is not some rigid form of arrangement that would bring them within our own defence organization as explained in the White Paper, but rather the closest practicable contact, not only in the sphere of the Services themselves, but also at the highest possible level; that is to say, whenever possible, contact between responsible Ministers. It is the aim of His Majesty's Government to do everything practicable under both of those heads.

We shall not give up either our persistent attempts to make the

[1] ibid. cols. 337-8.   [2] *Hansard* (Commons), vol. 428, col. 621.

United Nations organization function effectively . . . but, at the same time, we shall feel that we must make our forces such, first, that we can fulfil our commitments under the Charter of the United Nations; secondly, that we must have such forces within the British Commonwealth in addition as might enable us to hold a situation until such time as the general forces of the United Nations organization could come to the assistance of that part of the Dominions and Colonies which might perhaps be attacked. We shall take all those matters into full consideration, at all times, but that is our general objective.[1]

Developments in 1947–8

The United Kingdom White Paper of February 1948, *Statement Relating to Defence*,[2] gave further information regarding the execution of the proposals respecting Commonwealth defence co-operation which had been set out in the White Paper of October 1946, *Central Organization for Defence*.[3] It stated:

During the year, further improvements have taken place in the organization within the Commonwealth for the exchange of information on defence questions and for the common study of problems of mutual concern. United Kingdom Service liaison staffs have now been set up in Canada, the Union of South Africa, and in Australia, and will shortly be established in New Zealand. The establishment of British Service staffs in the Dominions, and of Dominion staffs in the United Kingdom, provides a system through which a standard of co-operation can be achieved which will measure up to the needs of modern defence strategy. It is hoped that it will before long be possible to have defence discussions with the new Dominions of India and Pakistan; in the meantime service representatives have been attached to the staffs of the United Kingdom High Commissioners. Mention has already been made of the change in the status of Ceylon and of the Defence Agreement which has been concluded between the Governments of Ceylon and the United Kingdom.[4]

During the month of November 1947, the Commonwealth Advisory Committee on Defence Science, which is composed of senior officers of the Services and of representative scientists from the United Kingdom and the Dominions, held a series of meetings in London. The discussions covered a very wide field, and valuable results were achieved. It is intended that meetings of the Committee shall be held at regular intervals in the several countries of the Commonwealth, and these will foster the growing understanding between them of the problems of defence science.[5]

The potentialities of these new weapons also enhance the need for greater co-operation within the Commonwealth. The security of the

[1] ibid. cols. 879–81.
[2] Cmd. 7327.
[3] Cmd. 6923; quoted on pp. 221-2, above.
[4] For text, see p. 275, below.
[5] Cmd. 7327, p. 9, paras. 49 and 50.

United Kingdom is one of the keystones of Commonwealth defence, but, equally, the United Kingdom alone, without the support of the Commonwealth, would lose much of its effective influence and power. If war should ever be forced upon us, besides defending these islands we should have to play our part in defending the resources on which the Commonwealth must rely. The control of communications and of strategic keypoints is essential to the achievement of this aim.[1]

The Commonwealth Advisory Committee on Defence Science had first been mentioned in 1946, when, on 31 May the Dominions Office had announced that an informal conference of British Commonwealth scientists and service representatives would be held, with Sir Henry Tizard in the chair, to make a specific and detailed examination of Commonwealth defence problems, the possibility of effective collaboration in research and large-scale defence investigations, and future exchange of information.[2] On 12 October 1947 the Ministry of Defence announced that 'a routine meeting' of these Commonwealth representatives would be held the following month.[3] On 20 October 1947 Mr Dedman, Australian Minister for Defence, had announced Australian participation in this conference, which followed the establishment, in Commonwealth countries, of special scientific bodies within the national defence departments.[4]

A major development in Commonwealth co-operation in defence science is the guided missiles project to which Mr Dedman the Australian Minister for Defence, referred in his speech of 4 June 1947,[5] and which was approved by the Government of Australia in September 1946. Mr Dedman had then announced the proposal to set up in Australia, as a joint venture with Britain, a range and other facilities for the testing of guided missiles. The Australian New Weapons and Equipment Development Committee and the Defence Scientific Advisory Committee, which he also mentioned, had been set up somewhat earlier, in April 1946, their main functions being 'to maintain a general survey of the scientific field and to bring before the Defence Committee, the Chiefs of Staff Committee, or the Council of Defence, for the notice of the Australian Government, scientific developments having either direct or indirect bearing on national defence, and to maintain liaison with their overseas counterparts'. In this connexion it was reported in May 1947 that Mr A. P. Rowe had been lent by the United Kingdom Government to Australia for one year as defence scientific adviser, and to be Chairman of the Defence Scientific Advisory Committee.

[1] ibid., p. 10 para. 56.
[2] *The Times*, 1 June 1946.
[3] ibid. 13 October 1947.
[4] ibid. 21 October 1947.
[5] See p. 259, below.

On 29 April 1948 Mr Dedman stated in the House of Representatives that the highest priority for labour and materials had been given to the long-range weapons project, and that an increase in the scope of research and development was under consideration. Sir Ben Lockspeiser, chief scientific adviser to the United Kingdom Ministry of Supply, had said that the research and development base at Salisbury in South Australia, where projectiles from the United Kingdom are assembled, was likely to become the main centre for British Commonwealth research in supersonic defensive rocket weapons. Interchange of staff with United Kingdom research institutions was increasing.

The United Kingdom *Statement on Defence*, 1949[1] continued the story of development in Commonwealth co-operation in defence, and also devoted attention to co-operation with foreign States. It stated in its introduction that the United Kingdom long-term plan must 'be appropriate to our obligations to the Commonwealth and Western Union and to any future arrangements concluded for the defence of the North Atlantic area'. It mentioned that Australian, New Zealand, and South African aircrews helped with the Berlin air-lift. After giving a résumé of combined operations activities during the year, it says:

Close liaison with the United States of America has been maintained. There has been an interchange of visits by officers connected with Combined Operations in the two countries and a team from the Combined Operations School has visited the United States Marine Corps School at Quantico as well as the Canadian Staff College at Kingston, Ontario.

On the general problem of international and Commonwealth co-operation, it stated:

The Charter of the United Nations defines as one of its main purposes the maintenance of international peace and security. . . . The general concept includes the building up of United Nations armed forces under the control of the Security Council to be used if need be for these purposes.

His Majesty's Government have from the outset done everything in their power to promote and assist this primary aim of the United Nations and will continue to do so. The degree of success realized has, however, proved a grievous disappointment and the establishment of collective security on a world-wide basis under the United Nations has not been achieved. In these circumstances, His Majesty's Government have necessarily devoted increased attention to co-operation with other members of the Commonwealth, the United States of America, and other like-minded Powers, and generally to the develop-

[1] Cmd. 7631.

ment of appropriate regional security arrangements as contemplated in Article 51 of the United Nations Charter.

In respect of Commonwealth action, it continued:

The meeting of Commonwealth Prime Ministers, which was held in London in October 1948, provided the opportunity for a valuable review of defence problems facing the various countries of the Commonwealth.

There was general approval of the existing arrangements for consultation between Commonwealth countries on defence matters. Recommendations for improving these arrangements have been submitted to the Governments for consideration, and substantial progress has been made in establishing a basis on which military co-operation could be developed. In consequence, His Majesty's Government in the United Kingdom hope that it will now be possible further to improve, within the framework acceptable to each individual Commonwealth Government, arrangements for military co-operation and for consultation on military planning.

Planning and consultation have taken place between individual Commonwealth authorities in respect of various areas which are of concern to them, and there have been frequent exchanges of visits by officers, officials and scientists between the countries of the Commonwealth.

Colonial Governments are already devoting an appreciable part of their resources to the maintenance of local defence forces. To prevent the dissipation of our armed strength and to free the United Kingdom forces for their true role, local forces must be built up to the extent necessary to deal with the present disturbed conditions. His Majesty's Government, in conjunction with the Colonial Governments concerned, are therefore examining the size and composition of the local forces required.

The statement then dealt with Western Union military arrangements, which have their relation to purely Commonwealth planing, and said:

United States and Canadian observers attend meetings of the Western Union Chiefs of Staff Committee, the Military Supply Board and the subordinate committees which work for these two bodies.

The Statement on Defence, 1950,[1] repeated the principles of collective defence and Commonwealth co-operation already described, and continued:

But now, in addition, specific engagements have been made with other peace-loving nations in the Brussels and North Atlantic Treaties. Collective self-defence was embodied in Article IV of the

[1] Cmd. 7895.

Brussels Treaty and in the Western Union defence organization set up under it. It was carried a significant stage forward in the North Atlantic Treaty signed in April 1949.[1] The initial stages of Western Union development was set out in last year's Statement on Defence and the work there described has been continued. . . . This will of course assist in the defence of the North Atlantic area. . . . The cost [of the United Kingdom's share in] these measures is reflected in the [increased] defence budget for 1950–1. In addition, we continue to give help to other Members of the Commonwealth in meeting equipment needs for which they themselves cannot provide. The . . . North Atlantic Treaty raised new problems and . . . the necessary organization has been established and is working. An overall strategic concept for the defence of the area has been drawn up and endorsed by the Council of the North Atlantic Treaty Organization.

Commitments under these two treaties were not the full tale of United Kingdom responsibilities. After describing the redistribution of forces required by the situations in the Middle East, Hong Kong, and Malaya, the White Paper described the situation regarding Colonial forces:

A review of the Colonial forces by the Chiefs of Staff Committee has been followed by consultations with the Colonial Governments concerned, and, in the case of the East and West African colonies, by a conference in London. The basic difficulty is that the cost even of the forces required for integral security is often beyond the means of the colony. Means of bridging the gap are under consideration.

No White Paper on defence was issued in February 1951. The story of the Commonwealth's participation in the major military event since February 1950—the United Nations' campaign in Korea—falls outside the scope of this handbook.

[1] See Chapter XVII, below.

CHAPTER X

CO-OPERATIVE ACTION FOR THE CONTROL OF ATOMIC ENERGY

International Action

WHILE the control of the use of atomic energy, as the greatest immediate problem posed by the advance of science, is of vital interest to every nation, two Commonwealth countries and one foreign country—the United Kingdom and Canada, and the United States—stand in special relation to it as the possessors of the essential practical knowledge. At the invitation of the President of the United States, Mr Truman, the Prime Ministers of the United Kingdom and Canada, Mr Attlee and Mr Mackenzie King, met him in conference in Washington in November 1945, and on 15 November they issued a three-nation declaration of policy.

In this declaration they stated with emphasis their view that responsibility rests with the whole civilized world for ensuring that the discovery of the means of utilizing atomic energy, with its vast potentialities for service and for destruction, should be used for good and not for evil. But, owing to the particular progress made by their own countries in developing and using atomic energy, they had agreed to take the initiative in considering the question of international action to prevent its destructive use and promote its beneficent uses. They recognized that the only complete protection against the destructive use of scientific discoveries, in all other fields as well as in the atomic field, lay in peace. They believed that the development of the peaceful ends of science should be promoted by the free interchange of scientific knowledge and ideas. As representatives of the three countries possessing the knowledge essential to the use of atomic energy, they declared their willingness to exchange information for peaceful ends with any country prepared fully to reciprocate; and urged the general adoption of the policy of complete reciprocity. But since the industrial and military techniques for using atomic energy are largely the same, they were not convinced that the release of industrial information could be justified in the absence of a system of effective, enforceable, reciprocal safeguards against its military use. In order to ensure the elimination of the destructive uses and promote the development of the beneficent uses of atomic energy, they believed that a United Nations Commission should immediately be set up to study and recommend upon the attainment of this end by whatever means of control, safeguards, and exchange of information.[1]

The history of the inconclusive and, so far, unfruitful labours of the United Nations Commission on Atomic Energy does not belong to this handbook. In the absence of successful control on a world basis, countries and groups of countries sought means of co-operation; and it followed from the facts that the United States and the countries of the British Commonwealth would be likely to collaborate.

After the war the United States, the United Kingdom, and Canada agreed to adopt a common policy with regard to the release of information on atomic energy. On 31 August 1948 the Ministry of Supply issued the following communiqué:

Britain, Canada, and the United States agreed at the end of the war to adopt a common policy for the release of scientific and technical information gained during their combined war-time development of atomic energy. The uniform declassification guide which was then prepared was revised at a conference held in Washington in November 1947.

It is in the mutual interest of the three Governments and of scientific workers both inside and outside the atomic energy programme to reconsider from time to time the boundary between that work which may be released without endangering the national security and that which must remain restricted in circulation. For this purpose a further meeting between representatives of the atomic energy organizations of Britain, Canada, and the United States will be held at the Atomic Energy Research Establishment, Harwell (Berks), on 6–8 September. The meeting will review the declassification guide in the light of technical developments in the past ten months.[2]

National control being a necessary preliminary to international control, the Member Nations of the Commonwealth have taken certain steps.

United Kingdom

In August 1945 the establishment of a committee to advise the Cabinet on all atomic energy questions was announced. This advisory committee was under the chairmanship of Sir John Anderson. It was dissolved on 8 August 1948, when the Ministry of Supply, the Advisory Council on Scientific Policy, and other bodies in the field took over its functions.

In 1946 the United Kingdom Government introduced the Atomic Energy Bill 'to empower the Minister of Supply to promote the development of atomic energy and to confer on him

---

[1] *New York Times*, 16 November 1945.
[2] *Manchester Guardian*, 1 September 1948.

powers of control over the unauthorized production or use of atomic energy and over the publication of certain information'. The Minister is charged with the general duty of development, and is empowered to promote research and production and to make grants or loans therefor. He may institute searches and surveys for fissionable materials, and provide for the cost. He is given wide powers compulsorily to take over mining rights, plant, contractual rights, inventions, and stocks of material, subject to payment of compensation. He may also compel the disclosure of information, and has powers of inspection and search for unauthorized possession of plant and materials. He may prohibit the disclosure of scientific and technical information, and the Comptroller-General of Patents is also given powers to restrict the publication of information regarding patents applied for. No resident in the United Kingdom may take out a patent outside the United Kingdom in respect of inventions concerned with the production, etc., of atomic energy without the written permission of the Comptroller-General. Fissionable material may be mined and worked only under Ministry of Supply licence; but the Minister is to ensure the availability of such material for research, educational, and commercial purposes unconnected with atomic energy production. Provisions for the acquisition of land, etc., under the Ministry of Supply Act, 1939, are extended to cover the purposes of the Bill. The fissionable materials prescribed for control include uranium, thorium, plutonium, neptunium, and their compounds, and the Minister may by order prescribe other substances. In the course of the second-reading debate on 10 October 1946, the Minister of Supply, Mr Wilmot, said that the Bill contained nothing inconsistent with the country's international obligations. Immediately the Bill was drafted, he added, copies were sent to the Dominions, and Bills were in the course of being prepared and passed in each of the Dominions with similar if not identical provisions.

The Radio-Active Substances Bill, introduced in the House of Lords on 25 April 1947, gave the Minister of Supply powers to control the manufacture, import, use, and possession of radioactive substances not covered by the previous Act. The Minister of Health was given power under the Bill to ensure that radioactive waste products are disposed of safely.

Certain Colonial Governments have taken steps to control the production, disposal, and utilization of radio-active material when it is believed to be present in their territories. On 21 March 1949 the Ministry of Supply announced the publication of a notice in all Colonial territories stating the conditions on which the Ministry would buy uranium ores and concentrates produced there in the next ten years. Where justified, the Ministry is prepared to assist Colonial mining development.[1]

The United Kingdom Government, under the 1946 Act, has established or taken over research and experimental plant, notably at Harwell.

Canada

The Canadian Government in 1946 established the Dominion Atomic Energy Control Board, under the chairmanship of General A. G. L. McNaughton. This measure superseded the various war-time measures of control and operation of fissionable materials by the Government. All discoveries of fissionable material made since the establishment of the Board passed compulsorily into its ownership. On 16 March 1948 the Minister of Reconstruction, Mr C. D. Howe, announced that private exploration and mining would again be allowed.[2] All mined ore would be purchased by one of the Government agencies under the aegis of the Board (such as the Eldorado Mining and Exploration Company operating at Great Bear Lake, Ontario, which was taken over by the Government during the war) at a guaranteed price dependent upon the uranium content of the material. This restoration of the right of private mining is in line with the majority recommendations of the second report of the United Nations Atomic Commission, to which Canada subscribed.

Australia

Under the Atomic Anergy (Control of Minerals) Act of 1946, the Australian Government took powers to control the production and distribution of uranium and other fissionable materials and their compounds. The establishment of a Cabinet Committee to study atomic warfare and its implications, consisting of the Prime Minister, the Ministers of the Interior and Works and the Postmaster-General, was announced on 12 January 1948. The Committee will also study the problems of guided projectiles and their effects. The Prime Minister, Mr Chifley, told a press conference that the United Kingdom Government had made available to this committee its confidential analyses of bomb damage by all types of projectiles. The Australian Government also announced at the same time its intention to offer money rewards for discoveries of atomic minerals up to a maximum of £A25,000 according to the extent and content of the discoveries. During the

---

[1] *The Times*, 22 March 1949.
[2] On 12 July 1948 Mr Howe told a press conference that no spectacular finds had recently been made and the El Dorado field continued to be the main source of supply; but that indications of plentiful radio-active material had been found in Saskatchewan (*The Times*, 13 July).

war certain mining activities had been undertaken at Mr Churchill's request, and the cost had been borne by the United Kingdom.[1] Mr Dedman, Minister for Defence announced in May 1947 that the Australian Council for Scientific and Industrial Research was planning close collaboration with United Kingdom scientists in the matter of atomic energy development, and would keep in touch with the United Kingdom experimental station at Harwell.

New Zealand

In December 1945 the New Zealand Government introduced legislation for Government control of atomic energy-producing materials, including mining, distribution, and working.

Union of South Africa

Control of the exploitation of fissionable materials was imposed by the Union Government by War Measure No. 65 of October 1945, and covered South West Africa as well as the Union. In the Speech from the Throne on 16 January 1948 it was announced that the Government would introduce legislation to replace this War Measure, which was due to lapse on 30 June. The passage of the legislation was delayed by the change of government, and Dr Malan's Government later introduced substantially the same Bill as had earlier been proposed. When the Government moved the second reading on 23 August 1948, the Minister of Mines and Economic Development, Mr Eric Louw, said:

Uranium had hitherto been controlled under war regulations, but it was essential that a stable control be established by special legislation. The Bill as introduced was substantially the same as that drawn up by the previous Government. It provided for State control of uranium and the generation of atomic energy and for a State monopoly of the exploitation of any other radio-active mineral. The main source of supply in South Africa was in the gold mines, where uranium was a constant constituent of gold-bearing ore. State control of the material worked on private property called for the closest collaboration between the State and private interests, and he was glad to say that the gold-mining industry was co-operating most satisfactorily. He paid a tribute to the work of Dr Schonland, president of the South African Council of Scientific and Industrial Research, in tackling the problems of economically extracting uranium.[2]

The Bill received the full support of the Opposition.

Mr Louw announced on 6 June 1949 that United Kingdom and United States experts would shortly visit the Union to discuss

[1] *Manchester Guardian*, 24 July 1948; *New York Herald Tribune*, 3 February 1947.
[2] *The Times*, 24 August 1948.

the production of atomic energy. The Union Government had already engaged the services of a Canadian expert for highly scientific work on the uranium content of gold tailings. No uranium had yet actually been produced in the Union.

Union of India

On 8 April 1948 the Indian Legislature passed a Bill for the development and control of atomic energy. It provided for the establishment of an Atomic Energy Board given powers, under Governmental sanction, to institute secret research and take over the functions of the Board of Research in Atomic Energy which had been set up in June 1947. Important deposits of thorium had for some time been known to exist in the State of Travancore, and by agreement with the State a joint Advisory Committee, consisting of three members appointed by the Union Government and three by the State Government, was set up to assist both governments.

CHAPTER XI

DEFENCE POLICIES OF THE MEMBERS OF THE COMMONWEALTH

The United Kingdom

WHEN the United Kingdom Government presented its White Paper on Defence to Parliament in February 1946,[1] they announced that their proposals for a central organization for defence would follow. These proposals were presented in October 1946.[2]

The October White Paper briefly reviewed, in paragraphs 2–10, the United Kingdom's defence arrangements in the past, including the statement on the functions of the Committee of Imperial Defence and of the Minister for the Co-ordination of Defence, quoted above.[3] The need for inter-service planning had been recognized by the Salisbury Committee, and it had been steadily developed between 1924 and 1939 under the Joint Staff system. No overall planning authority existed, however, and a step was taken to fill that gap in 1939, when the Committee of Imperial Defence set up a Policy Committee with the Prime Minister in the chair. 'It was a first attempt to separate . . . matters of high policy and strategy from those of supply and production.'[4] This committee was later assisted by a sub-committee of the Minister for the Co-ordination of Defence, the three Service Ministers, the three Chiefs of Staff, and the Secretary of State for Foreign Affairs, which reviewed the plans prepared in the event of war, and reported back to the Policy Committee.[5]

When war broke out in September 1939, a War Cabinet was immediately constituted, and it was assisted by a committee with similar functions to the previous Policy Committee which, like its parent body the Committee of Imperial Defence, ceased operations. The new committee was the Defence Committee (Operations), and during most of the war it consisted of the Prime Minister[6] in the chair, the Deputy Prime Minister, the Foreign

---

[1] Cmd. 6743.

[2] *Central Organization for Defence*, Cmd. 6923.

[3] p. 220. (A fuller account of the pre-war arrangements, up to 1934, may be found in the first issue of this handbook.)

[4] Lord Chatfield in the debate on Cmd. 6923, 16 October 1946, *Hansard* (Lords), vol. 143, col. 278.

[5] ibid.

[6] When Mr Churchill assumed office, he was also Minister of Defence, following the abolition in April 1940 of the post of Minister for the Co-ordination of Defence.

Secretary, the Minister of Production, the three Service Ministers and the Chiefs of Staff; with other Ministers attending when their spheres of responsibility were concerned. 'This Committee examined the military plans prepared by the Chiefs of Staff and the Joint Staffs and took decisions on behalf of the War Cabinet. A parallel body, the Defence Committee (Supply), dealt with the main lines of the production programmes. The duties of the Prime Minister as Minister of Defence were never defined.'[1] The Chiefs of Staff in their corporate capacity issued unified operational instructions and guided strategy. The detailed administration of the three arms was in the hands of the three Service Ministries, and they and the Commanders-in-Chief executed the Chiefs of Staff's directives.

The corporate authority of the Chiefs of Staff in the higher direction of the war, under the immediate supervision of the Prime Minister, was further consolidated, after the entry of the United States into the war, by the institution of the Combined Chiefs of Staff in Washington, by the appointment of Anglo-American Supreme Commanders, and by the close relations which developed between the President of the United States and the Prime Minister of the United Kingdom.[2]

The Prime Minister, in his capacity of Minister of Defence, took over as his staff the military secretariat of the War Cabinet, which in turn had taken it over from the Committee of Imperial Defence.

Thus no Ministry of Defence was created. When the United Kingdom Government came to consider its post-war plans, it stated that 'above all, experience during these years [of war and preparation against the threat of war] has shown the need of a Minister who has both the time and the authority to formulate and apply a unified defence policy for the three services'.[3] The Government therefore proposed a major change from the pre-war organization: the establishment of a Ministry of Defence.

The form of the new organization proposed may be summarized as follows:
(a) The Prime Minister will retain the supreme responsibility for defence.
(b) The Defence Committee, under the Chairmanship of the Prime Minister, will take over the functions of the old Committee of Imperial Defence, and will be responsible to the Cabinet both for the review of current strategy and for co-ordinating departmental action in preparation for war.
(c) A new post of Minister of Defence, with a Ministry, will be created. The Minister of Defence will be responsible to Parlia-

[1] Cmd. 6923 (1946), p. 3.   [2] ibid. p. 4.   [3] ibid. p. 6.

ment for certain subjects, which are defined in paragraph 26 below, affecting the three Services and their supply. In addition, he will be Deputy Chairman of the Defence Committee; and he will also preside over meetings with the Chiefs of Staff whenever he or they may so desire.

(d) The Chiefs of Staff Committee will remain responsible for preparing strategic appreciations and military plans, and for submitting them to the Defence Committee; and the Joint Staff system will be retained and developed under their direction.

(e) The Service Ministers will continue to be responsible to Parliament for the administration of their Services in accordance with the general policy approved by the Cabinet and within the resources allotted to them.

While the national organization for defence remains the responsibility of the Prime Minister and the Cabinet as a whole, the new Minister of Defence has important functions.

Apart from his duties as Deputy Chairman of the Defence Committee, it is proposed that the Minister of Defence should, as such, be responsible for the following functions:

(a) The apportionment, in broad outline, of available resources between the three Services in accordance with the strategic policy laid down by the Defence Committee. This will include the framing of general policy to govern research and development, and the correlation of production programmes.

(b) The settlement of questions of general administration on which a common policy for the three Services is desirable.

(c) The administration of inter-Service organizations, such as Combined Operations Headquarters and the Joint Intelligence Bureau.

The Minister will bring his proposals under (a) before the Defence Committee and the Cabinet. He will present the Cabinet's decisions on these to Parliament, and will decide questions arising between the three Services in their application. He will not be responsible for the subsequent detailed execution of the approved programmes, which will be the task of the Service and Supply Ministers. As a consequence of (b), he will answer questions in Parliament on matters common to the three Services or to the three Services and the Ministry of Supply.[1]

The Defence Committee had ten permanent members: the Prime Minister (chairman), the Minister of Defence, the Lord President of the Council, the Foreign Secretary, the Chancellor of the Exchequer, the three Service Ministers, the Minister of Labour, and the Minister of Supply; with the Chiefs of Staff in attendance. Other Ministers attended by invitation when their subjects were under discussion. The Defence Committee was assisted by a system of sub-committees mainly at the official level

[1] Cmd. 6923, pp. 7–8.

and on the lines of the pre-war sub-committee system of the Committee of Imperial Defence.

The Minister of Defence had the function of co-ordinating into a considered whole, the service estimates in terms of finance, material, and man-power for presentation to the Defence Committee of the Cabinet. This apportionment of resources was made in the light of the Chiefs of Staff's advice on total strategic requirements for the year under review. The Minister of Defence had the assistance on production questions of a standing Ministerial Production Committee, over which he presided, composed of the Service Ministers and the Ministers of Labour and Supply. This committee was in turn assisted by a Joint War Production Staff of serving officers and officials of the service and civil ministries concerned.[1] The Joint War Production Staff also assisted the Minister's Production Committee in the study of all aspects of war potential, a task with which the Committee was also specially charged. This Committee could co-opt the President of the Board of Trade and other Ministers concerned to assist its work on this subject.

The Minister of Defence also assumes control of all inter-service bodies concerned with planning, intelligence, and staff training which have grown up with the development of the Joint Staff system: for example, Combined Operations Headquarters, the Joint Intelligence Bureau, and the Imperial Defence College.

The relations between the Minister of Defence and the Chiefs of Staff were described as follows:

The Chiefs of Staff organization has been highly developed during the war and its value has been fully proved. No change is therefore contemplated in the organization of the Chiefs of Staff Committee, which will continue as at present, together with the Joint Staffs for strategic planning, intelligence, and administrative planning. The Chiefs of Staff Committee will retain their responsibility for preparing strategic military plans and submitting them to the Defence Committee. On all technical questions of strategy and plans it is essential that the Cabinet and Defence Committee should be able to have presented to them directly and personally the advice of the Chiefs of Staff, as the professional military advisers of the Government. Their advice to the Defence Committee or the Cabinet will not, therefore, be presented only through the Minister of Defence. At the same time, the organization on which they rely in their collective capacity will be within the new Ministry, and the Chiefs of Staff will meet under the chairmanship of the new Minister whenever he or they may so desire. Thus, it will be after such consultation with them that he will formulate his proposals for the apportionment of resources between the three Services. Before any major strategical plan is submitted to the

[1] ibid. p. 8.

Defence Committee, he will usually discuss it with the Chiefs of Staff though not with a view to acting as their mouthpiece in the Defence Committee.[1]

The White Paper described the method of dealing with problems of organizing research thus:

The problem here is to secure the continued and complete integration of military and scientific thought at all levels and to see that, in planning Defence Research as a whole, account is taken of the scientific effort of the country in other fields in order that our resources may be efficiently and economically used. For this purpose there will be a Committee on Defence Research Policy, consisting of those responsible, both from the operational and scientific angle, for research and development in the Service Departments and the Ministry of Supply. This will advise, on operational questions, the Chiefs of Staff, and, on wider aspects, the Defence Committee. Its Chairman will be a scientist of high standing, appointed for the purpose for a period of years. He will exercise his functions under the authority of the Minister of Defence, with whom will rest, as stated in paragraph 26, responsibility for the framing of general policy to govern research and development.[2]

Sir Henry Tizard was appointed the first Chairman of the Committee.

Questions of home security, which embrace many matters within the provinces of the civil ministries, were excluded from the functions of the Minister of Defence. The war-time Home Defence Committee has been reconstituted to assist the Defence Committee in its duty of linking home security problems to broad defence policy.[3]

Regarding staff, the White Paper says:

The Minister . . . will have as his principal advisers a Permanent Secretary, a Chief Staff Officer, the Chairman [whom he will appoint] of the Joint War Production Staff, and the Chairman of the Committee on Defence Research Policy. These will be assisted by a relatively small staff, partly civil and partly military, which among their other duties will provide the Secretariat for the Committees and Joint Staffs through which the Minister will mainly work.[4]

In the debate on the proposals in the House of Commons on 30 October 1946, the Prime Minister, Mr Attlee, speaking of the proposed Defence Committee as a development of Cabinet government, said that with present-day large Cabinets, with up to a dozen Ministers outside them,

experience has shown that a great many inter-departmental matters can be settled in committee and a great deal of preliminary work done,

[1] ibid. p. 9.   [2] ibid. p. 9.   [3] ibid. p. 10.   [4] ibid.

so as to free the Cabinet from an excessive amount of work over detail. Thus by bringing within that general structure the work that was formerly done by the Committee of Imperial Defence, it is possible to give the Defence Committee a power of decision which was denied to its predecessor.[1]

The White Paper proposals having been approved, the Ministry of Defence Bill, providing for the new Ministry and the creation of the post of Minister, passed through all its stages by the middle of December 1946.

In February 1946 the United Kingdom Government reverted to the pre-war practice of presenting to Parliament a general survey of defence policy,[2] and statements were again presented in February 1947, 1948, 1949 and 1950.[3] The later statements described the progress made with the execution of the proposals of October 1946.

The 1948 White Paper reviewed developments in defence organization.[4] The new Ministry had made full use of previously existing inter-service machinery as well as of the new arrangements outlined in October 1946. In the field of research and development, the Defence Research Policy Committee was constituted on 1 January 1947, and had been in full activity. It had devoted special attention to establishing priorities and ensuring concentration of work and material on projects of maximum importance.

A high proportion of the total expenditure on defence research and development is devoted to general aeronautical research and to the development of aircraft with improved characteristics of speed, range and carrying powers [including supersonic aircraft, both piloted and pilotless, and improved gas turbine engines]. Intimately connected with work on aeronautics is the effort being put into the development of controlled missiles of various kinds. One of the main objects of this work is to provide the most effective possible defence against aircraft attack. The Government of the Commonwealth of Australia is cooperating fully in this work by establishing a range and an organization in Australia, where it will be possible to carry out full-scale tests under most suitable conditions.[5]

Looking towards the future, the White Paper reaffirmed that the supreme object of British policy continued to be the prevention of war.

So far as it is possible to see ahead in present circumstances, His

[1] *Hansard* (Commons), vol. 428, cols. 622–3.
[2] Cmd. 6743 (1946).
[3] Cmds. 7042 (1947), 7327 (1948), 7631 (1949), 7895 (1950).
[4] pp. 8–9.
[5] Cmd. 7327, p. 7.

Majesty's Government are satisfied that it will be necessary to maintain the principle of universal military service and the provisions of the National Service Act, 1947. . . .

The latest White Paper (1950) took the same view.

The objectives of our defence policy derive directly from our obligations and commitments as a Great Power. It remains the firm intention of His Majesty's Government to maintain the forces which are needed to support its international policy, to ensure the security of the United Kingdom, to maintain its interests throughout the world, and to enable it to play its full part in the preservation of world peace. The forces which we maintain in peace must be sufficient to provide an adequate nucleus for expansion in war, to meet the need for garrisons overseas, including those engaged on occupational duties, and to furnish our contribution, when needed, to the United Nations forces. All these duties are the inescapable responsibilities of a Great Power intent on preserving peace.[1]

The 1949 'Statement', in its introduction, re-stated the United Kingdom's defence commitments in the light of the year's developments as follows:

The defence problem of to-day has three main features. First, there is the basic task of reconstruction, of building and equipping new and efficient units from the residue of our war-time forces and of fitting them into the framework of a long-term national defence plan—a plan which must allow for the introduction of new weapons and be appropriate to our obligations to the Commonwealth and Western Union and to any future arrangements concluded for the defence of the North Atlantic area. Secondly, there is the task of maintaining our existing forces from day to day in a condition in which they could resist aggression if suddenly and unexpectedly called upon to do so. Thirdly, and concurrently with the above tasks, arrangements must be made to meet a whole range of current commitments—the provision of forces of occupation in Germany, Austria, and Trieste; the extra forces necessary to reinforce the local security measures in such areas as Malaya, Hong Kong, West Africa and some of the ex-Italian Colonies; and finally the normal range of burdens which falls to the armed forces as a matter of course in peace-time.[2]

It mentioned that

the large-scale exercise of the Home Fleet in co-operation with the Royal Air Force and the Army in December last was designed to try out Fleet dispositions against the threat of atomic bombing and to test the organization for defending our shores against sea-borne attack.

[1] Cmd. 7327, pp. 10–11.
[2] Cmd. 7631, p. 2. In the 1950 White Paper these commitments were still current.

Of no less significance are the cold-weather trials carried out in northern waters by an aircraft carrier, destroyers, submarines and other vessels, designed to test the latest equipment under the rigorous conditions of the Arctic.[1]

Combined operations activities were considerable, and included liaison with United States and Canadian activities, as was mentioned above (p. 227). The Western Union Chiefs of Staff Committee took over the secretariat of the previous Military Committee established in London in May 1948, and had its inter-service planning committees, and technical sub-committees; and three Service Advisory Committees, one for each arm, 'which deal direct with the respective Service Departments in each country for executive action'.[2] The Western Europe Commanders-in-Chief Committee is under the chairmanship of Field-Marshal Viscount Montgomery. 'The main task of this body is to study the tactical problems of the defence of western Europe. It will not assume executive command of any forces in peace-time.'[3] The Western Union Military Supply Board works in close co-operation with the above bodies and 'has a permanent staff which comprises representatives of each country and is directed by a Supply Executive Committee'.[4] A Finance and Economic Committee, again working in co-operation with the above, has also been set up. The sum of £52,000 is borne on the United Kingdom Ministry of Defence vote for financing certain secretarial and other services in connexion with Western Union establishments located in London.[5]

Section VII, Research and Development, describes briefly the developments in research machinery:

Supervision and co-ordination of the programmes is the responsibility of the Defence Research Policy Committee which, under the chairmanship of Sir Henry Tizard, advises the Minister of Defence and the Chiefs of Staff on matters connected with the formulation of scientific policy in the defence field, and is responsible for presenting to the Minister of Defence an annual unified review of future defence research and development policy. The Controller of the Navy and the two Controllers of Supplies in the Ministry of Supply (responsible for munitions and aircraft production) are now members both of the Defence Research Policy Committee and of the Joint War Production Staff, which ensures a close co-operation between these two bodies. The position of Sir Henry Tizard, who is also Chairman of the Advisory Council on Scientific Policy, ensures a personal link with research on the civil side. The Defence Research Policy Committee is served by a permanent staff.[6]

[1] ibid.
[2] Cmd. 7631, p. 5.
[3] ibid.
[4] ibid.
[5] ibid. p. 7.
[6] Cmd. 7631 (1949), p. 13.

By 1950, research and development called for a still greater provision of funds. The full range of problems under this head submitted by the three services had increased, and the maximum scientific and technical effort which the Government felt justified in allotting to the work fell below their demands. The Development Research Policy Committee had the difficult tasks of selection and of recommending priorities.

CANADA

The first issue of this handbook included an account of Canada's defence policy and machinery up to 1933. Defence expenditure had fallen to $14.1 million.[1] The *Proceedings* of the 1937 Imperial Conference stated:

After considerable reductions in 1931 increased appropriations had recently been made for the Defence Services of the Dominion. The strength of the Canadian Naval and Air Forces had been increased, the militia had been completely reorganized and a policy of modernization and mechanization of equipment had been adopted. The industrial aspect of defence preparations had received close attention and a Committee of the Cabinet had been appointed to maintain active supervision of defence problems.[2]

Until 1939 the single Department of National Defence, under the control of one Minister and one Deputy Minister of National Defence, persisted. The following account of the position since the War of 1939–45 is mainly taken from an official pamphlet, *Canada's Defence*, issued in October 1947.[3]

On presenting the defence estimates to the House of Commons on 9 July 1947, Mr Brooke Claxton, Minister of National Defence, stated his country's needs and policy as follows:

Taking up first the question of the defence needs of Canada, Canada's defence forces may be required:
(1) to defend Canada against aggression;
(2) to assist the civil power in maintaining law and order within the country;
(3) to carry out any undertakings which by our own voluntary act we may assume in co-operation with friendly nations or under any effective plan of collective action under the United Nations.

Obviously our needs must be considered in the light of circumstances as they change from time to time. The factors bearing on this are numerous. Among them, the following are particularly important:

[1] p. 84 ff.
[2] Cmd. 5482, p. 17.
[3] Issued under authority of Hon. Brooke Claxton, M.P., Minister of National Defence, by the Department of National Defence.

(1) The geographical position of Canada;
(2) The capacity of any possible aggressor to make an attack;
(3) The dispositions of friendly nations;
(4) What may be called the 'international climate'.

Developments in war-like materials, particularly new weapons, have an important bearing on the whole position. . . . Distance and space still combine to give us great natural advantages for which we cannot be too grateful, but distance and space have been drastically reduced and are still shrinking; and the shaping of world events and the changing centres of power have put Canada in a more important strategical position than she has ever been in before. . . .

As the first aim of our foreign policy is peace, so the first aim of our defence policy is defence against aggression.

Repatriation and demobilization, the Minister continued, were virtually complete. Reorganization was still in progress, and five matters had particularly high priority: organization; training of officers; reserve training; research; and industrial organization. Among the long-term objects of his department and the services, the Minister enumerated: the progressively closer co-ordination of the three services, with joint intelligence and planning and close co-operation between defence, research, and civilian industry regarding weapons and industrial potential; maintenance of adequate numbers and standards of reserve forces and their equipment; organization of civil defence; and 'co-operation with the countries of the British Commonwealth, the United States, and other like-minded countries in working out common standards, planning and training'.

The pre-war organization of a single Minister and one Department was changed in 1940, when the additional posts of Minister of National Defence for Air and Minister of National Defence for Naval Services, with appropriate new departments, were created. The Defence Council, which had originally been created in 1923,[1] was reorganized to include the two new Ministers, the three Deputy Ministers, and the three Chiefs of Staff. A Chiefs of Staff Committee and numerous inter-service committees were also established; and there was, consequential upon war requirements, considerable reorganization of military districts and commands, and air commands.

After the war it was decided to revert to the system of having a single Minister of National Defence, charged, under the Department of National Defence Act (1927) with responsibility for the three services and all matters relating to defence.

The objects of unification included:
(1) The adoption of a unified defence programme to meet agreed strategic needs;

[1] See the 1934 issue of this handbook, p. 88.

(2) a single defence budget under which funds and resources would be allocated in accordance with the programme;
(3) the elimination of duplicatory and even competing services;
(4) consistent and equitable personnel policies;
(5) greater emphasis on defence research and closer co-ordination with other government departments and with industry.[1]

'The [civil] administration of the Department of National Defence is under the direction of the Deputy Minister as its permanent head responsible to the Minister.' There are two associate deputy ministers, for finance and supply and for personnel and pay questions; and three assistant Deputy Ministers responsible for subdivisions of these duties.[2]

The Defence Council, its war-time function of co-ordinating the work of three departments having ended with the re-establishment of a single department,

was reconstituted by P.C. 887 on 13 March 1947 and consists of the Minister who is Chairman, the Parliamentary Assistant, the Deputy Minister, the Associate Deputy Ministers, the three Chiefs of Staff and the Chairman of the Defence Research Board. The Chairman of the Personnel Members Committee, the Chairman of the Principal Supply Officers Committee or other officers attend as required; the Defence Secretary acts as its secretary.[3]

A War Committee of the Cabinet was established on 5 December 1939, and ceased to meet after the spring of 1945. In October 1945 it was succeeded by the Defence Committee of the Cabinet which, under the Prime Minister and the Minister of National Defence as Chairman and Vice-Chairman respectively, includes the Secretary of State for External Affairs, the Minister of Finance and the Minister of Trade and Commerce. The three Chiefs of Staff and the Chairman of the Defence Research Board attend, and other Cabinet Ministers, officers and officials are called as required. The Committee's terms of reference are 'to consider defence questions and to report to the Cabinet upon major matters of policy relating to the maintenance and employment of the three services'. On the less important matters which come before it, it gives directions to the Minister of National Defence to act.[4]

In line with the reversion to a single ministry,

a single National Defence Headquarters has been established. The Navy, Army and Air Force have been organized so that all their activities are channelled in three main divisions:

[1] Canada, Department of National Defence, *Canada's Defence Programme* 1949–50 (Ottawa, King's Printer, 1949) pp. 16–17.
[2] ibid. p. 19.
[3] ibid. pp. 17–18.
[4] ibid. pp. 18–19.

(1) planning, intelligence, training, and operations, corresponding to the General Staff or 'G' branch of the Army;

(2) personnel and pay, corresponding to the Adjutant General's or 'A' branch in the Army; and

(3) supply and equipment, corresponding to the branches of the Quartermaster-General and Master General of the Ordnance in the Army, which have been combined.

The officers and staffs of the Navy, Army, and Air Force dealing with these sets of matters are headed up in three inter-service committees:

The Chiefs of Staff Committee,

The Personnel Members Committee, and

The Principal Supply Officers Committee.[1]

The Chiefs of Staff of the three services and the Chairman of the Defence Research Board constitute the Chiefs of Staff Committee, which renders periodical appreciations of the military situation to the Defence Committee of the Cabinet and the Minister for National Defence. The Personnel Members of the three services are similarly associated on their committee with a Defence Research representative; and the pattern is paralleled in the Principal Supply Officers Committee.

'Intelligence activities common to the three services are being undertaken by the Joint Intelligence Bureau, which reports to the Joint Intelligence Committee, a sub-committee of the Chiefs of Staff Committee.'[2] A National Defence College for senior officers' courses was set up at Kingston, Ontario, in 1948.

The Defence Research Board, already referred to, was set up under the provisions of an amendment of 1 April 1947 to the Department of National Defence Act.[3] The Board consists of a full-time chairman and eleven members. Five of these are *ex officio* members; the three service Chiefs of Staff, the President of the National Research Council and the Deputy Minister of National Defence; six are appointed. For research in matters having also a civilian interest, the Board uses existing governmental research facilities; for purely military research, it has its own laboratories. 'The primary task of Defence Research is to make available to the armed forces all the scientific resources of Canada and of other friendly countries. In carrying out this task, Defence Research maintains close liaison with the United Kingdom and the United States.'[4]

The principles of defence co-operation between countries of the British Commonwealth have been outlined above.[5] In addition, Canada has special arrangements, somewhat similar in pro-

[1] ibid. p. 20.
[2] ibid. p. 27.
[3] R.S.C. 1927, c. 136.
[4] *Canada's Defence Programme*, 1949–50, p. 33.
[5] See p. 154 ff.

cedure, with the United States. The starting-point from which these arrangements developed was the establishment, by agreement between Mr Mackenzie King's Cabinet and the late President Roosevelt, of the Permanent Joint Board on Defence in August 1940. The Canadian Prime Minister and the President met at Ogdensburg, N.Y., and on 18 August issued the following joint statement:

> The Prime Minister and the President have discussed the mutual problems of defence in relation to the safety of Canada and the United States. It has been agreed that a Permanent Joint Board on Defence shall commence immediate studies relating to sea, land and air problems including personnel and matériel. It will consider in the broad sense the defence of the north half of the Western Hemisphere. The Permanent Joint Board on Defence will consist of four or five members from each country, most of them from the Services. It will meet shortly.[1]

The names of the six United States and five Canadian members of the Board were announced on 22 August 1940, and they met for the first time at Ottawa on 26 August.

The statement of 18 August 1940 was followed on 20 April 1941 by the 'Hyde Park Declaration' by the same two national leaders; a declaration which Mr Mackenzie King called the 'simple and logical extension, to the economic sphere, of the Ogdensburg Agreement . . . the economic corollary of Ogdensburg.'[2] The kernel of the declaration was contained in the following sentence:

'It was agreed as a general principle that in mobilizing the resources of this continent, each country should provide the other with the defence articles which it is best able to produce, and, above all, produce quickly, and that production programmes should be co-ordinated to this end.'[3] The statement went on to take account of currency conditions and requirements; and of the operation of Lease-Lend, so that Great Britain 'and all defenders of democracy' should benefit by increased aid through the co-ordination of programmes. On 17 June 1941 the United States and Canadian Governments jointly announced the establishment of Joint Economic Committees, having liaison officers with the State Department and the Department of External Affairs, to study means of maximizing efficient co-ordination of defence production programmes, and of mitigating post-war dislocation in the United States and Canadian economies.

---

[1] World Peace Foundation, *Documents on American Foreign Relations* (New Jersey, Princetown University, 1939–49) vol. 3, p. 160.

[2] ibid. pp. 164, 167; quoted from Mr Mackenzie King's statement in the Canadian House of Commons, 28 April 1941.

[3] ibid. p. 162.

Between June 1939 and November 1940, the Rush-Bagot Agreement of 1817 for naval disarmament on the Great Lakes was e-interpreted by mutual consent to permit, under stated safe-{ uards and with full exchange of information, of the use of Great Lakes shipyards by the United States and Canada for naval construction.[1]

A protocol of 27 March 1941 to the Agreement of the same date between the United States and the United Kingdom regarding the leasing to the United States of bases in Newfoundland, expressly protected Canada's interests in the defence of Newfoundland.[2]

The construction of a military highway through Canadian territory to Alaska was one of the matters put by the Canadian and United States Governments in the hands of the Permanent Joint Board on Defence for investigation and recommendation. On 26 February 1942 the Board approved a recommendation, based on purely military considerations, for the construction of the highway, and the two Sections of the Board as a result proposed to their respective governments, in general terms, a route for the highway. Both governments approved the proposal.

On 17 March 1942 the United States Minister in Ottawa addressed a formal proposal of terms for the construction to the Canadian Secretary of State for External Affairs (which office was held by the Prime Minister), and these terms were accepted by Mr Mackenzie King's Cabinet on 18 March.

The terms thus agreed were as follows: the United States Government undertook the building and war-time maintenance of the highway and agreed to:

(a) Carry out the necessary surveys for which preliminary arrangements have already been made, and construct a Pioneer Road by the use of United States Engineer troops for surveys and initial construction.

(b) Arrange for the highway's completion under contracts made by the United States Public Roads Administration and awarded with a view to ensuring the execution of all contracts in the shortest possible time without regard to whether the contractors are Canadian or American.

(c) Maintain the highway until the termination of the present war and for six months thereafter unless the Government of Canada prefers to assume responsibility at an earlier date for the maintenance of so much of it as lies in Canada.

(d) Agree that at the conclusion of the war that part of the highway which lies in Canada shall become in all respects an integral part of the Canadian highway system, subject to the understanding that there shall at no time be imposed any discrimina-

[1] ibid. pp. 169-78.   [2] See p. 276, below.

R

tory conditions in relation to the use of the road as between Canadian and United States civilian traffic.

The Canadian Government for its part agreed 'to acquire rights of way for the road in Canada (including the settlement of all local claims in this connexion), the title to remain in the Crown in the right of Canada or of the Province of British Columbia as appears more convenient'. The Government of Canada further agreed to waive or remit federal and local taxation of United States personnel and material employed, and restrictions on their entry; the United States Government undertook responsibility for the repatriation of their nationals in due course.

Additional practical points affecting the southern terminus of the highway, the right to construct eight airstrips, and the grant of an additional stretch of highway originally planned as a purely Canadian road, were agreed in notes exchanged in May 1942, August–September 1942, and November–December 1942.

On 27 January 1943, notes were exchanged covering the post-war disposition of defence installations constructed in Canada by the United States Government. The notes took the form of an agreement on general principles based on a recommendation of the Permanent Joint Board on Defence, to which the matter had been referred. The Board pointed out that details of disposition had been in a number of cases specifically agreed as part of the terms of construction, but recommended in principle:

. . . the approval of the following formula as a general fair and equitable basis to be used by reference whenever appropriate in the making of agreements in the future and to cover such defence projects, if any, the post-war disposition of which has not previously been specifically provided for:

A. All immovable defence installations built or provided in Canada by the Government of the United States shall within one year after the cessation of hostilities, unless otherwise agreed by the two Governments, be relinquished to the Crown either in the right of Canada or in the right of the Province in which the same or any part thereof lies, as may be appropriate under Canadian law.

B. All movable facilities built or provided in Canada by the Government of the United States shall within one year after the cessation of hostilities, unless otherwise agreed by the two Governments at the option of the United States Government:

(1) be removed from Canada; or

(2) be offered for sale to the Government of Canada, or with the approval of the Government of Canada, to the Government of the appropriate Province at a price to be fixed by a Board of two appraisers, one to be chosen by each country and with power to select a third in the case of disagreement.

C. In the event that the United States Government has foregone its option as described in B (1), and the Canadian Government or the Provincial Government decides to forego its option as described in B (2), the facility under consideration shall be offered for sale in the open market, any sale to be subject to the approval of both Governments.

D. In the event of no sale being concluded the disposition of such facility shall be referred for recommendation to the Permanent Joint Board of Defence or to such other agency as the two Governments may designate.

The principles outlined above shall reciprocally apply to any defence projects and installations which may be built in the United States by the Government of Canada.

All foregoing provisions relate to the physical disposition and ownership of projects, installations, and facilities and are without prejudice to any agreement or agreements which may be reached between the Governments of the United States and Canada in regard to the post-war use of any of these projects, installations, and facilities.[1]

The above agreements indicate the main co-operative defence projects undertaken in the interests of joint defence by Canada and the United States during the war. During 1944 the Canadian Government purchased, under the agreement of principle set out above, all the United States projects, although certain United States pesonnel remained at weather stations, etc., in the far north.

After the end of the war, it remained for the two countries to decide whether arrangements for co-operation in defence were to be continued and, if so, which procedures should be retained. The decisions arrived at were stated by the Prime Minister, Mr Mackenzie King, in the House of Commons on 12 February 1947, and again took the form of a joint declaration with the United States Government.

I wish to make a statement on defence co-operation with the United States. This statement is also being made to-day by the Government of the United States. It is regarding the results of discussions which have taken place in the Permanent Joint Board on Defence on the extent to which the war-time co-operation between the armed forces of the two countries should be maintained in this post-war period. In the interests of efficiency and economy, each Government has decided that its national defence establishment shall, to the extent authorized by law, continue to collaborate for peace-time joint security purposes. The collaboration will necessarily be limited and will be based on the following principles:

(1) Interchange of selected individuals so as to increase the familiarity of each country's defence establishments with that of the other country.

1 Canada, *Treaty Series*, 1942, nos. 13, 21 ,22 and 26; 1943, no. 2.

(2) General co-operation and exchange of observers in connexion with exercises and with the development and tests of material of common interest.

(3) Encouragement of common designs and standards in arms, equipment, organization, methods of training and new developments. As certain United Kingdom standards have long been in use in Canada, no radical change is contemplated or practicable and the application of this principle will be gradual.

(4) Mutual and reciprocal availability of military, naval and air facilities in each country; this principle to be applied as may be agreed in specific instances. Reciprocally each country will continue to provide, with a minimum of formality, for the transit through its territory and territorial waters of military aircraft and public vessels of the other country.

(5) As an underlying principle all co-operative arrangements will be without impairment of the control of either country over all activities in its territory.

While in this, as in many other matters of mutual concern, there is an identity of view and interest between the two countries, the decision of each has been independently in continuation of the practice developed since the establishment of the Permanent Joint Board on Defence in 1940. No treaty, executive agreement or contractual obligation has been entered into. Each country will determine the extent of its practical collaboration in respect of each and all of the foregoing principles. Either country may at any time discontinue collaboration on any or all of them. Neither country will take any action inconsistent with the Charter of the United Nations: the Charter remains the cornerstone of the foreign policy of each. . . .

In August 1940, when the creation of the Board was jointly announced by the late President Roosevelt and by myself as Prime Minister of Canada, it was stated that the Board 'shall commence immediate studies relating to sea, land, and air problems including personnel and material. It will consider in the broad sense the defence of the north half of the western hemisphere.' In discharging this continuing responsibility the Board's work led to the building up of a pattern of close defence co-operation. The principles announced today are in continuance of this co-operation. It has been the task of the Governments to assure that the close security relationship between Canada and the United States in North America will in no way impair but on the contrary will strengthen the co-operation of each country within the broader framework of the United Nations.[1]

In his comments on the declaration, the Prime Minister said:

The principles of co-operation announced . . . parallel closely the procedures which have long been applied between the nations of the British Commonwealth. . . . The similar arrangements envisaged between Canada and the United States in no way interfere with or replace our Commonwealth connexions in matters of defence training

[1] *Canada's Defence Programme* 1949–50, pp. 37–9.

and organization. Given the geographical position of Canada, it is important that measures of co-operation should be undertaken both with the United States and the United Kingdom.[1]

The Prime Minister concluded with an account of the factors underlying his Government's decisions regarding the Canadian North:

It is apparent to anyone who has reflected even casually on the technological advances of recent years that new geographic factors have been brought into play. The polar regions assume new importance as the shortest routes between North America and the principal centres of population of the world. In consequence, we must think and learn more about those regions. When we think of the defence of Canada, we must, in addition to looking east and west as in the past, take the north into consideration as well. Our defence forces must, of course, have experience of conditions in these regions, but it is clear that most of the things that should be done are required apart altogether from considerations of defence. We must know more about such fundamental facts as topography and weather. We must improve facilities for flying. We must develop better means of communication. The general economic development of the north will be greatly aided by tests and projects carried out by both civilian and defence services. As the Government views it, our primary objective should be to expand our knowledge of the north and of the conditions necessary for life and work there with the object of developing its resources.

Canada's northern programme is thus primarily a civilian one to which contributions are made by the armed forces. This has been the pattern for many years. Thus the army years ago installed and has continued to maintain communication systems in the Northwest Territories. It is now responsible for administering the Alaska highway, now known as the Northwest Highway System, extending from Dawson Creek to the Alaska boundary. The R.C.A.F. has been responsible for taking aerial photographs to be used in the production of maps and charts. It has also been given the responsibility of administering the airfields of the northwest staging route from Edmonton north which are used for civil aviation. More recently, a small winter experimental establishment was set up at Churchill where various tests on clothing, equipment, transport, and so on, are being conducted which will be of general benefit to all who live in the north. Since the United States, as well as Canada, recognizes the need for greater familiarity with northern conditions, we have arranged for its Government to participate in the work of this establishment.[2] It may

[1] ibid. p. 40. The United States Senate on 8 December 1947 ratified the Pan-American Mutual Defence Treaty, to which Canada is not a party. Mr Mackenzie King had already informed the Canadian House of Commons that the effect of the Treaty would not be to alter or extend the policy of American-Canadian collaboration which he had previously announced (*The Times*, 27 May 1947).

[2] A press statement said that there were 110 Americans and 315 Canadians at Churchill (*The Times*, 19 February 1947). Mr St Laurent stated that the United States personnel were under the supreme command of the Canadian

be that other tests and projects will require to be undertaken on a joint basis, in order to extend with a maximum of economy and effectiveness, our knowledge of the north. Through such extension we will acquire the basic data that are needed to make more accessible the economic resources of this region and which will be more valuable for defence purposes as well.[1]

Supplementary to the Permanent Joint Board on Defence, a Canadian Joint Staff Mission, representing the three services and defence research, is maintained at Washington. It was announced in February 1947 that arrangements for exchanges of officers had been made, to start with the temporary attachment of twelve United States Army officers to Canadian Army H.Q. in Ottawa and fourteen Canadians to Washington H.Q.[2] The United States and Canadian Governments would co-operate in operating nine Arctic weather stations to be established by the latter Government.[3] On 9 March 1949 the House of Representatives passed a measure authorizing the United States Government to co-operate with Canada in building a radar screen round North America at a cost of $U.S. 161 million.[4] Mr Brooke Claxton stated that none of this appropriation would be expended in Canada, but that the two countries had dovetailed their plans and that Canada would undertake proportionately comparable expenditures.[5] Canada has Joint Liaison Officers in London, and liaison visits of senior United Kingdom officers to Ottawa are regularly made. On 21 October 1946 it was announced that an interchange of a General Officer appointment between the Imperial Defence College in London and the Canadian Staff College had been arranged, and the first appointments would be operated from February 1947. It was announced in February 1949 that the established scheme by which Army officers of each country serve in the training establishments of the other would be continued for a further two years.[6] Canadian troops formed part of the British Zone Occupation Forces in Germany during 1945–6; they were withdrawn by 1947. On 29 April 1948, in the House of Commons, the Minister of

---

Commandant of the area but were responsible to their own officers for matters of internal discipline (*The Times*, 5 March 1947, report of the Canadian House of Commons debates on U.S. Army Courts' powers).
[1] *Canada's Defence Programme*, 1949–50, p. 41.
[2] *The Times*, 19 February 1947.
[3] *The Times*, 5 March 1947. One more station was established in 1950. The central joint weather station is at Resolute Bay, Cornwallis Island, whence more remote stations are supplied by air lift with personnel reliefs, provisions, scientific equipment, and fuel oil. In 1950 the Royal Canadian Air Force co-operated in the annual air lift, hitherto carried out by the United States Army Air Force (*The Times*, 8 April 1950).
[4] *The Times*, 10 March 1949.
[5] ibid. 29 March 1949.
[6] ibid. 26 February 1949.

National Defence, Mr Brooke Claxton, and the Secretary of State for External Affairs, Mr St Laurent, both reminded the House that the principles of the Canadian-United States Joint Declaration continued in operation; referring particularly to the fifth principle, that all joint defence undertakings in either country are completely under the control of the country on whose territory they are situated.[1]

The Canadian defence estimates debated during March 1949 showed that the armed forces were at the highest strength ever reached in time of peace: Navy, 7,981; Army, 18,523; Air Force, 14,307. Defence expenditure for 1949–50 would be 50 per cent higher than for 1948–9 at $375 million, and, in addition, approval was sought for future commitments on plans to run beyond the fiscal year up to $211 million.[2] Since union in 1949, Newfoundland, already to a large extent integrated with Canadian defence planning, has become formally a part of it. 'The island . . . commands the eastern approaches to our country, and Labrador is our north-eastern land frontier.' The identity of existing Newfoundland units has been maintained, and the organization of a Naval Reserve Division at St John's has begun.[3]

Later Canadian commitments in regional defence plans enabled the Government to define its defence objectives more precisely, although the general objectives remain as stated in 1948. 'The right place to defend Canada and what Canadians believe in is as far away from Canada as possible. . . . The defence of Canada and the defence of western Europe are ultimately one operation. . . . Canada is a member of two regional groups—the North American Group and the North Atlantic Ocean Group. . . . All branches of the defence of this continent have been surveyed by the United States and Canada together and the plans worked out are under continuous review.'[4]

A Joint Canada-United States Industrial Mobilization Planning Committee was set up by an exchange of Notes between the two Governments on 12 April 1949. This Committee will co-operate with the Permanent Joint Board on Defence in all matters of industrial mobilization and planning. In the course of a broadcast on 7 August 1950 on his Government's measures for the fulfilment of Canadian obligations under the United Nations Charter in respect of hostilities in Korea, the Prime Minister, Mr Laurent, referred to the existence in Canada of defence production capacity beyond the needs of Canada's own requirements,

[1] Canada, House of Commons Debates, vol. 87, no. 73, cols. 3438 and 3443.
[2] *Canada's Defence Programme*, 1949–50, pp. 15–19.
[3] ibid. p. 38.
[4] ibid. pp. 11–12. See also Chapter XVII, below.

and to the importance of the new planning committee in this connexion. He also mentioned that Canada had 'developed an airborne brigade group highly trained for operations in the north and designed to share in the immediate protection of this continent'.

The Speech from the Throne at the opening of Parliament on 30 January 1951 stated:

. . . the dangers of the international situation and the magnitude of the defence effort required as a deterrent have, in the opinion of my Ministers, created an emergency situation. You will accordingly be asked to approve legislation vesting in the Governor-in-Council additional powers to ensure adequate defence preparations to meet the present emergency and to prevent economic dislocation resulting from defence preparations.

The Speech also stated that approval would be sought: for Canadian participation in the integrated force for the defence of Europe being organized by the North Atlantic Treaty signatories, under the supreme command of General Eisenhower; for substantially increased defence expenditure; and for the establishment of a Department of Defence Production.

AUSTRALIA

The principles of the Australian Commonwealth defence policy as presented by Mr Bruce at the Imperial Conference of 1926[1] are summarized in the first edition of this handbook. It was recognized that the safeguarding of the Empire trade routes was a matter of prime importance and that equality of status implied some responsibility for sharing the common burden of defence.

No changes of principle in defence policy were shown in the report to the Imperial Conference of 1937, which was as follows:

The basis of Australian defence policy was described as participation in Empire naval defence for the protection of sea-borne trade, as a deterrent to invasion and as a general measure of defence against raids, combined with local defence to provide a further deterrent to and a defence against invasion and raids. The great importance from the Australian point of view of the Singapore base was noticed. The Conference was informed of the large increases in the defence votes in Australia under a Three Years' Programme commenced in 1934 and that a new Four Years' Programme overlapping the last year of the other programme had been put in hand. It was stated that the guiding principles of the Imperial Conferences of 1923 and 1926 had

[1] Cmd. 2769, pp. 170-9.

been adopted by His Majesty's Government in the Commonwealth of Australia as the basis of its policy and the main features of the programmes that sought to implement them were as follows:

(i) *Naval principles providing for the maintenance of adequate naval strength, and the provision of naval bases and facilities for repair and fuel*

The construction of a new cruiser and two new sloops.

The rearmament of the fixed defences and provision of air co-operation.

Facilities for naval repairs and oil storage.

(ii) *Responsibility for Local Defence*

In addition to strengthening the fixed defences of the important ports, the Australian Government had recently provided a special increase in the Army vote to bring the Field Army of seven divisions up to its minimum nucleus establishment. The strength of the permanent forces was also being increased and improvements were being effected in the efficiency, armament and equipment of the Army.

The Air Force would complete this year Part I of the scheme laid down by Sir John Salmond, and have a first line strength of eight squadrons and ninety-six aircraft.

The building up of the Munitions Supply organization had reached the stage that the Government factories had developed the capacity for the production of the various types of the ordinary requirements of the Army, Navy, and Air Force, and these resources were being further expanded. A survey of civil industry was also being carried out to determine the possibilities of capacity for production, and to prepare plans for mobilizing its resources in an emergency.

The Government had recently arranged for the establishment of the aircraft industry on a sound basis and this would be an important adjunct to defence.

As affecting the whole field of defence, great importance was attached by the Australian Delegation to the development of co-operation in defence matters between the several parts of the British Commonwealth.[1]

In 1938, as a result of tension in Europe, a greatly increased defence programme was introduced to cover the next three years, so that, at the outbreak of war a year later, progress had already been made in strengthening the armed forces and in making Australia more self-contained by the expansion of munitions factories and the development of secondary industries. (The Pacific Defence Conference held in New Zealand in April 1939 is described on p. 262.)

In 1944 Australia and New Zealand were parties to the Can-

[1] Cmd. 5482, pp. 17-18.

berra Pact[1] which, although mainly concerned with the prosecution of the war and with post-war aims, also contained an important statement on joint defence policy. Clause 13 of the Pact reads: 'The two Governments agree that within a general framework of world security a regional zone of defence comprising the South-West and South Pacific areas shall be established and that this zone should be based on Australia and New Zealand stretching through the arc of islands north and north-east of Australia to Western Samoa and the Cook Islands.'

A comprehensive defence policy for Australia was outlined by the Prime Minister, Mr Chifley, at the Prime Ministers' Conference in London in 1946, and a full account of his proposals is given in the section on Collective Defence on p. 211 ff. At the opening of Parliament in November 1946 these proposals were embodied in the Speech from the Throne:

Future defence policy will be governed by the forces to be placed at the disposal of the United Nations for the maintenance of international peace and security, including regional arrangements in the Pacific; the forces to be maintained by Australia under arrangements for co-operation in Empire defence; and the forces to be maintained by Australia to provide for self-defence.

My Government intends that the organization and strength of the post-war defence forces will proceed on a basis that recognizes that Australia will make a larger contribution towards the defence of the British Commonwealth. It is my Government's view that this could best be done in the Pacific, and that the approach to a common scheme of defence for this area should be by agreement between the United Kingdom, Australia and New Zealand, British Commonwealth plans being related to those of the United States, and other nations with possessions in this area. An arrangement with the United States Government for the joint use of bases in the Pacific on the principle of reciprocity would be welcomed by my Government, and discussions have been proceeding towards that end.

During the discussion of machinery for co-operation in Empire defence at the Conference of Prime Ministers last April, the Australian Government proposed that there should be assigned to Australia the function of developing the defence aspect of matters relating to regional security in the Pacific in which the United Kingdom, Australia, and New Zealand are concerned, with provision for overseas representation on the Australian machinery. Corresponding provision would also be necessary for dominion representation on the parallel machinery of the United Kingdom. Action is now being organized along these lines.

The whole question of post-war defence policy is affected by the impact of scientific development on the types of weapons and armament for the various services. As a first step, my Government has

[1] See p. 381, below.

approved of the creation of scientific and technical bodies to maintain the closest liaison for Empire co-operation in research, design, development and production of munitions and aircraft.

In the meantime, Australia's defence effort will be the maintenance of the strength and organization necessary with existing weapons; to provide for commitments in the interim period for the Australian component of the British Commonwealth Occupation Force in Japan, and for forces on the mainland for administrative and maintenance purposes, as well as to provide a basis for carrying forward the organization of the peace-time forces.

My Government will make full and adequate provision for post-war defence. The size of each service will be determined by the blending of the Navy, Army, Air Force and Supply services in a balanced scheme which provides in the most effective manner for our self-defence, and for the fulfilment of our obligations under the Charter of the United Nations.

Following this general statement of policy, Mr Dedman, the Minister for Defence, gave details of the Government's programme to the House of Representatives on 4 June 1947. It was based, he said, on the acceptance of the principle that an assured programme over a period of years was the necessary foundation for planning, expenditure, and balanced development. The Government proposed allocations over the next five years totalling £A250 million, annual allocations being: navy, £A15 million; army, £A12·5 million; air force, £A12·5 million; research and development, £A6·7 million; Departments of Munitions and Supply and Shipping, £A3·5 million. Compulsory defence training would be ended, and the programme aimed at permanent forces rising to about 49,000 (army, 19,000) and a citizen force of just over 50,000 (including some 200 in the citizen air force). Both the permanent and citizen forces would be obtained by voluntary enlistment. Naval forces in commission would comprise 2 cruisers, 2 light fleet carriers, 6 destroyers, and 19 ancillary vessels, including frigates and mine-sweepers. Ships in reserve would total 79, including 1 cruiser, 2 destroyers, 6 frigates, and 31 mine-sweepers. The air force would consist of 16 squadrons, with 439 operational aircraft in reserve, and 698 training and miscellaneous aircraft. The large amount allocated to defence research was in conformity with the intention to develop and distribute British Commonwealth resources. Mr Dedman said that the United Kingdom and Commonwealth Governments were in the closest consultation on the best way in which Australia could help with scientific developments affecting defence. To achieve a blending of service and scientific advice the Government had recently added to the higher defence machinery a Scientific Advisory Committee and a New Weapons and Equipment Development Committee. The main item in the programme of defence research and development would be the guided missiles project.[1]

Co-operation with the United States for defence in the Pacific continued to play an important part in Australia's defence policy. After discussions and visits with the United States Admiral of the Pacific Fleet in June 1947, a joint statement issued in Canberra by Mr Butler, the United States Ambassador to Australia, and Dr Evatt, the Australian Minister for External Affairs, reaffirmed the mutual interests of the two countries in the Pacific. The discussions were 'to ensure the continuance of the closest co-operation between the United States and Australian services which existed during the war. . . . They are the natural outcome of this close association . . . and being purely defensive in character are completely in accord with the principles and purposes of the United Nations.'

During the Budget debate in the House of Representatives in September 1948 Mr Dedman again emphasized that 'Australia's role in Empire defence was to develop into a main support area in the Pacific'. He announced further that the British Commonwealth Occupation Force in Japan would soon be entirely Australian, and the Government had gladly accepted that responsibility. He revealed 'a degree of British Commonwealth co-operation in defence never attempted before' and in support of this mentioned that the United Kingdom and New Zealand had joint service representatives in the Australian Defence Department and that strategic planning for common defence measures had thus been commenced. Reciprocal arrangements had been made for the Australian Government to be represented in the higher defence machinery of Britain and New Zealand.

It was announced on 7 June 1949 that the Council for Defence had recommended to the Cabinet an increase of £A20 million in the last three years of the defence plan, making the total for the five years £A270 million. Mr Dedman stated that the first two years' expenditure had been £A63 million, £A8 million less than forecast; but the annual rate of expenditure would probably rise in the next three years. Mr Armstrong, the Minister for Supply, said that satisfactory progress was being made with the guided missiles range in South Australia.

On 1 June 1950 the Admiralty announced the permanent transfer to the Royal Australian Navy of five Royal Navy destroyers, which had been lent to Australia since 1945. The transfer would be without charge, but Australia would bear the cost of

---

[1] See p. 226, above.

converting the vessels into fast anti-submarine frigates (about £2 million).

The Prime Minister, Mr R. G. Menzies, made three broadcast speeches on defence on 20, 22, and 25 September 1950. Events in Korea, he said, had made clear that the free world must face a new technique of oppression, closely integrated despite the geographical dispersion of actual theatres of activity. To confront this technique, it must be clearly recognized 'that for the democracies the days of isolation or of independent action are as dead as the dodo. Australia's defence policy must be part of a world democratic defence policy, or it is nothing.' His Government would reintroduce compulsory national defence training early in 1951. As regards the regular forces, enlistment in the army must in future involve the undertaking to serve anywhere in the world, as was already the case in the naval and air forces. 'The democratic world cannot afford . . . the withdrawal into useless isolation of some of the best troops in the world.' The regular army establishment would be increased to two mixed brigade groups as soon as possible. Present establishment was one group, and that, with one battalion already committed to Korea, was 4,000 under strength. A recruiting campaign would be initiated to bring this first brigade group up to strength as a mobile striking force, and to recruit the second group as a depot and for overseas reliefs of the first group. The Citizen (volunteer) Military Force would have a target of 50,000, and volunteers must undertake to serve overseas if required. With the regular units, it would form a potential expeditionary force. 'This is a major and crucial change in Australia's defence preparations.' The third element in the army would be the National Service trainees, to be called up by quotas for an initial 98 days' training, with 26 days' further training in each of the two years after the call-up year. Regarding the navy, the sound programme put in hand by the previous Government would be hurried on and extended. National Service trainees might choose naval service, and would have 124 days' initial training and a fortnight in each of the succeeding four years. For the Royal Australian Air Force, the Government would establish an Active Reserve of 10,000 ex-R.A.A.F. personnel, and extend Citizen Air Force training. To encourage recruiting in the regular services, rates of pay had been reviewed and suitable increases (of which the Prime Minister gave numerous details) were being made.[1]

---

[1] *Current Notes*, vol. 21, no. 9, pp. 658–69.

Administration

The services are administered by:

The Department of Defence, consisting of the Minister for Defence, the Secretary, with Assistants.

The Council of Defence, which is the statutory peace-time body for advice to the Government on defence and organization. It consists of the Prime Minister, the Minister for Defence, the Minister for External Affairs, the Minister for the Navy, Munitions, and Aircraft Production, the Minister for the Army, the Minister for Air, the Minister for Post-War Reconstruction and the Leader of the Government in the Senate. Officers regularly summoned would be the Chief of the Naval Staff, the Chief of the General Staff, the Chief of the Air Staff, and the Secretary of the Department of Defence. Other Ministers are invited to be present if the aspect of defence policy or organization has a direct relation to their ministerial responsibilities.

The Defence Committee, consisting of the Chiefs of the three services, and the Secretary and Financial Secretary of the Department of Defence. The Chairman of this Committee is the Secretary of the Defence Department.

NEW ZEALAND

The first edition of this handbook described New Zealand's defence policy as it evolved at the Imperial Conferences of 1923 and 1926, and the organization of its armed forces. The absolute dependence of New Zealand upon its sea-borne trade has always been stressed, and for this reason New Zealand readily agreed to contribute annual instalments towards the cost of the Singapore base.

The Pacific Defence Conference, 1939

The co-ordination of imperial defence in the Pacific areas has been continuously discussed between the United Kingdom and the Dominions since the last Imperial Conference in 1937. Under the stress of tension in Europe in 1938 and 1939 New Zealand took the initiative in calling a Conference to consider Pacific questions of common concern to Australia, New Zealand, and the United Kingdom with special reference to defence questions. Accordingly, the Pacific Defence Conference met at Wellington, New Zealand, in April 1939, and was opened by Lord Galway, the Governor-General of New Zealand. The delegates were the defence chiefs from each of the three countries concerned.

The aim of the Conference was to work out the details of an up-to-date common defence scheme, by which increased emphasis would be placed on the expansion and closer co-ordination of the services of the three countries concerned. The scheme would include plans for the closest co-operation of air and sea defences from India through Singapore and Australia to New Zealand and the island territories and colonies to the north and west of New Zealand. Other important features of the scheme would be the munitions supply between the various defence centres in the Western Pacific defence chain, and the provision for the maintenance of adequate lines of communication and transport along the whole chain in an emergency.

The decisions of the Conference were secret and the outbreak of war a few months later put New Zealand's defence policy on a war-time basis.

Post-War Policy

After the war a new defence policy, which stressed the need for close liaison with the United States in defence matters, was outlined by the Governor-General and by Mr Frederick Jones, the Minister of Defence.

Speaking at the opening of Parliament in June 1946, Sir Bernard Freyburg, V.C., the Governor-General, said that Mr Nash, the Minister of Finance, would continue discussions with the United States authorities on the mutual use of island bases, in accordance with the New Zealand Government's desire to be associated closely with the United States and with other Members of the British Commonwealth in responsibility for the defence of the South Pacific. New Zealand was willing to accept a greater proportion of responsibility than hitherto in the defence of the British Commonwealth.

Mr Jones made a comprehensive statement on defence policy in a speech on 5 April 1948.

Our primary task in defence is to make the most effective contribution we can to the security of our own country. We cannot limit our immediate interest to New Zealand. It must extend to that vital area, the islands to the north of us. We must at the same time provide that our forces are so organized and balanced that they can, with other countries of the British Commonwealth or other nations of the Pacific, if and when regional arrangements are developed, make a useful and effective contribution to combined forces. In deciding the size and composition of our armed forces the object is to establish a basic organization which in an emergency will develop with speed and efficiency the full war potential of New Zealand. Our military organization and plans for the future must take into account the possible effect of new weapons and scientific developments . . . the New Zealand armed forces must be so organized that we may play our part in the defence of the British Commonwealth and discharge our obligations to the United Nations. In addition, and as a prerequisite to these tasks, they must be able to contribute in a large measure, should the necessity arise, to the security of the South Pacific area and the defence of New Zealand territory. . . . Our immediate concern is the security of trade and communications, particularly in the Pacific. The Navy and the Air Force must be organized to discharge this role immediately in the event of emergency. To do so effectively, it is essential to maintain bases in the South Pacific Islands, notably Fiji, from which the defensive forces can operate.

The Minister said that positive steps had been taken to secure co-ordination of plans among the armed forces, and also between them and civil departments. Close liaison was maintained with other Commonwealth countries, and there were joint service liaison staffs in London and Melbourne. In addition close liaison would be maintained with the United States.

Defence Science

The Minister emphasized the importance in war of pre-eminence in science, and announced the establishment of a Defence Science Organization for the purpose of integrating scientific research with the armed forces.

The organization provides for a Defence Science Advisory Committee composed of the most eminent scientists in various fields drawn both from government departments and the universities. This committee is linked with similar committees in other British Commonwealth countries, and is charged with advising the Government and the Chiefs of Staff generally on all scientific questions affecting defence.

In addition, a Defence Scientific Corps, the members of which would be recruited from university graduates with high qualifications, was to be established. They would be appointed for a period of five years, and while in the Corps would be employed on the advice of the Defence Science Advisory Committee on defence science projects within the Commonwealth. They would have unique opportunities of gaining higher academic qualifications at overseas institutes within the Commonwealth.

Fiji

The importance of Fiji to the defence of Australia and New Zealand was recognized at the Pacific Defence Conference of 1939, and during the War of 1939–45 New Zealand assumed full responsibility for the defence of Fiji. In pursuance of this policy an agreement was reached in November 1948 between New Zealand and Fiji for the settlement of the Colony's £750,000 war debt to New Zealand and for sharing between the two countries future costs of the defence of Fiji. In announcing this agreement, Mr Nash, acting Prime Minister of New Zealand, said that Fiji would maintain her naval and military forces at strengths to be determined by the New Zealand Chiefs of Staff and would set aside £F100,000 annually for this purpose. New Zealand would pay whatever was required for the naval and military defence of Fiji in excess of this contribution, and would pay the whole cost of Fiji's air defence.

New Zealand Air Force

During a visit of inspection to New Zealand in July 1948 the Chief of the Air Staff of the R.A.F., Lord Tedder, said:

The role of the New Zealand Air Force in war is to contribute to the defence of the main support area in the South Pacific and the vital strategic areas associated with it. It should be so designed and equipped that in the absence of a threat to this support area it can contribute to the defence of neighbouring strategic areas more immediately threatened. . . . Subject to inter-governmental agreement, I am of the opinion that one of the most important roles of the New Zealand Air Force will be to maintain air force bases in Fiji. For this reason I agree that it is desirable that New Zealand should maintain advance air force elements in Fiji in war-time.[1]

Mr Jones, the Defence Minister, reporting on the visit of the Chief of the Imperial General Staff, Viscount Montgomery, in July 1948, said that he (Viscount Montgomery) gave advice with regard to the army, as follows:
(1) To base everything on the Territorial Army.
(2) To maintain sufficient regulars to train the Territorial Army, and no more.
(3) If we can maintain a flow of men through the Army with even three months' training our defensive organization will be reasonably efficient.
(4) Training must be linked with the needs of industry and seasonal trades.[2]

Defence Organization

The development of a higher defence organization in New Zealand has been progressive since 1933, when the New Zealand Committee of Imperial Defence was formed. This Committee was succeeded in 1936 by the Organization for National Security,

---

[1] *New Zealand Herald*, 15 July 1948.   [2] ibid.

whose functions were merged with those of the War Cabinet Secretariat, formed in 1940. After the end of the War of 1939–45 and the consequent dissolution of the War Cabinet, the arrangements outlined below came into being. It resembles the higher defence organizations developed in the United Kingdom, Canada and Australia, and is designed both to secure a co-ordinated approach to major defence problems in the broad sense, and to promote the maximum co-ordination between the three services themselves.

Decisions in matters of defence policy are made by the Cabinet, but in reaching these decisions the Cabinet is assisted by the discussion in, and the conclusions of, the Council of Defence. The Council of Defence is presided over by the Prime Minister and comprises the Ministers of Finance, Defence, Rehabilitation, Labour and Employment, Supply, and the Chiefs of Staff of the three services. Besides dealing with New Zealand's defence policy and organization, the Council also keeps under review questions of defence co-operation with the United Kingdom and other Members of the Commonwealth, and deals with any military matters affecting New Zealand which may arise through membership of the United Nations.

SOUTH AFRICA

Up to 1921 the defence of the Cape Peninsula, including that of the Simonstown naval base, was the responsibility of the Imperial Government, and the British troops stationed there and at other stations in the Union were available for use in the case of any internal war emergency. After the outbreak of the 1914–18 war the Union Government undertook the whole responsibility for the safety of South Africa, including the Cape Peninsula defences. With the exception of the command staff and a few details, the garrison of British troops was temporarily, as it was then intended, withdrawn. After the war, the question of the entire or partial resumption of the defence responsibilities previously discharged by the British Government was the subject of negotiations between the British and Union Governments, and the decision was then reached that the Union Government would undertake the whole responsibility for the defence of the Union. The British Government handed over to the Union these defences together with a large quantity of war material and stores, as well as the landed and other property.

The tension in Europe in the autumn of 1938 was the occasion for a detailed exposition of defence policy by Mr Pirow, the

Defence Minister. Speaking in the House of Assembly on 7 September 1938, he said that any approach to the problem of national defence must be from a purely South African angle, taking into consideration factors which were not found in other portions of the Commonwealth. With 60 per cent of the population Afrikaans-speaking, no defence policy would command the support of the bulk of the people unless its scope were explicitly confined to the protection of South Africa and its vital interests. Another factor was the moral certainty that the Union or its nearest neighbours could never become the main theatre of a major war.

Dealing with practical military problems the Minister explained that they would have to meet an enemy either in the bush or beyond their northern boundary, or along their coastline, if he attempted a landing in force or attacked the ports. The defence of the coastline envisaged a land army comprising a large proportion of the total forces, and a number of fortified harbours. This army would be more liberally equipped than the bush frontier forces with medium and heavy artillery and armoured vehicles and would have attached to it whatever mounted forces any particular situation might demand.

The fortification of South Africa's harbours was based on a 1928 report of the Committee of Imperial Defence, and Mr Pirow was able to announce that the Government had decided to go beyond these recommendations in various respects. He further informed the House that a joint committee of defence and railway experts was examining the possibility of a subsidy by the Defence Department to the railways for the purpose of acquiring and working certain heavy presses and a forging plant, which would be in a position to engage in aspects of armament manufacture at present beyond the means of local industry.

The defence of South Africa was again considered when Field-Marshal Viscount Montgomery, Chief of the Imperial General Staff, visited the Union in 1947 for defence talks with Field-Marshal Smuts, then Prime Minister and Minister of Defence, and Union defence chiefs. The main topics were the Union's defence potential and its role in Commonwealth defence plans. With its raw materials and strategic position on the safest east-west sea routes it was considered that the Union could be a valuable distribution base. Field-Marshal Montgomery's opinion was that two of the main factors in securing the defence of the Union were the dispersal of industries and a planned system of strategic communications. With the latter object in view the Government appointed, in October 1948, a liaison officer between the National Transport Commission and the Department of Defence in order to co-ordinate transport and defence policy.

An important feature of the defence system was to be the arterial roads joining Cape Town to Kenya, which is the main British military supply depot for Africa south of the Sahara.[1]

As Minister of Defence, Field-Marshal Smuts spoke frequently of the importance of the Cape routes in Commonwealth communications and of military recruitment and military training. In the Senate on 27 May 1947, he said that 'the Cape route would be one of the cardinal points of world defence. . . . The land forces were being kept going on new foundations, all the latest developments in the art of war having been adopted.' Again on 8 May 1948, he said 'the defence of South Africa is definitely the highest priority in the business of this country. . . . I attach the greatest importance to our Defence Force and to our young men and women who from year to year enrol and who will play their part in the future for the defence of South Africa.' In appealing for recruits at this time he said he was anxious to maintain the defence organization in as strong a condition as possible.

It (Communism) may come to Africa. We are not only interested in this part of the continent, but in all Africa. What comes to Africa can also come to us. We are, therefore, very anxious to see that we do not have to face this movement of aggressive infiltration penetrating into all our organization and walks of life here in South Africa.[2]

In Dr Malan's Government, which succeeded that of Field-Marshal Smuts in June 1948, Mr F. C. Erasmus was appointed Minister of Defence. While there was no marked change in defence policy, considerable changes were carried out in the organization of the defence forces. Speaking shortly after his appointment Mr Erasmus appealed to Afrikaans-speaking youth to join the Union's defence forces, both to build up a force in keeping with the country's independence and to improve the balance between English- and Afrikaans-speaking men. He invited them to come forward so that a strong force could be built up—one which would not be merely a link in the defence force of any other country.[3]

In the Speech from the Throne on 21 January 1949, it was stated:

There is unfortunately little evidence of any decrease in tension in the general international situation, but my Ministers have no reason to believe that the present differences between the Great Powers cannot be resolved without war. Pending such a settlement, however, my Ministers welcome the steps being taken by the Western democracies

[1] *Sunday Times*, 17 October 1948.
[2] *Cape Times*, 20 April 1948.
[3] ibid. 19 June 1948.

of Europe and America for the protection of that distinctive way of life which unites them and which is shared by the Union. My Ministers are prepared so far as the particular interests of South Africa are concerned, to co-operate with those democracies in the taking of such steps. . . . Special attention continues to be given to the organization and welfare of the Union Defence Forces.[1]

Soon after his appointment Mr Erasmus announced that in future no Bantus or other non-Europeans in South Africa would receive military training or be allowed to carry arms. They would be permitted instead to join the Essential Services Protection Corps in a non-military capacity.[2]

Mr Erasmus also spoke of giving the 'platteland' a greater share in the defence of South Africa. He announced the Government's intention of bringing about a high level of military preparedness in the country, in the cities and on the platteland. This was to be done by reviving and reorganizing the Defence Rifle Associations, which had flourished before the 1939–45 war, and by entrusting the platteland with arms.[3]

For weather-station purposes, South Africa occupied the Prince Edward and Marion Island, 1,400 miles south of Cape Town, in January 1948.

INDIA

India's defence policy was summarized in 1938 by a writer in the preparatory papers for the British Commonwealth Relations Conference held in that year as follows:

The primary function of India's defence forces is the discharge of India's domestic military liability, which comprises local naval defence security from invasion, and the maintenance of equilibrium on the North-Western and North-Eastern frontiers, and the maintenance of law and order in India itself in support of the civil power. . . . It will be seen that India's defence problems differ materially from those of the Dominions and necessitate the maintenance of a comparatively large Standing Army to deal with potential dangers which are ever present and call for immediate military action when they materialize.

A certain number of the Indian States also maintain State forces from within their own revenues, some of which would be available for general defence purposes in the event of an emergency.

India's liability for Imperial defence outside India has not been clearly defined, but generally speaking in the spheres directly affecting the safety of India, say in the zone lying between the Persian Gulf and Singapore, the United Kingdom Government could count on fullest

---

[1] *Weekly Newsletter* (Pretoria).
[2] *Manchester Guardian*, 28 June 1948.
[3] *Cape Times*, 1 November 1948.

co-operation. In spheres further afield there is no reason to suppose that India would not again in the future lend her forces for Imperial service overseas.

At this time responsibility for defence policy lay with the Secretary of State for India in the United Kingdom and with the Governor-General in Council in India.

On 3 September 1939 the Viceroy proclaimed a state of war and India automatically came into the war by virtue of this proclamation. The Defence of India Act was passed shortly afterwards, on 27 September. It was introduced as a war measure and gave the Central Government certain new powers in connexion with defence.

The Indian Independence Act of 1947 gave to India full responsibility for her defence policy for the first time, although a Minister for Defence, Sardar Baldev Singh, had already held office in the Interim Government.

In answer to a question in the House of Commons[1] on 25 February 1947, Mr Attlee, Prime Minister of the United Kingdom, said:

The responsibility for the security of India from external aggression will fall upon India from the date when full power is transferred. If India decides to remain within the British Commonwealth, the position as between His Majesty's Government and India will be similar to that now existing between His Majesty's Government in the United Kingdom and the British Commonwealth. If India decides to leave the British Commonwealth the continued security of India will be a matter of great interest to the British Commonwealth. His Majesty's Government will naturally be very willing to enter into discussions with India as to mutual assistance in matters of external defence, subject to the obligations of both parties under the United Nations Charter.

At the time of the transfer of power a Joint Defence Council was set up by the Governor-General consisting of the Governor-General of India, the Defence Ministers of India and of Pakistan, and the Supreme Commander of His Majesty's Forces in India and Pakistan. The Governor-General of India was the independent Chairman of the Council. The main functions of the Council were the division of the Indian Forces between the two new Dominions and their reconstitution as separate Dominion Forces, and the allocation, transfer, and movement of men and material belonging to the Indian Forces for the purposes of such reconstitution.

A sub-committee of the Joint Defence Council, the Armed

[1] *Hansard* (Commons), vol. 433, col. 1879.

Forces Reconstruction Committee, was the instrument for dividing the Indian armed forces. The proposed basis for division approximately allocated two-thirds of the total personnel and material of the armed forces to the Union of India and one-third to Pakistan. The division of personnel on a territorial-cum-optional basis involved the reorganization of many regiments so that they should contain only nationals of their respective Dominion (apart from the British officers whose services the Dominion retained).

It was announced by the Joint Defence Council in November 1947 that the British Government would close the Supreme Commander's headquarters forthwith, instead of on 1 January 1948, because of difficulties between the two Dominions. Notwithstanding this withdrawal, the Joint Defence Council was to continue to exist, with two Ministers, instead of one, from each Dominion.

Before partition the Indian armed forces had contained a large British element. The new Government retained only a small number of British officers, of whom the majority were experts and advisers on training or on technical matters. The obligation to compensate European and certain categories of Indian officers of the Indian Army for the premature termination of their employment due to the transfer of power was undertaken by His Majesty's Government in the United Kingdom.[1]

The transfer of power also necessitated the consideration of the position of the Gurkha regiments of the Indian Army, which in peace-time had been entirely officered by British soldiers. The future of these units was the subject of long negotiations between the Interim Government of India and the Governments of the United Kingdom and of Nepal. The sequel to these negotiations was an agreement among the three Governments, by which eight battalions of Gurkhas were allotted for service under His Majesty's Government in the United Kingdom and nineteen battalions—of which seven were temporary—were allotted to the army of the Dominion of India. No Gurkha was to be compelled to serve against his will either under His Majesty's Government or the Dominion of India. The agreement was signed on 9 November 1947.

India's change of status naturally led to considerable alterations in defence administration. Before the Interim Government took office in September 1946, the Commander-in-Chief had been the head of all three services and Defence Member of the Viceroy's Council. This latter function terminated with the appointment of a Defence Minister. After 15 August 1947 each

[1] Statement by Lord Listowel in the House of Lords, May 1947.

service was given its own Commander-in-Chief, who was also Chief of Staff of his service. On the establishment of the Republic on 26 January 1950, the President assumed the supreme command of the armed forces of India. A defence committee of the Cabinet was established, consisting of the Prime Minister, the Deputy Prime Minister, and the Ministers for Defence, Finance, and Transport. The Defence Committee of the Cabinet is assisted by subordinate committees at different levels, notably: the Defence Minister's Committee under the chairmanship of the Minister, with the three service Chiefs, the Defence Secretary, and the Financial Adviser (Defence) as the other members; and the Chiefs of Staff Committee. The Defence Ministry has established a Defence Science Research Organization serving the three services. The Republic of India has also participated in the Commonwealth Conference on Defence Science.

Sardar Baldev Singh, the Defence Minister in the new Central Government, was responsible for the reorganization and training of the armed forces necessitated by the withdrawal of the British element and the division of the forces with Pakistan. The Ministry of Defence announced,[1] soon after partition, that machinery was to be set up to provide military training for students of various universities aiming to build up potential reserves of officers for the three armed services. Some months later, on 31 August 1948, Parliament passed a Bill providing for the constitution of a territorial army for India. The role which it was to perform was: (1) to provide a second line of defence and source of reinforcements for the regular army; (2) to assist in internal defence duties in a national emergency; (3) to be responsible for anti-aircraft and coastal defence, and (4) to give the youth of India an opportuniy for military training. In moving the Bill, Sardar Baldev Singh said that the territorial force would comprise technical and administrative units pertaining to all arms and services of the regular army and would in due course form a balanced force in itself, under its own officers, except for a few regulars for instructional work.

Before 1947 responsibility for general naval defence lay with the Royal Navy, and the Royal Indian Navy was a small force primarily for local defence. After the transfer of power, the Indian Government put in hand plans for naval development. A cruiser and several destroyers have been acquired. Vice-Admiral Parry, Commander-in-Chief of the Indian Navy, said[2] in this connexion that 'for some years to come the problem of training officers and men to meet the needs of our greatly expanding Navy will be one of the most formidable problems'. He said that the aim was to train a navy 'capable of taking part in any opera-

[1] *The Times*, 6 December 1948.　　[2] *India Record*, 5 February 1949.

tion'. Plans for the development of an adequate air force are also in hand.

It was announced in December 1948 that General K. M. Cariappa would succeed General Sir Roy Bucher as Commander-in-Chief of the Indian Army.

Speaking on the role of India's defence forces in Parliament in March 1948, the Prime Minister, Pandit Nehru, said that they were the ambassadors of a free nation. The Indian Army had in the past fought on many battlefields and had won a name for itself. But now in a sense it was a new army. It had become the army of independent India and this change had placed a tremendous responsibility on the armed forces of the country. India's defence forces were for the entire country and not for the protection or service of any particular community or province. Of relations with Pakistan, he said that the Government of India would gladly consider the question of joint defence with Pakistan when the time was ripe. . . . The question of joint defence was important from the point of view of both India and Pakistan.

PAKISTAN

With the passing of the Indian Independence Act of 1947 the new Dominion of Pakistan became solely responsible for the defence of its frontiers. It was from the outset provided with a substantial nucleus of trained and armed forces, for the partition of India involved the division of the Indian armed forces between India and Pakistan on a territorial-cum-optional basis. This division was carried out by the Armed Forces Reconstruction Committee, already described above, under the presidency of Field-Marshal Sir Claude Auchinleck. Pakistan retained a small number of British officers, mainly for technical and training purposes.

By January 1948 the Pakistan Military Academy was opened and active planning was in progress for the establishment of a Staff College, and an Infantry School, and for the building of ordnance factories. Mr Liaqat Ali Khan, Pakistan's Prime Minister and Minister of Defence, speaking in the Pakistan Parliament on 15 May 1948, said that he hoped soon to have two million men and women in the Pakistan National Guard, which was formed with the object of helping the armed forces in time of emergency, and to give them training in the use of all forms of arms for the sole purpose of defending the country. The importance of military training as a part of defence policy is stressed by all Pakistan spokesmen.

The Governor-General, Khwaja Nazimuddin, speaking at the Constituent Assembly on 16 December 1948, said:

In the uncertainties of the present world we cannot afford to neglect our defences. The idea of collective security and pacific settlement of disputes which formed the basis of the United Nations has yet to be translated into action. We have, therefore, to depend upon ourselves for maintaining the integrity of our frontiers. The demands made by our defence requirements on our undeveloped economy are extremely heavy, but we should be prepared to make every sacrifice to safeguard our freedom. . . . People of all ranks and status, official and non-official, have impressed upon me the necessity of making adequate provision for the defence of Pakistan, and they have assured me that they are prepared to contribute whatever is needed for this purpose. This assurance has come from the people of East and West Pakistan alike. I also agree with them and the Prime Minister that financial considerations should not stand in the way of making adequate provision for our defence.

After partition, the Government of Pakistan withdrew its military forces from the garrisons in the tribal territories of the North-West frontier. The regular garrisons of the administered districts of the frontier were also considerably reduced. The defence of the frontier was to be conducted by the Civil Armed Forces, supported by mobile regular troops located in centrally situated areas suitable both for peace-time training and for rapid deployment to the frontier.

CEYLON

A small defence force was maintained by Ceylon before it attained independence, but in the main Ceylon relied upon the United Kingdom, to which a small defence subsidy was paid. Under the Constitution of 1946 the responsibility for defence was transferred to the Prime Minister as Minister of Defence, though the United Kingdom retained powers of control. These powers were removed by constitutional amendments in 1947, and, when Ceylon became independent on 4 February 1948, the Prime Minister became solely responsible to the Cabinet and the Parliament for the defence of the island. By reason of its important strategic position and dependence on sea and air communication, Ceylon requires to collaborate with the other nations of the Commonwealth for its own defence. For them, in turn, Ceylon is an important link in the chain of sea and air communications, since an unfriendly Power which seized bases in Ceylon could seriously interrupt sea and air routes in the Indian Ocean and the Bay of Bengal. These common interests found expression in a Defence Agreement between Ceylon and the United Kingdom of 11 November 1947. It runs as follows:

(i) The Government of the United Kingdom and the Government of Ceylon will give to each other such military assistance for the security of their territories, for defence against external aggression and for the protection of essential communications as it may be in their mutual interest to provide. The Government of the United Kingdom may base naval and air forces and maintain such land forces in Ceylon as may be required for these purposes, and as may be mutually agreed.

(ii) The Government of Ceylon will grant to the Government of the United Kingdom all the necessary facilities for the objects mentioned in Article I as may be mutually agreed. These facilities will include the use of naval and air bases and ports and military facilities, and the right of service courts and authorities to exercise such control and jurisdiction over members of the said forces as they exercise at present.

(iii) The Government of the United Kingdom will furnish the Government of Ceylon with such military assistance as may from time to time be required towards the training and development of Ceylonese armed forces.

(iv) The two Governments will establish such administrative machinery as they may agree to be desirable for the purpose of co-operation in regard to defence matters, and to co-ordinate and determine the defence requirements of both Governments.

Ceylon has a first-class naval harbour in Trincomalee, while Colombo is a busy commercial port. During the war several large aerodromes, capable of dealing with the large bomber and reconnaissance fleets intended to be used for the recapture of Malaya, were built, and some of them are being maintained.

In the course of his Speech from the Throne on 12 July 1949, the Governor-General, Lord Soulbury, said:

Proposals for the establishment of Ceylon's Defence Forces have reached an advanced stage. During the last session the Army Bill was passed into law. Among the legislative measures which will be submitted for your consideration during the present session will be a Bill for the establishment of a Ceylon Naval Force, a Bill for the establishment of a Ceylon Air Force and a Bill to define the relationship between Ceylon's forces and the visiting forces of any other country.

Part III

MACHINERY
OF COMMONWEALTH PARTICIPATION
IN INTERNATIONAL ACTION

CHAPTER XII

PARTICIPATION IN INTERNATIONAL
CONFERENCES AND ORGANIZATIONS

BEFORE the War of 1914–18, the British Empire operated as a diplomatic unity, and His Majesty's Government in the United Kingdom conducted high policy on its behalf, subject only to an agreement to inform and consult with the Dominions whenever it deemed this expedient and desirable. Although there was Dominion representation at some technical conferences before 1914,[1] the real watershed between the old system and the new developed during the War of 1914–18. In June 1916, Canadian and Australian representatives attended the Economic Conference in Paris, and in 1915, 1917, and 1918, United Kingdom ministers undertook that in due course the terms of peace would be fully discussed with the Dominions. In March 1917 the Imperial War Cabinet, invitations to which had been sent to the Dominion Governments the previous December, met for the first time, and this was the significant step. The Dominion members of the Imperial War Cabinet attended a meeting of the Supreme War Council at Versailles in July 1918, and the Cabinet became the British Empire Delegation to the Paris Peace Conference under conditions of participation very advantageous to the Dominions by comparison with those obtained by the lesser foreign Powers.[2] With the full support of the United Kingdom Government, the logical subsequent steps were taken; the Dominions signed the Peace Treaties, which were not ratified until the Dominion Parliaments had signified approval; and became original members of the League of Nations.

The War of 1914–18 had shown that the old system was anomalous in the new conditions, and the transition from the diplomatic unity of the British Empire to the diplomatic autonomy of its self-governing parts was smoothly enough effected from the British point of view during 1914–19. But from the point of view of foreign Powers the new system was puzzling and far more anomalous than the old. Sometimes they found themselves dealing with the familiar unit, the United Kingdom, without being quite certain how much of the Empire it also represented; sometimes, when there was separate Dominion representation, India although not fully self-governing, sent representatives, but Newfoundland did not. A diplomatic unity had declared war; a diplo-

---

[1] See p. 336, below.   [2] See account on p. 341, below.

matic multiplicity proposed to conclude peace. It was not surprising that foreign Powers suspected a manœuvre to obtain five or six votes where one had in the past sufficed, and therefore presented some opposition to the new system. The opponents in the United States Senate of the Treaty and the Covenant actually embodied their opposition in a reservation to those instruments, the fourteenth or 'Lenroot' reservation: that the United States would not consider itself bound by any League decision 'in which any member of the League and its self-governing Dominions, Colonies or parts of Empire cast more than one vote'.

Representation in the League of Nations

The opposition of foreign States, and the fact that the new system was, although operative in principle, still at a formative stage, explained the variable representation and enumeration of the British Commonwealth and Empire for some years. The formula for its participation in the Peace Conference at Paris is described elsewhere.[1] The formula for membership of the League of Nations was intermediate between the old and the new systems. The British Empire was an original member and had a permanent seat on the Council; the Dominions (except Newfoundland) and India were original members with full rights as sovereign States in the Assembly. In the list of original members in the annex to the Covenant, the Dominions and India were set out, not in alphabetical order, under the general heading 'British Empire'. At the Assembly meetings, however, delegates of the other British countries did not sit with the United Kingdom delegation, but in correct alphabetical order among all the States members. These variations created some theoretical legal difficulties with regard to the position of the British representative on the Council, but the practice was straightforward. He represented the United Kingdom and those parts of the British Empire which were not separate members of the League. As such he did not represent the Dominions (except Newfoundland) and India, but bore their interests in mind and consulted them when such interests might be affected. 'The essential point . . . was that no Dominion Government had any responsibility for what was done by the British Empire delegate on the League Council.'[2] In due course, moreover, it became an established understanding that one of the Dominions should occupy a non-permanent seat on the Council. An interpretative memorandum conceding Dominion right to election to the Council had been obtained by Sir

[1] See p. 336, below.
[2] See A. Berriedale Keith, *The Dominions as Sovereign States* (London, Macmillan, 1938) pp. 88-9.

Robert Borden from Mr Lloyd George, M. Clemenceau, and President Wilson at Paris,[1] and in 1927 Canada was the first Dominion to be elected to a non-permanent seat. When the Canadian term ended in 1930, the Irish Free State was elected; Australia followed in 1933, and New Zealand in 1936.

Three Dominions were mandatory Powers: Australia and New Zealand accepted 'C' mandates from the League of Nations for the territory of New Guinea and Western Samoa respectively, and South Africa for South West Africa. Australia and New Zealand were mandataries jointly with the United Kingdom for the island of Nauru.

The case of Newfoundland may here be dealt with. Actually since 1919, and in the eyes of international society at least since 1927, the equality in all major matters of the Dominions with other States members of the League was recognized. The position of Newfoundland up to 1934 (when its Dominion status was suspended at the island's request) in the League, in international conferences, and in treaty-making, was summarized in 1938 by Professor Berriedale Keith as follows. It

differed essentially . . . from that of the ordinary Dominion, which is a member of the League of Nations, and therefore in a very definite sense an individual unit of international law. In the case of the great international conferences it was not the practice for Newfoundland to be given special representation; the British representatives act for it as they do for Southern Rhodesia, Malta, and the Crown Colonies and Protectorates. On the other hand, it must be remembered that, while for other parts of the Empire the United Kingdom makes the final decision in these issues of acceptance or not of treaty obligations, it only adhered for Newfoundland with the assent of that Dominion. Nor in theory would that Dominion have been refused the right to conclude a treaty through her own representative. . . . It must, however, be remembered that the obligation to consult the Dominions on treaty matters involved the right of any of them to object to separate action by Newfoundland. . . . The Dominion was entitled to the régime of discussion . . . at the Imperial Conference and to consultation on all issues of general concern. . . . It is not doubtful that a British declaration of war would have at once applied to Newfoundland, and for the purposes of the Permanent Court of International Justice, as for representation in the League of Nations Council and Assembly, Newfoundland was dependent on the action of the British Government. It was not a unit which could be deemed responsible internationally to a foreign Power for any action taken by it contrary to treaty; for that the United Kingdom was bound to answer [as it was also *vis-à-vis* League action or obligations].[2]

---

[1] See p. 343, below.
[2] Keith, *Dominions as Sovereign States* pp. 607–8.

T

The Irish Free State came into existence officially on 6 April 1922, and was therefore not an original member of the League of Nations. In the Commonwealth it had explicitly the same status as Canada, and could therefore claim the same position in foreign relations. The Irish Minister for External Affairs applied formally for League membership on 20 April 1923, and the Irish Free State was admitted on 10 September. It was elected to a non-permanent seat on the Council in 1930, having previously vainly sought election in 1926.

Although the principle was established from the start (and any doubts in the minds of foreign Powers were in due course dissolved) that the Dominions as States members of the League occupied positions of absolute independence of the Government of the United Kingdom and of each other,[1] some theoretical legal points in their relationships were never resolved. The question whether one Member of the Commonwealth could invoke the Covenant of the League in a dispute with another Member never arose.[2] In consequence, the procedural questions involved— mainly whether the other Commonwealth countries should be regarded as interested parties and therefore precluded from voting on the issue—remained undetermined.

The 'Inter Se' Doctrine in League Affairs

The matter is closely connected with the *inter se* doctrine of Commonwealth relations, which in fact did arise in League affairs. Briefly, the *inter se* doctrine is that mutual relations of Members of the Commonwealth are *sui generis*, unique and especially intimate, and therefore differ from international relations, strictly speaking.

One of the bases of the doctrine is that the acceptance in common of the Crown prevents intra-Commonwealth relations being strictly international. It is manifested in a number of formulae— e.g. representatives of Commonwealth countries in each other's capitals are called High Commissioners and not Ambassadors, though their status and privileges are closely assimilated to those of Foreign Heads of Missions[3]—and has had practical usefulness as a ground for refusal to extend Imperial preferential trade concessions to foreign Powers with whom Commonwealth countries have, in other trade matters, most-favoured-nation relationships.

The *inter se* doctrine arose formally in League of Nations affairs in the shape of a difference between the Irish Free State

---

[1] ibid. p. 592.
[2] The question is fully discussed by P. J. Noel-Baker, *The Present Juridical Status of the British Dominions in International Law* (London, Longmans, Green, 1929) pp. 305–18.
[3] See pp. 169–70, above.

and the United Kingdom. On 11 July 1924 the Irish Free State representative at Geneva presented the Anglo-Irish Articles of Agreement of 1921 for registration with the League, holding that Article 18 of the Covenant applied. His Majesty's Government in the United Kingdom immediately addressed a note of protest to the Secretary-General of the League stating:

> Since the Covenant of the League of Nations came into force, His Majesty's Government have consistently taken the view that neither it, nor any conventions concluded under the auspices of the League, are intended to govern the relations *inter se* of the various parts of the British Commonwealth. His Majesty's Government consider, therefore, that the terms of Article 18 of the Covenant are not applicable to the Articles of Agreement of 6 December 1921.

The Government of the Irish Free State replied:

> The obligations contained in Article 18 are, in their opinion, imposed in the most specific terms on every member of the League and they are unable to accept the contention that the clear and unequivocal language of that Article is susceptible of any interpretation compatible with the limitation which the British Government now seek to read into it.

The Articles of Agreement were published in the League of Nations Treaty Series, and the United Kingdom note and the Free State's reply in the next volume.

The Permanent Court of International Justice

In 1920, under the Statute of the Permanent Court of International Justice, the Dominions were granted the rank of distinct States. But one vestige of the pre-1914 system remained under the Statute. The right of a party to a dispute before the Court to have a national judge appointed to sit—if it has not a national already on the Court—did not extend to a Dominion if a British judge was sitting. In March 1929 the United Kingdom Government suggested that this provision of the Statute should be amended in the sense of making it clear that a judge of a Dominion party to a case might sit in addition to one representing the United Kingdom or the British Empire when the case was before the Court. But certain foreign Powers opposed the alteration and it was not made.

The International Labour Organization

The International Labour Organization was established in 1919, when all original members of the League of Nations—and therefore the Members of the British Commonwealth at that date (except Newfoundland) and India—were original members. Membership of the League carried with it (although it was not necessary for) membership of the Organization, and the Irish Free State in due course became a member.

The International Labour Organization continued to function throughout the War of 1939–45, the office being transferred from Geneva to Montreal in 1940. The governing body met throughout the war years, except in 1942, when a session of its Emergency Committee was held. Regular sessions of the International Labour Organization Conferences were suspended from 1940 to 1943, but were resumed in 1944, with a session at Philadelphia. Following the dissolution of the League of Nations, the organization became a Specialized Agency in relationship with the United Nations by an Agreement under Article 57 of the Charter which entered into force on 14 December 1946.

The United Kingdom, the Dominions (except Newfoundland), and India were all members of the Organization in 1939, and their membership continued. Pakistan and Ceylon joined on becoming fully self-governing Members of the Commonwealth.

The Conference on Inland Waterways, Barcelona, March–April 1921

It has been noted above that 'the British Empire' headed the list of the British States signatories to the Covenant of the League of Nations, with the Dominions and India, not in alphabetical order, enumerated below and slightly indented by the printer.[1] In the year or two immediately following the War of 1914–18, 'the British Empire', without qualification, appeared as the high contracting party in instruments concluded as a result of technical or functional conferences on which, of British countries, the United Kingdom alone was represented. At the Conference on Inland Waterways in March–April 1921 held at Barcelona, another variant of still fluid Commonwealth practice was employed. The United Kingdom, New Zealand, and India were represented and signed separately three agreements concluded: the Convention and Statute on the Régime of Navigable Waterways of International Concern,[2] the Convention and Statute on Freedom of Transit,[3] and the Declaration recognizing the Right to a Flag of States having no sea-coast.[4] 'The British Empire (with New Zealand and India)' was the form of words employed to describe

---

[1] For an account of how this arrangement for printing the names was adopted, see J. T. Shotwell, *At the Paris Peace Conference* (New York, Macmillan, 1937) pp. 174 and 414–17.
[2] Cmd. 1993 (United Kingdom Treaty Series, no. 28, 1923).
[3] Cmd. 1992 (United Kingdom Treaty Series, no. 27, 1923).
[4] Cmd. 1994 (United Kingdom Treaty Series, no. 29, 1923).

the high contracting party; and, on signing, the United Kingdom Plenipotentiary expressly declared that his signature was not binding on three Dominions unrepresented at the Conference— Canada, Australia, and South Africa—and that he reserved the right to declare, on ratification, whether the United Kingdom ratification included Newfoundland.

The Washington Conference on the Limitation of Naval Armaments, 1922

The procedure established at the Paris Peace Conference set a precedent for the procedure for Dominion representation at the Washington Conference. At the outset, however, a check to this precedent might seem to have offered for when, in the autumn of 1921, the President of the United States issued the invitations to the Conference, an invitation was extended to the Government of the United Kingdom alone. The United States stressed the fact that it was in diplomatic relations only with Great Britain.

For a time it looked as though certain of the Dominions might stand aloof from the Conference and decline to be bound by any resulting treaty or convention. In the end, however, due regard was had to the importance and significance of the Conference, and it was decided that the Dominions should overlook the omission. Accordingly the British Government suggested a British Empire Delegation which was satisfactory to the Dominions, and His Majesty appointed the Dominions members of the British Empire Delegation on the advice of his Dominion ministers. The United States Government made no objection. Arising out of this arrangement separate full powers were issued by the Crown to the representatives of the Dominions and, in the formal parts of the treaties resulting from the Conference, each Dominion plenipotentiary signed on behalf of the Government which he represented. Thus Lord Balfour signed twice, once without specification on behalf of His Majesty's Government in the United Kingdom, and a second time on behalf of the Government of the Union of South Africa, since he had been appointed representative for this Dominion.

A comparison is immediately invited between the procedure adopted at the Paris Peace Conference and that followed at Washington. There was, technically, this difference: at Washington the Dominions did not obtain dual representation which, at Paris, had given them a peculiarly effective position. Although at Washington the Dominions were as effectively represented on the British Empire Delegation as they had been at Paris, they were not on this occasion represented by delegations of their own. On the other hand, Sir Robert Borden declared that 'the status and distinct consideration that the Dominions had received at Paris were accorded them at Washington'.[1] At both conferences Dominion delegates represented the British Empire delegation on various sub-committees; and in all essentials the position of the Dominions was the same in both cases.

The subject-matter of the Washington Conference, however, made it necessary for the representatives of the British Commonwealth and Empire to work as a unit because any accord on the quantitative limitation of naval forces would have been vitiated had the Dominions been free to pursue unregulated naval construction, which would have appeared to the foreign Powers concerned as disguised accretions to British naval strength.[2]

The Lausanne Conference, 1922–3

It has been mentioned above that foreign Powers did not always readily accept the situation in which several of His Britannic Majesty's Dominions claimed the right to conclude peace when one diplomatic unit, the British Empire, had declared war; and the Lausanne Conference is a case in point.[3]

The precedent created at Paris and maintained at Washington to the extent above described was not followed in any respect in the composition of the British Empire Delegation at the Peace Conference held at Lausanne between the Allied Powers and Turkey. It would appear that France raised objections to the separate representation of the Dominions at this Conference and the British Government yielded. Be that as it may, on 27 October 1922 it was intimated to the Dominions that arrangements had been made for the British Empire to be represented by two Plenipotentiaries (Lord Curzon was to be one, and the British High Commissioner for Constantinople the other); that the Dominions would be kept informed of the general lines of policy which the British delegates would follow and of the course of the negotiations: and that in due course they would be asked to sign any new treaty and the conventions regulating the position of the Straits.

This intimation gave rise to an exchange of views between the

---

[1] Robert L. Borden, 'The British Commonwealth of Nations', *Yale Review*, July 1923.

[2] Keith, *Speeches and Documents on the British Dominions* (London, Oxford University Press, 1932) pp. 67–73; *The Dominions as Sovereign States*, p. 17; A. G. Dewey, *The Dominions and Diplomacy* (London, Longmans, 1929) vol. 11, pp. 80–93; A. J. Toynbee, *The Conduct of British Empire Foreign Relations Since the Peace Settlement* (London, Oxford University Press for the Royal Institute of International Affairs, 1928) p. 83 ff.; Sir Robert Borden's report on the Conference, *Canadian Sessional Papers*, 1922, no. 47; and Sir John Salmond's report, *New Zealand Parliamentary Papers*, 1922, A. 5.

[3] Details in Toynbee, op. cit. pp. 85–92.

Governments of the United Kingdom and of Canada; while, on the one hand, the British Government insisted on the suggestion that the procedure adopted was in substance the same as that followed at Versailles, the Canadian Government, on the other, made it quite clear that it viewed the Lausanne procedure in a quite different light. While no exception was taken to the course pursued, the warning was explicit:

> The extent to which Canada may be held to be bound by the proceedings of the Conference, or by the provisions of the treaty or any other instruments arising out of the same, is necessarily a matter for the Parliament of Canada to decide, and the rights and powers of our Parliament in the particulars must not be held to be affected by implication or otherwise in virtue of information with which our Government may be supplied.[1]

The United Kingdom Government then, with the concurrence of the other Dominions, decided to restrict the signature to the actual British Plenipotentiaries, and Canada acquiesced. When, however, ratifications were to be exchanged, whereas the Government of India, New Zealand, Australia, and South Africa signified their concurrence, Canada once more stood out: she had not been a signatory; she could scarcely, therefore, be expected to give parliamentary approval to the treaty and without such approval the Canadian Government could take no responsibility as to ratification. It was added, however, that they would 'take no exception to such course as His Majesty's Government may deem it advisable to recommend'. The Irish Free State also hesitated to concur in ratification. Actually the Free State ratified the treaty in July 1924, but it was made clear that no active obligation of any sort was undertaken and that she was mainly concerned to have the state of war existing between the British Empire and Turkey terminated.

The Inter-Allied Conference on Reparation, London,
July–August 1924

The background of this Conference was of interest on account of the position taken by the United States and the terms of the British Commonwealth's response thereto. The withdrawal of the United States into isolationism, its rejection of the Covenant of the League, and its reservations to the Versailles Treaty, had hampered subsequent relations between the Allied and Associated Powers. It has been seen above that the advent into international diplomacy of the Dominions had received some checks

---

[1] Cmd. 2146 (1922), p. 4; also quoted in Keith, *Speeches and Documents on the British Dominions,* 1918–31, p. 326.

from other Powers, including the United States, to which Canada was especially sensitive. The pattern of inter-Allied relations was distorted by the attitude of the United States; and that of intra-Commonwealth relations by rigidities of international procedure.[1] Attempts to improve the situation in both these respects was made in 1923–4.

The Imperial Conference of October 1923 investigated fully, from the Commonwealth angle, the problems attendant on negotiation, signature, and ratification of treaties, and made a considerable advance towards their clarification.[2] The resolution which the Conference adopted was mainly concerned with promoting exchange of information and views, but referred to representation at international conferences in the following sentence:

In the case of treaties negotiated at international conferences, when there is a British Empire delegation, or when, in accordance with the now established practice, the Dominions and India are separately represented, such representation should also be utilized to attain this object [i.e. maximum consultation].[3]

Meanwhile there had been indications that the United States might be modifying its aloofness. One of the Senate's reservations to the Versailles Treaty was that the United States should not participate in the Reparation Commission without express consent of Congress—which was not forthcoming—and so far only an American unofficial observer had attended. But on 29 December 1922 the American Secretary of State, Mr Hughes, had hinted that Americans might take part in expert investigations,[4] and this hint had been confirmed on 11 October 1923 by President Coolidge. The United Kingdom Government responded with a dispatch containing the following passage:

It is in the firm belief that the American Government have it in their power to render a great service to the security and peace of the world that His Majesty's Government, speaking in the name of the whole British Empire as represented in the Imperial Conference now assembled in London, desire to associate themselves with the renewed proposal of the President, and they will be glad to receive from the American Government any suggestion that the latter may be disposed to offer.[5]

---

[1] Hancock, *Survey of British Commonwealth Affairs*, vol. 1, p. 287.
[2] See pp. 344–6, below, for details.
[3] Imperial Conference, London, 1923, *Summary of Proceedings*. Cmd. 1987, p. 13.
[4] In an address to the American Historical Association at New Haven.
[5] *Survey of International Affairs*, 1924, p. 49 ff.

The course of this potential diplomatic rapprochement between the United States, Europe, and 'the whole British Empire' did not run smoothly. The Negotiations with the European Allies were long and delicate, and until they were unanimous the United States Government felt unable to invite 'competent American citizens . . . to participate in an economic inquiry'; however, success was finally achieved.

There were also difficulties inside the Commonwealth. During the preparations for the London Reparation Conference, a preliminary meeting of delegates of Great Britain and the Dominions was held in order to arrange for representation at the Conference itself. The Dominion representatives intimated at the outset of the preliminary meeting that, in their opinion, representation should follow the finding of the 1923 Imperial Conference and the precedents set at Versailles and Washington, whereby each Dominion would be separately represented by its delegate, bearing full powers from His Majesty to act, in respect of the Dominion, in the name of His Majesty. It was subsequently intimated by the Prime Minister of Great Britain that it would not be possible for more than three representatives of the British Empire to be present at the Conference proper, 'since this would result in our total representation largely outnumbering that of foreign countries',[1] and it was suggested that those three would necessarily be members of His Majesty's Government in the United Kingdom. The Canadian representative intimated that this arrangement would not satisfy the Dominion; it was open to the same objections as Canada had already raised about Dominion representation at the Lausanne Conference.[2]

It was found impossible to arrive at definite arrangements before the Inter-Allied Conference opened, and at the first plenary session (16 July 1924) the Dominions were not separately represented. On 18 July, however, the Secretary of State for the Colonies announced:

It has been settled that representatives of any of the Dominions so desiring, and of India, shall become members of the British Empire Delegation at the Conference on the panel system, and it has also been arranged for the representatives so appointed to be present at the meetings of the Conference on days when it is not their turn to sit as members of the British Empire Delegation. This will ensure that they are fully acquainted with all that goes on in the Conference. The plan adopted is a special one for this particular Conference and is not to be regarded or quoted as a precedent.[3]

[1] Inter-Allied Conference: Exchange of telegrams between the British and Canadian Governments regarding representation of the Dominions; Canada, *Sessional Papers*, 1924, no. 309, p. 8.
[2] ibid. p. 11.
[3] *Hansard* (Commons), vol. 176, col. 750.

Thus, from 18 July 1924 onwards, the Dominions (with the exception of the Irish Free State) and India were represented at the Reparation Conference in accordance with this plan, and in addition the whole panel of delegates from Great Britain, the Dominions, and India, from which the British Empire delegation was drawn, held a plenary private meeting every day so long as the Conference lasted.

This was the last time the Paris Peace Conference 'panel' system was revived and used in British Commonwealth representation at an international Conference.[1]

The situation regarding Dominion participation in international conferences and organizations had now virtually crystallized. The new system was in force in practice, and it was re-examined and its rules formulated by the 1926 Imperial Conference, which supplemented the work of the 1923 Conference.[2] The character of Dominion participation in League of Nations activities as fully independent States Members was no longer in question and need not be further pursued. Attention is given below only to major international negotiations, outside the League machine, which presented any special features.

The Locarno Conference, 1925

When the Geneva Protocol for the Pacific Settlement of International Disputes of 1924 lapsed, a regional security arrangement for Western Europe was sought. The United Kingdom Government concluded

that the best way of dealing with the situation is, with the co-operation of the League, to supplement the Covenant by making special arrangements in order to meet special needs . . . by knitting together the nations most immediately concerned . . . by means of treaties framed with the sole object of maintaining, as between ourselves, an unbroken peace.[3]

In the subsequent negotiations which led to the Conference of Locarno on 5 October 1925, and during the Conference, the respective attitudes of the United Kingdom and the Dominions were in accord with the tenor of this statement, and with the agreement reached at the 1923 Imperial Conference. The United Kingdom Government kept the Dominion Governments fully informed throughout, by cable and dispatch but not by personal consultation. The Dominions left the conduct of negotiations in the hands of the United Kingdom Government, and reserved

[1] Keith, *Dominions as Sovereign States*, p.585 n.
[2] See pp. 346–9, below, for the text of the Resolution.
[3] Mr (later Sir) Austen Chamberlain's speech to the League Council on 12 March 1925 (League of Nations, *Official Journal*, April 1925, pp. 444–50).

their decisions as to whether they should become parties to any agreement that might emerge. By Article 9 of the Treaty of Mutual Guarantee in the body of agreements forming the Locarno Pact, to which the United Kingdom Government was a full party, the adherence of the Dominions and India was explicitly left optional,[1] and none in fact adhered.

The Conference for the Limitation of Naval Armaments, Geneva, 20 June to 4 August 1927

The Washington Conference had succeeded in negotiating the limitation of construction of battleships and battle-cruisers, and the United States Government wished to follow this up by applying the parities principle agreed at Washington to auxiliary craft from cruisers downwards. President Coolidge therefore issued invitations on 10 February 1927 to Great Britain, France, Italy, and Japan to meet in conference to examine this question. France and Italy refused; Japan accepted.

The nature of the question was of vital interest to the whole British Empire, whose global requirements in auxiliary craft were conditioned by the need to protect its extensive communications. The United Kingdom Government accepted the President's invitation in an agreed note after consultation with the Dominions.[2] The United States Government, which had refused to issue individual invitations to the Dominions to attend the Washington Conference, did issue them for the Geneva Conference.[3] Each Dominion (except Newfoundland) sent a delegation and the Government of India nominated Mr Bridgeman.

No agreement emerged from the Conference.

The Hague Conference, 1929–30

The Committee of Experts on reparation payments and inter-Ally debts (the 'Young Committee', February–June 1929) had before it, among the matters for consideration, Great Britain's claim for arrears of £200 million for the United Kingdom, and £2½ million for the Dominions' share of reparation allocated to them in 1921. During the arduous processes of the Committee's reduction of Allied claims, Great Britain gave way on the £200

---

[1] Keith, op. cit. p. 21: 'While the treaty was concluded for the King without limitation of area, it was expressly laid down that "the present treaty shall impose no obligation upon any of the British Dominions nor upon India, unless the Government of that Dominion or of India signifies its acceptance thereof".'

[2] Sir Austen Chamberlain in the House of Commons, 28 February 1927, *Hansard* (Commons), vol. 203, cols. 29–30. At that date the Irish Free State had not communicated its views, but it was represented at the Conference by its Minister of External Affairs, Mr Desmond Fitzgerald.

[3] P. J. Noel-Baker, *The Present Juridical Status of the British Dominions in International Law*, p. 162.

million, but stood firm on the Dominions' £2½ million. A formula emerged by which, through altering the proposed dates on which the Dawes Plan would end and the Young Plan begin, the Dominions' claims were protected.[1] The nominations of financial experts to serve on the Young Committee were made by His Majesty's Government in the United Kingdom. It was made clear by Mr Churchill, the Chancellor of the Exchequer, and by his successor in the Labour Government, Mr Philip Snowden, that the Young Committee's Report did not commit His Majesty's Government.[2]

The apparent weight of concessions under the Young Plan which would fall on British shoulders had aroused public misgiving, and at the first session of the Hague Conference called to negotiate on the Plan, which met on 6 August 1929, Mr Snowden's firm stand on British claims was supported in the United Kingdom and Dominion press. The convening Governments— Great Britain, France, Italy, Belgium, Japan, and Germany— had agreed that the conclusions of the Young Report concerned, *inter alia*, Canada, Australia, New Zealand, South Africa, and India, and their Governments were invited to take part at the Hague Conference in the negotiations and agreements affecting these Dominions. At the first session only Canada was directly represented. The other Dominion Governments concerned did not avail themselves then of the invitation to be represented individually.[3] Mr Bruce, Prime Minister of Australia, stated on 9 August 1929 that the Commonwealth Government had been consulted and supported Mr Snowden's stand. At the second session, which opened on 3 January 1930, Australia and New Zealand were directly represented.[4] The fourteen agreements which emerged were signed by representatives of all the Dominions invited.

The International Conference for the Limitation and Reduction of Naval Armaments, London, 1930.

At the Naval Conference of 1930, the Dominions were for the first time expressly associated with the issue of invitations to a conference.

Informal Anglo-American conversations on naval limitation and reduction had been in progress when on 2 July 1929 it was

[1] R. J. Stopford and J. Menken, 'The History of German Reparations from the Dawes Plan to the Young Report', *Survey of International Affairs*, 1929, pp. 145, 149–50.
[2] Mr Churchill, House of Commons, 9 May 1929; Mr Snowden, House of Commons, 26 July 1929.
[3] *The Times*, 4 January 1930.
[4] Cmd. 3484 (1930) pp. 4–8.

declared, in the King's Speech at the opening of Parliament, to be the earnest hope of His Majesty's Government in the United Kingdom to ensure, in co-operation with his Governments in the Dominions, the Government of India, and the Governments of foreign Powers, an early reduction of armaments throughout the world.[1] The Dominion Governments notified the United Kingdom Government by early October that they concurred in the proposal to invite the United States, France, Italy, and Japan to meet the British Empire in conference in London in January 1930. On 7 October 1929 a note of invitation was delivered, via their ambassadors in London, to these four Powers inviting them to send delegations to meet representatives of the United Kingdom and the self-governing Dominions of the British Commonwealth in London in the third week in January.[2]

Pending the issue of the Conference, the Government of the United Kingdom, without formally consulting the Dominions, suspended new work and slowed down current work on the Singapore naval base. The Prime Minister, Mr MacDonald, stated that the Dominions would be fully consulted before any decision affecting the base scheme as a whole might be taken.[3]

The Conference opened on 21 January 1930 in London. New Zealand, South Africa, the Irish Free State, and India were represented by their High Commissioners in London; Canada by her Minister of National Defence, Colonel Ralston; and Australia by her Minister for Trade, and Customs, Mr Fenton. With these representatives were associated technical advisers. As in 1921 and 1927, the British representatives acted together as constituting one major naval Power.[4] On 7 February 1929, the United Kingdom Government issued to the Conference, with the Dominion delegates' approval, a memorandum on their policy at the Conference;[5] and they were all kept *au courant* with the American–Japanese conversations during the Conference, which contributed much to the successful conclusion of Part III (not signed by France and Italy) of the ultimate Naval Treaty, which allocated auxiliary tonnage for the British Empire, the United States, and Japan.[6] Ratifications were deposited by all the British countries—except the Irish Free State, which delayed till 31 December—on 27 October 1930.

[1] *Survey of International Affairs*, 1929, pp. 39–41.
[2] ibid. pp. 46–7.
[3] ibid. p. 60, and *Hansard* (Commons), 18 November 1929, vol. 232, col. 35.
[4] Keith, *Dominions as Sovereign States*, p. 578.
[5] *Survey of International Affairs*, 1930, p. 43.
[6] ibid. pp. 55, 59, 69.

The Conference on the Limitation of Naval Armaments,
London, 9 December 1935 to 25 March 1936

At this Conference the question of the status of the Dominions and India was raised by a foreign Power, Japan; and the United Kingdom and the United States exchanged notes on the application of the principle of naval parity.

By Article 23 of the Washington Naval Treaty of 6 February 1922 in certain circumstances, and under Article 23 of the London Naval Treaty of 22 April 1930 automatically, the Powers concerned were committed to summoning a new naval conference before the end of 1935. The circumstances provided for by the former Treaty having arisen through its denunciation by Japan in 1934, His Majesty's Government in the United Kingdom fulfilled their double obligation by issuing invitations, on 24 October 1935, to the signatories of the two Treaties to attend a conference in London in December. Canada, Australia, New Zealand, South Africa, and the Irish Free State were represented by their High Commissioners in London, and India by the Under-Secretary of State for India, Mr R. A. Butler, as their principal delegates: supported, as in 1930, by naval advisers and experts.

The Conference was opened on 9 December 1935 by the Prime Minister of the United Kingdom, Mr Baldwin. The Dominions' representatives indicated at the opening session that they associated themselves generally with the United Kingdom Government's views. Before Christmas it had appeared that the Japanese delegates had been instructed to insist on their country's absolute right of naval parity and a common upper limit of naval construction; and they presently questioned the multiple representation at the Conference of the British Empire—whether it was one, or potentially seven, units of naval power. To the Japanese query whether each Dominion should be counted as 'an independent country', the South African and Irish Free State delegates made replies. The former emphasized the position of his country as a sovereign State, member of the League of Nations, but deprecated the raising of the issue of status 'which might possibly lead to different interpretations of the Statute of Westminster'. The latter said that his country had been a separate High Contracting Party to the 1930 Naval Treaty, and that its position was in no way different from that of any other States signatory to the Treaty participating in the present conference; nor would his country accept any other interpretation of its status.[1]

[1] United States Department of State, Conference Series, no. 24, *The London Naval Conference*, 1935 (Washington, 1936) pp. 142 and 232. Quoted by Robert B. Stewart, *Treaty Relations of the British Commonwealth* (New York, Macmillan, 1939) pp. 194-5.

The Japanese Government withdrew from the Conference on 16 January 1936, and seven of the remaining participants agreed upon the terms of a treaty, which was signed on 25 March 1936 on behalf of the United Kingdom, the United States, France, Canada, Australia, New Zealand, and India. Italy, the Irish Free State, and South Africa did not sign, the two British Dominions declining on the declared ground that their countries did not possess navies or intend embarking on a programme of naval construction. Ratifications in respect of the other Members of the Commonwealth were deposited on 29 July 1937. As a clarification regarding the principle of parity in its application to the fleets of the United States and the British Empire, an exchange of letters took place on 24 March 1936 between the heads of the United States and United Kingdom delegations. Mr Norman Davis put it on record that the two delegations were agreed 'that the principle of parity as between the fleets of the Members of the British Commonwealth and of the United States of America shall continue unchanged'. Mr Eden replied confirming his Government's full agreement 'that there must be no competitive building between our two countries, and that neither country should question the right of the other to maintain parity in any category of ship'.[1]

The Conference regarding the Régime of the Black Sea Straits, Montreux, 22 June to 20 July 1936

The objections of Canada to the procedure for negotiation, signature, and ratification of the Treaty of Lausanne, and the Canadian Government's eventual acquiescence in signature on behalf of the British Empire, have been referred to above. On 10 April 1936 the Turkish Government sent identical notes to the Powers signatory to the Lausanne Treaty,[2] (to which instrument the Convention on the régime of the Straits was annexed) requesting them to enter into negotiations with it for the modification of the demilitarization clauses of the Lausanne Convention. The United Kingdom replied on 16 April, expressing their willingness to negotiate as soon as they had consulted the Dominions.

Italy refused the Turkish invitation, but the representatives of the other actual signatories and of Australia met at Montreux on 22 June 1936. Letters were sent by the Governments of Canada, New Zealand, South Africa, the Irish Free State, and India intimating that their Governments did not intend to send delega-

---

[1] U.S. Department of State, op. cit. pp. 443–4.

[2] And also to Yugoslavia: see *Survey of International Affairs*, 1936, pp. 596, 604.

tions, but would accept the conclusions of the Conference. The Australian chief delegate, Mr Stanley Bruce, whose Government was considered to be the least directly concerned of those represented at Montreux, was elected President of the Conference. The new Straits Convention was signed on 20 July 1936.

The Conference regarding Abolition of the Capitulations in Egypt, Montreux, 12 April to 8 May 1937

The procedure for British Commonwealth representation at this Conference is cited by Professor Robert B. Stewart as interesting on account of the diversity of practice employed.[1] It is also interesting as an example of the revision by several diplomatic units of an instrument concluded by a single diplomatic entity, but which bound and benefited those units at the date of its original signature.

The United Kingdom, acting on behalf of all the dominions of the British Crown, had, in the eighteenth and nineteenth centuries, concluded various capitulatory agreements affecting or with Egypt which accorded privileges to all British subjects. The legal question now appeared whether His Majesty's Government in the United Kingdom, by revising or terminating the agreements, could release Egypt from its obligations in regard to Dominion nationals. Moreover, in 1914 the United Kingdom had unilaterally declared Egypt to be a British protectorate, and it was arguable that earlier capitulatory agreements had *ipso facto* lapsed. But in 1922 the United Kingdom Government had, again by unilateral declaration, pronounced Egypt to be an independent sovereign State, and had declared the capitulatory privileges to be a reserved question pending satisfactory treaty agreement. Negotiations in 1927–8 and 1929–30 broke down, but a treaty was successfully concluded between Egypt and the United Kingdom in August 1936. An annex to that treaty contained arrangements framed with the object of bringing about the abolition, after a reasonable transitional period, of the capitulations.[2] Clause 3 of the annex declared that His Majesty's Government in the United Kingdom did not oppose the intentions of the Egyptian Government, and would use their influence with the other capitulatory Powers in that sense.

Putting aside general legal questions about the position of the Dominions as Powers benefiting from but not actually signatory to the capitulations agreements, the position in respect of the British Commonwealth would seem clear enough. Under established convention, His Majesty could not undertake engagements

---

[1] *Treaty Relations of the British Commonwealth*, p. 197.
[2] Cmd. 5360 (Treaty Series, no. 6, 1937).

for the Dominions without their express consent, and must act in the matter on the advice of his Dominion Governments. In fulfilling the undertaking given to the Egyptian Government, that His Majesty's Government in the United Kingdom would use their influence with the other capitulatory Powers, they would proceed in the same manner towards the Dominion Governments as they used towards the Governments of foreign States; the established Commonwealth channels of communication being used in one case, the established foreign diplomatic channels in the other.

The Governments of the Dominions duly received invitations to attend the Conference. All except Canada accepted. The Governments of Australia, New Zealand, and India requested Captain Euan Wallace, M.P., leader of the United Kingdom delegation, to represent them. The Union of South Africa and the Irish Free State were separately represented. The Canadian High Commissioner in London sent to the President of the Conference, on behalf of the Government of Canada, a letter to be placed on record at the Conference, which stated that the Government of Canada, 'in the lack of any interest special to Canada', would not be directly represented, but would accept any convention drawn at the Conference 'which is signed and ratified in respect of other Members of the British Commonwealth of Nations'.[1] Full powers were issued to all the plenipotentiaries of the Commonwealth countries, and Captain Wallace signed the Convention resulting from the Conference four times, in his fourfold capacity. Full powers for the Irish Free State's delegate were issued by His Majesty; those for the South African delegate were issued under the powers given by the Royal Executive Functions and Seals Act, 1934.

[1] Cmd. 5491, p. 71.

CHAPTER XIII

THE COMMONWEALTH AND THE UNITED NATIONS

SOME account of Commonwealth participation in a variety of Agencies for the prosecution of the war of 1939–45, including intra-Commonwealth as well as international bodies, will be found in a separate subsection. The following account of 'United Nations' action and conferences, in the sense in which the term came to be used following the signing of the Declaration of the United Nations at Washington on 1 January 1942, is roughly divided into: co-operative action preliminary or preparatory to the framing of the Charter; the San Francisco Conference; and some account of Specialized Agencies. It also includes one inter-Allied meeting—that at St James's Palace on 12 June 1941—which does not fall strictly into the category but was preparatory to action within it.

The First Inter-Allied Meeting, London, 12 June 1941

The starting-point of much *ad hoc* United Nations action was a meeting, convened by His Majesty's Government in the United Kingdom, of representatives of Governments and exiled forces in the war against Germany. This meeting, with the Foreign Secretary, Mr Anthony Eden, presiding, was held in St James's Palace, London, on 12 June 1941. Representatives of the Governments of Canada, Australia, New Zealand, and South Africa, of the exiled Governments of Belgium, Greece, Luxembourg, the Netherlands, Norway, Poland, and Yugoslavia, of the Provisional Government of Czechoslovakia, and of General de Gaulle, leader of the Free Frenchmen, were invited and attended. They agreed upon and issued a declaration of Allied solidarity in the struggle against aggression.[1]

The Second Inter-Allied Meeting, London, 24 September 1941

Representatives of the European Governments and the Free French who had met at St James's Palace on 12 June 1941, met again on 24 September, when Mr Maisky also attended as the representative of the U.S.S.R. The meeting was again presided over by Mr Eden, the United Kingdom Foreign Secretary. The Dominion Governments did not send representatives on this occasion. The Governments represented declared their adherence

[1] Text in Cmd. 6285 (1941).

to the principles of the Atlantic Charter. Mr Eden then described action taken and projected to prepare plans for supplying necessities to countries, now occupied, after their liberation. While each Allied Government and authority must be primarily responsible for the needs of their own people, machinery for the co-ordination of plans would contribute to their success. He therefore proposed that each of the Allied Governments and authorities should prepare estimates of requirements in order of priority, and work out in concert plans for the most efficient employment after the war of available shipping resources; and:

That as a first step a bureau should be established by His Majesty's Government in the United Kingdom with which the Allied Governments and authorities would collaborate in framing estimates of their requirements and which after collating and co-ordinating these estimates would present proposals to a committee of Allied representatives under the chairmanship of Sir Frederick Leith-Ross.

The Governments represented accepted the proposals as a whole, with the exception of the Soviet Government which, while having no objection to the principles of collaboration suggested, did not feel able to accept the proposal for the bureau.

The Inter-Allied Post-War Requirements Bureau was duly established, with its inter-Allied directing committee, under Sir Frederick Leith-Ross. The secretariat was provided by the United Kingdom civil service, but was extensively assisted by experts from the other Governments. The Dominions were members of the directing committee, and generally played a notable part in the work of the bureau.

The United Nations Declaration of 1 January 1942

At Washington on 1 January 1942, twenty-six nations at war with Germany subscribed to a declaration of common purposes.[1] The signatories included all the belligerent Members of the British Commonwealth. The declaration stated that the signatory Governments, 'having subscribed to a common programme of purposes and principles embodied in the . . . Atlantic Charter . . . each Government pledges itself to employ its full resources . . . against those members of the Tripartite Pact with which such Government is at war'; and to co-operate with the other signatories and not to make a separate peace or armistice.

This declaration, which was not accompanied by any formal conference or ceremony, was signed in Washington by representatives of the Governments accredited to the United States. The State Department also expressed its willingness to 'receive state-

[1] Complete text in Cmd. 6388 (1942).

ments of adherence to [the declaration's] principles from appropriate authorities which are not governments'.[1] The declaration provided also for the adherence of any country subsequently entering the war, or rendering material assistance in the 'struggle against Hitlerism'.

The Washington Conference of the United Nations on Relief and Rehabilitation, November 1943

In his statement to the Inter-Allied Meeting on 24 September 1941, Mr Eden said that the United States Government would be kept fully informed of the work being done in London on the co-ordination of relief and supply plans. After the United States entered the war, President Roosevelt announced the establishment of an Office of Foreign Relief and Rehabilitation Operations on 21 November 1942, under Mr Herbert Lehmann, ex-Governor of New York State, who took office on 4 December. This United States agency operated in French North Africa after the Anglo-American landings there.

The experience of this office and the work of the Leith-Ross Committee provided a basis for more extensive planning, and the United States Government drew up an agreement on post-war relief after discussion with the Commonwealth countries, the U.S.S.R., and China. This draft agreement was issued by President Roosevelt's Administration, on 10 June 1943, to all the United Nations. At the invitation of the United States, representatives of forty-four United Nations, including Australia, Canada, India, New Zealand, the Union of South Africa, and the United Kingdom, met at Washington in November 1943, and at the White House on 9 November signed the Agreement for United Nations Relief and Rehabilitation Administration.[2] By this agreement, the Administration was established under a Council, consisting of a representative of each signatory,[3] to meet at least twice yearly; and a Central Committee, consisting of representatives of China, the U.S.S.R., the United Kingdom, and the United States, in more or less permanent session as the directing executive body, under the chairmanship (without a vote) of the Director-General. The agreement provided for regional Councils for Europe and the Far East, each with a regional Committee consisting of representatives of the countries in, or directly concerned with, the area. 'The Committee of the Council for Europe shall replace the Inter-Allied Committee on

---

[1] *The Times*, 5 January 1942.
[2] Cmd. 6491 (Treaty Series, no. 3, 1943).
[3] The Agreement provided for the subsequent admission to membership and representation on the Council of later signatories.

European post-war relief established in London on 24 September 1941, and the records of the latter shall be made available to the Committee of the Council for Europe.'[1]

The First Session of the Council of Unrra, Atlantic City, New Jersey, 10 November to 1 December 1943

Representatives of the forty-four Governments and authorities signatory to the Agreement of 9 November met the following day at Atlantic City, New Jersey, in the First Session of the Council of the United Nations Relief and Rehabilitation Administration. They reached agreement on the broad lines of policy for the administration, and, with the assistance of a number of committees and sub-committees, on a considerable volume of more detailed arrangements. Their agreement was embodied in forty-one resolutions accepted by the Council.[2]

Resolution No. 18 laid down that the Committee of the Council for Europe should consist of the members of the Council for Europe (or their alternates), therefore including the United Kingdom; and in addition, of members representing Brazil, Canada, and the United States. Resolution No. 19 set out the composition of the Committee of the Council for the Far East, in which the following Commonwealth countries were included: Australia, India, New Zealand, and the United Kingdom. Later, the seats of the two regional offices were initially established in London and Sydney. The headquarters office of Unrra was in Washington, and the United Kingdom and the Dominions were usually represented at the Council meetings by their Minister or Minister Resident, and India by its Agent-General.

The Inter-Allied Committee and secretariat under Sir Frederick Leith-Ross were dissolved, and the secretariat taken over, if the individuals wished, by the European Regional Office of Unrra in London. Sir Frederick Leith-Ross became Deputy Director of Unrra in Europe.

Unrra was responsible, until its activities were wound up at the end of June 1947, for the organization of a number of regional meetings and area offices, in which British Commonwealth personnel played their full part, and Commonwealth countries made important contributions to Unrra funds and supplies.

The United Nations Conference on Food and Agriculture, Hot Springs, Virginia, May 1943

The United States Government issued invitations to forty-four other Governments, including the Members of the Com-

---

[1] Cmd. 6491, p. 4, para. 5.
[2] Cmd. 6497 (Miscellaneous, no. 6, 1943).

monwealth (Eire excepted and including India), to meet on 18 May 1943 at Hot Springs, Virginia, to consider the goal of freedom from want in relation to food and agriculture.

The Conference accepted an extensive programme of recommendations and resolutions, including the key recommendation 'that the Governments and authorities here represented establish a permanent organization in the field of food and agriculture'.[1] The Conference further resolved:

That in order that every practicable step may be taken to attain these and the other appropriate objectives set forth in the declaration and specific recommendations of the Conference, an Interim Commission . . . be established.

That each of the Governments and authorities here represented be entitled to designate a representative on an Interim Commission, and that the Interim Commission be installed in Washington not later than 15 July 1943.[2]

The Interim Commission was duly established and held its opening session at Washington on 14 July. All the Commonwealth countries (Eire excepted) and India took part. The Commission's main task was to draft a constitution for the proposed permanent organization. 'The Interim Commission duly drafted and presented for acceptance by Governments a draft constitution, together with their First Report to Governments which set out the views of the members of the Interim Commission on the functions of the proposed organization, its administrative structure and its management.'[3]

The First Session of the Food and Agriculture Conference of the United Nations, Quebec, 16 October to 1 November 1945

Under the terms of Article XXI of the [draft] Constitution [of the permanent organization], not less than twenty acceptances of the Constitution were required to enable the Interim Commission to arrange for its formal signature and for the Organization itself to be brought into being. By September 1945, the Governments of twenty-five of the United Nations had notified their intention to accept the Constitution. The Interim Commission, which was also charged with the task of arranging the First Session of the Conference of the F.A.O., accordingly issued a formal invitation on 14 August 1945, to the forty-five nations present at Hot Springs to participate in the First Session at

---

[1] Food and Agriculture, *Final Act of United Nations Conference, Hot Springs, Virginia, 18 May–3 June 1943.* Cmd. 6451 (Miscellaneous, no. 3, 1943) p. 17. (Section reports were published in Cmd. 6461, 1943.)
[2] ibid.
[3] *Documents Relating to the First Session of the Food and Agricultural Conference of the United Nations.* Cmd. 6731 (Miscellaneous, no. 3, 1946) p. 3.

Quebec, Canada, on 16 October. The Canadian Government had offered to act as host.[1]

The Members of the British Commonwealth which had been represented at Hot Springs were among the twenty-five Governments which had signified their acceptance of the draft Constitution. Of these twenty-five, twenty-three had deposited formal acceptances, and sent representatives to Quebec with full powers to sign, by 16 October 1945. The opening of the First Session of the Conference was preceded by the ceremony of signing the Constitution, and the Commonwealth countries were among the twenty-three which then signed.

The Conference was notable for the harmony and expedition with which it agreed on the establishment of the Food and Agriculture Organization and its programme. Sir John Boyd Orr (United Kingdom) was nominated first Director-General, and accepted with enthusiasm. The Executive Committee included several members of Commonwealth countries. 'The Conference adopted a Resolution [No. 9] embodying a broad declaration of policy to the effect that the F.A.O. should so order its procedure and practice as to achieve the closest relationship with the United Nations and other Specialized Agencies established in connexion with it', and authorized the Director-General to negotiate the necessary agreements. 'At the time of the Conference the institutions of the United Nations organization had not come into being and final and detailed decisions in this connexion could not, therefore, be reached.'[2]

In the interval between the First and Second Sessions, a draft agreement covering the relationship between the F.A.O. and the United Nations had been negotiated. The draft was framed in accordance with Article 57 of the Charter of the United Nations and Article XIII of the Constitution of the F.A.O., and provided for the recognition of the F.A.O. as a Specialized Agency for the purposes set out in its basic instrument. The Second Session approved the draft agreement. With the acceptance of the status of Specialized Agency, the F.A.O. passes into the field of the *United Nations Yearbook* and out of the scope of the present compilation.

The Second Session of the Conference of the F.A.O. held at Copenhagen from 2–13 September 1946, considered the admission of Eire to membership of the Organization, which was approved, and Eire then sent a delegation, headed by the Minister of Agriculture, to Copenhagen.

[1] ibid.   [2] ibid. pp. 11–14.

The Preliminaries to the United Nations Conference

The preliminaries to the United Nations Conference at San Francisco, 21 April–29 June 1945, extended over the previous four years. The St James's Palace Conference of 12 June 1941 may be regarded as the starting point; details have already been given above. The next formulation of prospective United Nations aims in regard to a future peace settlement was bilateral, and remarkable in that one party was not a belligerent.[1] The Prime Minister of the United Kingdom, Mr Winston Churchill, and the President of the United States of America, Mr Franklin D. Roosevelt, met on the high seas, outside territorial waters, on board H.M.S. *Prince of Wales*, on 10 August 1941, and drew up and declared the 'Atlantic Charter'.[2]

The United States declared war on 8 December 1941, and on 1 January 1942 all States then at war with the Axis, which included all now Members of the British Commonwealth, signed the Declaration of the United Nations, affirming their adherence to the principles of the Atlantic Charter.

Mr Churchill, President Roosevelt, Premier Stalin, and Generalissimo Chiang Kai-shek met at Moscow on 19–30 October 1943, where they agreed upon and issued the 'Declaration of the Four Nations on General Security', which referred to future international organization, *inter alia*, as follows:

That their united action pledged for the prosecution of the war against their respective enemies, will be continued for the organization and maintenance of peace and security;

That they recognize the necessity of establishing at the earliest practicable date a general international organization, based on the principle of the sovereign equality of all peace-loving States and open to membership of all such States, large or small, for the maintenance of international peace and security.

The first three leaders met again at Teheran for four days and, on 1 December 1943, signed there a confirmatory declaration on 'common policy' in the conduct of the war and their aim of securing 'enduring peace'.[3]

---

[1] Although this was the first occasion on which the United States was associated with a belligerent in a public statement on peace aims, its Government had already devoted study to these questions. See U.S. Dpartment of State, *Report to President on the Results of the San Francisco Conference*, 1945 (Department of State Publication, no. 2349) pp. 20–5.

[2] Dated 14 August 1941.

[3] Text in Royal Institute of International Affairs, *United Nations Documents, 1941–5* (London, 1946) p. 24.

The Dumbarton Oaks Draft, 1944

Meanwhile, in Washington, an Advisory Committee on Post-War Foreign Policies, assisted by a Division of Special Research in the Department of State, by other Departments, and by two non-partisan Congressional groups and various unofficial experts, had prepared the basis upon which certain proposals for a future world organization were drawn up.[1] President Roosevelt ventilated the main outlines of the proposals in a statement issued on 15 June 1944, and on 18 July 1944 they were submitted in draft to the Governments of the United Kingdom, the U.S.S.R., and China.

The three Governments responded by submitting comments to the Department of State, and these three documents, with the American proposals, were the basis of conversations between the four Governments held at Dumbarton Oaks from 21 August to 7 October 1944. The conversations were at the official level, being held between United States, United Kingdom, and Soviet Union officials between 21 August and 28 September, and between United States, United Kingdom, and Chinese officials from 29 September to 7 October. The following announcement was issued on 9 October by His Majesty's Government in the United Kingdom, identical communiqués being issued simultaneously by the other three participating Governments:

(1) His Majesty's Government in the United Kingdom have now received the report of their delegation to conversations held in Washington between 21 August and 7 October with the delegations of the United States of America, the Union of Soviet Socialist Republics and the Republic of China for the maintenance of peace and security.

(2) There is annexed hereto[2] a statement of tentative proposals indicating in detail the wide range of subjects on which agreement has been reached at the conversations.

(3) The Governments which were represented in the discussions in Washington have agreed that, after further study of these proposals, they will as soon as possible take the necessary steps with a view to the preparation of complete proposals which could then serve as a basis of discussion at a full United Nations Conference.

The preliminaries for the San Francisco Conference were thus in train. The Dumbarton Oaks proposals provided an almost complete basis for discussion, except on some minor and three major points: no formula for voting was included; there was no draft on international trusteeship; although an international court was briefly proposed, no draft statute was provided.[3] The

---

[1] *Report to President on Results of San Francisco Conference*, p. 24.

[2] Not printed here. Text in Cmd. 6560 (1945).

[3] A Committee of Jurists met in Washington from 9 to 20 April 1945 and prepared a draft on which the Conference worked.

proposals were circulated to forty-six States for consideration and comment, in preparation for the Conference, by the States responsible for drafting them; these four States were called 'the Sponsoring Powers'. In the United States, comment on a large scale was invited from unofficial organizations and experts.[1]

The Yalta Voting Formula, 1945

The leaders of three of the Sponsoring Powers, the United States, the U.S.S.R., and the United Kingdom, met at the Crimea Conference in February 1945. On 11 February they issued a comprehensive statement on their deliberations, covering military operations and occupation, and European policy; and including the following:

We are resolved upon the earliest possible establishment with our Allies of a general international organization to maintain peace and security. We believe that this is essential, both to prevent aggression and to remove the political, economic, and social causes of war through the close and continuing collaboration of all peace-loving peoples.

The foundations were laid at Dumbarton Oaks. On the important question of voting procedure, however, agreement was not there reached. The present conference has been able to resolve this difficulty.

We have agreed that a Conference of United Nations should be called to meet at San Francisco in the United States on 25 April 1945, to prepare the charter of such an organization, along the lines proposed in the informal conversations at Dumbarton Oaks.

The Government of China and the Provisional Government of France will be immediately consulted and invited to sponsor invitations of the Conference jointly with the Governments of the United States, Great Britain, and the Union of Soviet Socialist Republics. As soon as the consultation with China and France has been completed, the text of the proposals on voting procedure will be made public.

On 24 March 1945 this statement was amplified by the issue of the text known as 'the Yalta voting formula', together with an invitation to the Conference sent by the United States Government to forty-five other States.[2] The voting formula was as follows:

C. Voting. (1) Each member of the Security Council should have one vote. (2) Decisions of the Security Council on procedural matters should be made by an affirmative vote of seven members. (3) Decisions

[1] For an account of the preliminary discussions inside the United States, see *Report to the President on Results of San Francisco Conference*, pp. 25–31.

[2] The final membership of the San Francisco Conference was 50: the United States and 45 originally invited, and 4 (Byelorussia, the Ukraine, Argentina and Denmark) invited by the Conference.

of the Security Council on all other matters should be made by an affirmative vote of seven members, including the concurring votes of the permanent members; provided that, in decisions under chapter 8, section A, and under the second sentence of paragraph 1 of chapter 8, section C, a party to a dispute should abstain from voting.

The United States Government, as the organizing Power, also invited participating Governments to nominate nationals to act as members of the secretariat of the Conference, which they desired should be international in composition: several Governments responded.

The British Commonwealth Consultations of May 1944

The foregoing may be called the international background to the San Francisco Conference and the Charter of the United Nations. Among the Members of the British Commonwealth, the usual channels of communication were supplemented by a conference of Commonwealth Prime Ministers held in May 1944, which discussed the progress of hostilities and the form of a future world organization.[1] Mr Mackenzie King, the Prime Minister, told the Canadian House of Commons on 14 August 1944 that the Commonwealth statesmen had discussed fully and agreed upon the broad essentials of world organization, and that the United Kingdom representatives at Dumbarton Oaks would be fully aware of the views of all the nations of the British Commonwealth. Mr Peter Fraser, Prime Minister of New Zealand, spoke in similar sense when he returned from Europe.

The Canadian official report gives the following additional information.

The Prime Ministers' Meeting in London in May 1944, discussed proposals framed by the United Kingdom Government. The United Kingdom Government, after revising these proposals in the light of the discussions, submitted them to the Governments of China, the Union of Soviet Socialist Republics, and the United States of America. Corresponding papers prepared by these three Governments were also circulated among the four Great Powers. Following a study of the revised United Kingdom memorandum, the Canadian Government gave the United Kingdom Government a considered expression of its views on some of the more important questions which were about to be discussed between the four Powers.[2]

The Canadian official report states:[3]

---

[1] See p. 114, above.
[2] Canada, Department of External Affairs, *Report on the United Nations Conference on International Organization* (Conference Series, no. 2, 1945), p. 7.
[3] p. 7.

Canada was not represented at Dumbarton Oaks, but the United Kingdom delegation met every day with representatives of the diplomatic missions in Washington of Canada, Australia, New Zealand, South Africa, and India. Thus the Canadian Government received day-by-day reports on the progress of the discussions and, in return, made its own views known to the United Kingdom delegation, both at the daily Commonwealth meetings and by telegrams to the United Kingdom Government.

Following the publication of the Dumbarton Oaks proposals on 9 October 1944, Dominion statesmen urged their countrymen to study them. Mr Mackenzie King recommended 'careful and earnest study' and hoped that proposals of such transcendent importance would not be made matter for party controversy. He added that Parliament would be given the fullest opportunity for discussion before Canada entered into any final commitment for participation in a general international organization.[1] Mr Fraser welcomed the Dumbarton Oaks proposals as a good beginning for a world-wide organization, and also recommended their careful examination before the final formulation of this country's views.[2] Field-Marshal Smuts, Prime Minister of South Africa, described the proposals as a step forward towards the establishment of the rule of law.[3]

The Australian statesmen reported in the same sense, and made it clear that no commitments had been undertaken.[4] The Australian and New Zealand Governments, in Article 14 of the Canberra Pact,[5] had already laid it down as 'of cardinal importance' that they should play their part in the planning of the world organization as foreshadowed at the Moscow Conference. Representatives of the two Governments met early in November 1944 and adopted certain resolutions regarding the nature of the future international organization.[6] These resolutions were communicated to the United Kingdom and other Governments; they formed the basis of much of Australia's policy at the San Francisco Conference. The Australian report says:

The work of the British Commonwealth meeting fell into three main groups. There was both a general and a detailed discussion of the Dumbarton Oaks proposals: a discussion on problems relating to colonial trusteeship: and a general exchange of information regarding various aspects of the current international situation.

[1] *New York Times* and *The Times*, 10 October 1944.
[2] *New York Times*, 13 October 1944.
[3] *Christian Science Monitor*, 8 December 1944.
[4] Australia, United Nations Conference on International Organization held at San Francisco 25 April–26 June 1945, *Report by the Australian Delegates* (Canberra, Government Printer, 1945).
[5] See p. 382, below.
[6] *Report by the Australian Delegates*, Annex A.

The Report went on to state the Australian Government's position regarding the trusteeship proposals.[1]

Misconceptions regarding Commonwealth Representation

The idea that the Commonwealth is still a diplomatic unity dies hard. Following the disclosure by the *New York Herald Tribune* of 29 March 1945 of an unpublished agreement at Yalta between Mr Churchill, Mr Roosevelt, and Mr Stalin, the White House on the same day issued a statement that:

The Soviet representatives at the Yalta Conference indicated their desire to raise at the San Francisco Conference of the United Nations the question of representation for the Ukrainian Soviet Republic in the assembly of the proposed United Nations' organization. The American and British representatives at the Yalta Conference were requested by the Soviet representatives to support this proposal when submitted to the Conference of the United Nations at San Francisco. They agreed to do so, but the American representatives stated that if the United Nations' organization agreed to let the Soviet Republics have three votes the United States would ask for three votes also.[2]

'Mr Stettinius, Secretary of State, in a statement to the press, said the reason why the proposal was not included in the joint report on the Crimea Conference was that the report was confined to decisions. The three-vote plan would have to go to the Conference and could not be called a decision.'[3]

The matter was kept secret also because President Roosevelt wished to discuss it with members of the United States delegation to San Francisco. The strong reaction in the American press following the disclosure was due more to the secrecy in which the subject had been wrapped than to the actual proposal. 'It had been communicated late in the previous week to some of the United States delegates to San Francisco. This resulted in a leak which was reflected in one newspaper—the *New York Herald Tribune*'.[4]

On 3 April President Roosevelt, without explanation, announced his intention to drop the plan to ask for three votes for the United States, but said he would continue to support Russia's request for three votes.[5]

Certain sections of the American press took the opportunity provided by this episode to revive the allegation that Great Britain controlled the British Commonwealth Members' votes

---

[1] ibid. pp. 10, 22-4, and Annexes R–U.
[2] *The Times*, 31 March 1945.
[3] *Daily Telegraph*, 31 March 1945.
[4] *Sunday Times*, 1 April 1945.
[5] *New York Herald Tribune*, 4 April 1945.

and thus had multiple representation. This allegation was firmly refuted by the Dominion statesmen in their opening speeches at their meeting in London on 4 April 1945.

The Commonwealth Statesmen's Views on their Countries' Roles

The Commonwealth statesmen's meeting opened in London on 4 April 1945, with Lord Cranborne in the Chair. All the Ministers took the occasion firmly to deny that any concerted Commonwealth policy was being prepared. In his opening speech, Lord Cranborne stated:

The present meeting will be concerned mainly with plans for the new World Organization. . . . I should make it clear, in case there may be misunderstanding in any quarter outside this room, that the purpose of these talks is not to 'gang up' against other nations or to obtain any sectional advantages for ourselves. That would be contrary to the whole spirit in which His Majesty's Government in the United Kingdom and His Majesty's Governments in the Dominions and the Government of India are going to this Conference. We are not entering this World Organization merely for what we can selfishly get out of it. We are entering the World Organization for what we can contribute to it. . . .

It is . . . quite possible both to be a citizen of the world and a member of a family. We are a family, and it is natural that we should wish to deliberate together so as to ensure that, as far as possible, we see eye to eye on the difficult problems we have to face, and may be able to make severally and jointly the greatest contribution in our power.

The High Commissioner for Canada, Mr Vincent Massey, restated the Chairman's point.

This meeting of representatives of the British Commonwealth is, of course, a normal event which is in full accordance with our traditional and reasonable practice. Any other interpretation placed upon it would be wrong and misleading. As the Chairman has said, the nations of the British Commonwealth will not go to San Francisco as a bloc bent on concerting their votes in opposition to those of others. They are not the only group of countries which has met to consider each others' views in advance of the great Conference. Nor has there been failure to talk things over with some of our friends outside the Commonwealth.

Australia's position was stated by Mr F. M. Forde, the Deputy Prime Minister.

Their[1] participation in the San Francisco Conference and ultimately their membership of the World Organization will be as autonomous nations, each participating in its own right. Within the Organization

[1] i.e. the Commonwealth countries.

they will accept obligations not as a group but as individual members, exercising their respective constitutional powers in accordance with the principles expressed in the Balfour Declaration.

Furthermore, the nature of the obligations to be assumed and the rights to be enjoyed by the members of the British Commonwealth within the Organization will vary. One member of the Commonwealth will be a permanent member of the Security Council and will rank among the Great Powers. Others may qualify as non-permanent members of the Council, and at any given time some of them will not be members. . . . The nations of the British Commonwealth may thus be cast into three different roles and look at the operations of the Organization from three different standpoints. If they are to join in a common effort to make a success of the Organization, preliminary discussion is desirable.

Sir Firoz Khan Noon stated India's views thus:

Although on paper India may not be a Dominion I feel it is sometimes necessary to point out that even His Majesty's Government does not know that under their very noses India has grown practically to Dominion status. . . . We are here to represent India and not His Majesty's Government, and we are going to San Francisco also to represent India. . . . His Majesty's Government gave us no instructions for any of these meetings; we have instructions from our own Government. . . . Therefore although on paper India may not be a Dominion, in practice India is a Dominion, and we feel we are here as equal partners with representatives of the other Dominions, as we have been in almost all international gatherings before. . . . There can be no difference between any of you gentlemen from the Dominions and ourselves from India regarding the establishment of a World Peace Organization. . . . We know you are for the future peace of the world and the avoidance of war, and so are we.

Field-Marshal Smuts in his opening speech commented on some of the special features of the proposals prepared for the United Nations Conference. Warning that he saw indications that allied unity was waning, he stressed the need for it to continue and for the Great Powers to work together for the success of the World Organization. He continued:

Recognition of the special position of the Great Powers is right. It corresponds with the realities of the situation. . . . We have now seen that they who wield the power must also carry a special responsibility. . . . The [Security] Council now becomes something very different from the old Council of the League of Nations. It is no longer a body for gate-crashing by the smaller Powers; it is no longer a body at which to seek prestige for ambitious minor States; it is a body which now has a special duty for world peace, for world security; and the Great Powers have heavy special duties thrown on them, such as they never had under the old League. . . . Some concessions will have to be made by the smaller Powers. . . . In status we are all sovereign Powers, but in function we are not all equal. . . . I know that there was something like consternation after Dumbarton Oaks when it became known that there was to be this special position and special functions for the Great Powers, but it was right. . . .

It is a new set-up. It means sacrifice for us, and it means what is much more difficult to secure, unanimity among the Great Powers. If San Francisco fails then I see nothing but stark disaster before mankind. War . . . has become the most awful menace that the human mind can conceive . . . and it will be worse in the future. . . . We go to San Francisco in that sober spirit.

So far as this Commonwealth is concerned, I think it is perhaps the most responsible group in the world, though not the most powerful. It has a very special responsibility for the success of this vast attempt for world peace. . . . I think the British Commonwealth and Empire is capable of making quite the biggest contribution to the success of San Francisco.

Mr Forde and Mr Peter Fraser also referred to the position of the smaller Powers. Mr Forde said that the war record of the Dominions emphasized the desirability of the participation of small and medium Powers in the organization of security. These Powers also wished to see some strengthening of the Economic and Social Council, and they welcomed the inclusion in the San Francisco Conference Agenda of the subject of the protection of dependent territories and their development. He concluded: 'It is thus no part of our purpose to pretend that in all respects the proposals for the World Organization as they stand at present are entirely acceptable to the Australian people. For our own part however we shall approach them with no paltry thought of moulding them to our own special advantage.' Mr Fraser emphasized the attachment of the British Commonwealth countries to the aim of freedom for all in a better world. Those countries had not met to concert selfish action, but to take what might be the last chance to build secure peace and victory.

Many of the points made in the opening speeches were reaffirmed in the final communiqué issued on 13 April 1945 by the Commonwealth statesmen's conference. Its text is as follows:

On the eve of the meeting of the United Nations at San Francisco which is to consider the establishment of a new world organization to secure and maintain peace, we, the representatives of the countries of the British Commonwealth, have met together in London.

We are convinced that only the maintenance after the war of the close co-operation between the United Nations which has brought, and is bringing, success to their arms can prevent the recurrence of strife between the Governments and peoples of the world. The countries of the British Commonwealth stand ready to play their full part in an international organization for the purpose of preserving international peace and security and promoting human welfare.

We have examined, generally and in detail, the tentative proposals resulting from the Dumbarton Oaks conversations and we have had a valuable exchange of views. We are agreed that the proposals provide the basis for a charter of such an organization, fully recognizing that in certain respects they call for clarification, improvement, and expansion.

Each of the countries assembled here will be represented at the San Francisco Conference. Through their representatives it will be the purpose of the peoples and the Governments of the British Commonwealth in all the continents to work for the establishment of a world order which will be worthy of the immense sacrifice made by our peoples and designed to unite the nations in assuring to all men in all the lands economic and social advancement in conditions of freedom, peace, and concord.[1]

After his return to New Zealand, Mr Peter Fraser reported as follows:

The purpose of the British Commonwealth discussions was not to arrive at decisions, but to secure elucidation of one another's viewpoint and to gain first-hand information on the Dumbarton Oaks proposals from the representatives of the United Kingdom Government, which had helped to formulate them. It was made clear to the public during the London talks that the meeting of British representatives in no way implied any intention or desire to create a 'British Empire bloc' which would confront the other United Nations with an agreed policy and a unified vote on all issues.

It was after the discussions at this meeting that Field-Marshal Smuts made the draft upon which the Preamble to the United Nations Charter was based.

The United Nations Conference, San Francisco,
    21 April to 29 June 1945

The exceptional features in the preparations for the calling of this Conference thus included: the long history of the concept of the Charter, dating back to the lowest ebb of the United Nations' military fortunes, and including a declaration of policy by a (then) non-belligerent; the process of formulation, and presentation for public discussion, of the proposals which went to the Conference; and the special position given by the Yalta voting formula to the Great Powers sponsoring the proposals. The procedure of the Conference itself was not less exceptional. 'Every nation represented at San Francisco was in a state of

---

[1] *Manchester Guardian*, 14 April 1945.

war when the Conference began.'[1] Following public plenary sessions, the Conference divided into four Commissions (whose meetings were also public), which subdivided into twelve Technical Committees working on their sections of the proposed Charter and twenty-six sub-committees for specific tasks. The overall guidance of the Conference was in the hands of a Steering Committee, on which every participating country was represented, as they were on each Commission and Technical Committee. Every item in the draft proposals and the thirty amendments submitted (after consultation at the opening of the Conference, from 25 April to 4 May) by the Sponsoring Powers were fully discussed by the representatives of the assembled States, each of which had one vote in Commission and Committee.

It will be seen that the procedure of the San Francisco Conference was one never before adopted by States in the consideration of such vital problems. The Sponsoring Powers submitted their proposals to the fullest vote and everything in the Charter was passed in the Technical Committees by a two-thirds majority before the final text was adopted unanimously at the Plenary Session. [By contrast] at the Conference at Paris of 1919, the Covenant of the League of Nations was drawn up in a committee in which the Principal Allied and Associated States had a majority of representatives, and even then it was not admitted that disputed questions could be decided by vote. In the two Plenary Sessions in which the Covenant was approved, no opportunity was given to those States not represented in the Committee to make alterations in the text. Finally, the Covenant was made part of a general Treaty.[2]

The part played in the Conference deliberations by the Commonwealth countries was important, constructive, and markedly individual. As has already been mentioned, the draft basis of the Preamble to the United Nations Charter was prepared by Field-Marshal Smuts. The careful statement of the protection accorded by the Charter to the domestic jurisdiction of member States, now contained in the seventh Principle (Chapter I) was strongly and successfully advocated by Australia and New Zealand. Chapters XI, XII, and XIII of the Charter, on Dependent Territories and Trusteeship, for which the Dumbarton Oaks meeting had not provided a draft, were based on a working draft compiled by the United States Delegation from proposals submitted by the Sponsoring Powers, France and Australia: the last-named took a distinctive part in this and in the subsequent discussions on the Chapters. 'The general declaration in Chapter

XI is the first comprehensive statement of Colonial policy to be included in an international instrument. Its inclusion is due to the initiative of the United Kingdom and Australia, who took the lead in the drafting of this Chapter.'[1]

In the debates on the Security Council, Australia likewise took a prominent part, submitting an amendment for removing the process of pacific settlement from the requirement of unanimity of the permanent members which, though it was ultimately rejected (by a vote from which many delegations abstained), enlisted marked support in discussion.[2] Australia was also active in the debates on regional security arrangements.

Canada was largely instrumental in introducing an entirely new Article 44, by which the Security Council, once it has decided upon the employment of armed force in a dispute, must admit separately to its deliberations, and accord a vote to, each State not a council member whose armed contingents the Council has called upon and intends to use.[3] Canada and New Zealand obtained the insertion of useful provisions regarding secretariat regulations and standards (Article 100). New Zealand and Australia also recommended an important change from the Dumbarton Oaks text on the Security Council regarding procedures to make armed contingents available, by which the Security Council shall take the lead in negotiating special agreements with the member State (or group of member States) in this matter.[4] All the Commonwealth countries made important contributions to the text on the Economic and Social Council; and India provided the Chairman of the Technical Committee (Committee 11/3) concerned, Sir Ramaswami Mudaliar, who guided its deliberations with outstanding skill and distinction. In accordance with British Commonwealth practice at international conferences, its Members' delegates consulted frequently and freely during the period of the San Francisco Conference.

Some Special Features of the United Nations Charter

The San Francisco Conference thus may be seen to have had exceptional features, and so had the resultant Charter. Apart from the character of the instrument as a whole, there are points of interest in relation to the narrower field of Commonwealth treaty practice. The opening to the Preamble, 'We the peoples of the United Nations', was, of course, modelled at American

---

[1] ibid.
[2] *Report to President on San Francisco Conference*, p. 76.
[3] Canadian *Report on United Nations Conference on International Organization*, pp. 37–9.
[4] The substantive Australian amendment was seconded by Canada, ibid. pp. 39–40.

instance on the opening words of the Constitution of the United States. The final paragraph of the Preamble:

Accordingly, our respective Governments, through representatives assembled in the city of San Francisco, who have exhibited their full powers found to be in good and due form, have agreed to the present Charter of the United Nations and do hereby establish an international organization to be known as the United Nations.

is in inter-governmental and not Heads-of-States form. The whole Preamble is in marked contrast to the account of contracting parties which precedes older instruments of extensive international character as, for example, the General Act of Berlin. The signatures of plenipotentiaries are preceded by Article 111: 'In faith whereof the representatives of the Governments of the United Nations have signed the present Charter,' and signatures are appended under the names of the countries arranged in order of the English alphabet.

In Chapter I, Article 2, 'Principles', the sovereignty of the signatory States is stressed: 'The Organization is based on the principle of the sovereign equality of all its Members.' Again, in Article 78, dealing with trusteeship, is found: 'The trusteeship system shall not apply to territories which have become Members of the United Nations, relationship among which shall be based on respect for the principle of sovereign equality.' The American commentary says, regarding the sovereign principle: 'The expression "sovereign equality" was understood to mean that States are juridically equal and that they enjoy the rights inherent in their full sovereignty.'[1]

Chapter XVI, Miscellaneous Provisions, brings out the overriding character of the Charter obligations:

Art. 102. (1) Every treaty and every international agreement entered into by any Member of the United Nations after the present Charter comes into force shall as soon as possible be registered with the Secretariat and published by it.

(2) No party to any such treaty or international agreement which has not been registered in accordance with the provisions of paragraph (1) of this article may invoke that treaty or agreement before any organ of the United Nations.

Art. 103. In the event of a conflict between the obligations of the Members of the United Nations under the present Charter and their obligations under any other international agreement, their obligations under the present Charter shall prevail.

Regarding Article 102, the United Kingdom commentary

---

[1] *Report to President on San Francisco Conference*, pp. 39–40.

says: 'No definition is given of the term "agreement" and the rules for the application of this Article will have to be worked out by the General Assembly itself.'[1] The United States commentary makes it clear that, in its view, the provisions for treaty registration and the non-recognition of unregistered treaties spring from that American dislike of 'secret diplomacy' of which the late President Woodrow Wilson was the notable exponent.[2] The question of what organ should determine issues of inconsistency arising under Article 103 was raised at the Conference, but not dealt with.

The requirement for ratification was drawn in a conveniently comprehensive form to cover all States' procedures: 'Article 110. (1) The present Charter shall be ratified by the signatory States in accordance with their respective constitutional processes.'

The Charter came into force upon the deposit of the ratifications of the Sponsoring Powers and France; and a majority of the other signatory States. The British Commonwealth signatories ratified in the following chronological order:

New Zealand	19 September 1945
Australia	24 September 1945
United Kingdom	20 October 1945
India	30 October 1945
Union of South Africa	7 November 1945
Canada	9 November 1945

The United Nations Monetary and Financial Conference, Bretton Woods, New Hampshire, 1–22 July 1944

The Bretton Woods Conference was preceded by some eighteen months of technical discussions at the official level. Informal conversations preceded the first preparatory step, which consisted in the simultaneous publication of Lord Keynes's proposal for a 'Clearing Union' and Dr Harry White's plan for a 'Stabilization Fund of the United and Associated Nations' in April 1943 in London and Washington respectively. The United States Treasury then held a series of bilateral conversations with officials of other Governments, including the Governments of the belligerent Members of the British Commonwealth, and followed these up by arranging a general exchange of views at Washington in June 1943, at which some twenty countries were represented. This meeting was followed by further conversations, bilateral and group, in the course of which Canada put forward proposals on similar general lines to those already made by the United Kingdom and United States officials.

[1] Cmd. 6666.
[2] *Report to President on San Francisco Conference*, pp. 153–5.

Since the area of general agreement was found to be considerable, attention was next given to matters of technique and amounts, and the experts' agreement on these questions was embodied in a Joint Statement on the Establishment of an International Monetary Fund of the United and Associated Nations and issued on 21 April 1944. A tentative draft of proposals for an International Bank for Reconstruction and Development had already been published on 24 November 1943. Final preparations for the Conference were made at informal discussions held at Atlantic City from 15 to 30 June 1944.[1]

The United States Government issued the invitations to the Conference, which opened at Bretton Woods on 1 July 1944. In all, there were present: forty-four representatives of Governments; the French Delegation; and the Danish Minister at Washington in his personal capacity. Mr Henry Morgenthau, Chairman of the United States Delegation, was elected President of the Conference.

The purpose of the Conference at Bretton Woods was to provide an opportunity for joint examination and discussion of the above-mentioned drafts [of 21 April 1944 and 24 November 1943] on behalf of the Governments of the participating nations, with a view to formulating proposals on a sufficiently considered and definite basis for submission to the Governments of the forty-four nations which sent delegations to the Conference. It was made clear from the beginning that, whatever proposals might be crystallized, and whatever plans might be formulated at the Conference, there would be no obligation, actual or implied, on any Government to become a party to any such plans. There is thus no impediment to the proposals being examined and dealt with purely on their merits.[2]

The final plenary session of the Conference took place on 22 July. The Conference authorized the publication by the United States Government of the Articles of Agreement of the International Monetary Fund and of the International Bank of Reconstruction and Development, drawn up as a result of the work of its Technical Commissions and Committees;[3] recommended the 'earliest possible' liquidation of the Bank for International Settlements; and invited the Governments represented at the Conference to take certain steps to prevent the effective concealment of assets and loot by enemy countries and enemy nationals.[4]

[1] United Nations Monetary and Financial Conference, Bretton Woods, New Hampshire, U.S.A., 1–22 July 1944, *Documents Supplementary to the Final Act.* Cmd. 6597 (1945), pp. 10–11.
[2] United Nations Monetary and Financial Conference, Bretton Woods . . . *Report by New Zealand Delegation and Text of Final Act* (Wellington, 1944), p. 1.
[3] Texts in Cmd. 6546 (1944).   [4] ibid. pp. 12–13.

Under Article XX of the International Monetary Fund Agreement, the Agreement was to enter into force when Governments having 65 per cent of the total of quotas agreed in Article III and set out in Schedule A had signed, but not earlier than 1 May 1945.[1] The International Bank Agreement was to enter into force, under its Article XI, when the signatures of Governments subscribing 65 per cent of total subscriptions had been deposited,[2] but again not earlier than 1 May 1945.

In accordance with the terms of the invitation to the Conference, the Articles of Agreement of the Fund and the Bank were submitted for consideration by the Governments, and gave rise to some controversy. By 27 December 1945, twenty-eight Governments had signified their acceptance of both Agreements, and, since their quotas and subscriptions represented a sufficient proportion of the totals, the Agreements then came into force. Australia did not sign either Agreement until 8 August 1947, and New Zealand has not signed.[3] The inaugural meetings of the Boards of both Agencies were held on 8–18 March 1946 at Savannah, Georgia. Agreements on the status of the Fund and the Bank as Specialized Agencies in relationship with the United Nations, under Article 57 of the Charter, were subsequently negotiated and came into force on 15 November 1947.

Upon the departure of Burma from the British Commonwealth and the attainment of fully self-governing status by Ceylon, the United Kingdom gave notice to the Fund and Bank that these countries had ceased to be territories on whose behalf the United Kingdom accepted the Articles of Agreement. Ceylon and Pakistan have since adhered to the Agreements.

The International Civil Aviation Conference, Chicago, 1 November to 7 December 1944

The War of 1939–45, like the War of 1914–18, raised a number of urgent problems of civil aviation. British Commonwealth countries gave attention to these questions at an early stage of the war. Before 1939 only two major international air conventions were operative. The first had been drawn up at Paris in 1919, and failed of ratification by the United States; nor was the U.S.S.R. among the thirty-three States parties to the Convention. The other, the Havana Convention of 1928, was applicable only to the American Republics. War-time experience made felt the need for more comprehensive international action.

[1] ibid. pp. 17–18, 37, 41.
[2] ibid. pp. 47, 63, 65.
[3] The United Kingdom, Canada, and South Africa signed on 27 December 1945.

The latest pre-war statement on British Commonwealth co-operation in civil aviation matters was the resolution of the Imperial Conference of 1937, as follows:

(1) Appreciating the many benefits, direct and indirect, immediate and potential, to be secured by nations possessing substantial and extensive civil aviation enterprises, the Conference is unanimous in its approval of the Members of the British Commonwealth of Nations pursuing a vigorous policy in regard to their air services, embracing expansion within each of their territories and interconnexion between Members.

(2) In order to promote arrangements whereby air lines of the Members of the British Commonwealth of Nations will link them together, the Conference affirms the willingness of the countries represented to co-operate with each other to the greatest possible extent.

(3) In emphasizing the importance of continued co-operation in the development of air services connecting the territories of the various Members, the Conference recognizes that the most effective method of co-operation and efficient organization can best be settled by the Governments concerned in each particular case as it arises, but any method should recognize, where desired by a Government, local control not only over services operating within its own territory but also, by agreement with the other Governments concerned, in adjacent areas in which it is particularly interested.

(4) It is agreed that, whenever an application received by one Member for facilities for foreign air services is likely to affect another Member, there should be consultation between the respective Governments concerned before facilities are granted; and if an agreement has been reached between the Commonwealth Governments concerned as to the service to be required in return for such facilities, the Commonwealth Government to whom the foreign application has been made will use its best endeavours to secure the reciprocal facilities agreed upon.

(5) The Conference notes with approval the practice followed by Nations of the Commonwealth whereby, when operational rights are granted to a foreign air line, the concession expressly provides for reciprocal rights as and when desired; and suggests for consideration the desirability of including in such concessions a general safeguard of the right of the Government, at its option, to take over the ground organization within its territory on suitable terms.[1]

On 11 March 1943 Sir Archibald Sinclair, Secretary of State for Air, said in the House of Commons that 'some form of international collaboration will be essential if the air is to be developed in the interests of mankind as a whole, trade served, international understandings fostered and some measure of international security gained'. Up to 1938, the attitudes of the United King-

---

[1] Cmd. 5482 (1937), p. 29.

dom and the United States had been broadly similar in favouring maximum freedom of commercial flight, but, by the passage of the Civil Aeronautics Act of 1938, the United States had turned towards a more restrictive policy. Canada, inevitably sensitive to divergencies between her southern neighbour and the United Kingdom, wished to promote their agreement, and welcomed the initiative of the Lord Privy Seal, Lord Beaverbrook, in calling a Commonwealth conference on air policy in October 1943.[1]

It appeared during this Conference that the different geographical situations of the Commonwealth countries had produced varying viewpoints on the scope and nature of international action. Canada particularly desired a new general air convention, and produced a draft. Australia and New Zealand, as terminal States on international air services linking them with both Europe and the Americas, favoured the negotiation of arrangements for the operation of main trunk air routes by an international authority. The Union of South Africa was mainly interested in questions of air transport expansion in the African continent. The conference was exploratory.

The Canadian Government laid its draft convention before Parliament in spring 1944. Meanwhile, on 21 January 1944, the Australian and New Zealand Governments had concluded the Canberra Pact,[2] containing a declaration of the two Governments' views on air transport. In clauses 17–23, the two Governments stated that they supported in principle the creation by agreement of an international air transport authority, with full authority to operate trunk routes. Within such a framework the Governments support the right of countries to conduct air transport services in territories within their national jurisdiction. Failing international agreement, the two Governments would support a system of government-owned air trunk routes within the British Commonwealth of Nations, controlled and operated by the Member Governments.

In April 1944 Mr Adolf Berle, the United States Assistant Secretary of State in charge of aviation, came to London for conversations with Lord Beaverbrook, as part of a United States initiative of having exploratory talks with principal air Powers in preparation for a general conference. The communiqué issued after these Anglo-American conversations stated that the two Governments 'are of the opinion that there is sufficient agreement between them to justify the expectations that final dispositions can be reached at an international conference'.[3] The United

---

[1] An account of Commonwealth air transport co-operative machinery, the Commonwealth Air Transport Council, etc., may be found in Chapter VII.
[2] See account in Chapter XVI. [3] *The Times*, 9 April 1944.

States Government issued invitations to fifty-five Allied and neutral States to meet at Chicago on 1 November 1944; fifty-two attended. The U.S.S.R. refused the invitation.

The Canadian, Australian, and New Zealand views were already known. The United Kingdom Government issued a White Paper on 8 October 1944.[1] It advocated as an objective a balance between world facilities and traffic offering, with equitable participation therein by operating countries, and the abolition of wasteful competitive practices and of subsidization of national air-lines. It proposed freedom of transit, and landings for non-traffic purposes, over and on national territory. It recognized the commercial carriage of passengers and goods between the country of origin of the aircraft and other countries, but excluded 'cabotage' in the sense of intermediate collection and discharge between two foreign countries or within a foreign country's territory. In common with the Canadian draft, it outlined a plan for an international air authority to define trunk routes, regulate frequencies, and fix rates.

The Chicago Conference sat for seven weeks and its subject gave rise to very considerable discussion. The main question of controversy was cabotage, or what the Americans christened 'the Fifth Freedom of the Air'. The United States also found the Australian–New Zealand proposal for internationally operated trunk routes unacceptable; and those countries, with India, then supported the Canadian alternative which already had United Kingdom support.

Complete agreement on all points was not achieved at the Conference, which eventually produced a convention and two agreements. The convention accepted the principle of national sovereignty over the air space above a State's territory (including colonial territories), and therefore that the operation of scheduled international air services required the consent of the countries of transit and destination. The signatories agreed to collaborate on all technical questions such as standards, auxiliary services and aids to navigation, etc., and to set up a permanent International Civil Aviation Organization (I.C.A.O.) to promote the achievement of the aims and the application of the principles of the Convention. A provisional organization (P.I.C.A.O.) for technical and advisory purposes was to be set up for the time until the ratifications of the Convention needed for the establishment of I.C.A.O. should have been deposited. P.I.C.A.O. was established at Montreal on 6 June 1945, and was duly succeeded, upon the deposit of twenty-six ratifications, by I.C.A.O. on 4 April 1946, with its headquarters also at Montreal.

[1] Cmd. 6561.

The two agreements drawn up at Chicago were: the Transit Agreement, which enables signatories mutually to accord each other right of innocent passage and technical (i.e. non-traffic) landing; the Transport Agreement enabling signatories to give each other the right of intermediate traffic (carriage of passengers and goods within the territories of contracting States and between one foreign contracting State and another). All the Commonwealth countries and Eire became members of I.C.A.O. and signed the first Agreement. Eleven States, none in the Commonwealth, have accepted the second Agreement.

I.C.A.O. deals with regional aspects of air transport by means of four regional offices which, with the headquarters as regional office for North America, effect liaison with contracting States in the regions. The Far East and Pacific regional office is in Melbourne. I.C.A.O. also organizes regional meetings for eight specified regions: European-Mediterranean; Middle East; Caribbean; South-West Pacific (held at Melbourne in February 1947); South American; South Atlantic; North Atlantic; North Pacific. Within the framework of I.C.A.O., the States interested in the North Atlantic area have agreed to combine, as a result of a conference held in London in September 1946, to maintain thirteen weather stations in their area. Nine were in operation by September 1948. Ten States, including Canada and the United Kingdom, combine to assist Iceland to maintain air navigation facilities and a weather service for the North Atlantic routes.

THE UNITED NATIONS WAR CRIMES COMMISSION

The Inter-Allied Commision and the Declaration
of St James's, 13 January 1942

On 25 October 1941, Mr Winston Churchill and President Roosevelt (whose country was still neutral) issued simultaneous, but not identical, denunciations of war crimes; and on 7 November 1941 Mr Molotov, for the Soviet Government, issued a note of denunciation and protest against war crimes. The first procedural step was taken on 13 January 1942, when the exiled European Governments in London and General de Gaulle signed a formal declaration placing punishment for war crimes 'through the channel of organized justice' among their principal war aims. The United Kingdom Secretary of State for Foreign Affairs, Mr Anthony Eden, was present, with representatives of Australia, Canada, India, New Zealand, and the Union of South Africa, and of the United States, the U.S.S.R., and China; none of these signed the declaration.

Subsequent Declarations

In June 1942 the signatories of the Inter-Allied Declaration of 13 January presented notes of denunciations and protest regarding war crimes to the Governments of the United Kingdom, the United States, and the U.S.S.R., and to the Holy See. The notes expressed the hope that the three Great Powers would take measures to deter and punish criminals.[1] These Great Powers replied on 8 September, 21 August, and 14 October respectively, stating that war criminals would be handed over to the courts of the countries where the atrocities were committed.[2]

Meanwhile the United Kingdom Foreign Office had ascertained from the European Governments represented on the Inter-Allied Commission on the Punishment of War Crimes (the body which had drafted the Inter-Allied Declaration) that they were agreeable to the establishment of a 'fact-finding Commission'. Aware of their *agrément*, the Lord Chancellor, Lord Simon, announced in the House of Lords on 7 October 1942, that a United Nations War Crimes Commission would be established; and, secondly, that the handing over of named criminals should be made a condition of the armistice.[3] On the same day, President Roosevelt made a similar announcement, pledging his Government's co-operation in the Commission's activities.

The last and major pronouncement at this stage was made as a result of the Moscow Conference, on 1 November 1943. Mr Churchill, President Roosevelt, and Mr Stalin made an agreed 'Declaration on Atrocities',[4] 'speaking in the interest of the thirty-two United Nations', of which the main points were: Perpetrators of atrocities to be handed over by Germany as part of the Armistice terms; judgement to be 'by the peoples they have outraged'; but major criminals 'whose offences have no particular geographical location' to be judged and punished by Allied action. This last began a new phase in the procedure against war crimes, the development of which was related to, but juridically distinct from, the work of the War Crimes Commission.

The Establishment and Organization of the War Crimes Commission

On 20 October 1943 a diplomatic Conference was called at the Foreign Office in London. It was attended by representatives of:

---

[1] U.N., War Crimes Commission, *History of the United Nations War Crimes Commission and the Development of the Laws of War* (London. H.M.S.O., 1948) p. 93.
[2] ibid. pp. 93–4.
[3] *Hansard* (Lords), vol. 124, col. 563.
[4] Text in Royal Institute of International Affairs, *United Nations Documents*, 1941–1945 (London, 1946) p. 15.

the European Governments in exile; the French Committee of National Liberation; China; the United States; and all the British belligerent countries. The meeting agreed unanimously to set up a War Crimes Commission, empowered to elect its own Chairman, establish its own procedure, and to set up panels for investigation. The scope and functions of the Commission were not at this date very closely defined, but its essential character—that of a fact-finding body, with no jurisdiction of any kind but acting as an investigating agent for the Governments concerned—was established at the meeting and remained substantially unchanged throughout its operations; although its actual work later grew to large proportions. The United Kingdom, by agreement, provided the Secretary-General; the rest of the appointments to the secretariat were left open for the time being. The participating Governments undertook to share the expense of the Commission on an agreed basis.[1]

The Commission, after three informal meetings, held its first official meeting on 11 January 1944, when Sir Cecil Hurst (United Kingdom) was elected Chairman; when ill-health compelled his retirement, Lord Wright (Australia) became Chairman on 31 January 1945. The secretariat was composed of nationals of the participating Governments. During 1944–5, national offices affiliated to the Commission were set up by the Governments to investigate and report to a committee of the Commission established for the purpose of examining and collating their reports. Australia, Canada, New Zealand, India, and the United Kingdom set up national offices in their capitals; the European Governments transferred theirs to their territories when liberated. Canada sent observers to the Commission from December 1944, as a preliminary to full membership. The Canadian national office was abolished on 28 May 1946, when its duties were taken over by a War Crimes Advisory Committee. The national offices of the other Commonwealth participants were variously organized, being attached to the External Affairs or Defence Departments, and, in the United Kingdom, to the Treasury Solicitor's Office.

Regional investigations by area panels or sub-commissions had been envisaged at the meeting at the Foreign Office on 20 October 1943; and on 10 May 1944 the Commission agreed to set up a Far Eastern Sub-Commission, which held its inaugural meeting on 29 November at Chungking. Australia, India, and the United Kingdom participated in the work of the Chungking Sub-Commission. The Sub-Commission completed its own work on 31 March 1947.

[1] *History of U.N. War Crimes Commission*, pp. 109–17.

Machinery for Executive Action

The punishment of the major criminals whose crimes had no particular geographical location was distinct from the work of the War Crimes Commission, and punishment was effected, as will be seen below, under jurisdiction conferred by a special instrument of international agreement. The War Crimes Commission, which had no jurisdiction of any kind, acted as the agency of co-operation with the Governments,[1] assisting them to exercise their jurisdiction over war criminals whose crimes had a definite connexion (as set out in the Moscow Declaration of 1 November 1943 and other related statements) with their own territory. In addition, the Commission developed an important function of dealing, in an advisory capacity, with questions of policy and law. 'Owing to the significance of many of the legal questions . . . examined, the Commission's advisory function tended, in course of time, to exceed in importance its original task of investigation.'[2]

The complementary co-operative activities of the Governments and the military authorities increased *pari passu* with the range of the Commission's activities and cannot here be described in detail. The most that can be done is to indicate in outline the machinery set up by the countries of the Commonwealth for purposes of co-operation in the punishment of war crimes.

In Europe, the occupation and military government planning unit of Supreme Headquarters, Allied Expeditionary Force (the 'German Country Unit' of SHAEF) had its legal division, entrusted with the tracing and apprehension of war criminals. The work of War Crimes branches and the Allied liaison teams was combined with that of a special agency established by SHAEF early in 1945, the Central Registry of War Criminals and Security Suspects (CROWCASS). The national military executive units involved worked as war-crimes agencies of this planning unit. In the case of the United Kingdom, the war-crimes agency was the Judge Advocate General's Office of the War Office and became a very considerable organization.[2] The jurisdiction of national military courts for war-crimes trials fell within the framework of two major ordinances (Proclamation No. 1 and Ordinance No. 2) of General Eisenhower, the Supreme Allied Commander in Europe. The jurisdiction and regulations for British military courts were laid down by the Royal Warrant of 14 June 1944, amended in respect of certain procedures on 4 August 1945 and 30 January 1946. On 14 June 1945 the Commander-in-

---

[1] Full details are given in ibid. Appendix 1 and Chs. VI, VII, XII, and XIV.
[2] ibid. p. 126.
[3] ibid. pp. 361, 366–76.

Chief, British Zone, assumed, for the zone, the powers previously held by the Supreme Commander, and the British military courts continued to function under the Royal Warrant, as before. Later, on 1 January 1947, British Zone Ordinance No. 68 established Control Commission Courts, also with jurisdiction in war crimes cases; that is to say, with concurrent jurisdiction. British Zone Ordinance No. 69 (31 December 1946) set up two grades of German Courts to try members of organizations declared criminal by the Nuremberg Tribunal.

Canadian regulations for the trial of war criminals were issued by Governor-General's Order-in-Council of 30 August 1945. They were confirmed by Act of Parliament passed on 6 August 1946, which was deemed retrospective to 30 August 1945.[1] The Canadian Military Tribunals so established were on much the same lines as those under the British Royal Warrant. Canada did not adhere to the Agreement and Charter of 8 August 1945,[2] and was therefore not entitled to claim trials under Article 10 of the Charter; nor was Canada bound, in strict law, by Nuremberg Tribunal decisions. 'However, whenever a member of such organizations [i.e. those declared criminal at Nuremberg] was detained by Canadian authorities, as prisoner of war or otherwise, and whenever such member was guilty of war crimes falling within the jurisdiction of Canadian courts, there was nothing to prevent such trials from taking place.'[3]

For Australia, the War Crimes Act[4] gave the Governor-General authority to constitute military courts for the trial of war criminals. The principles of this Act were similar to those of the British Royal Warrant of 14 June 1945.[5] In October 1945 the Governor-General delegated to certain senior staff officers and commanders in the field his power under the Act to convene military courts; in December 1945 these powers were extended to confirming the findings and sentences of such courts. Australia adhered to the Agreement and Charter of 8 August 1945, but Australian interest in war crimes was in practice almost entirely in the Far East, although Australian ex-prisoners of war contributed evidence to prosecutions in Europe.

Far Eastern Machinery

In the Far East, an Allied war crimes machinery was developed to carry out tasks similar to the European machinery, but its geographical extent was greater owing to the vastness of the

[1] No. 309, 2nd Session, XXth Parliament; 10 Geo. VI, c. 73.
[2] See p. 330, below.
[3] *History of U.N. War Crimes Commission*, pp. 325-6, 469.
[4] Assented to, 11 October 1945.
[5] ibid. p. 468.

area overrun by the Japanese. The main task of identifying, locating and apprehending war criminals in the Far East and the Pacific fell upon the British and United States military authorities. Two main centres were established, one in Singapore for the whole of South East Asia, run by the British, and one in Tokyo for the whole South-West Pacific area, run by the Americans. The two centres maintained liaison with each other, and with the other Governments and military authorities concerned in their areas, by means of the interchange of liaison teams, the attachment of national teams to the centres, etc. The British-run centre in Singapore came under the South East Asia Command (SEAC); the American-run centre was constituted at the headquarters of the Supreme Commander for the Allied Powers (SCAP) and was placed directly under General MacArthur.

In the Singapore (SEAC) centre, the Adjutant-General's branch was made responsible for administration, while the Judge Advocate General's branch acted in judicial and advisory capacity and provided legally qualified presidents and prosecutors for military courts. The centre had its investigating teams, and its War-Crimes Registry, Co-ordinating, and Legal Sections; and the United States, Australia, the Netherlands, and France maintained their own war-crimes sections attached to the centre. In all, twelve British military courts were constituted, in Singapore, Rangoon, Hong Kong, Malaya, and British North Borneo (the two last being on circuit). American cases within the centre's area were tried by the British courts with the assistance of a United States prosecuting officer; the Dutch, French and Australians set up their own courts. Australian courts sat in Singapore, British North Borneo, Labuan, and New Guinea.[1]

The establishment of Australian Government machinery for dealing with war crimes began on 8 June 1944, when the Government appointed a commissioner to conduct inquiries. In 1945, three more commissioners were appointed so as to constitute a Board of Inquiry under the chairmanship of the original commissioner, Sir William Webb. Following the delegation to the military authorities of the Governor-General's powers under the Australian War Crimes Act, a central War Crimes Office was set up at Army Headquarters at Melbourne, which established local war-crimes sections in Singapore[2] and Tokyo; and Australian military courts were established in Singapore, but not in Tokyo. The various Australian military commands established

---

[1] ibid. pp. 380–3.

[2] The Singapore Section was transferred to Hong Kong in September 1947, for the trial there of Japanese accused before Australian military courts.

local investigation teams in their area, and all these field units maintained close liaison with Melbourne. All branches of the Australian machine maintained liaison with the British (including Indian Army), American, Chinese, and Dutch war-crimes operations, and the Australian authorities negotiated the interchange of prisoners with them, and assisted them where necessary to complete their investigations.[1]

THE INTERNATIONAL MILITARY TRIBUNALS AT NUREMBERG AND TOKYO

The Nuremberg Tribunal

The preliminaries to war-crimes operations have been traced above as far as the Moscow statement of 1 November 1943.[2] Thereafter the task of prosecuting the major criminals became distinct from the procedures of the War Crimes Commission and the national Governments for bringing to trial the criminals associated with a particular place or area. That is not to say that the Commission did not concern itself with the creation of an International Tribunal—in fact, it began to consider the question during the earliest stages of its work—but that the jurisdiction of the Tribunals was established by special instruments.

The United States and Australian representatives on the Commission pressed strongly, at an early stage, for the consideration of the question of a special court to try the major criminals, and on 22 February 1944 the Commission instructed its Committee on Enforcement to begin discussions. Thereafter discussions, in the course of which various drafts on procedure, etc., were submitted by national representatives and considered, were continued until by 20 September 1944, a convention for the establishment of a United Nations Joint Court had been accepted and circulated. But meanwhile 'it had become clear that the creation of such a court would be subject to long delays', and Indian and United States proposals for interim courts to be established by the Supreme Commanders were considered.[3] At this stage the Canadian Government, hitherto not represented on the Commission, submitted, in December 1944, through its High Commissioner in London, the view that mixed military tribunals should be established quickly. On 4 January 1945 Mr Eden, the British Foreign Secretary, submitted the view of his Government. His Majesty's Government in the United Kingdom, he said, had

---

[1] *History of U.N. War Crimes Commission*, pp. 386–90.
[2] p. 324, above.
[3] *History of U.N. War Crimes Commission*, pp. 443–53.

throughout doubted both the desirability and the practicability of an Inter-Allied Court. Mixed military courts might be a practicable alternative, but the United Kingdom Government felt that it should first reach agreement in principle with the United States Government before committing itself to either course.[1]

The United States Government gave its support to the concept of an international military tribunal. It made no formal official statement on this before the conclusion of the London Agreement of 8 August 1945, but 'the establishment of this tribunal was due to the initiative of the United States Government'.[2] The appointment of Justice Robert H. Jackson as United States Chief of Counsel was announced by President Truman on 2 May 1945. The appointment of the United Kingdom opposite number, Sir David Maxwell Fyfe, was announced on 6 June 1945.

All this preparatory work led up to the London Agreement of 8 August 1945, to which the signatories were the United States, United Kingdom, French, and Soviet Governments. Under Article 5 of this Agreement, any of the United Nations might adhere, and, of the Commonwealth Members, Australia and New Zealand did so. The Agreement provided for the establishment for Germany of 'an international military tribunal for the trial of war criminals whose offences have no particular geographical location, whether individually or in their capacity as members of organizations or groups, or in both capacities'. The constitution, jurisdiction, and functions of the Tribunal were set out in an annexed Charter. The establishment of the tribunal under this Charter did not prejudice the jurisdiction of national courts on Allied or occupied territory, nor the return of war criminals to stand trial in the countries where they committed their crimes (Articles 6 and 3). The crimes within the tribunal's special jurisdiction under the Charter were: crimes against peace; war crimes in the sense of violations of the laws of war; and crimes against humanity (Article 6 of the Charter). Groups or organizations might be declared criminal by the tribunal (Article 9), and signatory States had the right to bring members thereof to trial before national, military, or occupation courts (Article 10).[3]

Compulsion upon Germany to hand over war criminals was provided by Article 11 of the terms of unconditional surrender. The Italian surrender, signed on 29 September 1943, had contained a somewhat similar article for the handing over of 'Benito Mussolini, his chief Fascist associates', and all other suspects

---

[1] ibid. pp. 453–4.   [2] ibid. p. 454.
[3] *Agreement . . . for the Prosecution and Punishment of the Major War Criminals of the European Axis.* Cmd. 6668 (Miscellaneous, no. 10, 1945).

listed by the United Nations. The powers given under Article 11 of the German surrender were extended to Austria by subsequent agreement between the Four Powers.

The Tokyo Tribunal

The Tokyo Tribunal did not derive its jurisdiction from a specially drawn international instrument, as did the Nuremberg Court. During the Potsdam Conference a proclamation defining the terms of surrender for Japan was issued, on 26 July 1945, by the President of the United States and the Prime Minister of the United Kingdom, the President of China concurring. This proclamation included a statement that 'Stern justice shall be meted out to all war criminals'. When the surrender came to be signed in Tokyo Bay on 2 September, the Japanese accepted the terms of the Potsdam Declaration and undertook to obey any orders made by the Supreme Allied Commander for carrying them out. The actual instrument establishing the Tribunal at Tokyo was a Special Proclamation of the Supreme Commander signed by him on 19 January 1946, to which was annexed a Charter for the Court.

The Special Proclamation, in its Preamble, refered to the Potsdam Declaration and the surrender terms:

Whereas, the Governments of the Allied Powers at war with Japan on 26 July 1945 at Potsdam, declared as one of the terms of surrender that stern justice shall be meted out to all war criminals including those who have visited cruelties upon our prisoners;

Whereas, by such Instrument of Surrender, the authority of the Emperor and the Japanese Government to rule the State of Japan is made subject to the Supreme Commander for the Allied Powers, who is authorized to take such steps as he deems proper to effectuate the terms of surrender;

Whereas, the undersigned has been designated by the Allied Powers as Supreme Commander . . .

Whereas, the Governments of the United States, Great Britain, and Russia at the Moscow Conference, 26 December 1945, . . . with the concurrence of China have agreed that the Supreme Commander shall issue all orders for the implementation of the terms of surrender;

Now, therefore, I, Douglas MacArthur . . . do order and provide as follows: . . .

There followed three Articles: (1) providing for the establishment of the International Military Tribunal for the Far East; (2) providing that its constitution jurisdiction, and functions should be as set forth in the Charter; (3) providing that the jurisdiction of other international, national or military courts be not prejudiced thereby.[1]

[1] Text in *Documents on American Foreign Relations*, vol. 8, pp. 353-4.

Article 2 of the Charter[1] provided that: 'The Tribunal shall consist of not less than six members nor more than eleven members, appointed by the Supreme Commander ... from the names submitted by the Signatories to the Instrument of Surrender, India, and the Commonwealth of the Philippines.'

Under Article 3, the President of the Tribunal was appointed by the Supreme Commander from among the members. The indictment[2] was drawn by the United States, China, the United Kingdom, the U.S.S.R,. Australia, Canada, France, the Netherlands, New Zealand, India and the Philippines against twenty-eight Japanese accused. The President of the Court was Sir William Webb, Chief Justice of the Supreme Court of Queensland.

[1] Text in ibid. pp. 354–8.
[2] Text in U.S. Department of State, *Trial of the Japanese War Criminals* (Washington, U.S.G.P.O., 1946) pp. 45–64.

CHAPTER XIV

THE NEGOTIATION AND RATIFICATION OF TREATIES

The Negotiation of Treaties Before 1914

THE power to make treaties was a corollary of responsible government, and necessarily inherent in full Dominion status. The description of the procedure for Commonwealth representation at international conferences given in the preceding section involved also some account of negotiation and ratification of multilateral treaties since 1918. Before 1914, it might be said that all treaties entered into by the United Kingdom and involving other dominions of the Crown were in a sense multilateral, but the onus of discharging the obligations they involved lay, in international law and in the eyes of all foreign States, upon the United Kingdom, and the full development of the British Commonwealth and Empire from a diplomatic unity to an association of separate diplomatic entities was spread over many decades. Professor Robert B. Stewart traces it, in a fully documented study, from Lord Durham's Report of January 1839 for one hundred years, showing how the process developed first in the commercial and technical fields in both bilateral and multilateral negotiation.[1]

The Growth of Procedures for the Recognition of Divergent Interests within Imperial Diplomatic Unity

The first signs of the emergence of multiplicity of interests and views were in the field of tariff policy, and led to the Colonies claiming representation in commercial negotiations involving their interests. Their claims gave rise, on 11 November 1865, to a Foreign Office statement of the conditions on which Colonial representatives might be associated with the United Kingdom's trade negotiations, mainly through permission to make representations regarding colonial interests involved. Perhaps the main interest, for the future, of this dispatch was that it foreshadowed the establishment of a much later convention. The Imperial Conference of 1923 stated the *desideratum* 'that no treaty should be negotiated by any of the Governments of the Empire without due consideration of its possible effects' on

---

[1] R. B. Stewart, *Treaty Relations of the British Commonwealth* (New York, Macmillan, 1939), see especially Ch. II for a summarized account; and Keith, *The Dominions as Sovereign States*, Ch. I.

other parts or the whole of the Empire; and that, to this end, there should be the fullest exchange of views between the Governments. Lord Ripon's dispatch of 1865 laid down the *desideratum* that no Colony should obtain advantage from, or give advantage to, a foreign country at the expense either of other Colonies or of the Empire as a whole. Supervision of the fulfilment of this requirement was, however, laid by Lord Ripon upon Her Majesty's Government in the United Kingdom: 'guardianship of the common interests of the Empire', he said, 'rests with them.'

Practice, however, occasionally went beyond the Foreign Office statement, as when in 1871 Sir John Macdonald was appointed, with full powers issued by Queen Victoria, as one of her plenipotentiaries in the negotiation of the Treaty of Washington between Great Britain and the United States. But the position regarding colonial representation was still, for many more years, somewhat fluid and no general power was conceded.

In 1877 the United Kingdom Government decided generally to adopt the usage of requesting foreign Powers parties to commercial treaties to accord the United Kingdom the right to adhere in respect of any Colonies individually within a stated time, usually one year, which gave time for consultation with the Colonies. The last case of the automatic inclusion of the Colonies in a commercial treaty without consultation was the Treaty of Friendship and Commerce with Serbia, 7 February 1880. Lord Kimberley, Secretary of State for the Colonies, circulated its text with a dispatch to the colonial Governors-General explaining: that the automatic inclusion had been 'inadvertent'; and that steps had been taken to ensure, in the future, that a clause permitting Colonies whose wishes had not been ascertained to contract out should be included in commercial treaties.[1] This clause became general practice thereafter in the terms of British commercial treaties. In 1882 eleven Colonies were excluded by name from the operation of Great Britain's Treaty of Friendship, Commerce, and Navigation with Montenegro; and thereafter the practice of naming certain Colonies and India for exclusion was not uncommon.[2]

The next logical step in the tacit recognition of the diversity in unity of the British Empire was to obtain for the Colonies the right of withdrawal from commercial treaties. In his Report on the Colonial Conference held at Ottawa in 1893, Lord Jersey recommended this course.[3] In 1899 it was agreed that the

[1] Further details may be found in Stewart, op. cit. pp. 97–8.
[2] The treaties mentioned, and a number of others showing variations in the use of the clause, etc. may be found in Hertslet, *Commercial Treaties*, vol. XV.
[3] C. 7553 (1894), pp. 5–6.

adherence of the self-governing Colonies to future commercial treaties should be qualified by a clause permitting them to withdraw separately under any provision contained in a treaty for its termination at a given date or alternative dates. This procedure was first used in a commercial convention concluded with Uruguay on 15 July 1899.[1] But there were *en vigueur* upwards of sixty commercial treaties signed before the exemption procedures came into use. 'There remained . . . the desirability of obtaining power to withdraw separately from [earlier] treaties, and that was first conceded by Greece in 1904 and later by nearly all the States.'[2]

There remained, in fact, one further matter to be dealt with in order to ensure that the Dominions obtained maximum advantage and freedom combined. This was to secure for them, in the same commercial instrument, the right of separate adherence and also most-favoured-nation treatment even in the absence of adherence. The necessary procedure came into use about 1904–5, when there began to be inserted, in treaties stipulating for separate adherence, another clause on the following lines:

Nevertheless, the goods produced or manufactured in any of His Britannic Majesty's Colonies, Possessions, or Protectorates shall enjoy in [the foreign country] complete and unconditional most-favoured-nation treatment so long as such Colony, Possession or Protectorate shall accord to goods of [the foreign country's] origin or manufacture treatment as favourable as it gives to the similar produce or manufacture of any other foreign country.

A provision on somewhat similar lines, *mutatis mutandis*, was also sometimes employed to ensure most-favoured-nation treatment of all British subjects (i.e. including Dominion citizens) in regard to the right to trade or reside in the foreign country, and to engage in merchant shipping transport with it.

A variant of the procedure described above was used as recently as 1930, when the Irish Free State Government declined to take advantage of its right to adhere to the Treaty of Commerce and Navigation between the United Kingdom and Roumania,[3] but asked that the British Minister in Roumania be instructed by the Foreign Office to ask Roumania to accord most-favoured-nation treatment to Irish Free State produce. The Roumanian Government agreed. The clause was frequently used in general commercial treaties between the United Kingdom and foreign countries during the nineteen-twenties.

---

[1] United Kingdom, Treaty Series, no. 15, 1900.
[2] Keith, *The Dominions as Sovereign States*, pp. 9–10.
[3] 6 August 1930, Cmd. 3945 (Treaty Series, no. 38, 1931). Full details are given in Stewart, op. cit. p. 108.

It was in the technical field that the Colonies and India first entered into strictly multilateral agreements. For example, since they all had separate national postal systems, they began in 1878 to send separate delegations to the International Congress of the Universal Postal Union. The position up to 1912 is summarized as follows by Professor A. Berriedale Keith:

Many instances had taken place in the past of the Dominions being represented in one way or another at General Conferences, but no issue as to international questions had arisen until 1906, when the question was raised how the delegates to the postal conference should be accredited. Ultimately, the device was adopted of giving authority to the colonial representatives from the Secretary of State for the Colonies in the same way as the British representatives were given power by the Postmaster-General, and the agreements were treated not as treaties proper, to be formally ratified, but merely as accords which were formally approved.[1]

The year 1912 saw the establishment of a new and important precedent, although its significance was not particularly noticed at the time. In that year the International Radiotelegraph Conference was convened in London, and it was held desirable that the Dominions should be separately represented, should have freedom of action and separate votes. Therefore full powers were issued to representatives of Canada, Australia, New Zealand, and the Union of South Africa, as well as to the United Kingdom representatives. The last received full powers 'expressed in the usual form without limitation of area of authority; [the other four] were confined to the representation of the interests of the Dominion concerned.'[2] This was the first occasion on which the British Empire took part in an international conference and signed a resulting multilateral instrument as five diplomatic entities instead of as a diplomatic unity.

The Procedure Adopted in 1907

In the year 1907, Mr W. S. Fielding and Mr L. P. Brodeur were appointed plenipotentiaries, with full powers without limitation of area, to negotiate a commercial treaty between Canada and France. In his instructions on 4 July to the British Ambassador in Paris, Sir Edward Grey, the British Foreign Secretary, stated that, as 'the selection of the negotiator is principally a matter of convenience', in the circumstances it would 'obviously be more practical' to leave that to the Canadians. A supplemen-

---

[1] Keith, *The Sovereignty of the British Dominions* (London, Macmillan, 1929) pp. 308–9.
[2] ibid.

tary Convention agreed in 1909 was negotiated on the same principle. The instruments, which were signed by the British Ambassador and the two Canadian plenipotentiaries, were ratified by both the Dominion and United Kingdom Governments.[1]

The same procedure was used as recently as 1923, when a 'Commercial Convention between Canada and Italy' was negotiated by Mr W. S. Fielding and Mr Ernest Lapointe. The 1907 instrument was entitled 'Convention regulating the Commercial Relations between Canada and France'; the 1893 instrument, which Sir Charles Tupper negotiated, 'An Agreement between Great Britain and France, for Regulating the Commercial Relations between Canada and France'. The procedures of 1907 are generally regarded as the climax, before 1914, of the process of Dominion recognition in commercial negotiations.

Imperial Diplomatic Unity in High Policy

The above examples of breaches of varying degree in the diplomatic unity of the British Empire were in the commercial or technical sphere. In the political field, the convenient device of using arbitral procedures to ensure adequate representation of Canadian interests in matters affecting its relations with the United States was resorted to on several occasions before 1914. For example, Lord Bryce in 1909 negotiated a treaty with the United States Government establishing an International Joint Commission, with three American and three Canadian members on equal footing, for the decision of issues affecting the United States–Canadian boundary waters. The Canadian commissioners were appointed by the King on the advice and recommendation of the Governor-General of Canada in Council. His Majesty's Government in the United Kingdom referred matters to the decision of the Commission only with the consent of the Governor-General in Council. 'The Treaty so clearly gives Canada control that even on 15 March 1928, the Prime Minister held change unnecessary.'[2] In 1914 a further treaty negotiated between the United Kingdom and the United States arranged for the establishment of an international commission of five to investigate and report upon any matter of dispute which might arise between Great Britain and the United States. In this treaty it was provided that, if the matter to be considered concerned a Dominion, the United Kingdom Government might nominate a Dominion representative in substitution for the United Kingdom member. Geographical contiguity made it likely that such matters would concern Canadian–American relations, but the treaty

---

[1] Texts in Hertslet, *Commercial Treaties*, vol. 35, p. 800.
[2] Keith, *The Sovereignty of the British Dominions*, p. 299.

provision covered representation of any Dominion whose interests might be affected.

The Dominions did not raise the question of their participation in general foreign policy, and their main reason was that they did not want to become involved in the resultant responsibilities.[1] If they asserted their international capacity in matters of high policy, they would have to be prepared to defend it. The situation before 1914 was summarized by Professor Berriedale Keith as follows:

> In point of fact it proved, on the whole, fairly easy in the period before the War of 1914–18 to combine the recognition of the final authority in external affairs of the Imperial Government with the claims of the Colonies. By 1914 it may fairly be said that the system had been moulded so that in matters commercial the Dominions had all the powers which they desired or required, and that in matters more directly political they had achieved most of what they wished and what could be obtained for them, and that future advance was open to them without any objection of the Imperial Government but was retarded by their own reluctance to engage themselves in matters which seemed of remote interest.[2]

The Discussions at the Imperial Conference of 1911

Before the 1914–18 war, however, one important case of multilateral negotiation over which the Dominions were not consulted did in fact occur, and gave rise to protests and discussion at the Imperial Conference of 1911. The instrument concerned was the Declaration of London, 1909, negotiated as a result of decisions of the 1907 Hague Conference, to certain points in which exception was taken by public opinion both in the United Kingdom and in the Dominions. The resolution of protest was tabled at the 1911 Conference by Mr Fisher, Prime Minister of Australia. It regretted the omission of consultation, and proposed that certain Articles of the Declaration of London should not be adopted by the United Kingdom. Sir Wilfrid Laurier, in the resulting discussion, although he upheld the principle of the desirability of consultation, insisted that the Dominions must not demand consultation as a matter of right because the right would carry with it the automatic obligation to give military support to the United Kingdom if events required.[3] After hearing a

---

[1] The implications of this attitude are analysed by A. Gordon Dewey in *The Dominions and Diplomacy* (Toronto, Longmans, Green, 1929). Although dissatisfaction with British diplomacy had 'become a popular tradition in Canada', he comments: 'Complain as he might of British ineptitude, no one was more loath than Sir Wilfrid [Laurier] to force the Dominion into the hazards of participation in problems of high policy' (vol. I, pp. 189–90).

[2] Keith, *The Sovereignty of the British Dominions*, p. 278.

[3] Imperial Conference, London, 1911, *Minutes of Proceedings*. Cd. 5745, pp. 113–17.

statement by the British Foreign Secretary, Sir Edward Grey, the Conference reached general agreement that the Dominions should be consulted regarding the agenda of future Hague Conferences, and accepted the following resolution:

(a) that the Dominions shall be afforded an opportunity of consultation when framing the instructions to be given to British delegates at future meetings of the Hague Conference, and the conventions affecting the Dominions provisionally assented to at the Conference shall be circulated among the Dominion Governments for their consideration; and (b) that a similar procedure, when time and opportunity and the subject matter permit, shall as far as possible be used when preparing instructions for negotiation of other international agreements affecting the Dominions.[1]

Commenting on the resolution, General Botha specifically related it to the sphere of treaties of general application.

It was at this same Conference that the Prime Minister of Great Britain, Mr Asquith, winding up the debate rejecting the New Zealand Prime Minister's proposal for some form of Imperial executive,[2] made the classic re-statement of imperial diplomatic unity. Sir Joseph Ward's proposals, he said,

would impair if not altogether destroy the authority of the Government of the United Kingdom in such grave matters as the conduct of foreign policy, the conclusion of treaties, the declaration and maintenance of peace, or the declaration of war and, indeed, all those relations with Foreign Powers, necessarily of the most delicate character, which are now in the hands of the Imperial Government, subject to its responsibility to the Imperial Parliament. That authority cannot be shared.[3]

That this statement represented the existing position was demonstrated in August 1914, when the British declaration of war, made by His Majesty on the advice of the United Kingdom Government alone, committed all the territories of the Crown to belligerent status, and was fully accepted by the Dominions. Under the impact of global war, unknown in the preceding hundred years of the *Pax Britannica*, the slow evolution of the international personality of the Dominions was sharply accelerated.[4]

The Position Regarding Extradition Treaties

Consultation and co-operation regarding the external relations of the British Commonwealth up to the 1914–18 war was thus well developed in the commercial field and also—although this

---

[1] ibid. pp. 15, 132.
[2] See p. 87-8, above.
[3] Cd. 5745, p. 71.
[4] See Chapters IV and XII.

had attracted less notice—in technical matters; while in more strictly political matters it had probably gone as far as the Dominions really desired. There remained one field in which development was less than might have been expected, considering how nearly it touched the internal sovereignty of the Dominions: namely, extradition practice. As late as the end of the 1914–18 war, the whole position was virtually governed by the Imperial Extradition Act of 1870, under which any new arrangement with a foreign State was brought under the operation of the Act by Order in Council.[1] If there was no local colonial legislation in operation, the Order in Council extended the Act to all British possessions; if there were a local Act in force, it could be saved, by Order in Council, under the provisions of Article 18 of the 1870 Act. Thus, when Canada passed a comprehensive Act in 1886, the operation of the Imperial Act was suspended in respect of Canada for so long as the Canadian Act should remain in force. As late as 1915 Professor Keith pointed out that no custom of consulting the Dominions had yet developed.

Extradition treaties with enemy States lapsed as a consequence of the War of 1914–18, and Article 289 of the Treaty of Versailles (to which treaty the Dominions and India were signatories) provided that they could be revived by notification from the victorious Powers. The United Kingdom's extradition treaties with Germany, Austria, and Hungary were revived, under the provisions of this Article, in their original form covering all British countries. New treaties had to be made with successor States, and those with Finland (30 May 1924), Latvia (16 July 1924) and Estonia (18 November 1925) contained the first use of a provision analogous to that so long used in commercial treaties, for the separate adherence of the Dominions and India; and also provision for separate termination. As in the older treaties, application for the surrender of a criminal has to be made to the chief authority in the British territory. In the Dominions, therefore, application would be made to the Governor-General, who would act in the matter upon the advice of the Dominion Cabinet. Older treaties have, since 1919, been extended, by convention between the original high contracting parties, to cover mandated territories. When the Dominion mandates have been included, the Dominions concerned have signed individually.

In general, it may be said that, up to 1939, the great majority of extradition treaties *en vigueur* date from the time when the Dominions were automatically included without either consultation or rights of separate adherence or withdrawal.

[1] Until 1870, there had been no such Imperial General Act; each new arrangement required the passage of a separate Act.

Developments Since 1918

It has been said that the development of Dominion treaty-making power was sharply accelerated by the War of 1914–18. In fact the *début* of the Dominions into international society took place at the most important international conference and treaty negotiation since the Congress and Treaty of Vienna, and constituted a striking recognition of their international stature.

The Paris Peace Conference and Treaty of Versailles

The Imperial War Cabinet[1] began its third plenary session on 25 November 1918, and addressed itself to the problems of the peace settlement. The Dominions, led by Canada, whose Prime Minister, Sir Robert Borden, had opened the subject in dispatches to Mr Lloyd George towards the end of October, claimed the right as effective belligerents and autonomous States to be represented at the Peace Conference. The United Kingdom Cabinet was nothing loth to accept the claim, and the Imperial War Cabinet, including India's representatives, transferred itself to Paris as the British Empire delegation.

Although the United Kingdom statesmen readily accepted the right of the Dominions to representation at Paris, foreign States were less ready. They recognized that—to quote a phrase of Sir Robert Borden's—the British countries 'secured a peculiarly effective position' as a bloc composed of separate constitutional units, each separately effective at the council table. The Principal Allied and Associated Powers had ruled that the smaller Powers should not take part in the Peace Conference proceedings except when their special interests were concerned in the discussions; but the Dominions, supported by the United Kingdom Prime Minister, achieved a composite arrangement and obtained a dual position which amounted to this: as 'Belligerent Powers with special interests', Canada, Australia, South Africa, and India were each represented by two plenipotentiary delegates; New Zealand was represented by one such delegate. In addition to this direct representation, it was stipulated that 'the representatives of the Dominions (including Newfoundland) and of India, can, moreover, be included in the representation of the British Empire by means of a panel system'.[2] As 'Belligerent Powers with special interests', their representatives were entitled to be summoned in their own right when questions in which they had a concern were being discussed. As participants by way of the panel system in

---

[1] This body is described on pp. 90–2, above.
[2] Keith, *Speeches and Documents on the British Dominions*, p. 14.

the British delegation, the Dominion representatives took part in all sessions and commissions, the British Empire being classed as a 'Belligerent Power with general interests'. Further, Dominion representatives sat on various commissions dealing with special problems. Thus the Dominions, at the Conference, may be said unquestionably to have obtained far greater opportunity of having their wishes expressed than did the minor Powers which were co-belligerent in the war. The inclusion of India was, to the foreign Powers, a crowning piece of illogic under which the constitutional anomalies of the British Empire had to be accepted by international society.

From representation at Paris to signature of the Peace Treaties was a short and obvious step. Sir Robert Borden again took the initiative, and circularized the other Dominion Prime Ministers on 12 March 1919. In his dispatch he proposed that, in the preamble to and the signature of the Treaty of Versailles, there should be a general heading 'British Empire', under which the United Kingdom, the Dominions and India should be enumerated; and the plenipotentiaries should sign each under his country's sub-head. He desired that the Dominion plenipotentiaries should individually sign the Treaties, and that the Dominion legislatures should ratify them in respect of their own countries. He wrote:

The procedure is in consonance with the principles of constitutional government that obtain throughout the Empire. The Crown is the supreme Executive in the United Kingdom and in all the Dominions, but acts on the advice of different constitutional units; and under resolution of the Imperial War Conference, 1917, the organization of the Empire is to be based upon equality of nationhood.

The principle was conceded, although not quite in full. In the event, the United Kingdom was not enumerated: its plenipotentiary signed for the British Empire; the others, each for the Dominion he represented. It will be observed that the 'Heads-of-States' form was not used. This mode of signature, in fact, reproduced the principle on which representation at the Conference had been secured, by the panel system combined with individual Dominion representation as 'Belligerent Powers with special interests'. The Treaty was ratified by His Majesty only after the Dominion Parliaments had signified approval.

The same principle, but slightly extended in the direction desired by Sir Robert Borden, was applied in the case of the Covenant of the League of Nations. The Dominions were original and independent members voting separately in the League Assembly. The British Empire (not the United Kingdom) was a permanent member of the Council. But Sir Robert Borden obtained from M. Clemenceau, President Wilson, and Mr Lloyd George a ruling on Article 4 of the Covenant granting the right of Dominion election to non-permanent seats on the Council.[1]

Since the evolution of Dominion status had now brought the Dominions into high policy, the stage had been reached when forms and formulae had a more than intra-Commonwealth significance and had begun to interest foreign States. As Professor Hancock comments: ' "Are you one or are you many?" foreigners asked; and the British answered innocently—or were they so very innocent?—"We are one, and we are many".'[2] We have seen above that yet another formula appeared at the Barcelona Conference on Inland Waterways in 1921: 'the British Empire, with New Zealand and India'.[3] In 1923, when Mr Fielding signed Canada's trade agreement with Italy, the 1907 procedures were used, and he rejected a suggestion that a United Kingdom co-signatory was unnecessary, saying that he appreciated the honour of signing with the Foreign Secretary.[4] Yet, in 1922, Canada had raised objections to the procedures proposed for the Lausanne Conference, and in 1923, just after the commercial agreement with Italy had been signed, Canada objected to the procedure which Mr Fielding had chosen being used again in connection with the signature of the so-called 'Halibut Treaty' with the United States.

The 'Halibut' Treaty of 1923

The Halibut Treaty illustrates a number of important points in intra-Commonwealth co-operation and international practice. In the first place, its concern was political and territorial as well as commercial and technical. Secondly, it was entirely negotiated by a Dominion Cabinet Minister, Mr Ernest Lapointe. He negotiated and signed under the full powers issued by His Majesty for this purpose, and these full powers contained no mark of any limitation on his representation, or indication that he signed in any other capacity than would have been filled if the British Ambassador at Washington had signed with him, or alone. The issue of Imperial full powers without limitation of area was identical with pre-war practice, but the sole Canadian signature was a new departure. Prior to signature on 2 March

---

[1] See H. G. Skilling, *Canadian Representation Abroad* (Toronto, Ryerson Press, 1945) pp. 156–9, for a full account. Canada was first elected to a Council seat in 1927.

[2] Hancock, *Survey of British Commonwealth Affairs*, vol. i, p. 67.

[3] See p. 284, above.

[4] Keith, *Sovereignty of the British Dominions*, p. 370.

1923, communications passed between the British Ambassador at Washington and the Governor-General of Canada. The Ambassador stated that he had received instructions from the United Kingdom Government to act as co-signatory with Mr Lapointe, and the Governor-General replied that, as the Treaty solely affected Canada and the United States, Mr Lapointe's signature would be sufficient. In consequence of these exchanges, the United Kingdom Government withdrew their instructions to the Ambassador, and Mr Lapointe signed alone. The Treaty was ratified by His Majesty under the Great Seal of the United Kingdom.

Thirdly, the differing titles given to what is called for convenience 'the Halibut Treaty' illustrate the international aspect. The draft of the treaty prepared in the State Department was called: 'Convention between the United States of America and Great Britain concerning Halibut Fishery', and it appears in the United States Treaty Series so entitled.[1] In the United Kingdom Treaty Series it is designated a 'Treaty between Canada and the United States'.[2] This question of nomenclature is not much more than casual, but in this case it was associated, though probably not of intent, with a more important point. The United States Senate, when invited to ratify, proposed a gloss on the text in the form of an understanding that 'none of the nationals or inhabitants on boats or vessels of any other part of Great Britain shall engage in the halibut fishery contrary to the provisions of the treaty'. Canada very naturally objected, and finally the Senate abandoned the interpretation, but ratification had by then been delayed for a year and a half, until 22 October 1924.

The Resolution of the Imperial Conference of 1923

The conjunction of events—the new procedures used in the case of the Halibut Treaty, Canadian views on representation at the Lausanne Conference,[3] and the recent variations in procedure outlined above—made it apparent that the whole subject of the negotiation, signature, and ratification of treaties required clarification. The Imperial Conference of 1923, which opened on 1 October, addressed itself to the problem. The subject was fully investigated by a committee under the chairmanship of the United Kingdom Secretary of State for Foreign Affairs, the other members being the Secretary of State for the Colonies, the Prime Ministers of Canada, Australia, New Zealand, the Union of South Africa, and Newfoundland, the Minister of External Affairs of the Irish Free State, and the Secretary of State for India (as leader of the Indian Delegation). The Committee

---

[1] No. 701.   [2] No. 18 of 1925.   [3] See p. 286, above.

drew up a Resolution, which was accepted by the Conference, as follows:[1]

I. (1) *Negotiation*

(*a*) It is desirable that no treaty should be negotiated by any of the Governments of the Empire without due consideration of its possible effect on other parts of the Empire, or, if circumstances so demand, on the Empire as a whole.

(*b*) Before negotiations are opened with the intention of concluding a treaty, steps should be taken to ensure that any of the other Governments of the Empire likely to be interested are informed, so that, if any such Government considers that its interests would be affected, it may have an opportunity of expressing its views, or, when its interests are intimately involved, of participating in the negotiations.

(*c*) In all cases where more than one of the Governments of the Empire participates in the negotiations, there should be the fullest possible exchange of views between those Governments before and during the negotiations. In the case of treaties negotiated at International Conferences, where there is a British Empire Delegation, on which, in accordance with the now established practice, the Dominions and India are separately represented, such representation should also be utilized to attain this object.

(*d*) Steps should be taken to ensure that those Governments of the Empire whose representatives are not participating in the negotiations should, during their progress, be kept informed in regard to any points arising in which they may be interested.

(2) *Signature*

(*a*) Bilateral treaties imposing obligations on one part of the Empire only should be signed by a representative of the Government of that part. The Full Power issued to such representative should indicate the part of the Empire in respect of which the obligations are to be undertaken, and the preamble and text of the treaty should be so worded as to make its scope clear.

(*b*) Where a bilateral treaty imposes obligations on more than one part of the Empire, the treaty should be signed by one or more plenipotentiaries on behalf of all the Governments concerned.

(*c*) As regards treaties negotiated at International Conferences, the existing practice of signature by plenipotentiaries on behalf of all the Governments of the Empire represented at the Conference should be continued, and the Full Powers should be in the form employed at Paris and Washington.

(3) *Ratification*

The existing practice in connexion with the ratification of treaties should be maintained.

II. Apart from treaties made between Heads of States, it is not unusual for agreements to be made between Governments. Such agree-

---

[1] Cmd. 1987, pp. 13-15.

Z

ments, which are usually of a technical or administrative character, are made in the names of the signatory Governments, and signed by representatives of those Governments, who do not act under Full Powers issued by the Heads of the States: they are not ratified by the Heads of the States, though in some cases some form of acceptance or confirmation by the Governments concerned is employed. As regards agreements of this nature the existing practice should be continued, but before entering on negotiations the Governments of the Empire should consider whether the interests of any other part of the Empire may be affected, and, if so, steps should be taken to ensure that the Government of such part is informed of the proposed negotiations, in order that it may have an opportunity of expressing its views.

The Resolution was submitted to the full Conference and unanimously approved. It was thought, however, that it would be of assistance to add a short explanatory statement in connexion with part I (3), setting out the existing procedure in relation to the ratification of Treaties. This procedure is as follows:

(*a*) The ratification of treaties imposing obligations on one part of the Empire is effected at the instance of the Government of that part.

(*b*) The ratification of treaties imposing obligations on more than one part of the Empire is effected after consultations between the Governments of those parts of the Empire concerned. It is for each Government to decide whether Parliamentary approval or legislation is required before desire for, or concurrence in, ratification is intimated by that Government.

The Recommendations of the Imperial Conference of 1926

In the interval before the Imperial Conference met again in 1926, a certain divergence of views arose as to the exact working of the 1923 Resolution. Accordingly the 1926 Conference returned to the question and, while approving generally the principles already laid down, examined 'some phases of treaty procedure . . . in greater detail in the light of experience in order to consider to what extent the Resolution of 1923 might with advantage be supplemented'. This examination was carried out by a sub-committee under the chairmanship of Mr E. Lapointe, Minister of Justice of Canada, which reported very fully.[1]

The substance of the sub-committee's recommendations on methods of negotiation were later conveniently summarized by the Imperial Conference of 1930 as follows:

(1) Any of His Majesty's Governments conducting negotiations should inform the other Governments of His Majesty in case they should be interested and give them the opportunity of expressing their views, if they think their interests may be affected.

(2) Any of His Majesty's Governments on receiving such informa-

[1] Cmd. 2768, pp. 20–7.

tion should, if it desires to express any views, do so with reasonable promptitude.

(3) None of His Majesty's Governments can take any steps which might involve the other Governments of His Majesty in any active obligations without their definite assent.

In the absence of comment, the negotiating government should, as indicated in the report of the 1926 Conference, be entitled to assume that no objection will be raised to its proposed policy.[1]

The sub-committee then dealt with the question of form as it had arisen on some recent occasions:

Form of Treaty

Some treaties begin with a list of the contracting countries and not with a list of Heads of States. In the case of treaties negotiated under the auspices of the League of Nations, adherence to the wording of the Annex to the Covenant for the purpose of describing the contracting party has led to the use in the preamble of the term 'British Empire' with an enumeration of the Dominions and India if parties to the Convention but without any mention of Great Britain and Northern Ireland and the Colonies and Protectorates. These are only included by virtue of their being covered by the term 'British Empire'. This practice, while suggesting that the Dominions and India are not on a footing of equality with Great Britain as participants in the treaties in question, tends to obscurity and misunderstanding and is generally unsatisfactory.

As a means of overcoming this difficulty it is recommended that all treaties (other than agreements between Governments) whether negotiated under the auspices of the League or not should be made in the name of Heads of States, and, if the treaty is signed on behalf of any or all of the Governments of the Empire, the treaty should be made in the name of the King as the symbol of the special relationship between the different parts of the Empire.

In the case of a treaty applying to only one part of the Empire it should be stated to be made by the King on behalf of that part.

The making of the treaty in the name of the King as the symbol of the special relationship between the different parts of the Empire will render superfluous the inclusion of any provision that its terms must not be regarded as regulating *inter se* the rights and obligations of the various territories on behalf of which it has been signed in the name of the King. In this connexion it must be borne in mind that the question was discussed at the Arms Traffic Conference in 1925, and that the Legal Committee of that Conference laid it down that the principle to which the foregoing sentence gives expression underlies all international conventions.

In the case of some international agreements the Governments of different parts of the Empire may be willing to apply between themselves some of the provisions as an administrative measure. In this case they should state the extent to which and the terms on which

[1] *Summary of Proceedings*, Cmd. 3717, pp. 27–9.

such provisions are to apply. Where international agreements are to be applied between different parts of the Empire, the form of a treaty between Heads of States should be avoided.

The sub-committee recommended that Full Powers for the plenipotentiaties for each part of the Empire should in each case be issued by the King on the advice of the Government concerned. In cases where some among His Majesty's Governments were only concerned in a minor degree, they might find it convenient to advise the King to issue Full Powers on their behalf to the plenipotentiary of another of his Governments more directly concerned; or to make provision in the treaty for their subsequent accession.

Regarding signature and ratification, the sub-committee recommended:

In the cases where the names of countries are appended to the signatures in a treaty, the different parts of the Empire should be designated in the same manner as is proposed in regard to the list of plenipotentiaries in the preamble to the treaty.

The signature of a treaty on behalf of a part of the Empire should cover territories for which a mandate has been given to that part of the Empire, unless the contrary is stated at the time of the signature.

In general, treaties contain a ratification clause and a provision that the treaty will come into force on the deposit of a certain number of ratifications. The question has sometimes arisen in connexion with treaties negotiated under the auspices of the League whether, for the purpose of making up the number of ratifications necessary to bring the treaty into force, ratifications on behalf of different parts of the Empire which are separate Members of the League should be counted as separate ratifications. In order to avoid any difficulty in future, it is recommended that, when it is thought necessary that a treaty should contain a clause of this character, it should take the form of a provision that the treaty should come into force when it has been ratified on behalf of so many separate Members of the League.

The sub-committee also studied the question of the representation of the different parts of the Empire at international conferences. Their conclusions were as follows:

(1) No difficulty arises as regards representation at conferences convened by, or under the auspices of, the League of Nations. In the case of such conferences all members of the League are invited, and if they attend are represented separately by separate delegations. Co-operation is ensured by the application of paragraph I 1 (c) of the Treaty Resolution of 1923.

(2) As regards international conferences summoned by foreign Governments, no rule of universal application can be laid down, since the nature of the representation must, in part, depend on the form of invitation issued by the convening Government.

(a) In conferences of a technical character, it is usual and always desirable that the different parts of the Empire should (if they wish to participate) be represented separately by separate delegations, and where necessary efforts should be made to secure invitations which will render such representation possible.

(b) Conferences of a political character called by a foreign Government must be considered on the special circumstances of each individual case.

It is for each part of the Empire to decide whether its particular interests are so involved, especially having regard to the active obligations likely to be imposed by any resulting treaty, that it desires to be represented at the conference, or whether it is content to leave the negotiation in the hands of the part or parts of the Empire more directly concerned and to accept the result.

If a Government desires to participate in the conclusion of a treaty, the method by which representation will be secured is a matter to be arranged with the other Governments of the Empire in the light of the invitation which has been received.

Where more than one part of the Empire desires to be represented three methods of representation are possible:

(i) By means of a common plenipotentiary or plenipotentiaries, the issue of Full Powers to whom should be on the advice of all parts of the Empire participating.

(ii) By a single British Empire delegation composed of separate representatives of such parts of the Empire as are participating in the conference. This was the form of representation employed at the Washington Disarmament Conference of 1921.

(iii) By separate delegations representing each part of the Empire participating in the conference. If, as a result of consultation, this third method is desired, an effort must be made to ensure that the form of invitation from the convening Government will make this method of representation possible.

Certain non-technical treaties should, from their nature, be concluded in a form which will render them binding upon all parts of the Empire, and for this purpose should be ratified with the concurrence of all the Governments. It is for each Government to decide to what extent its concurrence in the ratification will be facilitated by its participation in the conclusion of the treaty, as, for instance, by the appointment of a common plenipotentiary. Any question as to whether the nature of the treaty is such that its ratification should be concurred in by all parts of the Empire is a matter for discussion and agreement between the Governments.

The recommendations under the section *Form of Treaty* were followed up at the Council of the League of Nations. Sir Austen Chamberlain made a statement on 9 March 1927. He said that the Imperial Conference had agreed, for constitutional reasons 'with which I need not trouble the Council', that 'the acceptance by the Governments of the British Empire of treaties negotiated under the auspices of the League would be facilitated' if the innovations of Versailles were abandoned and a reversion made to the Heads-of-States form.[1] The Council of the League took note of the statement, the pre-Versailles practice was subsequently adopted, and the use of 'the British Empire' as the high contracting party, condemned by the 1926 Imperial Conference, entirely disappeared from instruments negotiated under League auspices.

Equality of Status in Operation: the Briand-Kellogg Pact, 1928

The resolutions of the Imperial Conferences of 1923 and 1926 may be regarded as the final crystallization of the long development of consultation and co-operation in treaty-making. The Dominions thenceforward (with the exception of Newfoundland)[2] made bilateral treaties and took their part in the making of multilateral treaties on a basis of complete equality with the United Kingdom and with each other, and the rules for mutual consultation and, where necessary, co-ordinated action were recognized and followed. The corollary of this crystallization is that each Dominion is responsible for the fulfilment of its treaty obligations, and that foreign States must look to them individually for the execution of their international duty, and make representations in respect of non-fulfilment, or other claims arising, to the Dominion Governments. The development of the Dominions' diplomatic services has facilitated direct communication with foreign Governments, but in cases where no Dominion representative is accredited to the foreign State concerned, the United Kingdom diplomatic machinery is used as a channel of communication, but without affecting the attribution of responsibility.

These treaty-making principles are illustrated by the case of the Briand-Kellogg Pact of 1928, the first major international instrument after the 1926 Imperial Conference, which is also of interest in that it was a multilateral instrument agreed without prior deliberation at an international conference. The proposal for a Treaty for the Renunciation of War came actually from the United States, following correspondence à deux between M. Briand, the French Minister for Foreign Affairs, and Mr Kellogg, the United States Secretary of State. The American Government addressed its démarche only to the United Kingdom Government, among the Commonwealth countries, on 13 April 1928. The British Foreign Secretary, Sir Austen Chamberlain, in his reply of 19 May, stated that:

---

[1] Full text of statement in League of Nations, *Official Journal*, vol. 8 (1927), p. 377.　　[2] The position of Newfoundland is described on p. 281.

the proposed treaty, from its very nature, is not one which concerns His Majesty's Government in Great Britain alone, but it is one in which they could not hope to participate otherwise than jointly and simultaneously with His Majesty's Governments in the Dominions and with the Government of India.

The United States Government accordingly addressed invitations to participate to the Canadian and Irish Free State Governments direct, through those countries' Ministers at Washington, and to the other Dominions, with whom they were not in direct diplomatic communication, through the Imperial Government. All had accepted the invitation by the middle of June 1928. As the next stage, Mr Kellogg sent a circular note to fourteen Governments—the five British Dominions and the Government of India being separately addressed, through the channels already used, among this fourteen—on 23 June 1928; and the treaty that was presented was signed at Paris on 27 August. The treaty was in Heads-of-States form, being concluded for the United Kingdom, the Dominions, and India in the name of the King Emperor; and their seven plenipotentiaries signed separately. Mr Mackenzie King, Prime Minister and Minister of External Affairs of Canada, and Mr Cosgrave, President of the Executive Council of the Irish Free State, both journeyed to Paris to sign personally. His Britannic Majesty executed seven separate instruments of ratification on advice tendered by the seven Governments during January and February 1929. These instruments were deposited simultaneously at Washington on 2 March 1929 by the Irish Free State and Canadian Ministers for their countries and by the British Ambassador for the other five. Certain reservations were tendered by the United Kingdom Government,[1] and the Dominions made it clear that they were not identified with them.

Commonwealth Treaty Procedures in Use by 1950

The established procedures for the negotiation, signature and ratification of treaties by the Dominions may be summarized as follows. It should be regarded as understood that the process of consultation with other Commonwealth Members laid down in the 1923 and 1926 Resolutions is observed, since it is an essential feature of Commonwealth co-operation. After the proclamation of the Republic in January 1950, the following general account ceased to apply to India.

A. Treaties and Conventions; other than inter-Governmental agreements of a technical or administrative character, which are not concluded in Heads-of-States form.

[1] See *Survey of International Affairs*, 1928, pp. 20-2.

1. All treaties and conventions between Heads-of-States concluded by the Dominions with foreign States are made in the name of the King and, when concluded, ratification is effected by the King.

(NOTE: A treaty concluded in the name of His Majesty does not regulate the relations of the Members of the Commonwealth *inter se.*

2. The negotiation of such treaties or conventions falls upon His Majesty's Government in the Dominion. The Dominion Government nominates a plenipotentiary to whom the King, on the Dominion Government's advice and at the instance of the Governor-General in Council, issues Full Powers. The Full Power thus issued indicates the Member of the Commonwealth in respect of which the obligations are to be undertaken, and the preambles and texts of treaties are so worded as to make their scope clear.

(NOTE: Full Powers for Australian, New Zealand, Pakistan, and Ceylon plenipotentiaries are issued under the Great Seal of the Realm. Under the Royal Executive Functions and Seals Act of 1934, Full Powers for South African plenipotentiaries are issued under the Royal Great Seal of the Union of South Africa, and His Majesty's sign manual, under the same Act, may be dispensed with if urgency or other serious reasons of State require. For Canadian plenipotentiaries, under the new Letters Patent governing the office and appointment of Governor-General which came into force on 1 October 1947, Full Powers could be issued by the Governor-General under the Great Seal of Canada, but it is understood that the Canadian Government do not contemplate any change in existing procedure in this respect.)

3. Treaties, when their terms have been agreed, are signed by the Dominion plenipotentiary.

4. Ratification is effected by His Majesty on the advice and at the express request of the Dominion Government; subject to the variations in procedure indicated in the note to (2) above.

B. Agreements other than treaties and convention in Heads-of-States form.

Agreements in this form (i.e. agreements between Governments) are not concluded in the name of the King, and Royal Full Powers are not required for negotiation, signature, or ratification. The necessary powers are usually issued by the Governor-General in Council, or by a Dominion Minister authorized thereto by the Governor-General in Council.

CHAPTER XV

THE DEVELOPMENT OF CO-OPERATION IN WAR-TIME

SINCE the object of British Commonwealth war-time co-operation was victory, it was natural that its forms should vary with the fortune and phases of the war. In the period of the 'phoney war' and the German *Blitzkrieg*, military operations were confined to Europe, and co-operative organization was predominantly Anglo-French.[1] The Dominions were getting their forces and economies on to a war footing, and consultation and co-operation with them was conducted almost entirely through the normal established channels. After the fall of France in June 1940 the Dominions' attitude was one of affording maximum help to the United Kingdom, rather than of asking for a share in the overall direction of the war. During this phase, however, the Delhi Conference[2] took place and certain steps were taken to organize the resources of the Commonwealth, notably the establishment of the Eastern Group Supply Council. No Imperial War Cabinet was established (pp. 94–9). The military system which obtained in time of peace was not formally altered or redefined, but the United Kingdom Cabinet took over the standing organization of the Committee of Imperial Defence. The military forces of the Commonwealth consist of the separately organized forces of its sovereign members, and their employment depends on the decisions of the several Governments. The foundation of common action had long been laid by the standardization of equipment and training, the interchange of officers, the training provided by the Imperial Defence College, etc. It remained in 1939 to obtain unity of command in actual operations; and to regulate, by law or order-in-council, certain administrative matters arising from overseas service and combinations of forces.

Naval Forces

The paramount position of the Royal Navy over a century led

---

[1] 'Before September 1939, Britain and France had bound themselves by treaty under certain clearly specified eventualities to wage war as Allies; they had defined with precision the military support which they would give each other; they had specified the combined machinery through which their combined war effort would be conducted' (W. K. Hancock and M. M. Gowing, *British War Economy*, London, H.M.S.O., 1949, p. 378).

[2] See p. 365-6, below.

to the evolution of Dominion naval forces in close co-operation with it: a tendency strengthened by the global character of naval warfare and the need to use bases in common. Unity of command had, in essence, been accepted in 1911, in a Memorandum agreed at the Imperial Conference.[1] Having laid down principles for common training systems, seniority of officers, etc., the Memorandum says: 'In time of war, when the naval service of a Dominion, or any part thereof, has been put at the disposal of the Imperial Government by the Dominion authorities, the ships will form an integral part of the British Fleet, and will remain under the control of the British Admiralty during the continuance of the war.' The Royal Australian Navy and the New Zealand Division of the Royal Navy (now the Royal New Zealand Navy) were transferred to the control of the Admiralty by their Governments at the outbreak of war; as were the ships of the Royal Canadian Navy employed in the Atlantic. The Royal Indian Navy also operated under Admiralty control from the outset. The Union of South Africa, which had depended on the Royal Navy for its maritime defence, organized a small mine-sweeping and patrol service, and units co-operated with the Royal Navy in the Mediterranean. As the Dominions had always applied the King's Regulations and Admiralty Instructions, there were no administrative questions to be regulated. Personnel was freely interchangeable, and officers' seniority was determined by the date of their commission, whichever navy they had originally entered.

Land Forces

The position in regard to land forces was not so closely co-ordinated. Agreement on policy and operations was obtained by consultation at Cabinet level, and the Governments then put forces at the disposal of the command. Mr Mackenzie King, the Prime Minister of Canada, expressed the principle thus: 'So far as the disposition of troops is concerned, the Canadian Government places no restriction whatever upon any decision that may be made, other than that the Government itself shall have the opportunity of knowing what is contemplated and an opportunity of expressing its views'.[2] Units remained under their own officers in their formations, but were under the operational command of the General Officer Commanding in any theatre. It was always clear that the home government retained ultimate control, but delegated it voluntarily, in consultation and agreement with the other governments of the Commonwealth.

[1] Cd. 5746.
[2] Referring to the First Canadian Division in the United Kingdom; 26 August 1941.

The legal position of Canadian troops in the United Kingdom was regulated by the Visiting Forces (British Commonwealth) Act, 1933,[1] and the almost identical United Kingdom statute of the same year.[2] The position was fully described to the Canadian House of Commons on 1 April 1941 by the Minister of National Defence, Mr Ralston.[3] The Act provided for the visiting forces to be either 'serving together' with United Kingdom forces—in which case the Canadian command remained separate—or 'serving in combination', in which case there was a single commander designated by the United Kingdom Government. A Canadian Order-in-Council of 3 April 1940[4] applied the 1933 Act in such wise that Canadian troops dispatched to the Continent of Europe were automatically classed as 'serving in combination'. Moreover, the appropriate Canadian commanders on the spot were authorized to detail forces or parts of forces under this command to serve 'in combination' with British forces in the United Kingdom. Thus General McNaughton, commanding the Canadian Corps in the United Kingdom, was designated by the Minister of National Defence as so authorized, and, through him, senior Canadian combatant officers also.[5]

The position with regard to 'visiting forces' in the cases of Australia and New Zealand was different. Neither had adopted the Statute of Westminster, and the Annual Army and Air Force Acts (Imperial) applied to their forces and to 'visiting forces' to their countries from the United Kingdom. To regulate the position vis-à-vis Canada and the Union of South Africa, Australia and New Zealand passed legislation on similar lines to the reciprocal legislation which had been passed in Canada and the Union following an agreement between those two countries at the 1930 Imperial Conference, which provided that a visiting force remained subject to the law of its country of origin.[6]

Financial Resources

The co-operative mobilization of crucial financial resources was given consideration before 1939, and measures were soon taken. After the economic crisis of 1931, the United Kingdom

---

[1] Can. Statutes, 23–24, Geo. V, C. 21.

[2] Provision for the discipline, etc., of 'visiting forces' was one of the matters considered by the Conference on the Operation of Dominion Legislation, 1929 (Cmd. 3479, p. 17). The Imperial Conference of 1930 found itself with insufficient time to consider the question in full, and recommended that the several governments should take appropriate action (Cmd. 3717, p. 26).

[3] Canadian House of Commons Debates, pp. 2047–9.

[4] P.C. 1066.

[5] Canadian Institute of International Affairs, Canada in World Affairs, 1939–41, by R. M. Dawson (London, Oxford University Press, 1943) pp. 297–307.

[6] Journal of the Parliaments of the Empire, vol. 21 (April 1940), p. 307.

Treasury established and operated an Exchange Equalization Account for currency transactions, and a mild measure of exchange control was operated through the banks as authorized dealers in currency. Despite the changed position of the London money market compared with the nineteenth century, it was still the hub of the world sterling exchange system, and a more or less effective 'sterling area' was therefore in existence. United Kingdom exchange control regulations were completed in draft by March 1939, and 'were promulgated in instalments between 24 August and 3 September'.[1] These regulations had been the subject of intra-Commonwealth discussions, and were based on the informal membership of the sterling area—a membership indicated by the habit of holding a considerable proportion of monetary reserves in the form of London sterling. 'In September 1939 this was still the qualification for membership. . . . Some foreign countries, such as Egypt, still remained in the sterling area; some Empire countries—notably Canada and Hong Kong —had passed outside it; but, by and large, the sterling area was now coterminous with the British Commonwealth and Empire. Its wartime definition was in form the result of Treasury action; but behind this were careful discussions which had started six months earlier in response to an Australian initiative. The sterling area rested upon the recognition of common interests and responsibilities by an association of sovereign governments. All the associates engaged themselves to impose within their own jurisdictions an exchange control of the United Kingdom brand. None of them was under any obligation to keep its currency unit in any fixed relation to the British £; what united them all was a common code of practice under which they remained unhampered from exchange control in their mutual transactions with each other, but maintained a united front in all their external dealings. They combined their earning power and pooled their earnings of 'hard' currencies, and entrusted them to the Exchange Equalization Fund, which held them as the reserve of the entire sterling area and issued to each member the sums that it required to satisfy its own economic needs. The sterling area was in fact a financial union, centred on London and managed by London.'[2] 'Hard' currencies were designated in lists issued from time to time.

The Effect of the Entry of the United States into the War

The whole picture changed after Pearl Harbour. The entry into the war of the United States, the largest producing country in

---

[1] Hancock and Gowing, op. cit. p. 109.
[2] ibid. p. 110.

the world, whose military effort when mobilized would also form the largest single contribution to Allied man-power and resources, naturally led to the switching of co-operative machinery to Washington on a large scale. At the same time, the military disasters in the Far East drew the Indian Ocean and Pacific areas deeply into the military picture, and the intensity of interest and effort in South Africa, Australia, and New Zealand was correspondingly sharpened. At the same time, Canada, whose war effort was already to a material extent integrated with United States policy by the establishment of the Joint Defence Board in August 1940, and the Joint Economic Committees set up on 17 June 1941 (see pp. 247–8, above), was the British Commonwealth country nearest to the main centre of co-operative activity. A natural result was that the Dominions became progressively more closely associated with the direction of the war effort.

Excluding the U.S.S.R., which at no time entered into comparable co-operative arrangements, the United States and the United Kingdom were the major partners in the new phase. They were by far the largest units in terms of man-power, manufacturing capacity, shipping resources, and finance. There were also overriding considerations of urgency which reinforced the natural tendency to a predominantly bilateral relationship. The United States authorities may have felt that urgent progress would be retarded if they had to deal, on cumbersome committees and boards, with representatives of all the lesser United Nations; in any case, it appears that they welcomed forms of organization which enabled them to deal with the British Empire as far as possible as a unit centring the co-ordination of its requirements, etc., on London.

As a result of this bilateral relationship, when a United States–United Kingdom co-operative agency was set up in Washington, a Commonwealth counterpart tended to be established in London. The exception to this was Canada, whose geographical contiguity and traditionally close relations with the United States, as well as her importance as a contributor to the United Nations' resources, made it more natural for her to co-operate with organizations located in Washington, and to be represented in London quite frequently by liaison officers. For example, in due course Canada became a member of the Combined Food Board and the Combined Production and Resources Board.

The Combined Boards

By direct agreement between the President of the United States and the Prime Minister of the United Kingdom, Combined Boards were first established in Washington in January

1942. This formal step had a background of informal co-operation in the period of American neutrality, so that after Pearl
Harbour the British-American partnership structure took shape
with a rapidity otherwise inconceivable. Three boards were then
set up: (i) the Munitions Assignment Board; (ii) the Combined
Shipping Adjustment Board; (iii) the Combined Raw Materials
Board.

On 27 January a White Paper was presented to Parliament
entitled 'Co-ordination of the Allied War Effort'.[1] It announced
that three boards had been established in Washington by the
President of the United States and the Prime Minister of the
United Kingdom. The three boards were called: the Munitions
Assignment Board, the Combined Shipping Adjustment Board,
and the Combined Raw Materials Board. These boards would
confer with representatives of the U.S.S.R., China, and such
other of the United Nations as might be necessary for effective
joint utilization of available resources. The manner in which the
Boards should operate was outlined as follows:

(1) *Munitions Assignment Board* was to operate under the
Combined Chiefs of Staff, but divided into two committees, one
in London and one in Washington under the leadership of Lord
Beaverbrook and Mr Hopkins respectively. The principle of
operation was that 'the entire munitions resources of Great
Britain and the United States were deemed to be in a common
pool', and the Board would advise on assignments and priority.
In each case the Committee was to be assisted by a secretariat
whose function was to survey every branch and to co-ordinate
with every sub-committee.

The two divisions of the Board in Washington and London
were later supplemented by a third, established in Ottawa for the
assignment of Canadian production. When Australia and India
achieved the production of disposable surpluses of munitions,
assignment committees were established in both countries. These
committees were composed of representatives of the United
Kingdom and the United States sitting with representatives of
the producing country.

The Munitions Assignment Board dealt with new production,
and the war ended before it had to face the problem of re-deploy-
ment of weapons from theatres of operations which had been
'mopped up'. The Board's task, as it was, was difficult enough,
because there were some forty claimants on the pool. To prevent
confusion, it was necessarily ruled that claims must not be submitted both to Washington and to London. Generally speaking,
on account of similarity of weapons and close association in the

[1] Cmd. 6332.

field, the countries of the Commonwealth and the European
Allies fell within the London group, and South American countries and China in the Washington group. The final agreement
in the case of Australia and New Zealand was that they should
claim assignments of Army and Navy equipment from London,
and Air Force equipment from Washington. These decisions
'did not, however, interfere with the processes of lend-lease
accountancy'.[1]

(2) *Combined Shipping Adjustment Board* was to operate under
Sir Arthur Salter and Admiral Land in Washington, and under
Lord Leathers in London. Shipping resources were to be pooled
in principle. The Board would consider adjustments in the distribution of shipping rather than the distribution of shipping
facilities as a whole, and shipping was to remain controlled by
the Ministry of War Transport and by the equivalent authority
in the United States.

Before the entry of the United States into the war the Ministry
of War Transport had, in consultation with the Dominion and
Indian Governments, co-ordinated and allocated all British shipping resources.

(3) *Combined Raw Materials Board* was to operate under Mr
Batt and Sir Clive Baillieu in Washington and Lord Beaverbrook
in London, and was to effect the speediest and most effective
use of raw materials. The Board received estimates and requirements and made all allocations accordingly.

The first two Combined Boards had their parallel divisions in
Washington and London, the London Boards consisting of
United States and United Kingdom representatives with Dominion liaison officers. Canada was the exception to the plan of co-
ordinating Commonwealth action in London, having pooled her
resources with the Washington Boards.

The third Board, for the allocation of raw materials, was in a
different position owing to the far greater importance of the
Dominion contribution of raw material resources, which made
it desirable that they should have their full share in their control. As a result, an Empire Clearing House located in London
was proposed.[2] The background to this proposal may be seen
in certain pre-existing conditions and organizations. On the one
hand, the operation since March 1941 of Lend-Lease had involved the establishment in Washington of machinery for
Dominion participation and for a combined British procurement
system. Dominion Missions in Washington (which grew, be-

[1] Hancock and Gowing, op. cit. p. 395.
[2] It was duly established and held its first formal meeting in March 1942;
see below.

tween the inauguration of Lend-Lease and the end of the war, from some two or three persons to several hundreds) already provided the United States authorities with detailed information on their countries' requirements. There was also in Washington, dating from the period before the operation of Lend-Lease, the British Purchasing Commission which was the co-ordinating agency for British Commonwealth purchases.[1] In London, from May 1941, there had been in operation the Empire Steel Supplies Committee. This Committee was charged with the co-ordination of total Empire steel supplies and requirements, and any deficit had to be met by external purchases, which were naturally made from the United States as the world's greatest steel supplier once the Continental European iron and coalfields (other than Swedish ore resources) were in German hands. The British Purchasing Commission at Washington acted as the agent for all Empire steel purchases, and its functions were a corollary of the co-ordination of supplies under Lend-Lease after that system came into operation. Mr Purvis was the head of the Commission, which after March 1941 acted as the Empire purchasing agent for all supplies and not only for steel.

The Empire Clearing House

It was against this background that the Empire Clearing House was set up under the auspices of the Ministry of Production, and held its first formal meeting in March 1942. Its Chairman was Lord Portal, and all the Dominions (except Canada), as well as Southern Rhodesia, were members, represented by persons on the High Commissioners' Staffs. Canada appointed an observer and worked with the Combined Raw Materials Board in Washington through Mr Batt, the Chairman of the Canadian–United States Joint Raw Materials Committee. The Empire Clearing House held plenary sessions once a fortnight. Later its work increased so that it became necessary to set up a working sub-organization which met about twice a week.

The functions of the Empire Clearing House were clarified by the middle of May 1942. It was more than merely a collecting centre for information; it had an active share in determining distribution. All Empire raw materials information, requests, etc., were routed through the Clearing House, except that the functions of the Dominion Missions in Washington as providers

---

[1] The British Commonwealth organization, which was built up for this purpose before American entry into the war, was the British Supply Council in North America; under it was the British Purchasing Commission, with subsidiary organizations, such as the Empire and Allied Requirements Committee on which were representatives of every country in the Empire.' (H. Duncan Hall, *The British Commonwealth at War*: Part II, no. 5 (iv), p. 52.)

of detailed information for Lend-Lease allocations were not affected. It worked out in practice that the Empire Clearing House mainly dealt with the Eastern Hemisphere, while the Combined Raw Materials Board in Washington (on which Sir Clive Baillieu was Ministry of Supply representative) dealt with supplies and requirements in the Western Hemisphere. There was, however, co-ordinated puchasing and allocation between them, more especially in the case of raw materials in short supply. In August 1942 the Empire Clearing House took over the functions of the Empire Steel Requirements Committee. Sir Clive Baillieu, who was kept systematically supplied with the necessary information by the Dominions' Missions in Washington, represented them on the Combined Raw Materials Board. In pooling and co-ordinating the information he had the assistance of an Empire Advisory Committee, without formal status, composed of representatives of the Dominion Missions.

The Combined Production and Resources Board

As the United States economy became more closely geared to war-time requirements, and much concentration of American production followed, there was a danger that civilian requirements, which were not covered by the three Combined Boards, might be squeezed out, with, probably, especially severe curtailing of the civilian requirements of the Dominions and the smaller United Nations. On 9 June 1942, therefore, the Combined Production and Resources Board was set up to cover certain resources not looked after by the existing Boards. It consisted of two members: the Chairman of the United States War Production Board, and the British Minister of Supply's representative in the United States. Canada was not covered by this representation. On 11 July 1942, in the Canadian House of Commons, Mr Mackenzie King welcomed the announcement of the Anglo-American Combined Production and Resources Board. He went on to say that in regard to co-operation in war production, Canada had worked through the medium of the Canada–United States Joint Economic Committees on a war-time agricultural programme, and through the Canada–United States Joint War Production Committee and War Supplies Limited on an industrial war production programme. 'Through what agencies and representatives their existing co-operation with both the United Kingdom and the United States could most effectively be co-ordinated with the new United Kingdom–United States Boards was receiving the considering of the Government.'[1] Later, on 10 November 1942, Canada was admit-

[1] *Journal of the Parliaments of the Empire*, vol. 23, July 1942, p. 496.

2A

ted to membership of the Combined Production and Resources Board, being represented by Mr C. D. Howe, Minister of Munitions and Supply.

The Commonwealth Supply Council

The new Combined Board had no complementary body in London, since the Empire Clearing House was concerned only with raw materials. After consultation with the Dominion and Southern Rhodesian Governments, the Commonwealth Supply Council was set up in London and held its first meeting on 28 October 1942. The official announcement stated:

> The first meeting of the Commonwealth Supply Council, which has been formed to co-ordinate the arrangements for supply throughout the Empire, was held yesterday. The Council's aim will be to bring together and develop existing machinery in order to assist and co-ordinate the common war effort in every way possible.
> The Minister of Production is chairman of the Council, which also includes the Secretaries of State for the Dominions, Colonies, and India, the President of the Board of Trade, and the Minister of Works and Planning. Australia is represented by Mr S. M. Bruce, New Zealand by Mr W. J. Jordan, High Commissioner; South Africa by Mr S. Waterson, High Commissioner; India by Sir Ramaswami Mudaliar; and Southern Rhodesia by Mr S. M. L. O'Keeffe, High Commissioner.
> Because of her special position in relation to North American production, Canada will not take direct part in the work of the Council, but will keep in touch with its proceedings. The work on raw materials hitherto done by the Empire Clearing House will be merged in the work of the Council.[1]

As well as taking over the functions of the Empire Clearing House, the Commonwealth Supply Council was concerned also with the finished goods which were dealt with in Washington by the new Combined Board. The Commonwealth Supply Council was composed of four committees of officials: (i) Munitions Committee; (ii) Non-Munitions Committee; (iii) Raw Materials Committee (which continued the functions of the Empire Clearing House); and (iv) Machine Tools Committee. Later, other committees were set up under the aegis of the Council: the Railway Equipment Committee (which originated as a sub-committee of the Munitions Committee); the London Food Committee; the Fertilizers Committee (which was a sub-committee of the Raw Materials and London Food Committees); and the Agricultural Machinery Committee (a sub-committee of the Non-Munitions Committee and the London Food Committee).

[1] *The Times*, 29 October 1942.

The Combined Food Board

The establishment of a Combined Food Board was announced at the same time as the establishment of the Combined Production and Resources Board, on 9 June 1942.

It was composed of the Secretary of Agriculture for the United States and the head of the British Food Mission; the latter represented the Minister of Food and acted under that Ministry's instructions. A joint statement to the press said: 'In principle, the entire food resources of the United States and the United Kingdom will be deemed to be in a common pool.'[1] The Board was formed to investigate, formulate plans, and advise the United Kingdom and United States Governments in regard to any question common to the two countries and the other allied nations concerning food, materials and implements for the production of food, and its transport. It particularly dealt with foods in short supply.

President Roosevelt said at a press conference that whereas the Production Board would be concerned chiefly with British and American production, the Combined Food Board's activities would cover all the United Nations.[2] In October 1943 Canada became a third member of the Board.[3]

The Combined Steel Committee

The creation of the Committee resulted from a visit made by a United States Steel mission to the United Kingdom under the auspices of the Combined Production and Resources Board. The mission brought to light many concrete differences in the production and use of steel between the United States and the United Kingdom. It recommended that better results could be obtained in both countries by pooling technical information and production and distribution methods.

On 14 December 1942 the Combined Steel Committee was set up by the United States, United Kingdom, and Canadian staffs of the Combined Production and Resources Board and the Combined Raw Materials Board. Mr Hiland G. Batcheller was appointed chairman with a staff of production experts from the three countries. The Committee worked in Washington.

Instructions given to the Committee were:

(i) To obtain, assemble, and co-ordinate information on iron ore and scrap, iron and steel production, and requirements of iron and steel of the United Nations in such form as will enable the supply and requirements position to be kept continuously under review by both boards.

[1] *New York Times*, 22 August 1942.
[2] *The Times*, 19 June 1942.   [3] Hancock and Gowing, op. cit. p. 404.

(ii) To consider and make recommendations on the means of increasing production and improving the efficiency of the use of steel and distribution facilities in the United Nations, including facilitating the exchange of technical information, information on trade practices and measures of conservation and limitation of use.

(iii) To consider and make recommendations on unified systems of definitions and terminology.

(iv) To recommend as necessary any action which should be taken by either board to adjust supplies and requirements to one another.[1]

An Anglo-American Mission made a survey of the steel situation in India, Australia, New Zealand, and South Africa. After five months' research the Mission reported its findings in November 1943 to the Steel Committee. The Mission made four recommendations to the combined Committees:

(i) An organization should be established in the United Kingdom to co-ordinate United States–United Kingdom information on steel controls and this information should be circulated to the Dominions.

(ii) The Dominions should advise this body of savings they have been able to make and the method used, for consideration and possible adoption by the United States and the United Kingdom.

(iii) To ease the burden of the United States and the United Kingdom and to save shipping space a careful study should be made of further surplus capacity, so that one Dominion might provide the requirements of another.

(iv) That when standardization of controls is completed all steps possible should be taken to facilitate action on requirements submitted to the United Kingdom and the United States by the various Dominions.[2]

The Principal Commonwealth Supply Committee

The establishment of the Commonwealth Supply Council did not entirely obviate difficulties regarding certain civil supplies which were dealt with by its Non-Munitions Committee. To remedy the situation, after consulting by circular dispatch with the Dominion, Indian, and Southern Rhodesian Governments, the Principal Commonwealth Supply Committee was established in Washington. It consisted of representatives of the Governments' supply missions, and at formal meetings the representatives were the heads of the Dominion, Indian, and Colonial missions, with the resident Minister as Chairman. It worked

---

[1] *The Times*, 15 December 1942.
[2] ibid. 8 November 1943.

through several sub-committees. The first three to be set up were: Combined Planning; Programming and Priority (later divided); and an Apportionment Committee.

After about a year these Committees were amalgamated into a Requirements Sub-Committee. Other sub-committees which had come into existence were concerned with Lend-Lease and planning. The amalgamation of the original three Committees was accompanied by the establishment of two new committees: Cash Procurement and Railway Facilities. The latter was paralleled in London by the Railway Equipment Sub-Committee of the Commonwealth Supply Council.

The Delhi Conference and the Eastern Group Supply Council

Reference was made earlier to British Commonwealth organizations established before the United States entered the war.

The opening of the Eastern Group Supply Conference at Delhi on 25 October 1940 marked a new development in the methods of consultation and co-operation between the countries constituting the British Empire. The object of the Conference, said Lord Linlithgow in his opening speech, was to form a plan to make British Commonwealth countries lying east and south of Suez into one unit in regard to production and interchange of goods. This area covered the theatres of war in the Middle East, also Egypt and the Islamic countries of western Asia.

The Conference met at the invitation of the Government of India. Delegations were present from the Governments of Australia, New Zealand, South Africa, India, Burma, Ceylon, Southern Rhodesia, Hong Kong, Malaya, and Palestine. Representatives from the Netherlands East Indies attended as observers, and Sir Alexander Roger represented the British Ministry of Supply mission ('Roger Mission'), which had been making a survey in India of Indian industry and industrial potential.

Preparations for the Conference were begun soon after the defeat of France and the entry of Italy into the war, which events severely hampered the use of the Mediterranean as a supply route. When the Conference assembled, Sir Muhammad Zafrullah Khan presided over its Central Committee and Sir Alexander Roger and Sir Walter Massy-Greene (head of the Australian delegation) were chairmen of the two main working committees under the Central Committee.

The aims of the Conference were to pool the resources of these countries needed for the prosecution of the war, so that by co-operation the participating countries would be as far as possible self-supporting as a group. The primary aim was to relieve Great Britain of such of her war burdens as these countries could bear, and any surplus production was to go to Great Britain.

The Conference confined itself to war production. It was concerned with direct war requirements (i.e. the actual needs of the defence services), and with indirect war requirements (i.e. essential needs of the civil population and connected commercial and industrial capacity).

Finally, it was the intention to set up a Standing Committee to see that the policies and principles were carried out.

The Conference ended its formal deliberations on 26 November 1940. The recommendations were not then disclosed since they had to be kept secret for security reasons. In view of this need for secrecy it was arranged that as far as possible the delegates forming the Eastern Group Supply Council (as the Standing Committee was called) should have been representatives at the Conference. A mission composed of delegates on the Eastern Group Supply Council under the chairmanship of Sir Alexander Roger made a survey of the resources available after visiting the countries concerned.

A Central Provision Office was established on 21 March 1941 in Delhi. It worked under military control, its function being to collaborate with the Eastern Group Supply Council on questions of war supply. It set up local provision offices in the countries represented at the Conference.

As a result of the Delhi Conference, the United Kingdom Government, with the cordial support of the Governments of the Dominions and India, established the proposed Standing Committee, under the title of the Eastern Group Supply Council, towards the end of 1940. The Governments of the United Kingdom, India, Southern Rhodesia, Australia, New Zealand, and South Africa were represented. The United Kingdom member, Sir Archibald Carter, acted as chairman. Military liaison with the Imperial General Staff was provided by the Comptroller-General of Army Provision being a member of the Council. Shortly before the fall of Singapore, the Netherlands Government was invited to join and appointed a representative. The area covered by the Council consisted of: India, Burma, Malaya, and the Netherlands East Indies; Australia and New Zealand; the Union of South Africa; Southern Rhodesia; and the Middle East. The purpose of the Council was to ensure the fullest use of its members' resources for the Eastern Group area, including the Middle East. Following military reverses in the Far East at the end of 1941 and the beginning of 1942, the resources commanded by the Eastern Group were drastically reduced, while at the same time India and Australia, being now in the area of hostilities, needed to use the whole of their production of manufactured goods. The situation was, moreover, altered by the creation of the Combined Boards, with their complementary bodies in London; and the functions of the Eastern Group Supply Council were inevitably reduced. Ultimately its activities were taken over by the Central Provision Office in Delhi, working in close co-operation with a Ministry of Supply Mission. The head of that Mission became Chairman of the Eastern Group Supply Council, which remained in being as a consultative body.

Middle East Supply Centre

Set up in April 1941 in Cairo by the Minister of State in the British War Cabinet, Mr Lyttelton, when the shipping problem had become acute, the importance of this regional political and supply organization which co-ordinated non-military with military requirements was increased when it became an Anglo-American body in 1942.

The object, primarily strategical, was to rationalize all supplies for the Middle East and to ensure that with the utmost economy in shipping space the peoples of the Middle East should receive vital requirements. By the control of imports, together with carefully considered advice from the Centre to the Governments of Middle East countries as to the development of local resources, the equitable distribution of available supplies, and the means by which they could render mutual aid to one another, it was hoped the area could be saved from suffering too severely from the changes in national economies bound to occur as the result of the exigencies of war.

Since M.E.S.C. was first established the area that comes within its scope has been very much expanded, and now includes Egypt, the Sudan, Tripolitania, Cyrenaica, Eritrea, Ethiopia, British and French Somaliland, Aden, Palestine, Syria, the Lebanon, Transjordan, Saudi Arabia, the Arab Sheikhdoms, Iraq, Persia and Cyprus. Malta also was at one time included. Territories in East Africa only come into the scope of the Centre's activities as one of the outside sources of supply, and Turkey only as a consumer of pooled resources.[1]

There was a representative of M.E.S.C. in each country.

On questions of policy requiring co-ordination with other civil or military administrations in the Middle East the Centre consulted with the Supply and Transportation Committee presided over by the British Minister Resident in the Middle East. Its functions were not executive but only advisory. It was the sole agency whose recommendations were accepted by the appropriate bodies in London and Washington, the Combined Boards and other agencies.

[1] *Bulletin of International News*, vol. 31, no. 16, pp. 620-1.

One of the chief aims of M.E.S.C. was to import essential foods for civilian and military requirements and to put into operation schemes for increasing the food production of these countries. A major problem with which the Centre had to deal was the question of how best to collect grain in the Middle East countries. Under a certain amount of pressure and advice from M.E.S.C. many of the Governments concerned set up collecting organizations, the necessary transport being provided through M.E.S.C. and the military authorities.

The M.E.S.C. was also concerned with industrial problems of development for producing greater self-sufficiency. On the medical side, a Middle East Medical Advisory Committee was set up in Cairo in association with the medical department of the Centre, on which the leading medical authorities in the British and American armies were represented.

The Joint Supply Council for the Union of South Africa

In September 1943 there was established the Joint Supply Council for the Union of South Africa, consisting of representatives of the Union, the United Kingdom, and the United States Governments. Its personnel consisted of the United States Minister to the Union of South Africa, the United Kingdom High Commissioner, and the Union's Director-General of Supplies, with alternates. Its function was to formulate programmes of requirements in the Union, mainly of supplies from the United States.

Area Programming

About the middle of 1943 the success of the Middle East Supply Centre led to various proposals for what was called Area Programming. The Middle East Supply Centre had been set up in April 1941 by the United Kingdom alone, on account of its special interests and responsibilities in the area. On 11 November 1942 it became an Anglo-American joint body.

The original conception of the Area Programming Committees was similar. They were to be Anglo-American bodies concerned with determining the programme of supply, either for all the requirements of an area or for a group of requirements; and with allocating the necessary shipping. They were conceived as a means of co-ordinating the requirements and resources of the Allied African territories, which were progressively liberated following the Anglo-American landing in French North Africa in November 1942. In the event their constitution was informal and variable. They were generally tripartite bodies: Franco-Anglo-American or Belgian-Anglo-American, and therefore do not concern this handbook. The same applies to the Anglo-American Joint Economic Mission to North Africa, and similar bilateral bodies. But the Comité de Programme for Madagascar was a quadripartite body, consisting of Free French, United States, United Kingdom, and South African representatives under the chairmanship of the French member, established in the late summer of 1943. Towards the end of 1944, a South African member was invited to join the tripartite Programme Committee for the Belgian Congo.

The British Commonwealth Air Training Plan

After Pearl Harbour the organization of military co-operation entered formally upon a new phase with the establishment of the Combined Chiefs of Staff in Washington. The supply organization—the Combined Boards, etc.—subsidiary to this military organization for the co-ordination of the war effort has been described above. The publication of official military histories and documents will in due course provide material for a picture of Commonwealth military co-operation in this phase. For the present it has been considered appropriate only to include in this handbook two examples of common action undertaken by Commonwealth countries: the British Commonwealth Air Training Plan, and the leasing of the Newfoundland bases. Both of these arrangements were started in the period before Pearl Harbour, and both have special and novel features.

The British Commonwealth Air Training Plan was an example of a new institution of Commonwealth co-operation produced by the war. During the five years of its existence over 130,000 air-crew were trained in Canada for service with the Royal Air Force, the Royal Australian Air Force, the Royal Canadian Air Force, and the Royal New Zealand Air Force. For various reasons the South African Government did not consider the plan applicable to the Union and their air force personnel received their full training in South Africa.

Before the outbreak of war in September 1939, there were plans for co-operation between the United Kingdom and Canada for the training in Canada of pilots for the Royal Air Force. On 1 May 1939 Sir Kingsley Wood, Secretary of State for Air in the United Kingdom, confirmed that the two Governments had agreed on a scheme 'under which Royal Air Force pilots will be sent to Canada for intermediate and advanced flying training under the auspices of the Canadian Department of National Defence. The duration of the scheme will be for three years and the number of pilots to be trained will not exceed fifty in any one year. The cost of training will be borne by the United Kingdom

Government.'[1] The Royal Canadian Air Force was at this time small, and recruitment and the training syllabus under the scheme were designed to meet Royal Air Force requirements.

After the outbreak of war a more comprehensive scheme was thought necessary, and accordingly Sir Kingsley Wood announced on 10 October 1939 that the Governments of Canada, Australia, and New Zealand had agreed to proposals made by the United Kingdom for the establishment and maintenance of air training schools in each of these Dominions, and they had further agreed that

the more comprehensive and technical facilities required for advanced training . . . will in the main be concentrated in Canada. Personnel from the elementary training schools in Australia and New Zealand, as well as a substantial proportion of the young men passing out of similar establishments in this country, will proceed to Canada to receive there, with similar personnel from Canadian schools, the advanced training which will fit them for service in the line. The young men so trained will join either the Air Force squadrons maintained by the respective Dominion Governments in the theatre of operations or our own Royal Air Force units, while those from this country who get their final training in Canada will, of course, come back to join the Royal Air Force squadrons in the field. . . .[2]

Missions from the United Kingdom, Canada, Australia, and New Zealand met in Ottawa in November 1939, and the British Commonwealth Air Training Agreement was signed there on 17 December 1939. The Government of Canada was designated as administrator of a co-operative air training scheme capable of producing, when fully developed, 520 pilots with elementary training, 544 pilots with service training, 340 observers, and 580 wireless operator-air gunners every four weeks. To meet this objective 3 Initial Training Schools were to be established, 13 Elementary Flying Training Schools, 16 Service Flying Training Schools, 10 Air Observer Schools, 10 Bombing and Gunnery Schools, 2 Air Navigation Schools and 4 Wireless Schools. In addition there were to be schools for the training of the necessary staff, and appropriate command, recruiting, and maintenance organizations. The first three flying schools were to open in May 1940 and all were to be in operation by the end of April 1942. It was stipulated that the United Kingdom would provide up to 10 per cent of the pupil intake necessary to produce the required number of aircrew graduates; Canada would supply about 70 per cent, Australia 10–12 per cent, and New Zealand 6–10 per cent.

[1] *Hansard* (Commons), vol. 346, cols. 1507–8.
[2] ibid. vol. 352, cols. 182–4.

The original scheme, which in fact was fully operational by September 1941, was to remain in force until 31 March 1943; but with the extension of the war to the Pacific area, conditions were altered, more especially for Australia and New Zealand, and a new agreement was signed by the four Governments at Ottawa on 5 June 1942.[1] The facilities in Canada were still to be used to the full, and the number of training units increased (from 58 to 67), but the proportion of men provided by each Dominion was revised. The United Kingdom was henceforth to provide up to 40 per cent of the pupils required to fill the courses, and the remaining 60 per cent were to come from Canada, Australia, and New Zealand together. The agreement was to run until 31 March 1945.

The Plan reached its peak at the close of 1943 with 73 British Commonwealth Air Training Plan and 24 Royal Air Force[2] flying schools in operation, complemented by 184 ancillary units. By the Power-Balfour Agreement between Canada and the United Kingdom of February 1944, it was arranged, in view of the large reserve of aircrew already trained or under instruction, to begin the gradual reduction of pupil intake and of the training schools. In October 1944 the closing of schools was accelerated so that the Plan might terminate, as scheduled, on 31 March 1945. By the end of 1944 the number of B.C.A.T.P. schools had been reduced to 50 and those of the R.A.F. to 2; schools and units remaining on 31 March 1945 were absorbed by the Royal Canadian Air Force.

Of the 131,553 aircrew trained under the Plan, the Royal Canadian Air Force contributed 54·4 per cent (72,835 pupils) of the total, the Royal Air Force provided 32 per cent (42,110 pupils), the Royal Australian Air Force 7·3 per cent (9,606 pupils), and the Royal New Zealand Air Force 5·3 per cent (7,002 pupils).

A number of United States citizens, of Frenchmen from North Africa, and Norwegians, Poles, Indians, and others were also trained under the scheme.

The needs at the beginning of the scheme were very great. One of the main needs was for trained personnel as instructors and ground staff at the training school. Canadian 'bush' pilots and United States commercial pilots supplied a nucleus of instruc-

---

[1] *Agreement* amending and extending the British Commonwealth Air Training Plan (Ottawa, King's Printer, 1942); *Supplementary Agreement* between Canada, Australia and New Zealand concurred in by the United Kingdom modifying the B.C.A.T.P. Agreement of 19 December 1939, 1 June 1942 (Ottawa, King's Printer, 1942).

[2] The R.A.F. flying schools were incorporated in the Plan by the 1942 Agreement.

tors, while veterans of the War of 1914–18 filled many of the administrative posts. The Royal Air Force also provided over 250 personnel for staff positions in the first months of 1940. Further expansion in staff was met largely by graduates from Plan schools who were trained as instructors and retained for duty in Canada. This policy was followed by all four partners in agreed proportions.

Construction engineering and equipment requirements also bore heavily on the Royal Canadian Air Force, which had a personnel of only 4,000 at the beginning of the war. Technical experts were drawn in from civilian life, and the United Kingdom Air Ministry lent specialist officers in the early days of the Plan. Construction in 1942 reached a peak expenditure of some $80 million (Canadian). The Royal Canadian Air Force sent liaison officers to the United Kingdom and the United States to facilitate the supply of aircraft and equipment. The United Kingdom inevitably fell short of its original supply undertakings in the summer of 1940 and later the Atlantic sinkings of supply ships made the flow uneven. But meanwhile the Canadian Department of Munitions and Supply had speeded up and increased Canadian manufacture of a considerable list of equipment items, so that in due course the provision of certain of these items exceeded the Plan's needs and Canada was able to export these surpluses to the United Kingdom.

The cost of the scheme, which was approximately $1,500 million, was borne in agreed proportions by the four participating Governments.

The Leasing of Air and Naval Bases

This handbook is concerned only with consultation and cooperation involving two or more Commonwealth countries, and therefore consultations in 1940 between His Majesty's Government in the United Kingdom and the Government of the United States regarding the leasing to the United States by the former of certain naval and air bases, or sites for them, are not within its scope except in so far as they related to bases in Newfoundland with which His Majesty's Government in Canada and the Commission of Government in Newfoundland were also concerned. It is, however, clear from the published correspondence between President Roosevelt and Mr Winston Churchill that the Canadian and Newfoundland Governments were informed while negotiations were still at the secret state. Mr Winston Churchill wrote to the President on 15 August 1940: 'It will be necessary for us to consult the Governments of Newfoundland and Canada about the Newfoundland base, in which Canada has an interest.

We are at once proceeding to ask their consent.' President Roosevelt, at a press conference on 16 August, said:

The United States Government is holding conversations with the Government of the British Empire with regard to the acquisition of naval and air bases for the defence of the Western Hemisphere and especially of the Panama Canal. The United States Government is carrying on conversations with the Canadian Government on the defence of the Western Hemisphere.[1]

On 20 August Mr Churchill stated in the House of Commons:

President Roosevelt has recently made it clear that he would like to discuss with us, and with the Dominion of Canada and Newfoundland, the development of American naval and air facilities in Newfoundland and in the West Indies. There is, of course, no question of any transference of sovereignty—that has never been suggested—or of any action being taken without the consent or against the wishes of the various Colonies concerned, but for our part His Majesty's Government are entirely willing to accord defence facilities to the United States on a ninety-nine years' leasehold basis, and we feel sure that our interests no less than theirs, and the interests of the Colonies themselves and of Canada and Newfoundland, will be served thereby.[2]

Regarding the Newfoundland leases, the sequence of events was as follows. The Canadian Prime Minister, very shortly after Dunkirk, announced in Parliament that Canada had undertaken the responsibility for the defence of Newfoundland.[3] In August 1940 the establishment of the United States–Canadian Permanent Joint Board of Defence and the leasing by the United Kingdom Government to the United States Government of bases at various points in the Western Hemisphere from Trinidad to Newfoundland were announced. Canadian forces moved in, with the consent of the Newfoundland Commission of Government, to protect the Gander airfield, the Botwood seaplane base, the mines at Bell Island, and the city of St John itself. The two Governments arranged that Newfoundland forces should operate under Canada's Eastern Command. A fighter base was later constructed by Canada at Torbay, near St. John's, on land bought by the Crown in right of Canada from private owners or granted by the Newfoundland Commission of Government; and subsequently Goose Bay was leased to Canada for the construction of a large new air base, the work being begun in July 1941 and completed by the winter. Canada advanced the funds and constructed a naval base for the British Admiralty at St John's; the title to it was expressly vested in the Admiralty, although it was adminis-

---

[1] W. S. Churchill, *The Second World War*, vol. 2, p. 361.   [2] ibid. pp. 408–9.
[3] Canada, House of Commons Debates, 1940, p. 954.

tered by the Royal Canadian Navy for the duration of the war. Canada constructed a subsidiary repair base at Bay Bulls, near St John's, with a 99 years' lease. The Goose Bay Agreement between the Government of Canada and the Commission Government of Newfoundland was actually signed on 10 October 1944. By its terms: the Government of Newfoundland leased to the King in right of Canada for 99 years from 1 September 1941 the area on Goose Bay in Labrador as described; the Government of Canada had the right 'to construct, maintain, operate, manage and control', and fortify and defend, the base; and to construct and maintain, in each case with the consent of and by agreement with the Newfoundland Government, feeder roads, water and power supply installations, radio stations, and docks and wharves. For the duration of the war, and such time as might be necessary after that, the base was to be managed and controlled by the Royal Canadian Air Force, and freely used by service aircraft of the United Kingdom and the United States, and by civil aircraft if necessary to the war effort. After the war the United Kingdom's right to use the base for military aircraft was to be the subject of consultation and agreement between the Governments of Canada and Newfoundland, and the United Kingdom; meanwhile, the United Kingdom's military facilities were to be continued. Civil and military aircraft of the Government of Newfoundland might use the base 'on terms not less favourable than those of the Government of Canada'. 'The laws of Newfoundland shall be applicable throughout the air base and to all persons therein or thereon.' The Governments of Canada, Newfoundland, and the United Kingdom should discuss the question of the civil and commercial use of the air base 'not later than twelve months after the war'. The Government of Canada might not transfer all or any part of its rights under the Agreement to any third party, unless with the consent of the Government of Newfoundland.

United States forces moved into Newfoundland later than the Canadian forces, after they had prospected base sites. Construction work began early in 1941, on four sites (constituting three bases): at Quidi Vidi, near St John's, and on a dock area in St John's harbour; at Argentia on the west side of the Avalon peninsula; and at Stephenville on the west coast. The Anglo-American correspondence about the leasing of these and the West Indian bases has been mentioned, and led to an exchange of Notes between the United Kingdom and the United States Governments on 2 September 1940: the United Kingdom Government set out proposed areas and terms of lease for the bases, which the United States Government accepted. The definitive agreement on the bases was signed on 27 March 1941: the two Notes and certain explanatory correspondence were annexed to it.[1] The agreement was between the Government of the United States and the Government of the United Kingdom 'in consultation with the Government of Newfoundland'.

By the terms of the agreement, the base areas were leased to the United States Government for 99 years from 1941. 'The United States shall have all the rights, power and authority within the Leased Areas which are necessary for the establishment, use, operation and defence thereof, or appropriate for their control, and all the rights, power and authority within the limits of territorial waters and air spaces adjacent to, or in the vicinity of, the Leased Areas, which are necessary to provide access to and defence of the Leased Areas, or appropriate for control thereof' (Article I), and may in addition, in case of war or special emergency, exercise rights necessary for the conduct of military operations in the territories (i.e. of Newfoundland, Bermuda, etc.) and surrounding air and water (Article II). The actual rights of survey, control, construction, etc., enumerated (the enumeration is not exhaustive) were similar to those in the Goose Bay Agreement (see above). The United States had extra-territorial jurisdiction in its Leased Areas (Articles IV–VIII) and full rights of ingress and egress (Article XIII); postal facilities (Article XVI); exemption for military and base personnel's goods from customs and excise (Article XIV); and exemption of base personnel from taxation by the territory, except in minor and special circumstances (Article XVII). Various articles covered ancillary rights and facilities. Security measures, surveys, questions affecting aids to navigation, use of public services, etc., prevention of abuses of customs exemption, and other matters affecting the rights of both the United States and the territories, were to be dealt with by the Governments of the territories and the United States authorities in consultation and co-operation. 'British commercial vessels may use the Leased Areas on the same terms and conditions as United States commercial vessels' (Article XI, (3)); and 'a Leased Area is not a part of the territory of the United States for the purpose of coastwise shipping laws so as to exclude British vessels from trade between the United States and the Leased Areas' (Article XI (4)). Commercial aircraft (except for military reasons) might not normally operate from the bases except by agreement between the contracting parties; but in the case of Newfoundland any agreement on this point was to be between the United States and Newfoundland Governments (Article XI (5)). All mineral and treasure trove rights, and

[1] Cmd. 6259 (United Kingdom Treaty Series, no. 2 of 1941).

antiquities, in the Leased Areas were reserved to the territories, which might not transfer them to a third party without the consent of the United States (Article XXV).

Canada's interest in the defence of Newfoundland was expressly recognized in a Protocol annexed to the Leased Bases Agreement, as follows:

1. It is recognized that the defence of Newfoundland is an integral feature of the Canadian scheme of defence, and as such is a matter of special concern to the Canadian Government, which has already assumed certain responsibilities for this defence.

2. It is agreed therefore that, in all powers which may be exercised and in such actions as may be taken under the Agreement for the use and operation of United States bases dated 27 March 1941 in respect of Newfoundland, Canadian interests in regard to defence will be fully respected.

3. Nothing in the Agreement shall affect arrangements relative to the defence of Newfoundland already made by the Governments of the United States and Canada in pursuance of recommendations submitted to those Governments by the Permanent Joint Board on Defence—United States and Canada.

4. It is further agreed that in all consultations concerning Newfoundland arising out of Articles 1(4) [practical application of general United States' rights outside the confines of the bases], II [special emergency powers], and XI(5) [operation of commercial aircraft from the bases] of the Agreement, or of any other Articles involving considerations of defence, the Canadian Government as well as the Government of Newfoundland will have the right to participate.

Some questions about the air bases at Gander in Newfoundland and at Goose Bay in Labrador was raised in the United Kingdom Parliament on 16 December 1943. These bases were created to meet military needs, the agreements involved were made under security silence, and members objected that the people of Newfoundland had not been consulted before 99-year leases of their territory were granted. The Under-Secretary for the Dominions made the following statement with regard to Goose Bay:

Nothing could be said about the arrangement or the Agreement which was made at that time because for operational reasons it had to be kept secret. The cost of construction of the airport [at Goose Bay] was entirely borne by Canadian funds. In return it was agreed that the Newfoundland Government should grant a lease to the Canadian Government for 99 years. The lease was to be for defence purposes and there was no transfer of Newfoundland sovereignty. The use of the airport for civil aviation will be considered after the war. The Government were unable to explain the position to the people of Newfoundland, but as soon as the agreement has been con-cluded it will be published.[1]

At the end of the war there were in Newfoundland the follow-ing military facilities on lease or transfer terms: (a) on 99-year leases to the United States under the agreement of 27 March 1941, the convoy escort base at Quidi Vidi; the naval and air base (operational for the largest battleships) at Argentia; and the air staging base at Stephenville: (b) on 99-year leases to the Crown in right of Canada: the air base at Goose Bay, and the naval repair (subsidiary) base at Bay Bulls: and, (c) on transfer to the Govern-ment of Canada for the duration of the war, the large air base at Gander ('Newfoundland Airport'), and the seaplane bases at Botwood and Gleneagles. There were also in existence a number of minor auxiliary facilities to the main bases, arranged between the Governments concerned; and certain commercial civilian air-line facilities, for example the agreement in respect of the New-foundland service of Trans-Canada Air Lines arranged in February 1942.[2]

The Post-War Disposition of the Newfoundland Bases.

By the agreement which came into force on 31 March 1946,[3] the Governments of Canada, Newfoundland, and the United Kingdom, 'having considered their respective interests in Western Hemisphere defence', made arrangements for the dis-position of the defence installations constructed on Newfound-land territory under the Air Bases Agreement of 17 April 1941.[4] The Canadian Government transferred the control and operation of the Gander Airport and the seaplane bases at Gleneagles and Botwood back to the Newfoundland Government,[5] and Canadian obligations in respect thereof ceased and were deemed discharged. All Canadian structures and supplies at Gander were transferred to Newfoundland ownership against payment of $1 million. Canada forewent its rights with respect to leases at Gander, Botwood, and Gleneagles under Article VII of the 1941 Agree-ment. Should Canada and Newfoundland both be involved in war, Canada could resume control of Gander for the duration of hostilities (Article 2 (h)). 'Title in fee simple to the lands of

[1] *Hansard* (Commons), vol. 395, cols. 1802–3.
[2] Canada, Treaty Series, 1942, No. 19; extended by Exchanges of Notes in 1943, 1944, 1945, and 1946.
[3] Agreement between the Governments of Canada, Newfoundland and the United Kingdom respecting Defence Installations in Newfoundland (Cmd. 6823, 1946; Canada, Treaty Series, 1946, No. 15).
[4] Classified 'Secret' and not yet published.
[5] The transfer to Canada had been for the duration of the war; but Canada had spent some $25 million on installations, and had been granted security of tenure up to fifty years in respect of them.

Torbay Airport and its subsidiary installations shall be vested in the Government of Canada in accordance with the understanding between the Governments of Canada and Newfoundland at the time of the construction of the Airport' (Article 4 (a)). Canada might continue to operate Torbay Airport for civilian service between Newfoundland and Canada, and for military purposes as required. The laws of Newfoundland, including civil aviation laws and regulations, applied to Torbay Airport and to all persons therein. Newfoundland civil and military aircraft might use the Airport on terms not less favourable than those applicable to Canadian aircraft. Provision was made for periodic consultation between Canada and Newfoundland and the co-ordination of defence requirements in the latter's territory; and Canadian and United Kingdom military aircraft might fly over Newfoundland and use bases there which were under Newfoundland or Canadian control without landing fees (Article 5 (a) and (b)). The agreement was to run for three years, and might then be continued by mutual consent, or terminated at 12 months' notice.

It had been stated in the Goose Bay and other agreements that the use of the leased or transferred bases for civil aviation after the war should be the subject of agreement. This matter was regulated as between Canada and Newfoundland by agreement on 29 July 1946.[1] It provided for the arrangements for a Canada–Newfoundland regional service, and for the operation over Newfoundland of a transatlantic service, by Trans-Canada Air Lines (Articles II and III). Necessary facilities at Goose, Gander, Torbay and Buchans airfields were agreed (Articles X, XI, XII, and XVI), and civil aircraft of Newfoundland were to have no less favourable terms at Buchans (Article XIII). Under the agreement of 31 May 1946, already quoted, Newfoundland had such terms at Torbay, and Gander had been transferred back to Newfoundland.

Following the agreement between Canada and Newfoundland of 11 December 1948,[2] whereby Newfoundland was united with Canada as a tenth Province on 31 March 1949, the various agreements between Canada and Newfoundland became of historical interest only. Canada became responsible for the defence of Newfoundland, and all the bases and facilities passed into the possession of the Dominion of Canada. Article 31 ('Miscellaneous Provisions') of the Agreement on the terms of union states: 'At he date of the Union, or as soon thereafter as practicable,

---

[1] Agreement between Canada and Newfoundland on Air Transport between Canada and Newfoundland (Canada, Treaty Series, 1946, No. 34) in force 29 July 1946.
[2] *Terms of Union of Newfoundland with Canada*, Cmd. 7605, 1949.

Canada will take over the following services . . . namely, . . .
(d) civil aviation, including Gander Airport . . . (f) defence.'
Article 33 states that

the following public works and property of Newfoundland shall become the property of Canada when the service concerned is taken
over, subject to . . . any interest other than that of Newfoundland in
the same. . . .

(b) The Newfoundland Airport at Gander, including buildings and
equipment, together with any other property used for the operation
of the Airport. . . .

(f) Military and naval property, stores and equipment.

There remained any questions relating to the United States
interests in Newfoundland which might arise in connexion with
the terms of union of Canada and Newfoundland. On 23 October
1947 the land area of the United States base at Argentia and the
maximum area of territorial waters necessary 'to exercise the
rights, power and authority conferred by Article 1' of the Bases
Agreement of 27 March 1941 had been redefined with 'the
approval of His Majesty's Governments in the United Kingdom,
Canada and Newfoundland'.[1] Following the Bermuda Agreement of 11 February 1946 between the United States and United
Kingdom Governments regarding air services between their
territories,[2] the latter Government, 'after consultation with the
Government of Newfoundland', informed the United States
Government that an airline or airlines designated by it might
enjoy at Gander Airport certain rights as set out in the Bermuda
Agreement.[3] The correspondence provided that, in the event of
any constitutional change in the status of Newfoundland, the
agreement embodied in the correspondence should cease to
apply and the United States Government would be at liberty to
negotiate a new arrangement with Newfoundland 'or such other
State as may be empowered to act in that connexion on behalf of
Newfoundland'.

On 4 June 1949 the Canadian and United States Governments
entered into an understanding regarding civil aviation at the
Newfoundland leased bases. It will be recalled that, under
Article XI(5) of the Bases Agreement of 27 March 1941, civilian
aircraft were not permitted to use the leased bases save in emergency or for military purposes.[4] Under the agreement of 4 June

---

[1] *Agreement between the United States of America and the United Kingdom,*
Department of State Treaty Series, Publication 3324. (Washington, U.S.G.P.O.,
1948).

[2] Cmd. 6747, 1946.

[3] *Exchange of Notes regarding the Use of Gander Airport by United States Air-
lines,* Cmd. 7157, 1947.

[4] See above, p. 375.

1949, the use of the bases for civil aviation purposes was made generally subject to such arrangements between the two Governments regarding authorized civil flying as might be in force; but owing to the military nature of the bases, certain supplementary provisions were necessary. By the terms of the understanding: civil aircraft might use the Stephenville base when operational conditions prevented their using Gander Airport (Article I), and might use Argentia as an alternative whenever 'the operating minima established by the Government of Canada for the civil use of the airport at Torbay did not permit' its use (Article III). Canadian civil aircraft 'engaged in domestic air services within Canada' may use Stephenville (Article II). The civil use of both Argentia and Stephenville might be restricted or refused for security or military reasons (Articles IV and V).[1]

Negotiations between the Canadian and United States Governments regarding other matters arising from the Bases Agreements were in progress at the time of writing.

---

[1] *Exchange of Notes constituting an Understanding relating to Civil Aviation at the Leased Bases in Newfoundland*, Canada Treaty Series, 1949, No. 15.

CHAPTER XVI

REGIONAL ORGANS OF CO-OPERATION

The Australian–New Zealand Agreement, 1944

THE Governments of Australia and New Zealand, each represented by several Cabinet Ministers and headed by their respective Prime Ministers, Mr John Curtin and Mr Peter Fraser, met at Canberra on 17 January 1944, to consider a comprehensive agenda concerning the relations between their two countries and their joint attitude to post-war problems and policy.

The discussions lasted till 21 January, on which date the Governments signed the Australian–New Zealand Agreement, 1944 (also sometimes called the ANZAC Pact or the Canberra Agreement) consisting of forty-four clauses. In announcing the Agreement, Mr Curtin said that the Conference marked an important step in working out improved methods of consultation within the British Commonwealth, and was also an important stage in Dominion autonomy in foreign policy. That the Dominions could act both as separate units and as Members of the British Commonwealth would not weaken but would strengthen the ties binding the nations of the Commonwealth.[1]

On 21 January Dr H. V. Evatt, Minister for External Affairs in the Government of Australia, said that in substance the two countries

have declared a Pacific Charter of permanent collaboration and co-operation. There has been nothing in the past in the nature of a conference dealing with the foreign policy of both Governments and their future plans for the peace, order, and good government of the region to which they both belong. . . . In the successful outcome of the present Australian–New Zealand consultations there may well be a precedent of considerable value to other members of the British Commonwealth, especially in the provision for alternate meetings of Ministers in the respective capitals.[2]

The aspects of the Agreement which he specially emphasized were the common foreign policy in matters of common concern; the establishment of a regional zone of defence within the framework of a general system of world security; the proposal for the

---

[1] The Times, 22 January 1944.
[2] Current Notes on International Affairs (Department of External Affairs, Canberra), January 1944, p. 24.

establishment of an international air transport authority; the principles regarding the administration of dependent territories and the proposal for a South Seas Regional Commission for advancing the interests of all native peoples; migration policy and the new and permanent machinery for collaboration and consultation.

The official title of the Agreement is 'The Australian–New Zealand Agreement, 1944'. Under the first six of its forty-four clauses, the two Governments agreed: to provide for the fullest exchange of information and views between them, and for the maximum degree of unity in the presentation of their views elsewhere; to act together in matters of common concern in the South-West and South Pacific areas; and to co-ordinate their present military effort to the highest degree compatible with the existence of separate commands.

In clauses 7–12, the two Governments declared their vital interest in the terms of any armistice and in the final peace settlement, and their desire for active participation in the conclusion of the terms thereof.

By clauses 13–16 'the two Governments agree that within the framework of a general system of world security a regional zone of defence comprising the South-West and South Pacific areas shall be established and that this zone shall be based on Australia and New Zealand stretching from the arc of islands north and north-east of Australia to Western Samoa and the Cook Islands'. The two Governments regarded as of cardinal importance that they should not only be members of any world organization, but should be associated with it in the formative stage. They were vitally interested in the policing of the South-West and South Pacific areas; and they recognized the principle that the war-time use of bases does not in itself afford any basis for post-war territorial claims or rights of sovereignty.

In clauses 17–23, the two Governments stated that they supported in principle the creation by agreement of an international air transport authority, with full authority over international trunk routes. Within such a framework the Governments support the right of countries to conduct air transport services in territories within their national jurisdiction. Failing international agreement, the two Governments would support a system of government-owned air trunk routes within the British Commonwealth of Nations, controlled and operated by the Member Governments.

The two Governments went on to state, in clauses 24–31, that they intended to resume the administration of their dependent territories upon the liberation of those territories, and would not recognize any change of sovereignty or control of any Pacific island except by international agreement to which the Governments of Australia and New Zealand were parties. The two Governments would apply in their dependencies, and they recognized as applicable to all colonial territories, the principles of trusteeship and of the Atlantic Charter; to which end international collaboration in welfare and development is necessary. They intended to promote the establishment of a South Seas Regional Commission including the United Kingdom, the United States, the French Committee of National Liberation, and Portugal, to secure the advancement and well-being of native peoples and their progress towards self-government. In clause 34, the two Governments agreed that a conference of nations with interests in the South-West and South Pacific should be called as soon as practicable for an exchange of views on security, development, and native welfare.

By clauses 32 and 33, the two Governments recognized the principle that all governments have the right to control emigration and immigration in territories within their jurisdiction; and the two Governments would support one another in maintaining this principle, and would co-operate in all matters concerning migration to their respective territories.

The two Governments agreed, in clauses 35–42, to establish permanent machinery of collaboration and co-operation in all aspects of policy, including close co-operation for defence; collaboration in all matters of external policy affecting the Pacific; the development of trade between Australia and New Zealand and the industrial development of the two countries; co-operation in achieving full employment in their two countries and high standards of social security there and throughout any territories for which the two Governments may have responsibility. They further declared their desire for the co-operation of other Governments in the Pacific area in achieving this last object.

The two Governments agreed that conferences at ministerial level should be held between them at least twice a year, in Canberra and Wellington alternately; these conferences to be supplemented by meetings and committees of departmental officers and experts, exchange of personnel, etc. To facilitate the carrying out of the provisions of the Agreement, the two Governments agreed to establish a permanent secretariat to be known as the Australian-New Zealand Affairs Secretariat. The Secretariat should consist of secretariats under this title to be established in Australia and New Zealand, each under the control of the respective Minister of External Affairs. These parallel bodies should provide for continuity and co-ordination of collaboration, and for carrying out the action agreed upon at the periodic conferences and meetings provided for under clause 37.

The first conference of Ministers provided for by clause 37 was held at Wellington on 30 October 1944.

The South Pacific Commission

In clauses 30 and 31 of the Australian–New Zealand Agreement the two Governments undertook 'to promote the establishment, at the earliest possible date, of a regional organization with advisory powers . . . to secure a common policy on social, economic, and political development directed towards the advancement and well-being of the native peoples'. After the war, at the meeting of Commonwealth Prime Ministers in May 1946, Mr Chifley, Prime Minister of Australia, submitted proposals for a South Seas Commission 'to recommend measures for increased participation by natives in administration and for such material development as increased production and industrial growth'.[1] Shortly afterwards invitations were issued jointly by the Governments of Australia and New Zealand to the Governments of the United Kingdom, the United States, France, and the Netherlands, all of which have direct territorial interests and responsibilities in the South Pacific, to a conference in Australia.

The South Seas Conference was duly opened in Canberra on 28 January 1947, and speaking at the time Mr Nash (New Zealand) gave a five-point summary of its purposes;[2] namely, the end of exploitation of the natives of the South Pacific, improved standards of living for the natives, increased production, better educational and health facilities, and the encouragement of cognate missionary activities. It was explicitly stated that the proposed Commission would not deal with any political matters or with questions of defence or security.

As a result of the Conference the South Pacific Commission was established.[3] The participating Governments are those of Australia, France, the Netherlands, New Zealand, the United Kingdom, and the United States, and their aim is 'to encourage and strengthen international co-operation in promoting the economic and social welfare and advancement of the peoples of the non-self-governing territories in the South Pacific region administered by them'. The territorial scope of the Commission comprises all the non-self-governing territories in the Pacific Ocean which are administered by the participating Governments and which lie wholly or in part south of the Equator and east of

---

[1] *The Times*, 4 May 1946.
[2] *New Zealand Herald*, 29 January 1947.
[3] Cmd. 7104, Canberra, 6 February 1947.

and including Netherlands New Guinea. There are under two million people in this region.

The establishment of a South Pacific Commission was in line with the general idea of regional co-operation which had been outlined in 1943 by Mr Oliver Stanley, then Secretary of State for the Colonies, in a speech in the House of Commons on 13 July. He said, 'What His Majesty's Government has in mind is the possibility of establishing Commissions for certain regions. Such Commissions would provide effective and permanent machinery for consultation and co-operation so that the States concerned might work together to promote the well-being of the colonial territories.' This idea had already taken shape in the Caribbean Commission, a regional organization established in 1946 to serve the peoples of the non-self-governing territories in the Caribbean. Four of the Governments participating in the South Pacific Commission (the United Kingdom, the United States of America, the Netherlands, and France) were already members of the Caribbean Commission. The agreement for the Caribbean Commission and the experience of the Commission were drawn upon in working out the most effective arrangements possible for the South Pacific Commission.

The Agreement establishing the Commission defines its constitution and sets up two subsidiary bodies, a Research Council and a South Pacific Conference.

The Commission is a consultative and advisory body and possesses direct executive powers only in so far as these are conferred on it by the participating Governments; for example, for research.

Articles III to V describe the constitution and functions of the proposed Commission. It shall consist of not more than twelve Commissioners. Each participating Government shall appoint two Commissioners and shall designate one of these as the Senior Commissioner. Irrespective of the place of meeting each Senior Commissioner shall preside in rotation, in the alphabetical order of the participating Governments. The Commission may meet at such times and in such places as it may itself determine, but it shall hold at least two regular sessions each year. The Commission has the following powers and functions:

(a) to study, formulate, and recommend measures for the development of and, where necessary, the co-ordination of services affecting the economic and social rights and welfare of the inhabitants, particularly in respect of agriculture, communications, transport, fisheries, forestry, industry, labour, marketing, production, trade and finance, public works, education, health, housing, and social welfare;

(*b*) to facilitate research in technical, scientific, economic, and social fields and to ensure co-operation between research bodies;

(*c*) to make recommendations for the co-ordination of local projects in any of the fields already mentioned and for the provision of technological assistance from a wider field not otherwise available to a territorial administration;

(*d*) to provide technical assistance, advice, and information for the participating Governments;

(*e*) to promote co-operation with non-participating Governments and non-governmental agencies having common interests in the area;

(*f*) to address inquiries to the participating Governments on matters within its competence;

(*g*) to make recommendations with regard to the establishment and activities of auxiliary and subsidiary bodies.

Articles VI to VIII describe the constitution and functions of the Research Council which, in view of the importance of research for the carrying out of the purposes of the Commission, is established as a standing advisory body. Members of the Research Council shall include a small number of persons highly qualified in the several fields of health, economic development, and social development.

The functions of the Research Council are:

(*a*) to maintain a continuous survey of research needs in the territories and to make recommendations on the research to be undertaken;

(*b*) to arrange for the carrying out of the research studies approved by the Commission, using existing institutions where appropriate and feasible;

(*c*) to co-ordinate the research activities of other bodies working within the field of the Commission's activities and to avail itself of the assistance of such bodies;

(*d*) to appoint technical standing research committees to consider problems in particular fields or research;

(*e*) to appoint *ad hoc* research committees to deal with special problems.

Articles IX to XII establish a South Pacific Conference with advisory powers as a body auxiliary to the Commission for the purpose of associating with the work of the Commission the local inhabitants and local official and non-official institutions. A session of the Conference is to be convoked within two years of the coming into force of the Agreement, and thereafter at intervals not exceeding three years. Each session of the Conference is to be held in one of the territories within the scope of the Commission, with due regard to the principle of rotation. Delegates to the Conference shall be appointed for each territory within the scope of the Commission, and there shall be at least two for each designated territory. They shall be selected so as to ensure the greatest possible measure of representation of the local inhabitants of the territory. The Conference may discuss such matters of common interest as fall within the competence of the Commission.

Articles XIII to XVI deal with the secretariat, the headquarters of the Commission, and finance. The secretariat shall consist of a Secretary General and staff and shall, as far as possible, be appointed from the local inhabitants of the territories within the scope of the Commission and with a view to obtaining equitable national and local representation. The staff of the secretariat shall not seek or receive instructions from any Government or from any other authority external to the Commission, but shall be international officials responsible only to the Commission.

The expenses of the Commission and its auxiliary and subsidiary bodies shall be apportioned among the participating Governments as follows: Australia 30 per cent, France 12 per cent, Netherlands 15 per cent, New Zealand 15 per cent, United Kingdom 15 per cent, United States 12½ per cent. Pending the adoption of a budget the expenses would be met from an initial working fund of £40,000, contributed in agreed proportions by the participating Governments.

The permanent headquarters of the Commission shall be within the territorial scope of the Commission, and pending the establishment of headquarters, the Commission shall be temporarily accommodated in or near Sydney. Preliminary arrangements for the establishment of the Commission should be undertaken jointly by the Governments of Australia and New Zealand.

Article XV requires that the Commission shall co-operate as fully as possible with the United Nations and with appropriate Specialized Agencies on matters of mutual concern; and that the participating Governments shall consult with the United Nations from time to time with a view to defining the relationship which may in future exist and to ensuring effective co-operation between the Commission and the appropriate organs of the United Nations and Specialized Agencies dealing with economic and social matters.

In Article XVII a saving clause stipulates that nothing in the Agreement shall be construed to conflict with the existing or future constitutional relations between any participating Government and its territories or in any way to affect the constitutional authority and responsibility of the territorial administrations.

Finally, the Conference recommended the South Pacific Commission, on its establishment, to consider projects on agriculture, economics, education, and social development, fisheries, forestry, health and medicine, labour, and the establishment of an up-to-date technical and scientific reference library.

An interim Organization was established in April 1947 soon after the end of the Conference, and a Preparatory Conference to arrange for the first session of the Commission was held in Sydney in November 1947. This first session was held in Sydney in May 1948. At the second session, also in Sydney, in October 1948, it was announced that the permanent headquarters of the Commission would be at Noumea in French New Caledonia. The Commission has held its subsequent meetings there.

The South Pacific Conference, provided for by Article IX of the Commission Agreement, was first held in Suva, Fiji, on 24 April 1950.

The Special Commission in South-East Asia

Before the war there had been no liaison on economic or political matters among the different countries of South-East Asia, and little or no machinery for the co-ordination of British interests and policies in the area. During the war the formation of the South-East Asia Command favoured the development of regional co-operation, and after the war this Command acquired many responsibilities of a non-military character in the area, such as the allocation of food supplies and the movement of coal and freight. It was in order to fill the vacuum that would be caused by the impending dissolution of this Command that the office of British Special Commissioner in South-East Asia was created in February 1946. Lord Killearn was appointed on 18 February 1946 with headquarters at Singapore. The normal functions of the Special Commissioner were to advise His Majesty's Government on the many problems arising in South-East Asia which affected foreign affairs.

In the first place, however, Lord Killearn will have a special task in connexion with the food situation, which is so important a factor in the world food problem that His Majesty's Government feel that it calls for urgent investigation and prompt action. Lord Killearn will therefore proceed to his new post at the earliest possible moment with special authority from the Cabinet to review the food situation with the various authorities concerned, to initiate and supervise immediate action, and to make such further recommendations as he may judge desirable.[1]

---

[1] Foreign Office Statement, *The Times*, 19 February 1946.

The area to be covered by the Commission comprised Burma, Ceylon, Malaya, British Borneo, Indo-China, Siam, Indonesia, and Hong Kong. In addition, close contact was to be maintained with the Government of India, the Dominion representatives at Singapore, and the United Kingdom High Commissioners in Australia and New Zealand. At the same time a special Cabinet Committee to concert action in the United Kingdom on matters within Lord Killearn's sphere was set up in London. It should be noted that the Special Commissioner had no executive authority.

On the political side the work of the Special Commissioner was limited to his part in advising the British military authorities in Java. From August 1946 his good offices were used to bring together the Dutch and Indonesians, but this task ended with the initialing of the Linggadjati Agreement in November 1946. Since that date advice to His Majesty's Government and the Colonial Government took the place of direct activity in the purely political sphere.

To deal with the food situation Lord Killearn convened a Conference of the Supreme Allied Commander and the governors of British territories in the area. It was there agreed to hold a monthly conference of representatives of these territories and also of non-British territories in the area, in order to ensure a fair distribution of the available rice supplies and to deal with other food problems. The meetings began with reviews of the situation of food supply and production in each country and allocations were then varied and cargoes diverted to deal with local difficulties.

This Liaison Conference was the Special Commissioner's chief instrument for carrying out his work.

The Chairman of the Liaison Conference also became Chairman of a sub-committee on rice of the International Emergency Food Council, with headquarters in Singapore. The Food Council used the Special Commissioner's organization for the work of rice distribution.

In addition to its work on rice, the Special Commission dealt with the state of nutrition in the participating countries, with the distribution of other imported foods, and also with fertilizers, coal, the exchange of surplus commodities and equipment, the allocation and control of shipping, pest control, etc. Efforts were made to increase food production and the supply of commodities such as coal.

In addition to the regular Liaison Conferences a series of conferences was convened on subjects of special importance in the area. They included such subjects as nutrition, fisheries, social welfare, and statistics. At the Social Welfare Conference representatives of the social affairs division of the Economic and Social Council of the United Nations, the Food and Agriculture Organization, the Economic Commission for Asia and the Far East, and the World Health Organization were present. This last had already in 1947 taken over the Commission's Health Intelligence Section, which collected and circulated information on the incidence of major infectious diseases in the seaports and airports of the area.

In connexion with the Economic Intelligence Section of the Commission, the secretary of the Economic Commission for Asia and the Far East proposed the establishment of working relations between the two bodies, with the mutual appointment of liaison officers and detailed examination of the Commission's economic work in order to avoid duplication. This proposal was adopted.

On 27 March 1948, Lord Killearn retired from the post of Special Commissioner. A press communiqué of 30 April stated:

It has now been decided that the amalgamation of the posts of Special Commissioner in South-East Asia and Governor-General, Malaya, shall take effect on 1 May. Mr Malcolm MacDonald will bear the title 'Commissioner-General for the United Kingdom in South-East Asia'. He will continue to communicate with the Secretary of State for the Colonies on matters with which he formerly dealt as Governor-General, Malaya, and will be responsible, as hitherto, for the co-ordination of administration and policy in relation to the Federation of Malaya, Singapore, North Borneo, Sarawak, and Brunei. He will be responsible to the Secretary of State for Foreign Affairs for the work previously carried out by the Special Commissioner's organization, and in his relations with the foreign territories with which he is concerned he will have the personal rank of Ambassador.[1]

Conference on Indonesia

In January 1949 a Conference was called at Delhi, on the initiative of the Prime Minister of India, Pandit Nehru, to consider the situation in Indonesia, where fighting had broken out between the Netherlands forces and the Indonesian Republic. The Conference was attended by the representatives of nineteen Asian nations, including five Members of the Commonwealth, namely, India, Pakistan, Ceylon, Australia and New Zealand. It was stated during the Conference that this was 'the first inter-governmental conference on the political level to be held in Asia'.

[1] *The Times*, 30 April 1948.

In his opening speech at the Conference Mr Nehru said:

We meet within the framework of the United Nations and with the noble words of the Charter before us. That Charter itself recognizes regional arrangements as a means to further international peace and security. Ours is therefore a regional conference, to which we invited both Australia and New Zealand, whose interest in the tranquillity and contentment of Indonesia is as great as that of any of us. Our primary purpose is to consider how best we can help the Security Council to bring about a rapid and peaceful solution of the Indonesian problem. We meet to supplement the efforts of the Security Council, not to supplant that body.[1]

The Conference passed a resolution making detailed recommendations to the Security Council for settling the Indonesian dispute, and a further resolution that the 'participating Governments should consult among themselves in order to explore ways and means of establishing suitable machinery, having regard to the areas concerned, for promoting consultations and co-operation within the framework of the United Nations'.

The Delhi Conference on the Crisis in Burma

In Burma, revolt by the Karens, who had since before Burma's independence been claiming autonomy, and Communist violence and lawlessness had thrown the country into a state of confused fighting and disorder resulting in grave economic difficulties. Early in 1949 the Prime Minister of Burma, Thakin Nu, approached the United Kingdom Government with a request for a loan to finance the export of the rice crop, which is vital to the Burmese economy, and 'for other purposes'.[2] After consultations held with the agreement of the Burmese Government, an informal conference was held in Delhi on 28 February 1949, 'to consider the situation in Burma'. The Government of the Union of India acted as convenor and sent invitations to the United Kingdom, Australia, New Zealand, Pakistan, and Ceylon. India had a particular interest in Burmese security since there are many Indians resident in that country and the question of mass repatriation had been raised, and because West Bengal is dependent on Burma for rice supplies.

Representative delegates to the Conference were: the Indian Prime Minister, the Australian Minister for External Affairs, the United Kingdom Secretary for Overseas Trade, the High Commissioner for Ceylon, and the Commissioner-General in South-East Asia. There were no Burmese observers present, and Pakistan was not represented because the date coincided with

[1] ibid. 21 January 1949. [2] *The Times*, 26 February 1949.

the introduction of the Dominion's Budget. After the meeting a statement was issued as follows:

There was a consensus of opinion that peace and prosperity can be restored to Burma primarily through conciliation. The meeting unanimously decided to address a joint communication to the Prime Minister of Burma in which certain suggestions have been made for exploring ways and means of finding a peaceful settlement. The conference agreed that the proposals should be followed up by the representatives of the United Kingdom and of the Dominions in Burma, and that there should be no further meetings in Delhi.[1]

The terms of the joint communication did not prove wholly acceptable to the Government of Burma, and the negotiations for financial aid broke down. But during April 1949 Thakin Nu reopened the matter when he visited the Prime Ministers of India and Pakistan at Delhi and Karachi. These exchanges were reported to the Commonwealth Prime Ministers meeting which opened in London on 21 April, and on 11 May the United Kingdom Secretary of State for Foreign Affairs, Mr Ernest Bevin, told the House of Commons that, during the course of the Commonwealth meeting, the Prime Ministers of the United Kingdom, India, Pakistan, and Ceylon had met together to consider the Burmese Prime Minister's request for assistance in the early restoration of law and order in Burma. They desired to give support to the Burmese Government in the rapid restoration of peace in the country, and machinery had been set up for the implementation of their intention. In answer to a supplementary question, Mr Bevin said that the decision whether or not to grant a loan to Burma would depend on the recommendations of the experts.

It was reported later that the ambassadors to Burma of the four Commonwealth countries co-operating in the matter of assistance to the Burmese Government would meet in Rangoon, with their expert advisers, to settle what should be done.[2] The Government of Burma issued a communiqué on 12 May, stating that it had requested and accepted assistance solely for the purpose of restoring law and order and 'setting the Union of Burma on the path of prosperity as an independent sovereign State.'[3]

[1] *The Times* and *Manchester Guardian*, 1 March 1949.
[2] *The Times*, 14 May 1949.
[3] *Manchester Guardian*, 13 May 1949.

CHAPTER XVII

REGIONAL SECURITY: THE NORTH ATLANTIC TREATY

THE North Atlantic Treaty was, like the Briand–Kellogg Pact of 1928, a major multilateral instrument agreed without the preliminary of an international conference; although it was, of course, preceded by many months of informal conversations and private negotiations.[1] Its origins are related to the Treaty of Alliance and Mutual Assistance between the United Kingdom and France[2] (the 'Dunkirk Treaty') signed on 4 March 1947, and the Brussels Treaty, signed on 17 March 1948 between Belgium, France, Luxembourg, the Netherlands, and the United Kingdom;[3] which instruments, having only one Commonwealth signatory, fall outside the scope of this handbook.

On the day when the Brussels Treaty was signed, President Truman addressed a joint session of the United States Congress, and in his speech welcomed the Treaty as a notable step towards peace, adding that the American people would extend to the free countries the support which the situation might require and that their determination to defend themselves would be matched by an equal determination on the part of the United States to help them to do so.[4] On the same day, the Prime Minister of Canada, Mr Mackenzie King, speaking at Ottawa, said:

This pact is far more than an alliance of the old kind. It is a partial realization of the idea of collective security by an arrangement made under the Charter of the United Nations. As such, it is a step towards peace which may well be followed by other similar steps until there is built up an association of all free States which are willing to accept responsibilities of mutual assistance to prevent aggression and pre-serve peace. . . . The Canadian Government has been closely following recent developments in the international sphere. The peoples of all free countries may be assured that Canada will play her full part in every movement to give substance to the conception of an effective system of collective security by the development of regional pacts under the Charter.[5]

---

[1] Cmd. 7692 (1949), pp. 2–3.
[2] Text in Cmd. 7217.
[3] Text in Cmd. 7599.
[4] U.S.A. Department of State *Bulletin*, vol. 20, no. 512 (24 April 1949), p. 532.
[5] *External Affairs* (Monthly Bulletin of the Department of External Affairs, Ottawa), November 1948, p. 4.

The United States Senate Foreign Relations Committee addressed itself to a study of the international situation, and reported its views in the form of Senate Resolution No. 239 to the Senate on 19 May 1948. The Resolution (often known as the 'Vandenberg Resolution') was accepted on 11 June by a non-partisan vote of sixty-four to four, and is as follows:

Whereas peace with justice and the defence of human rights and fundamental freedoms require international co-operation through more effective use of the United Nations:

Therefore be it RESOLVED, that the Senate reaffirm the policy of the United States to achieve international peace and security through the United Nations so that armed force shall not be used except in the common interest, and that the President be advised of the sense of the Senate that this Government, by constitutional process, should particularly pursue the following objectives within the United Nations Charter:

Progressive development of regional and other collective arrangements for individual and collective self-defence in accordance with the purposes, principles and provisions of the Charter;

Association of the United States, by constitutional process, with such regional and other collective arrangements as are based on continuous and effective self-help and mutual aid, and as affect its national security;

Contributing to the maintenance of peace by making clear its determination to exercise the right of collective self-defence under Article 57 should any armed attack occur affecting its national security.[1]

This resolution, although it expresses the policy of a foreign State, is given in full because its objectives (apart from the references to 'constitutional processes', which were designed to meet the requirements of the United States Constitution) were endorsed and welcomed at other times by the other signatory Governments to the North Atlantic Treaty, including Canada and the United Kingdom.

Supported by this resolution, the United States Administration inaugurated informal and exploratory conversations on 6 July at Washington with the Canadian Ambassador and the Ambassadors of the five States signatory to the Brussels Treaty. By the middle of September, general agreement had been reached on the principles and nature of a regional security treaty for the North Atlantic area. A hint of the progress of the discussions, and of his Government's policy, was given by the Canadian Secretary of State, Mr Lester B. Pearson, in a speech at Kingston, Ontario, on 21 September 1948. 'The Canadian Government', he said, 'has made it clear that it is not only willing, but anxious, to

[1] U.S.A., Department of State *Bulletin*, vol. 20, no. 512, pp. 532–3.

join the other North Atlantic democracies in establishing a regional collective security pact for the North Atlantic.' Its representatives had, for over two months, been participating in the discussions on this subject in Washington, and he could not say more—since the discussions were, by agreement, private—than that he had reason to believe they would be fruitful. In addition, since the end of July there had been a Canadian observer present at the deliberations of the Military Committee of the Brussels Powers. He continued:

> The Canadian Government has taken these steps towards the creation of an effective regional security system with, I am sure, the overwhelming support of the people of Canada, [knowing that] we would share not only our risks but our resources. It would, for instance, be the task of a North Atlantic security system, once it is established, to agree upon a fair allocation of duties among the participating countries, under which each will undertake to do that share of the joint defence and production job that it can do most efficiently. . . . Some sort of constitutional machinery must be established under which each participating country will have a fair share in determining the policies of all which affect all.

This did not mean necessarily that all signatories would be represented at all levels on all the organs of co-operation; that might be unworkable. 'But it does mean that every organ of the regional security organization will derive its powers from a constitutional grant of those powers to it by all the members of the organization.'[1]

The close relation between defence under the Brussels Treaty and defence under the proposed North Atlantic Pact, brought out by the Canadian Secretary of State, was re-emphasized when the Consultative Council of the Brussels Treaty (composed of the Foreign Ministers of the five signatories) met at Paris on 25 and 26 October 1948. The communiqué issued after the Council meeting said:

> The Council also made a preliminary study of the question of North Atlantic security and the conversations on this subject which took place at Washington during the summer. This examination resulted in complete agreement in the Council on the principle of a defensive pact for the North Atlantic and on the next steps to be taken in this direction.[2]

Formal negotiations for a North Atlantic regional security pact were opened in December 1948 between the seven Governments which had taken part in the preceding exploratory talks. On

[1] *External Affairs*, November 1948, pp. 5-6.
[2] *The Times*, 27 October 1948.

2C*

4 March 1949 the Government of Norway also joined in the negotiations. By 15 March agreement had been reached on the terms of a North Atlantic Treaty, and the eight negotiating Governments issued invitations to the Governments of Denmark. Iceland, Italy, and Portugal to join with them as original signatories of the instrument. On 18 March the eight countries, by agreement, published the draft treaty, which was thus available for parliamentary and public discussion before signature.[1] The draft having (in the words of the Belgian official commentator) 'subi de légères retouches', the final text was signed just over a fortnight later, on 4 April 1949, at Washington, by the eight negotiating and the four specially invited Powers: Belgium, Canada, Denmark, France, Iceland, Italy, Luxembourg, the Netherlands, Norway, Portugal, the United Kingdom, and the United States. Each plenipotentiary, on signing, mentioned in his speech that the intentions of his Government and the terms of the Treaty were in full accord with, and a development of, the principles and objects of the United Nations Charter.[2]

The signature of the Treaty was followed, on 5 and 6 April 1949, by an exchange of notes on military aid under its terms. The five signatories of the Brussels Treaty addressed a note to the Government of the United States, stating that, in their view, material aid from the United States was essential to the effective implementation of the new Treaty. The military strength of the European signatories must be reinforced without endangering efforts at West European economic recovery, and the transfer of military materials should, as far as possible, be arranged without creating inflation, or disturbing either the monetary exchange position or the intra-European system of payments. For their part, the European signatories would create a co-ordinated military organization, with a common strategic plan against aggression.

The United States Government replied that it was prepared to ask Congress for power to furnish military material and equipment in pursuance of the principle of mutual aid to countries implementing the principle of self-help; and asked for details of military requirements. The Governments of Denmark, Italy, and Norway, which had presented notes in terms similar to that of the Brussels Powers, received similar replies from the United States Government.[3]

[1] This procedure—though less elaborate and extended—may be compared with the opportunity given for discussion of the Dumbarton Oaks draft of the United Nations Charter; see pp. 305-13, above.
[2] The texts of these speeches may be found in *Chronique de Politique Etrangère*, vol. 2, no. 3 (May 1949), pp. 331-66.
[3] Texts in ibid. pp. 367-77.

The negotiation and signature of the Treaty did not pass without comment from the Soviet Government and its sympathizers elsewhere. On 31 March 1949, the Government of the U.S.S.R. addressed a long note on the terms of the Treaty (published in draft on 18 March) to the intending signatories. The note denounced the proposed Treaty as aggressive, and provocatively anti-Soviet in despite of the declared pacific intentions of the Soviet Government. Far from being in line with the Charter, the Pact 'sapped the very bases' on which the principles and objects of the United Nations rest. The note drew unfavourable comparisons between the genuinely pacific intentions of all pacts of non-aggression concluded by the Soviet Government and its friends, and the 'war psychosis' behind the North Atlantic Treaty. The new Treaty, moreover, was contrary to the terms of the Anglo-Soviet Treaty of Friendship of 1942, to the similar Franco-Soviet Treaty of 1944, and to the Yalta and Potsdam Agreements between the Soviet, American, and British Governments.

The Foreign Ministers of the signatory countries sent a joint note in reply on 2 April from Washington. It was very brief, saying that the Soviet note was full of misrepresentations and could not have been based on a study of the text of the Treaty, which itself was the best answer to the Russian allegations. Some of the signatory Governments also made individual replies in greater detail, among them the United Kingdom and Canadian Governments. The United Kingdom's note, after repeating the terms of the joint reply, denied that the new Treaty was in any way contrary to the terms of the Anglo-Soviet Treaty of 1942 or to the Potsdam agreement; and pointed to various acts by the Soviet Government which were incomprehensibly irreconcilable with those instruments. The Canadian reply took up and rejected the other Soviet charges, that the Treaty was aggressive and cut at the roots of the United Nations Charter.[1]

The substance of the Soviet charges was repeated by Mr Gromyko at the United Nations Assembly on 13 April, where Mr Warren Austin replied, rejecting the attack as 'calumnious propaganda'.

When the Treaty was presented to the Canadian House of Commons, on 28 March, for approval before signature, the Secretary of State for External Affairs, Mr Lester B. Pearson, gave an analysis of its Articles. Before he spoke, the Prime Minister, Mr St Laurent, made it clear that the Treaty was wholly in line with the Charter, and that the 'mainspring of the developments' leading up to the Treaty was the persistent Soviet

[1] The texts of these exchanges can be found in ibid. pp. 383–90.

policy of frustrating the usefulness of the United Nations while, at the same time, tightening its own grip on the States bordering its territory or under its influence; a policy which created 'fear of subversive Communism allied to Soviet might'. The Treaty would help free and peace-loving States to speak to Communist dictatorships in 'the only language they understand—the language that speaks from strength. . . . There is neither peace nor security for Canada if Western Europe, quite as much as any part of this hemisphere, is in danger.'

Mr Pearson opened his speech on similar lines before proceeding to describe the Articles of the Treaty. The Preamble and the first two Articles repeated, in other words, obligations already undertaken by the parties under the Charter of the United Nations: to settle disputes by peaceful means, to abjure aggression, to strengthen free institutions and promote economic collaboration. Articles 3 and 4 pledged the parties to strengthen by self-help and mutual aid their capacity to resist attack; and to consult together if attack threatened any one of them. Article 5 he described as the heart of the Treaty.

If, in spite of our precautions, there is armed attack on any of the Parties in either Europe or North America, all the members of the group will assist the one which is attacked. Each will do so, and I quote from this Article:
'by taking forthwith, individually and in concert with the other Parties, such action as it deems necessary, including the use of armed force, to restore and maintain the security of the North Atlantic area.'
It is specifically provided that action under this Clause shall cease as soon as the Security Council is able to take measures under the Charter to restore international peace.

Under this treaty, then, each North Atlantic nation declares that it will in future consider an armed attack against any one of its allies as an armed attack against its own territory. . . . That does not mean that Canada would automatically be at war if one of our allies were attacked. We would, however, be bound, in company with the other members of the alliance, to take promptly the action which we deemed necessary to restore and maintain the security of the North Atlantic area.

Article 6 defined the area concerned, which was the whole North Atlantic, north of the Tropic of Cancer, and also the Algerian department of France and any party's occupation forces in Europe. Articles 7 and 8 declared that the Treaty did not conflict with any engagement under the Charter, nor any other international engagement of any party. Mr Pearson went on:
'Article 9, to which I attach great importance, provides for the

setting up of a North Atlantic Council through which activities under the alliance shall be arranged. It further provides that the Council shall set up whatever subsidiary bodies prove to be necessary; in particular, it shall establish immediately a defence committee.' All the parties will be equally represented on the Council.

Article 10 provided for the admission of new adherents; Article 11 set out the procedure for ratification; Article 12 provided for a review of the Treaty after ten years in the light of the existing situation; and Article 13 set the minimum duration of the Treaty at twenty years.[1]

The Foreign Secretary in the United Kingdom Government, Mr Ernest Bevin, in a broadcast in London on 18 March 1949, had made a number of the points brought out by the Canadian statesmen. The United Nations had not fulfilled the world's hopes, largely owing to the way the Soviet Government used its right of veto in the Security Council. The North Atlantic Treaty, following the Brussels Treaty, was intended to safeguard Western Europe from piecemeal destruction such as it had suffered under Hitler; and to strengthen the defence of the Western Hemisphere.

The whole concept of the pact is to be regarded as a concrete expression of the identity of view long held among the Western nations. . . . It is founded on principles of democracy, individual liberty, and the rule of law between nations. There are no secret clauses. . . . It is an endeavour to express on paper the underlying determination to preserve our way of life. . . . It must not be thought, however, that the signing of this pact relieves us from, or minimizes, our obligations under the United Nations. . . . Nor does this minimize in any way our ties and responsibility to the great family of nations known as the British Commonwealth, while we of course have the duty to defend our overseas territories. Neither do we forget the ties of friendship and treaties we have in other parts of the world.[2]

It may be observed at this point that the North Atlantic Treaty presents the first occasion of a formal and, in its commitments, highly specific multilateral instrument of mutual defence and military aid concluded in peace-time between, among the signatories, two Members of the British Commonwealth of Nations.

In pursuance of Article 9, the United States joint Chiefs of Staff left for Europe on 29 July 1949 for consultations on the military organizations to be established. Talks between their representatives and the Canadian Chiefs of Staff had already

---

[1] The texts of the Canadian speeches and of the Treaty may be found in *External Affairs*, vol. 1, no. 4 (April 1949), pp. 3-24.

[2] *Listener*, 24 March 1949.

begun.[1] The United States mission met the United Kingdom Chiefs of Staff in London on 3 August, and also had talks there with the military representatives of Norway and Denmark. Similar conversations were held in Paris with representatives of France, Belgium, the Netherlands, and Portugal; and the United States mission also conferred with the Commanders-in-Chief Committee of the Brussels Treaty organization. The North Atlantic Treaty Council held its inaugural session in Washington on 17 September 1949, when it agreed that the following subsidiary organs be established:

A Military Committee composed of the Chiefs of Staff;

A Standing Group of the Military Committee, composed of representatives of the United States, the United Kingdom and France;

Five regional planning groups: (1) *North European* (Denmark, Norway, the United Kingdom); (2) *Western European* (the Brussels Treaty Powers); (3) *Southern European–Western Mediterranean* (France, Italy, the United Kingdom); (4) *North American* (Canada and the United States); (5) *North Atlantic Ocean* (Belgium, Canada, Denmark, France, Iceland, the Netherlands, Norway, Portugal, the United Kingdom, and the United States). The groups were not mutually exclusive; the United States may take part in Nos. 1, 2, and 3, and Canada, Denmark, and Italy also in No. 2.

On 28 September 1949, following a request made to it by President Truman on 25 July, the United States Congress approved a programme of military aid to the European signatories of the North Atlantic Treaty, totalling $1,314 million. Negotiations for bilateral agreements on their share of this aid were begun on 3 November between the United States on the one hand and the United Kingdom, France, Belgium, the Netherlands, Luxembourg, Italy, Denmark, and Norway. Canada, Iceland, and Portugal had not requested aid.

Of the five groups enumerated above, No. 1, the North European, has its headquarters in London, and held its first meeting there on 31 October 1949. No. 3 was set up on 8 November, following a two-day meeting in Paris between the Defence Ministers of the United Kingdom, France, and Italy. Meanwhile, the Treaty's Defence Committee had set up the North Atlantic Military Production and Supply Board, composed of representatives at the official level of each signatory. The Board held its first meeting in London on 1 and 2 November. Its permanent organization is in London, but it may meet elsewhere as

[1] It will be recalled that the United States and Canada already had a permanent Joint Defence Board; see pp. 247–8, above.

convenient. The Board is to report to the Defence Committee.

The establishment of the Board was approved and confirmed by the North Atlantic Council at its second meeting, held at Washington on 18 November 1949. The Council at this meeting also agreed to establish a Defence Financial and Economic Committee, having equal status with the Military Defence Committee, and reporting direct to the Council.[1]

At its meeting in London in May 1950, the North Atlantic Treaty Council agreed to set up a standing body of Deputies of Council members. This meeting also accepted the principle of a collective balance of NATO forces, and at the next meeting, in New York in September 1950, the Council accepted the principle of integrated force under a single command for the defence of Western Europe. At its meeting in Brussels on 18 and 19 December 1950, the Council agreed upon the establishment of this integrated force and the appointment of General Dwight D. Eisenhower as Supreme Commander. It also agreed upon the manner in which the German Federal Republic might participate in the force under the Supreme Commander.

---

[1] A diagram of the North Atlantic Treaty organization may be found on p. 9 of Cmd. 7883 (1950), *Collective Defence under the Brussels and North Atlantic Treaties*. See also Cmd. 8214 (1951), *The System of Command Established within the North Atlantic Treaty Organization*.

APPENDIX

THE STATUTE OF WESTMINSTER

An Act to give effect to certain resolutions passed by Imperial Conferences held in the years 1926 and 1930.[1] [11 December 1931]

WHEREAS the delegates of His Majesty's Governments in the United Kingdom, the Dominion of Canada, the Commonwealth of Australia, the Dominion of New Zealand, the Union of South Africa, the Irish Free State and Newfoundland, at Imperial Conferences holden at Westminster in the years of our Lord nineteen hundred and twenty-six and nineteen hundred and thirty did concur in making the declarations and resolutions set forth in the Reports of the said Conferences:

And whereas it is meet and proper to set out by way of preamble to this Act that, inasmuch as the Crown is the symbol of the free association of the members of the British Commonwealth of Nations, and as they are united by a common allegiance to the Crown, it would be in accord with the established constitutional position of all the members of the Commonwealth in relation to one another that any alteration in the law touching the Succession to the Throne or the Royal Style and Titles shall hereafter require the assent as well of the Parliaments of all the Dominions as of the Parliament of the United Kingdom:

And whereas it is in accord with the established constitutional position that no law hereafter made by the Parliament of the United Kingdom shall extend to any of the said Dominions as part of the law of that Dominion otherwise than at the request and with the consent of that Dominion:

And whereas it is necessary for the ratifying, confirming and establishing of certain of the said declarations and resolutions of the said Conferences that a law be made and enacted in due form by authority of the Parliament of the United Kingdom:

And whereas the Dominion of Canada, the Commonwealth of Australia, the Dominion of New Zealand, the Union of South Africa, the Irish Free State and Newfoundland have severally requested and consented to the submission of a measure to the Parliament of the United Kingdom for making such provision with regard to the matters aforesaid as is hereafter in this Act contained:

Now, therefore, be it enacted by the King's most Excellent Majesty by and with the advice and consent of the Lords Spiritual and Temporal, and Commons, in this present Parliament assembled, and by the authority of the same, as follows:

1. In this Act the expression 'Dominion' means any of the follow-

[1] 22 Geo. V, c.4.

ing Dominions, that is to say, the Dominion of Canada, the Commonwealth of Australia, the Dominion of New Zealand, the Union of South Africa, the Irish Free State and Newfoundland.

2. (1) The Colonial Laws Validity Act, 1865, shall not apply to any law made after the commencement of this Act by the Parliament of a Dominion.

(2) No law and no provision of any law made after the commencement of this Act by the Parliament of a Dominion shall be void or inoperative on the ground that it is repugnant to the law of England, or to the provisions of any existing or future Act of Parliament of the United Kingdom, or to any order, rule or regulation made under any such Act, and the powers of the Parliament of a Dominion shall include the power to repeal or amend any such Act, order, rule or regulation in so far as the same is part of the law of the Dominion.

3. It is hereby declared and enacted that the Parliament of a Dominion has full power to make laws having extra-territorial operation.

4. No Act of Parliament of the United Kingdom passed after the commencement of this Act shall extend, or be deemed to extend, to a Dominion as part of the law of that Dominion, unless it is expressly declared in that Act that that Dominion has requested, and consented to, the enactment thereof.

5. Without prejudice to the generality of the foregoing provisions of this Act, sections seven hundred and thirty-five and seven hundred and thirty-six of the Merchant Shipping Act, 1894, shall be construed as though reference therein to the Legislature of a British possession did not include reference to the Parliament of a Dominion.

6. Without prejudice to the generality of the foregoing provisions of this Act, section four of the Colonial Courts of Admiralty Act, 1890 (which requires certain laws to be reserved for the signification of His Majesty's pleasure or to contain a suspending clause), and so much of section seven of that Act as requires the approval of His Majesty in Council to any rules of Court for regulating the practice and procedure of a Colonial Court of Admiralty, shall cease to have effect in any Dominion as from the commencement of this Act.

7. (1) Nothing in this Act shall be deemed to apply to the repeal, amendment or alteration of the British North America Acts, 1867 to 1930, or any order, rule or regulation made thereunder.

(2) The provisions of section two of this Act shall extend to laws made by any of the Provinces of Canada and to the powers of the legislatures of such Provinces.

(3) The powers conferred by this Act upon the Parliament of Canada or upon the legislatures of the Provinces shall be restricted to the enactment of laws in relation to matters within the competence of the Parliament of Canada or of any of the legislatures of the Provinces respectively.

8. Nothing in this Act shall be deemed to confer any power to repeal or alter the Constitution or the Constitution Act of the Commonwealth of Australia or the Constitution Act of the Dominion of

New Zealand otherwise than in accordance with the law existing before the commencement of this Act.

9. (1) Nothing in this Act shall be deemed to authorise the Parliament of the Commonwealth of Australia to make laws on any matter within the authority of the States of Australia, not being a matter within the authority of the Parliament or Government of the Commonwealth of Australia.

(2) Nothing in this Act shall be deemed to require the concurrence of the Parliament or Government of the Commonwealth of Australia in any law made by the Parliament of the United Kingdom with respect to any matter within the authority of the States of Australia, not being a matter within the authority of the Parliament or Government of the Commonwealth of Australia, in any case where it would have been in accordance with the constitutional practice existing before the commencement of this Act that the Parliament of the United Kingdom should make that law without such concurrence.

(3) In the application of this Act to the Commonwealth of Australia the request and consent referred to in section four shall mean the request and consent of the Parliament and Government of the Commonwealth.

10. (1) None of the following sections of this Act, that is to say, sections two, three, four, five and six, shall extend to a Dominion to which this section applies as part of the law of that Dominion unless that section is adopted by the Parliament of the Dominion, and any Act of that Parliament adopting any section of this Act may provide that the adoption shall have effect either from the commencement of this Act or from such later date as is specified in the adopting Act.

(2) The Parliament of any such Dominion as aforesaid may at any time revoke the adoption of any section referred to in subsection (1) of this section.

(3) The Dominions to which this section applies are the Commonwealth of Australia, the Dominion of New Zealand and Newfoundland.

11. Notwithstanding anything in the Interpretation Act, 1889, the expression 'Colony' shall not, in any Act of Parliament of the United Kingdom passed after the commencement of this Act, include a Dominion or any Province or State forming part of a Dominion.

12. This Act may be cited as the Statute of Westminster, 1931.

INDEX